THE UNIVERSITY OF LOUISVILLE

THE UNIVERSITY OF LOUISVILLE

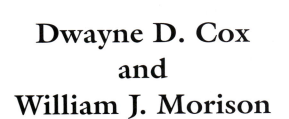

Dwayne D. Cox
and
William J. Morison

THE UNIVERSITY PRESS OF KENTUCKY

Publication of this volume was made possible in part by a grant
from the National Endowment for the Humanities.

Editorial and Sales Offices: The University Press of Kentucky
663 South Limestone Street, Lexington, Kentucky 40508-4008

04   03   02   01   00   5   4   3   2   1

All illustrations are from the University of Louisville Archives
unless otherwise indicated. CSC denotes Caufield and Shook
Collection, U of L Photographic Archives.

Frontispiece: Auguste Rodin's *The Thinker.*

Library of Congress Cataloging-in-Publication Data

Cox, Dwayne, 1950-
     The University of Louisville / Dwayne D. Cox and William J.
Morison.
          p.   cm.
     Includes bibliographical references (p.   ) and index.
     ISBN 0-8131-2142-6 (alk. paper)
     1. University of Louisville–History.   I. Morison, William James,
1943-   .   II. Title.
LD3131.L42C69   1999
378.769'44–dc21   99-28299

Manufactured in the United States of America

To the students, faculty, staff, and friends
of the University of Louisville past and present:

By your affection for and dedication to
the university and its work throughout all its years,
you have brought honor to your
families, city, commonwealth, and nation.

CONTENTS

FOREWORD

THE BICENTENNIAL CELEBRATION of the University of Louisville has stimulated interest in the story of an educational institution both venerable in time and increasingly vital to the life of a heartland community of a million people. One of the most important testimonials to the university's sustained curiosity about the past is the publication of a comprehensive history of the institution, a landmark achievement in that it is both an initial effort and a well-developed and well-documented account.

A university, like any other corporate entity, grows and develops along lines determined by its historic past. It can ignore this past not only, as the popular saying goes, at the peril of repeating it, but even more significantly at the peril of failing to understand its present and sallying forth in dismal ignorance into its future. Institutional memory, fortunately for the University of Louisville, has been well preserved in the University Archives, a treasure house of historic documents and recorded oral history, certainly available to the scholar and information-seeker and also to the occasional history buff. But institutional memory also needs to be more widely shared and directly available in home and office to those who respond daily to the challenges of university life and to those whose experiences and interests have been bound up with the university.

Such a history has to have the unity and continuity that only an institutional biography can pro-

vide. People and events must find their places in a sustained narrative that relates these components to an ongoing tide of historical development. The University of Louisville, for example, for the first three-quarters of a century of its history, was essentially a consortium of two professional schools devoted to the practical requirements of a professional career and, in the case of the medical school, to the research and development of the profession.

This pattern was unusual. The vast majority of modern universities were more firmly rooted in liberal arts colleges, often sponsored by religious denominations; in land grant schools devoted to the mechanical and agricultural arts; or in teachers' colleges concerned with staffing elementary and secondary education. Two results of importance flowed from this history at the University of Louisville. One was an emphasis on practical education in long-established and well-respected professions as the central driving force in the university; the other was a sense of virtual autonomy in the units. The history of the university, therefore, has been a sustained struggle for the key position of the College of Arts and Sciences and an equally persistent concern for the central direction and administrative control of the university.

The research for this institutional history was remarkable for its ingenuity. There were few available guideposts. The sources are essentially diverse, including minutes of boards and faculties, official reports and catalogs of the units, administrative memoranda, letters, legislative records, professional journals, biographies and biographical dictionaries, newspaper accounts, and personal interviews. It required extensive use of the archives of the university, materials in the Filson Club, and various collected documents extending to Frankfort, Lexington, and beyond.

The University of Louisville is deeply indebted to the authors, who were required to venture forth on an uncharted course where imagination and perhaps serendipity, coupled with good judgment and sustained effort, made possible this very important account of the university's fascinating story.

William F. Ekstrom
Executive Vice President Emeritus

PREFACE

THIS OVERVIEW OF U OF L'S history relies heavily on the extensive research and writing of Dwayne D. Cox, head of the Archives and Manuscripts Department for Auburn University Libraries. From 1975 to 1986, Dr. Cox was associate archivist at the University of Louisville. His 1984 dissertation at the University of Kentucky, under Professor Charles P. Roland, was entitled "A History of the University of Louisville." William J. Morison revised the manuscript and expanded it considerably, adding several chapters and many sections of chapters, and the two worked together to put the manuscript in its final form. Morison joined the faculty of U of L's Department of History in 1969, and in 1973 received the additional appointment as university archivist and later director of the University Archives and Records Center. He received his Ph.D. in history from Vanderbilt University in 1971.

The authors are indebted to a number of people who read all or portions of the manuscript and made invaluable suggestions. Among them are Mary Margaret Bell, Katherine Burger Johnson, Margaret Merrick, and Tom Owen, all associate archivists at the University of Louisville and members of its library faculty; current or retired U of L faculty members Dale Billingsley, Eugene Conner, Dario Covi, Wood Currens, Allen Dittmer, William F. Ekstrom, J. Blaine Hudson III, Ellen McIntyre, and Paul Weber; current, former, or retired U of L staff members David L. Baker, John Chamberlain, Elaine Whelan,

Clarita Whitney, Polly Wood, and Linda Wilson; current or former students Charles Brown, Jennifer Johnson Franklin, Kent Jennings, Newton McCravy, and Philip B. Setters; and Kentucky historians Clyde Crews of Bellarmine College, James Klotter of Georgetown College and Samuel W. Thomas of Louisville.

The manuscript also profited from the work of several former members of the staff of the University Archives, especially Janet Hodgson, enjoying retirement in Montana; L. Dale Patterson, Archivist/ Records Administrator for the United Methodist Church Archives; Sherrill Redmon, Director of the Sophia Smith Collection at Smith College; and Deborah Skaggs, Manager, Information Management and Administrative Services for the Frank Russell Company.

Daniel Hall, Vice President for University Relations, and Michael Mangeot, Executive Director of the Bicentennial Celebration, encouraged the book's publication and provided funds for the three research assistants. The U of L Alumni Association, under the direction of Tara Singer, played an important role by promoting the project in its early stages and providing financial support. Rodney Williams, longtime alumni director and now director of special alumni programs, refused to let his failed eyesight alter his determination that U of L's bicentennial celebration not end without the publication of a scholarly history. Truth be told, Williams was convinced that such a history would ultimately be seen as one of the most important and enduring products of the bicentennial season. He read draft after draft and alternated enthusiastic praise with pleadings that the coverage of this or that episode be expanded or reduced. If, for example, the story herein of the school's fraternities and sororities is undeservedly skimpy, it is not Williams' fault. At Williams' behest, Larry C. Ethridge, of ULAA's board of directors, read the manuscript at various stages and made good suggestions. Williams also enlisted the aid of former U of L president Donald C. Swain, who read the manuscript and shared his consistently incisive and constructive comments with the authors.

The authors also wish to express their appreciation for the assistance given by Terry Birdwhistell, University of Kentucky Archives; Shirley Botkins, Jefferson County Public Schools Archives; Lynn Hollingsworth, Kentucky Historical Society; Mark Wetherington and James Holmberg, Filson Club; Sue Lynn Stone, Western Kentucky University Archives; Betsy Morelock, Kentucky State University Archives; David Morgan, Jefferson County Archives; Sharon Receveur, City of Louisville Archives; and, from the University of Louisville, Mary Kay Becker, Gary Freiburger, and Diane Nichols, Kornhauser Library; Glenda Neely, Ekstrom Library; James C. "Andy"

Anderson, William J. Carner, and Susan M. Knoer, Photographic Archives; Karen Howe, Office of University Counsel; Marilyn Odendahl and Jennifer Recktenwald, University Communications; and Ronald Van Stockum, former Assistant to the President, all of whom tracked down elusive information and made other useful contributions.

Katherine Burger Johnson and Jennifer Johnson Franklin also served as research assistants, along with Sherri Pawson, Archives Office Manager, who every day for two years went the extra mile to resolve never-ending problems. The three of them worked tirelessly to identify illustrations, write captions, and help the authors improve the manuscript.

The authors, of course, accept full responsibility for the final product, which may contain errors of fact and undoubtedly contains errors of judgment.

Finally, the authors thank William E. Bigglestone, whose archival labors and scholarly writings at Oberlin College provide a model for anyone interested in documenting the history of a college or university with a balance for sympathy and critical objectivity, and they express their gratitude to their wives, Beth Cox and Ellen McIntyre, for their encouragement, advice, and sacrifice. These few words cannot wholly describe their indebtedness to these three people.

ONE

JEFFERSON SEMINARY
1798-1829

ON APRIL 3, 1798, eight men declared their intention to establish the Jefferson Seminary in Louisville, and called on their fellow citizens to join them in pledging funds to buy "a small Lot of Land," erect "the necessary Buildings," and supply "other requisite Expenses" for the academy they envisioned. Thus began a community effort to provide an advanced level of education for the young people of a frontier settlement barely two decades old. Near the end of the eighteenth century these early Louisvillians took the first steps on a journey that would link them to the modern University of Louisville.[1]

The eight founders were prominent citizens of Louisville, then a town of fewer than four hundred residents at the Falls of the Ohio River. Richard Clough Anderson, Alexander S. Bullitt, William Croghan, John Thruston, William Taylor, and James Meriwether had served as army officers during the American Revolution. Anderson moved to Kentucky in 1784 and was a delegate to the Kentucky statehood convention of 1788. Bullitt, a nephew by marriage of Virginia governor Patrick Henry, represented Jefferson County at Kentucky's constitutional conventions of 1792 and 1799. Meriwether was a veteran of Colonel George Rogers Clark's 1778-1779 Illinois campaign against the British, a county commissioner, and a state legislator. Thruston served as a town trustee, as did the Irish-born Croghan, married to Clark's sister, and Taylor, a cousin of U.S.

presidents James Madison and Zachary Taylor. Henry Churchill, a Jefferson County Circuit Court Judge, later became a member of the Kentucky House of Representatives. John Thompson also served in the state legislature and was subsequently a judge in Louisiana.[2]

When these men sounded the call for Jefferson Seminary, Louisville bore some of the rough edges of its days as an isolated military outpost established by Colonel Clark in 1778 during the war for independence. The settlement, then the farthest west in the new nation, was the northern terminus of the Wilderness Trail, which entered the Kentucky country through the Cumberland Gap to the southeast. Jefferson Seminary was chartered just six years after Kentucky became the new nation's fifteenth state in 1792, during George Washington's first term as president. A little over a year before the school's birth, a traveler called Louisville an "inconsiderable V[i]llage" that "may in time be of Consequence."[3]

On February 10, 1798, the Kentucky General Assembly, with its *Act for the Endowment of Certain Seminaries of Learning,* had chartered a network of six academies, naming the proposed Jefferson Seminary as one. No religious connotation was implied by the term seminary. In fact, it was among the earliest academies in the commonwealth not administered by a religious body. The Louisville school was awarded a land grant of six thousand acres by the state legislature, which appointed Anderson, Bullitt, and the oth-

Jefferson Seminary Subscription List, April 3, 1798. The original trustees called for donations to help create an academy in Louisville, a town on the new nation's western frontier.

ers as trustees. These men were authorized to sell a portion of the land, located below the Green River in the southern part of the state, and use the proceeds "for the purpose of erecting their public buildings, purchasing a library and philosophical apparatus, provided that the lands hereby granted shall not be surveyed on any lands set apart for any Indian tribe." With their April 3, 1798, announcement of the fundraising campaign, the work to establish Jefferson Seminary could begin in earnest. They themselves pledged $715.[4]

Nearly three years later, however, the founders had little to show for their labors. A lottery authorized in December 1798 by the state legislature to raise $5,000 for a building fund had come to nothing. In December 1800, perhaps in an attempt to invigorate the nascent school, the legislature added eight new trustees, doubling the size of the board. The new members were Robert Breckinridge, Fortunatus Cosby, Abner Field, Abraham Hite, Gabriel J. Johnston, James F. Moore, Samuel Oldham, and John Speed.[5]

With the effort to raise enough money for a site and building stalled, the legislature in 1804 again reorganized the board, which now included Thomas Barber, John Bates, Jonathan Taylor, and David L. Ward, along with Anderson, Breckinridge, Bullitt, Churchill, Field, Hite, Johnston, and Oldham. The endeavors of this group likewise proved futile, and in 1808 the legislature, responding to complaints that some trustees had not "acted in conformity with the laws heretofore in force," added James Ferguson to the board and dropped Barber, Churchill, and Taylor.[6]

While only Richard C. Anderson and Alexander S. Bullitt served on the board continuously through those frustrating early years, the names of many of the seminary's trustees reverberate throughout the history of the community. Their names now grace major city streets and other sections of the surrounding landscape. These Kentucky pioneers' most enduring legacy, however, may have been their inception of a dream that ultimately connected them, however tenuously, to the University of Louisville.

In the fall of 1813, with the necessary funds finally raised

Mann Butler (1784–1852) headed Jefferson Seminary, edited two Louisville newspapers, helped found the town's first library and its first free public school, and taught in other academies in Louisville and Kentucky. In 1834 he also published what one scholar called "the first generally reliable history of Kentucky." Butler left the state around 1845 and died in a railroad accident in Missouri. (Filson Club Historical Society.)

nally raised and a building site purchased, Jefferson Seminary opened in temporary quarters under the direction of Edward Mann Butler, the dominant figure in the history of the school. Raised in England and in Baltimore, Maryland, Mann Butler embraced the life of schoolmaster and scholar; his best known work was *A History of the Commonwealth of Kentucky* (1834). He taught mathematics at Transylvania University in Lexington, and then lived in Louisville intermittently between 1813 and 1845.[7]

In September 1814 the seminary held classes in a new brick building erected by the trustees on the west side of Eighth Street between Green (now Liberty) and Walnut (now Muhammad Ali) Streets. Other brick buildings also had risen in Louisville, heretofore a town of log and frame structures. Its

A mid-twentieth-century artist's rendering of the Jefferson Seminary building, constructed in 1814.

first churches had appeared during the last five years, along with a theater, newspapers, factories, warehouses, and other business establishments. An increasingly active river trade had been punctuated by the dramatic appearance at the wharf in 1811 of the *New Orleans,* the first steamboat on the western waters. In another five years, Louisville's steamboat trade would be in full swing and its population would reach four thousand.[8]

During Jefferson Seminary's first year, tuition rose from $17.50 to $20 per five-month session. The curriculum consisted of English, French, Latin, Greek, geography, and trigonometry as applied to surveying and navigation. Both males and females attended; in April 1815 a student listed only as "Miss C. Sneed" won honors in French in a public examination.[9]

Controversy over the purpose of the institution arose early as Butler found himself trying to educate too many pupils, many of whom he considered unqualified. Eventually he refused to accept more than thirty-five students without an assistant. Then

two years later the frustrated professor announced he was leaving Jefferson Seminary, probably because the school did not fit his definition of a "select limited academy." Butler was succeeded for a time by William Tompkins (1794-1858), later an attorney and magistrate.[10]

Faculty turnover, internal dissent, and financial instability hindered the school's progress. In 1819 physician and naturalist Henry McMurtrie's *Sketches of Louisville* reported that it was not "so well patronized as it deserves," owing in part to an "eternal hunger and thirst after money" which discouraged large seminary enrollments. After Butler left, the board began an unsuccessful effort to raise operating funds from the sale of its land holdings. In 1821 the trustees engaged a new principal, Charles Plunkitt McCrohan, who claimed credentials from Trinity College in Dublin, Ireland. According to a second-hand account, McCrohan had come to Louisville following his capture in January 1815, while serving as a lieutenant in the British army at the Battle of New Orleans. By January 1826, he had departed, after which point the school operated under the direction of two heads, Mann Butler, who had returned, and Harvard-educated Francis Edward Goddard. Not long afterwards, though, this teaching partnership dissolved when Goddard apparently questioned Butler's knowledge of trigonometry. Butler again resigned, but by 1828 he had returned for a final stint at the seminary.[11]

While mentions of the new academy survive in a few scattered accounts of Louisville residents, the school seems to have gone unnoticed by travelers who stopped in Louisville in the second and third decades of the nineteenth century. They were more likely to observe muddy streets like "ponds . . . up to the knees"; the "cordiality" of the townspeople, the fondness of many for drinking and gambling, and their prevailing racial prejudice and the presence of slave auctions; "splendid, substantial, and richly furnished" homes; and, overall, "the warehouses, the stores, the smell of the landing even, the ship-yards, . . . the great and growing importance of the place."[12]

Debates on the purpose of the academy and whom to educate continued. By the mid-1820s the school also had come under attack in the local press. Shadrach Penn Jr., editor of the *Louisville Public Advertiser,* was a Jacksonian, and his sheet welcomed contributions which accused the seminary of being an enemy of the "common man." Because the state had established the school and provided land holdings to finance its operation, the "mechanics and laborers of Louisville" resented its curriculum, which did not provide for teaching students "to read, and to write and to cipher." One commentator wrote that "we can now have our children taught to gabble in an unknown tongue, . . . and to despise us, because we cannot understand them." The seminary's curriculum was modified in order to gain "the fostering hand of public patronage," but criticism continued until 1829, when the school closed for good.[13]

In that same year Louisville established its first system of public or "common" schools, which all white children between the ages of six and fourteen were entitled to attend free of charge. Penn wanted more Louisville youth taught the basics, rather than a few wealthy ones taught the frills. The faculty of the

Shadrach Penn Jr., editor of the Louisville Public Advertiser, *criticized the Jefferson Seminary for being an elitist institution. (Filson Club Historical Society.)*

new school system was charged with promoting "morals, decency, and good conduct" among scholars.[14]

With Jefferson Seminary's demise, the state earmarked half of its assets to establish a "high school" in Louisville. Then, as will be recounted in more detail in the next three chapters, in 1837 the city established the Louisville Medical Institute and the Louisville Collegiate Institute for the purpose of educating students beyond the "high school." The Collegiate Institute's name soon changed to Louisville College, and the college eventually inherited that portion of the seminary estate set aside for the high school. In 1846 by act of the General Assembly the Louisville College and the Louisville Medical Institute were combined, and a law school was added, to form the University of Louisville. Thus the University of Louisville was ultimately the heir of Jefferson Seminary and Louisville College.[15]

The relationship between Jefferson Seminary and the University of Louisville has long been well known among historians of Louisville, as books pub-

An ageless Minerva has glared at successive generations of U of L students since at least the early 1850s. Not insensitive to fashion, however, this Roman goddess of wisdom more than once has restyled her hair, replaced her warlike bonnet, and adorned herself with ever-older founding dates: first 1846 (left), then 1837 (center), and, for the last fifty years, 1798 (right). The current university seal has been used since the early 1950s. It was designed by Vienna-born Kentucky artist Victor Hammer, who also created the present seals of the City of Louisville and the Louisville Free Public Library.

lished in 1882 and 1896 called attention to this "lineal connection." So did an 1899 history of education in Kentucky, a 1932 history of municipal higher education in the United States, and the 1930s research of U of L historian William C. Mallalieu. Yet none of these studies portrayed the seminary as a true predecessor of the university and none advertised a 1798 founding date for the modern institution. They assumed that what became the University of Louisville originated in 1837, with the beginning of the Louisville Medical Institute and the Louisville Collegiate Institute. After all, if one defined institutional lineage solely in terms of an unbroken connection, a 1798 founding date would be difficult to defend. This definition obviously prevailed in 1937, when the university celebrated its centennial.[16]

Actually, prior to the 1930s, the founding date emblazoned on the university's seal was 1846, the year the institution acquired its modern name. Faced with financial and other problems associated with the lengthening depression decade of the 1930s, U of L president Raymond A. Kent, who had assumed his post just a few months before the stock market crash of October 1929, launched a fund-raising and public relations campaign that included changing the school's official founding date from 1846 to 1837.

On April 3, 1932, the university marked its "ninety-fifth anniversary" with a "Founders' Day Celebration" and a week of concerts, plays, and exhibits, and began laying plans to celebrate its centennial in the spring of 1937.[17]

Meanwhile, a faculty member began research on a general history of the school. William C. Mallalieu had received his doctorate in history from Johns Hopkins University in 1925 and, three years later, accepted an appointment in the Department of History at the University of Louisville. In 1933 he announced plans to publish a history of the school for the forthcoming centennial celebration.[18]

By early 1937, Mallalieu had completed a draft of the centennial history. It included an introductory chapter on the university's origins, followed by separate sections on the medical school, the law school, the liberal arts college, and additional academic divisions. As the centennial celebration approached, however, other responsibilities drew Mallalieu away from his manuscript. He eventually relinquished his work to the Kentucky Writers' Project, part of a federal New Deal program designed to provide work for the unemployed, in hopes that the book could be completed for the centennial festivities.[19]

Mallalieu did manage to publish one article—a

thorough, clear, and accurate statement—on the origins of the university. In his account, the histories of the Medical Institute and the Collegiate Institute were closely intertwined with the city's political, economic, and cultural development. Mallalieu also understood the relationship of Jefferson Seminary and Louisville College to the University of Louisville, but he did not maintain that the university had been born in 1798.[20]

The Writers' Project, meanwhile, continued work on the centennial history. Urban R. Bell, state project director, initially predicted completion by April 1937, but university officials scrutinized each chapter, despite Bell's complaints that the result might be a "puff story." President Kent cautiously insisted all department heads read the manuscript. Some suggestions offered by school officials improved the work, but they also impeded its progress. President Kent reported to Bell in August 1938 that he considered the existing draft poorly written, inadequately documented, and factually inaccurate. Furthermore, the Writers' Project had omitted significant information in some cases and provided excessive detail in others. Bell promptly remanded some of the criticisms to an assistant for correction.

In early 1939, the project editors in Washington returned one draft of the book with "extensive editorial criticism" and a comment that "several cooks stirring the broth" had led to a jerky narrative. The difficulty of meeting project standards and institutional demands made work on the book considerably more difficult.[21]

The centennial passed without the history. In fact, the entire event was nearly canceled because of the Ohio River flood that inundated the city and closed the university early in 1937. Plans continued, however, and the program, held first on Founder's Day, April 3, 1937, and then at other times during the spring, featured an impressive series of lectures on recent scientific developments, the history of higher education, and the role of education in society. Speakers included Simon Flexner, an 1887 graduate of the medical school and director emeritus of the Rockefeller Institute for Medical Research; Will Shafroth, advisor to the American Bar Association's

Council on Legal Education; and Horace Mann Bond, dean at Dillard University. Bond discussed the black liberal arts college as a social force, in recognition of the university's Louisville Municipal College for Negroes (LMC), at that time a segregated, undergraduate division. He was a son of James Bond, who had been instrumental in the founding of LMC, and he was the father of civil rights leader Julian Bond.[22]

Centennial publicity was not without its hyperbole, as it touted U of L as "the oldest municipal university in the United States." The school possessed some claim to this distinction, although not without qualification. Even *Time* magazine, while conceding the honor to U of L, recognized that the boast was in dispute. In the 1830s the city of Louisville had provided land, a building, and library appropriations for the Medical Institute, but the school did not receive annual municipal support. The Collegiate Institute and Louisville College, on the other hand, enjoyed regular appropriations from the city budget, at least for part of their brief histories. After 1846 the mayor and city council appointed the University of Louisville's board of trustees, even though the school was legally declared a private rather than a public institution in 1854. U of L's trustees, in fact, resisted municipal control throughout the nineteenth century. Not until the early twentieth century did the University of Louisville receive a continuing annual appropriation from the city budget. By the time of the 1937 centennial, the city and the university enjoyed a close and mutually beneficial relationship.[23]

Although Mallalieu supported U of L's claim, he recognized that the College of Charleston in South Carolina, chartered in 1785, also possessed a strong argument for being the country's oldest municipal university. Beginning in 1837, the city of Charleston had pledged continuous financial support for the school. Passed to city control that year, the college remained in more or less uninterrupted operation after that time. While the South Carolina school lacked the professional programs offered by the University of Louisville during the nineteenth century, for most of the same period Louisville could not claim a liberal arts division. In his authoritative history of municipal higher education in the United States, published in 1932, Roscoe H. Eckelberry argued that the College of Charleston possessed a better claim to this disputed honor.[24]

In 1939 the *Centennial History of the University of Louisville* finally appeared as part of the American Guide Series. Building on the work done by Mallalieu, the authors had examined a variety of sources, unearthed new material, and usually dealt openly with controversial issues. On the other hand, the organization and writing were uninspired. The authors produced an account stocked with information on the university's past, but they seldom related the school's development to the history of the city, the state, or higher education in general. Although the Writers' Project noted the relationship of Jefferson Seminary to the Louisville College and then to the University of Louisville, the title of the volume itself indicated that its authors did not adopt 1798 as the university's date of origin.[25]

The 1937 centennial observance ended with everyone seemingly satisfied about the university's founding date. Ten years later, however, in May 1947, Charles Peaslee Farnsley, an attorney and university trustee with a refreshing curiosity about the school's history, and Leslie Shively, alumni secretary, revealed the discovery of "new evidence" supporting 1798 as its date of origin, making the University of Louisville "one of the 12 oldest universities in the nation." Farnsley, who would become mayor of Louisville less than a year later, had indeed unearthed some additional information about Jefferson Seminary, but he had no evidence indicating it was any closer to being the progenitor of the University of Louisville than had already been recognized.[26]

Most of Farnsley's "new evidence" had been gathered by George A. "Doc" Hendon, an attorney put on the university payroll to conduct research on the history of Jefferson Seminary. In 1947 and 1948 Hendon diligently consulted a variety of sources in fleshing out the story of the predecessor school. He even inspected primary historical documents in archives at the University of Chicago library and later described the entire project as "much more fun . . . than fixing somebody's fenders."

His reports were filled with references to the history of Jefferson Seminary culled chiefly from early nineteenth century newspaper notices, but his claims on behalf of the school were frequently exaggerated and misleading. The authors of the Jefferson Seminary charter, for example, had borrowed heavily from the wording of Virginia governor Thomas Jefferson's 1779 "Bill for the More General Diffusion of Knowledge." Hendon concluded, therefore, that the seminary represented "a seed of democracy, coming to the frontier from Thomas Jefferson, and planted and nurtured by his friends."[27]

Bolstered by the evidence Hendon had gathered, Farnsley and U of L's new president, John W. Taylor, prepared to celebrate the university's sesquicentennial—its 150th anniversary—in conjunction with Taylor's inauguration ceremonies in February 1948. Taylor made the announcement, and on July 30, 1947, the *Courier-Journal* reported that the University of Louisville had aged thirty-nine years in a day. Plans for a celebration were already underway. Thus in February 1948 the University of Louisville held its sesquicentennial celebration, only eleven years after its presumed centennial.[28]

At the festivities held downtown at the Armory on February 9 and 10, "the assembled group of dignitaries" included poets, generals, and senators, many of whom received honorary degrees or sesquicentennial medals as part of the celebration. With a journalistic grin, however, the editors of *Time* magazine recalled that the university had celebrated its first century only eleven years earlier with "three months of banquets and festivities." Someone was reported to have remarked that Kentucky colleges aged faster than Kentucky bourbon. Soon after the celebration, Frank L. McVey, a former president of the University of Kentucky, criticized the University of Louisville's adoption of a "remote date" of origin. McVey even questioned the use of 1837 or 1846 as the founding date, since the modern liberal arts college had not opened until 1907.[29]

While U of L's decision to move its founding date back thirty-nine years, from 1837 to 1798, may have provoked kidding from *Time* magazine and skepticism from the University of Kentucky, the championing of a new date of origin was met with little resistance at home. On the eve of the celebration, a *Courier-Journal* feature dubbed the University of Louisville "a brain child" of President Thomas Jefferson and claimed that the school was entering "the second half of its second century . . . mellowed by the warmth of history."[30]

With its classrooms full of returning veterans and its Arts and Sciences faculty dotted with rising stars, the University of Louisville was flush with postwar exuberance. The institution showed little hesitation as it leapfrogged back past the 1837 founding date to the 1798 chartering of the Jefferson Seminary, thereby signifying its dedication to the liberal arts. The university's renewal of its link with a frontier academy born a few years after the close of the Revolutionary War era tied it even more strongly to its city, named during the war for Louis XVI of France, who gave crucial aid to the American rebels. The College of Arts and Sciences suddenly became the "oldest" school within the university, and U of L's seal was changed to read "chartered in 1798."

Louisville has had no more enthusiastic champion of its city and university than Charles Farnsley. "When you first saw him in his antebellum frock coat, straw hat, dazzling white shirt, and string tie, accompanied by his gallant and courtly manner," recalled U of L art history professor Walter L. Creese, who rented rooms in Farnsley's house on the edge of campus on Confederate Place, "you would be unbelieving that the South could rise that soon again." As city mayor from 1948 until 1953, he polled residents door to door to ascertain their opinions, held weekly "beef sessions" to hear their complaints, and won approval for a tax on workers for the improvement of city services. As a university trustee he coveted the prestige an ancient founding date lent to his alma mater and constantly prodded the school to become a Harvard on the Ohio.[31]

Besides, Farnsley knew the public relations value of a significant anniversary. An indefatigable booster, he was comfortable with celebrating an anniversary when he could and when it suited his purposes. It suited U of L's purposes in 1937, when the school needed to raise money during the Great Depression; and it suited the institution's purposes in 1948, with

Charles Farnsley served as Louisville's mayor from 1948 until 1953 and from time to time as a U of L trustee. His "push to relocate the founding of the University of Louisville" back to 1798 was accompanied by "energetic chronological research." Farnsley "was content to stop at 1798 because he learned that the original land negotiations evidenced the imprint of his greatest hero, Thomas Jefferson. He kept a vertical chart listing the founding dates of the earlier universities, the U of L coming at the end. Then as his search through the documents enabled him to attain a fresh conclusion, he'd push the position of the U of L a few slots up on the chart and cry out, 'We're gaining on them!'" (Walter L. Creese, U of L art history professor, "Remembering Mayor Charles P. Farnsley" [1997].)

the depression and World War II behind it, when the school's new young publicity-oriented president was to be inaugurated. Farnsley did not finish his tinkering with seals and founding dates in 1948. As mayor in the early 1950s he came up with a new seal for the city, this one bearing a founding date of 1778, two years earlier than the one the city had previously celebrated.[32]

Julius J. Oppenheimer, then dean of the College of Arts and Sciences, later recalled that the idea of changing the university's founding date to 1798 belonged "absolutely, pure and simple" to Charlie Farnsley. Farnsley was convinced Louisville could be the site of an institution of enviable worth and quality. It was a dream he shared with the founders of Jefferson Seminary one hundred fifty years earlier.[33]

Only two of the original trustees of Jefferson Seminary lived to see it close in 1829. One remained when its successor school, Louisville Collegiate Institute, was established in 1837. None witnessed the creation of the University of Louisville proper in 1846. But they did fashion an academy where none existed before, and they and their descendants and others built Louisville into one of the West's more prominent cities. They wanted a community that valued education. Their confident declaration of April 3, 1798, was the genesis of the vision from which a modern university grew.

The story of how the University of Louisville came to claim 1798 as its founding date is at least as interesting as the history of Jefferson Seminary itself. With the celebration of the sesquicentennial, the actual strength of the connection between the two schools became, in many ways, beside the point. Prior to 1948 it would have been possible to tell the story of the University of Louisville with little or no reference to Jefferson Seminary. Subsequent to Charlie Farnsley's effort to link the two, it became impossible.

TWO

"FIRST AMONG THE MEDICAL SCHOOLS OF THE WEST"

B Y 1830 LOUISVILLE boasted a population of more than eleven thousand residents, making it the commonwealth's largest community. Just two years earlier it had been incorporated by the state legislature as Kentucky's first city. Although the decade began with the Falls City bereft of its academy, a new generation of leaders capitalized on the prosperity generated by the burgeoning steamboat trade. Building upon the work of their forebears, they moved Louisville quickly to a position of prominence among the nation's western cities.

In rapid succession the city saw the completion of the Portland Canal in 1830, bypassing the Falls of the Ohio; the planning of an ambitious courthouse, begun at Sixth and Jefferson Streets in 1836; the construction of grand hotels, churches, banks, thoroughbred racetracks, stately mansions, streets lit by gas lamps; and in 1837, two blocks south of the Jefferson Seminary building, the formation of schools that together became the University of Louisville in 1846.[1]

The lion's share of the credit for the creation of the University of Louisville proper belongs to James Guthrie. Born in Bardstown, Kentucky, Guthrie read law with Judge John Rowan, who later became a U.S. senator from Kentucky and the first president of the Louisville Medical Institute. Guthrie moved to Louisville in 1820, was elected a town trustee in 1824, and served on the first board of directors of the newly chartered Louisville & Portland Canal Company in 1825. By the early 1830s he headed a city committee appointed to investigate the possibility of establishing a medical school in Louisville.[2]

The actions that resulted in the incorporation of the University of Louisville in 1846 originated with the dream of Guthrie and his contemporaries for urban leadership in the trans-Appalachian West. From the perspective of the late 1700s and early 1800s, this vision was well-founded. Louisville's strategic location at the Falls of the Ohio River placed the city in an ideal position to profit from the advent of steam navigation. As the economic future brightened, Guthrie and other city leaders sought to demonstrate cultural leadership as well. In 1837 they established separate medical and liberal arts colleges, which were combined nine years later as the University of Louisville.

In this enterprise, Louisville profited from the decline of Lexington, which lacked a navigable waterway. President Andrew Jackson's 1830 veto of the Maysville Road, which would have connected Lexington with the Ohio River, further isolated that town from the avenues of commerce. In addition, Lexington's infant industries never recovered from the financial panic of 1819, caused in part by the excessive land speculation and bank activity following the War of 1812. Transylvania University had emerged in the 1780s and had established a medical school, the oldest west of the Appalachians, in 1799. The institution was Lexington's major cultural asset, but in recent years it had come under political and religious attack.[3]

Led by James Guthrie, the Louisville city council moved quickly to exploit Lexington's plight. First, it proposed moving Transylvania's medical department to Louisville, which offered a larger supply of cadavers and a teaching hospital. Several Transylvania medical professors supported this plan, primarily because they saw a better economic future in Louisville. Not surprisingly, the proposition outraged many in Lexington. In 1837 the state legislature soundly rejected the transfer proposal and also refused to charter a new medical school in Louisville.[4]

Not discouraged, the city council then resurrected an 1833 charter for the Louisville Medical Institute, an inactive organization that possibly lacked the legal authority to confer degrees. Further, the council offered land and $30,000 for the construction of a school building. The *Louisville Public Advertiser* followed with its own brand of boosterism: "What a valuable addition to our population would four or five hundred respectable students form!—think of the mass of money they would expend here!—and then of the fame and influence we should acquire."

On March 30, 1837, Charles Caldwell, leader of the Transylvania defectors, delivered a public address calling for the immediate creation of a medical school at city expense. The following month the city reaffirmed its earlier pledge and added $20,000 for books and equipment. The Louisville Medical Institute (LMI) opened that fall with three of its original six faculty members drawn from Transylvania: Charles Caldwell, John Esten Cooke, and Lunsford P. Yandell, who served as the school's first dean. They would soon be joined by such luminaries from Transylvania and elsewhere as Charles Wilkins Short, Daniel Drake, and Samuel David Gross. It was an estimable faculty that opened the school's first year in October 1837 with one hundred students.[5]

To lead this enterprise, the trustees chose as the first president of the board Judge John Rowan, one of the more distinguished Kentuckians of the early national period. Rowan's family came from Virginia and eventually settled in Bardstown, Kentucky, where he studied under the noted frontier educator James Priestley. Rowan went to Lexington to read law, was licensed in 1795, and returned to practice in Bards-

Louisville Medical School faculty, 1837-1838.

town, where he developed into an accomplished criminal lawyer and orator. A Jeffersonian Republican, Rowan represented Kentucky in the U.S. House of Representatives from 1807 until 1809, and in the U.S. Senate from 1825 until 1831. While he lived in Louisville, Rowan also maintained a residence in Bardstown, "Federal Hill," linked by folklore to the Stephen Collins Foster ballad, "My Old Kentucky Home," which in 1928 became Kentucky's state song.[6]

The Louisville Medical Institute was a ringing success. The city council approved James Guthrie's plan to finance a building on Chestnut Street between Eighth and Ninth. The cornerstone of the Greek Revival building, designed by noted Kentucky archi-

John Rowan (1773–1843), first president, Louisville Medical Institute, 1837–1842. Rowan served in the U.S. House of Representatives and Senate and was the first president of the Kentucky Historical Society, organized in 1836. On the morning of February 3, 1801, Rowan killed Dr. James Chambers in a duel that grew out of a drinking dispute in a Bardstown tavern. Chambers had impugned Rowan's mastery of classical languages.

of the early LMI faculty. Senior in age, fierce in debate, and well-known within the medical profession, Caldwell possessed fearless confidence in his own rectitude. He published widely on a variety of medical topics and would live to see three, at least, discredited: polygenesis, the separate creation of the races; vitalism, the belief that a mysterious principle regulated body chemistry; and phrenology, the study of the skull's shape to deduce mental capacity. Caldwell held that there were three perfect heads in the American republic. One of them rested on the shoulders of Henry Clay and another belonged to Daniel Webster. Modesty prevented the professor from identifying the owner of the third.[8]

Charles Wilkins Short, another early Louisville Medical Institute faculty member, had come to Transylvania in 1825 as professor of materia medica (pharmacology). He sympathized with the decision

Charles Wilkens Short (1794–1863) studied under Caspar Wistar in Philadelphia. When Short left Transylvania for the Louisville Medical Institute, one observer likened his move to "taking a strong timber from an enemy's ship." (Samuel David Gross, Biographical Sketch of Charles Wilkins Short [1865].)

tect Gideon Shryock, was laid on February 22, 1838. Between 1838 and 1861, the school produced nearly 1,500 medical doctors. At the start of the 1844 term, Professor Short gleefully reported that enrollment at the Louisville Medical Institute had left Transylvania far in the background. Although Kentucky provided many more of the institute's students than any other state, each term found significant numbers of enrollees arriving by steamboat from areas ranging from the Great Lakes to the Gulf of Mexico. The tuition revenue generated by the Medical Institute allowed it to build an excellent faculty. With some degree of truth, the institution's supporters declared it "first among the Medical Schools of the West."[7]

No one disputed Charles Caldwell's leadership

In 1854 Daniel Drake (1785–1852) published Principal Diseases of the Interior Valley of North America, *his medical masterpiece. (Drake,* Pioneer Life in Kentucky *[1870].)*

fessional responsibility, for he was quick to point out the shortcomings of medical education and practice in the trans-Appalachian West and he was ready with recommendations for overcoming them. Furthermore, he was a renowned scholar. While in Louisville, Drake completed much of the research and writing for his study of the relationship between climate, geography, and disease in the Mississippi and Ohio Valleys. Finally, he edited the *Western Journal of Medicine and Surgery,* an excellent professional journal that spread the name of the Louisville Medical Institute throughout the region. Among other things, the *Western Journal* carried pioneering articles by Edward Jarvis on medical statistics and the humane treatment of mental illness.[10]

Samuel David Gross was another noted faculty member during those formative years. Gross came to the Louisville Medical Institute faculty in 1840 from

of Caldwell, Yandell, and Cooke to move to Louisville in 1837, but feared losses from the sale of his Lexington property if he followed them. At the same time, William Short, his uncle and trusted advisor, urged him to leave Transylvania behind. After visiting Louisville in the spring of 1838, Short joined the Medical Institute faculty for its second term, which began that fall. One observer likened his move to "taking a strong timber from an enemy's ship." A skilled teacher, respected scholar, and quiet leader, Short made his scientific reputation as a botanist. He specialized in field work and classification. Asa Gray, father of American botany, named the North Carolina wildflower *Shortia galacifolia* in his honor.[9]

Daniel Drake's appointment in 1839 to the Louisville Medical Institute probably added more to the faculty than the acquisition of any other member. Drake possessed a keen and articulate sense of pro-

Samuel David Gross (1805–1884), author of System of Surgery, *was one of America's greatest surgeons and a founder of the American Medical Association.*

the Cincinnati Medical College, shortly after publishing a well-received book on pathological anatomy. He remained in Louisville for all but one of the following sixteen years, later recalling this time as one of the more productive periods in his professional life. While in Louisville, Gross conducted research on abdominal wounds, using dogs as his subjects. He boarded the animals in the basement of the medical building, which soon became infested with fleas. Gross complained that these parasites "skipped about in every direction," causing at least one faculty member to wear his boots over his trousers "to prevent them from effecting an entrance to his body."[11]

During the 1850s the medical school also boasted two distinguished chemists, J. Lawrence Smith and Benjamin Silliman Jr. The New Orleans editor J.D.B. De Bow placed Smith at the head of American chemists, and an authority on science in the Old South cited him as one of the region's outstanding minds. Although Silliman spent most of his professional career at Yale University, while affiliated with the University of Louisville he conducted the research that led to his landmark description of the distillation, purification, and uses of petroleum.[12]

The medical school's first session in 1837 was held in the city workhouse while construction proceeded on its permanent home at Eighth and Chestnut. During this period Professor Yandell confessed that, when feeling low-spirited, he would visit the construction site, where he rekindled confidence by visualizing the structure's "splendid & graceful proportions." When completed, the building offered ample classroom, office, and laboratory space. Furthermore, it housed a library, a medical museum, and basement anatomy rooms "brilliantly lit at night, with gas, making dissection, at such time, as satisfactory as by daylight." Even the reserved Professor Short claimed that no medical school facilities anywhere in the nation could rival LMI's. One orator considered the building physical evidence that, in Louisville, intellectual pursuits had eclipsed the rougher passions of the frontier.[13]

Yet the Louisville Medical Institute probably accepted any white male who paid his fees. No female or person of color need have applied. (Decades would pass before a female student would be admitted, and more than a century before an African American would attend.) Many of its students had poor academic backgrounds and limited social skills. Short warned them not to read frivolous books, smoke cigars, or talk during lectures, which some undoubtedly did. Drake complained that western medical students often lacked intellectual discipline and professional dedication. An earnest opponent of strong drink, Drake also organized the Physiological Temperance Society of the Louisville Medical Institute. At least for a time, he succeeded in persuading about half the medical class to swear off alcoholic beverages. Drake warned anyone who would listen that strong drinks lacked nutritional value, harmed the body and the mind, and stimulated the baser passions.[14]

Henry Clay Lewis, an 1846 graduate who later immortalized his alma mater in his humorous writings as the "Louisiana Swamp Doctor," recalled that many of his fellow students devoted little attention to their studies, but added that they became more serious as final examinations approached. In truth, nineteenth-century medical students entered school at a relatively late age, and some supported themselves as physicians' apprentices. Not surprisingly, they had adult vices and were unintimidated by faculty authority.[15]

Once enrolled, students attended two years of lectures to complete their degree requirements. The term began in October and ended in March, and the second year merely repeated the first. In 1837 students paid $15 directly to each instructor for a matriculation ticket. The school assessed a $5 general fee, and second year students paid a $20 graduation fee. Room and board were available for about $3 per week. Drake advocated a three-year course of progressive difficulty, which did not become the norm in American medical schools until late in the century.[16]

Courses fell into three categories: basic sciences, which included chemistry, anatomy, and physiology; diagnosis, in which the instructor expounded some theory of the origin of disease; and treatment, which included surgery and materia medica. At this time, physicians had no knowledge of the germ theory of

Medical students purchased tickets like these to attend lectures in basic science, diagnosis, and treatment. Dissection was optional.

disease or the role of insect vectors in its transmission. Most medical schools taught that heat, humidity, and decaying vegetable matter produced a "miasma," or harmful atmosphere, that carried epidemic disease. Furthermore, many believed that all disease arose from an imbalance of the body's "humors," or fluids: blood, phlegm, yellow bile, and black bile. John Esten Cooke, one of the original Transylvania defectors, was among those who taught this theory. He advocated bleeding and purging as sovereign remedies because these procedures balanced the humors. In 1844, when other medical educators were abandoning such approaches as his dependence on high doses of calomel (a mercury compound used as a cathartic before it was found to be toxic), Cooke retired involuntarily in the face of heavy professional criticism.[17]

The availability of anatomical material had provided one argument for establishing a medical school in Louisville. In a period of social and legal opposition to such activity, students and faculty sometimes robbed graves or broke into the city morgue to obtain bodies, an indication of the importance attached to dissection. Not surprisingly, many of their subjects came from the lower rungs of the city's social and economic ladder, especially transients, slaves, and free blacks, who together probably represented a disproportionate part of the cadaver supply. The school also employed a demonstrator of anatomy, who acquired cadavers and oversaw dissecting sessions. One occupant of this position was Tobias G. Richardson, who later taught medicine at Tulane University and published a standard textbook on human anatomy. Most

of the dissecting work took place in the evening, following the day's lectures, when four to six students could work on each cadaver. Some cut while others read aloud from the anatomy textbook.[18]

The Louisville Marine Hospital, built in 1825 at Chestnut and Preston Streets and long under city control, provided another effective argument for establishing a medical school in the city. From the beginning the Medical Institute faculty enjoyed free access to this facility, renamed Louisville City Hospital in 1836, and offered clinical lectures there. In 1840 they even added a 400-seat amphitheater at their own expense. Experience at the City Hospital undoubtedly exposed students to the harsh side of medical

Charles A. Hentz, an LMI student, depicted himself on foot and Dr. George Wood Bayless, demonstrator of anatomy, on horseback with a corpse on a midnight grave-robbing expedition. (Hentz Family Papers, Southern Historical Collection, University of North Carolina at Chapel Hill.)

Medical students often posed for photographs with their cadavers, as did this 1880s group in an outdoor cadaver lab at the Louisville Medical College (left) and this 1906 group from the Hospital College of Medicine (right). (Filson Club Historical Society; U of L Kornhauser Health Sciences Library.)

The original Louisville Marine Hospital of the 1820s became the central section of the enlarged Louisville City Hospital, which opened in February 1870. One of the institution's functions, caring for ill and injured river men, had been taken over by the United States Marine Hospital, established in Portland about 1851. A new structure on the same spot replaced City Hospital in 1914. Its name was later changed to Louisville General Hospital. Now the location of the U of L School of Medicine, this site has been the heart of the city's medical center for 175 years. (Yater, Two Hundred Years at the Falls of the Ohio.*)*

On the night of December 4, 1868, William Garvin, born in Ireland in 1795, second president of the Louisville Medical Institute, 1842–1843, lost his life when the Louisville and Cincinnati steamers America *and* United States *collided on the Ohio River above Warsaw, Kentucky. (*Harper's Weekly, *courtesy of the Filson Club Historical Society and the University of Kentucky Special Collections and Archives .)*

practice in a rough-and-tumble society. In 1842, for example, one student reported the case of a man who had suffered a knife wound to the right eye. The blade passed through the lid, evacuated "the humors," and penetrated the sinus cavity behind the upper jaw.[19]

The faculty required each degree candidate not only to attend a course of clinical lectures but also to submit a thesis on some medical topic. Short complained that too many students wrote "long dissertations, often in illegible characters, on subjects which they knew little or nothing about." Perhaps in response to his colleague's complaints, Drake urged students to work on their theses between sessions, when they had more time for research, reflection, and

revision. He even suggested possible topics, such as native medicinal plants, regional medical problems, and the relationship between chemistry and medicine. The faculty published some students' theses, including one on the antiseptic qualities of creosote. This work included a history of the substance, a review of the medical literature, and a case study of its use on the inflamed leg of a free black laborer. One admirer of Caldwell pursued his mentor's interest in cerebral physiology, although his work fell mainly in the realm of pseudo-science.[20]

Degree candidates also stood for a final oral examination. This consisted of a fifteen-minute private session with each of seven professors. One student,

Henry Clay Lewis, likened the ordeal to being "without a friend or a dollar thousands of miles from home." In his case, the examination included questions on the pros and cons of vitalism and the types and amounts of drugs to administer in specific situations. One faculty member considered Lewis talented but overconfident, and used the examination to administer a dose of humility. Short believed the school produced some medical doctors "not very well entitled to the honor," but concluded that Louisville's graduates were as well trained as any. Most of those who took the examination passed, but some students never reached that point. Even Lunsford P. Yandell's son, David W. Yandell, who would become a stellar member of the faculty after the Civil War, almost failed to graduate.[21]

At the time of John Rowan's death in 1843, the Louisville Medical Institute, with its library and clinical amphitheater, was at the peak of its prosperity. During the last year of his life, Rowan relinquished the institute's presidency and was succeeded for a brief time by Louisville businessman William Garvin, who operated a dry goods business, Garvin, Bell and Company, which prospered during Louisville's antebellum mercantile expansion to the south and west. In 1843 James Guthrie succeeded Garvin as president. Meanwhile, the Louisville Medical Institute had come under attack by local physicians and political opponents, who advocated its merger into a comprehensive university. Eventually, this pressure weakened the medical school, but it also led to the founding of the University of Louisville.

THREE

FROM FRONTIER ACADEMY TO CITY COLLEGE

A<small>T THE OPENING</small> of the Louisville Medical Institute, Charles Caldwell declared that the city had left behind its coarse, frontier origins. He envisioned a municipal university as the capstone of the public schools, offering degrees in medicine, law, theology, and liberal arts. Chartered by the state, this "great and commanding university" would be the commonwealth's premier institution of higher education. It must be located in Louisville, Caldwell declared, for that place alone among Kentucky cities could provide the necessary financial support.[1]

The city council agreed. In November 1837, in the wake of the founding of the Louisville Medical Institute, the council created the Louisville Collegiate Institute (LCI). Again James Guthrie played the leading role. The council stipulated that if the state legislature chartered a comprehensive university in Louisville, control of the medical school's property and operation would pass to the new institution. At this point the medical faculty, flush with the promise of their new enterprise, offered no objection.[2]

The Louisville Collegiate Institute was seen as the forerunner of the liberal arts division of the proposed university. On paper, it resembled many other American colleges of the mid-nineteenth century. The school catalog described a four-year course with training in ancient and modern languages, English literature, history, natural and physical sciences, and moral and political economy, all of which trained citizens

Benjamin Franklin Farnsworth (1793–1851), first president of the Louisville Collegiate Institute, 1837–1838.

"for a republican and christian country." The Louisville Collegiate Institute opened in May 1838 in the old Jefferson Seminary building on Eighth Street under Benjamin Franklin Farnsworth, a Baptist schoolmaster, who had been appointed president on December 2, 1837.[3]

The Louisville Collegiate Institute received some municipal support, but relied largely on tuition and fees, as did the medical school. Unfortunately, neither its funding nor its curriculum lived up to its promise. The school attracted few students and, as had its predecessor, Jefferson Seminary, struggled to survive. Farnsworth lasted less than a year. Citing failing health, he retired in 1838 and moved to his daughter's home near Lexington.[4]

John Hopkins Harney, previously a member of LCI's faculty, succeeded Farnsworth. Self-educated, Harney early developed a talent for mathematics. At age seventeen, his clever solution to a difficult surveying problem earned him the principalship of an academy in his home town of Paris, Kentucky. Young Harney saved his money and soon set out for Miami University in Oxford, Ohio, where he graduated in 1827 in belles-lettres and theology. Upon graduation, he went to Indiana Seminary (predecessor of Indiana University) as professor of mathematics, and in 1833 he moved to Hanover College in Indiana. There he began work on his *Algebra*, published in 1840.[5]

In that same year, 1840, the Louisville Collegiate Institute was rechartered as Louisville College, with Harney continuing as president. Friends of the school knew a way had to be found to put it on a sound financial footing. They considered this act a significant step toward an integrated, comprehensive university, and they hoped the trustees of such an institution would be empowered to allocate funds accordingly.[6]

Unlike the Louisville Collegiate Institute and its successor, Louisville College, the Louisville Medical Institute had prospered. Its building and lot, both donated by the city, were large and impressive. Its library included many volumes purchased in Europe especially for the school, and its anatomical collection was remarkable. Some of its professors made upwards of $4,000 per session in lecture fees. Some Louisville officials argued that the medical faculty owed more than mere gratitude to the city council for its generosity toward the school. They maintained that a portion of the profits gleaned by the medical faculty should be diverted to support the struggling liberal arts college.[7]

John Hopkins Harney (1806–1867), second president, Louisville Collegiate Institute, 1838–1840; president, Louisville College, 1840–1844. By 1846, when Louisville College and the Louisville Medical Institute merged to form the University of Louisville, Harney had established himself in a new field, journalism. He founded the Louisville Democrat, *which he edited until his death. Harney's editorial protestation of arbitrary unionist actions during the Civil War brought him a short term in a Union jail, and following the war he criticized retaliatory measures taken against former Confederates. The* Democrat *dissolved soon after Harney's death, and was absorbed by a new newspaper, the* Louisville Courier-Journal.

Shadrach Penn Jr., still editor of the Democratic *Louisville Public Advertiser*, cried loudest for the financial and administrative combination of the medical school and the college, with full public control of the merged institution. The medical faculty, supported by George Prentice, editor of the pro-Whig *Louisville Journal*, claimed this attack upon their autonomy had been perpetrated by political opponents jealous of the faculty's financial success.[8]

George Prentice published the Louisville Journal, *where he supported the cause of the Louisville Medical Institute faculty.* (History of the Ohio Falls Cities [1882].)

Friends of Louisville College found allies among local physicians. William A. McDowell, an authority on tuberculosis, undoubtedly resented not having been offered a position on the faculty of the Louisville Medical Institute, most of whose members were brought in from outside the city. In 1840 a pamphlet issued by McDowell and others accused the LMI fac-

ulty of low standards, resulting in poor stewardship of the building provided by the city and a lack of public confidence in the institution. Two years later McDowell and his allies brought their complaints before the city council, calling for a transfer of the Louisville Medical Institute to the managers of the Louisville College, which was under municipal control. A bitter exchange followed. At one point, Professor Yandell declared that McDowell could no more cure tuberculosis than he could "make a pig's stump tail grow out again."[9]

In 1844 Louisville College inherited the portion of the estate of Jefferson Seminary designated for the use of higher education in Louisville, but this action came too late to save the school. By then it had closed its doors with little immediate hope of survival. It was clear that the key to winning control of the Louisville Medical Institute was to secure a charter for a comprehensive university in Louisville, which by the agreement of 1837 between the city and the Medical Institute would subordinate the medical school to the trustees of the new university.[10]

After several unsuccessful attempts to have the college recognized as a comprehensive university, to which the trustees of the Medical Institute would be obliged to surrender their property under the agreement of 1837, LMI's opponents took action. On their behalf, the city council late in 1845 petitioned the state legislature to charter a new institution in Louisville, a comprehensive university that presumably would take financial control of the medical school and revive the liberal arts college.[11]

FOUR

THE EMERGENCE OF A UNIVERSITY

CITY OFFICIALS and other friends of the college won the battle but lost the war. Over the objections of the LMI faculty, the state legislature in 1846 combined the Louisville Medical Institute and the languishing Louisville College to form the University of Louisville. It was the first use of this modern name. Unfortunately for the insolvent college, however, the new charter made no provision for the financial invasion of the medical school.

In addition to leaving each division financially autonomous, the charter made no allowance for public financial support. This left both the medical school and the college to survive on tuition and private benevolence. Furthermore, although the mayor and the city council would appoint the university's eleven trustees, the city had little authority over the school other than requiring it to submit an annual report. Finally, the board of trustees would elect one of its members as president, a voluntary position which ensured a lack of central authority. The 1846 charter compromised the interests of the contending parties, with the medical faculty getting the better part of the bargain.[1]

To lead this new University of Louisville, the trustees chose Judge Samuel Smith Nicholas as its first president. The son of a prominent Virginia family, Nicholas was orphaned early and left with meager means. He took a position in the offices of an uncle's maritime firm in Baltimore and studied French and Latin in his spare time. Nicholas sailed to China and

Samuel Smith Nicholas (1797–1869), first president of the University of Louisville, 1846–1847, was the son of George Nicholas, a drafter of Kentucky's first constitution and the commonwealth's first attorney general. During the Civil War, S.S. Nicholas grew increasingly reflective and published several essays on legal and constitutional issues. Although a Unionist, Nicholas never reconciled himself with the coercive measures the United States used to prosecute the Civil War successfully.

LOUISVILLE UNIVERSITY.

The city of Louisville provided the Louisville Medical Institute building as an enticement to the Transylvania University medical faculty. A decade later, the city added a second structure to "University Square," this one intended for the Academic Department of the new University of Louisville. In 1856 this building was occupied by what became Male High School, and later still by Central High School. (Ballou's Pictorial Drawing-Room Companion, *October 1856.*)

South America with his uncle's fleet and eventually moved to Frankfort, Kentucky, to read law. In 1825 he settled in Louisville, where he became an agent and attorney for the Bank of the United States. Nicholas served on the Court of Appeals bench from 1831 to 1837 and thereafter for a time on the Louisville chancery court. Later in his career, he turned down a nomination to the United States Supreme Court.[2]

Under the new 1846 charter, the struggling Louisville College, which apparently had not held classes for the last two years, became the Academic Department of the University of Louisville. Using the proceeds from the sale of the Jefferson Seminary property, the city moved quickly to erect a new building on what was now called University Square next to the Medical Department at Eighth and Chestnut

Streets. Designed in the Greek Revival style by architect John Stirewalt, the new three-story college building remained idle for a time, save for a mathematics class taught by a professor who groused about the leaky roof. This lack of activity irritated city government officials, opponents of the new Medical Department, and friends of the Academic Department. The board of trustees discussed plans to finance the Academic Department, but no funds materialized other than tuition and fees, which had proven inadequate in the past.[3]

The 1846 charter also added a Law Department, which from its beginning achieved at least moderate success. The school's few faculty members offered late afternoon classes, first in the unfinished courthouse, then for a brief period in the new Academic

Department building, then in rented quarters. They created few records of their activity. Degree candidates attended two courses of lectures, participated in mock court sessions, and took a written final examination, but received their primary training through apprenticeships. They worked as clerks for practicing attorneys and studied for the bar examination as time allowed.[4]

The faculty was composed entirely of practicing attorneys who considered teaching an avocation rather than a profession. They were local men, more absorbed with the practical functions of bench and bar than with the halls of academe. The original law professors included no more dedicated teacher than Henry Pirtle, who, like many of his colleagues, had never taken a formal law degree. Pirtle functioned as both dean and registrar, though he held neither title, and remained with the school until his retirement in 1873.[5]

Joining Pirtle on the first law faculty were Garnett Duncan, who served in the U.S. House of Representatives from 1847 until 1849, and Preston S. Loughborough, who used his expertise in jurisprudence to publish a definitive compilation of early Kentucky statutes. Initially classes met in the basement of the Jefferson County Courthouse. The Law Department attracted fewer students than the medical school, but enough to generate operating revenue.[6]

Meanwhile opponents of the new University of Louisville Medical Department, including those who believed it operated too independently of public control, moved forward. In 1848 Joshua Barker Flint, who had been dismissed from the Louisville Medical Institute faculty eight years earlier, led a campaign to charter another medical school in the city. The state legislature rejected the idea, but two years later Flint and his allies borrowed the charter of a dormant institution and opened the Kentucky School of Medicine. The new school, operated in conjunction with Transylvania University, offered the traditional winter term in Louisville and a summer session in Lexington, which enabled students to complete the two required sessions in one calendar year. Yandell predicted that "Flint and his new corps" would cause no alarm, but in two years he complained bitterly about

The Kentucky School of Medicine representd an alliance between Transylvania University and the Louisville physicians who resented the medical faculty of the University of Louisville.

unfair attacks upon the medical faculty of the University of Louisville. The rival school appealed to enough potential physicians to cause a significant decline in the University of Louisville's enrollment during the 1850s.[7]

Efforts to place the university under public control and divert a portion of the medical school's revenue to a common account continued. John Hopkins Harney, who earlier had been president of Louisville College and now was editor of the *Louisville Democrat*, led the campaign.

By 1850 Louisville had become the nation's tenth largest city. In that year the city proposed that the financially insolvent Academic Department become part of the public, or "common," schools. Although financially practical, this move was opposed by President James Guthrie, who wanted to maintain the autonomy of the department and provide funding through other means. Guthrie, who in 1847 had followed Nicholas as president of the university, found his administration beset by legal conflicts over the school's liberal arts division. Guthrie argued his case before the state legislature, but in 1851 the General Assembly, under prodding from Harney and his associates, approved a new charter for Louisville. It called for direct election of the university's trustees, central control of all school finances, and revival of the moribund Academic Department as the capstone of the public schools.[8]

There was still a question of constitutionality, however, and in 1854 the Kentucky Supreme Court overturned the city's charter as it applied to the University of Louisville. Citing the United States Supreme Court's 1819 ruling in the Dartmouth College case, the opinion held that the university was a private corporation controlled by the original board of trustees. Like Dartmouth, its charter was immune from revisions imposed by outside agencies, including the state legislature.[9]

The Academic Department still lacked funds, however, and a disgusted Louisville city council shifted its support to a public high school. Thus in 1855 the university trustees and those of the public schools agreed to place the Academic Department in the hands of the latter board and to turn over the department's building for the high school. The Medical Department and what became known as Male High School, the latter actually an academy more advanced than the modern high school, existed side by side on University Square at Eighth and Chestnut Streets through Guthrie's long presidency, with the Male students often attending medical lectures. The two schools operated under separate boards, and for many years Male's board of trustees awarded bachelor's degrees to its graduates. In 1860 another act of the state legislature stipulated that the University of Louisville could receive no municipal support while it remained under private control.[10]

Time and circumstances took their toll on the medical school during the 1850s. Short and Drake had resigned in 1849. In 1850 Caldwell, still lecturing at the age of seventy-eight, was abruptly dismissed in a move probably engineered by Professor Lunsford P. Yandell, who opposed Caldwell's promulgation of the theory of vitalism. His forced retirement left a deep wound. A few years later Gross finally left, unhappy with the loss of able colleagues and displeased with some of their replacements. Age, feuds, and jealousies had weakened a fine faculty, men who had ably championed the medical school during its first decade. On the last day of 1856 the school suffered another loss: a faulty stovepipe in the chemistry laboratory caused a fire, destroying the grand original building and many of the school's historical records. It was replaced by a new structure judged finer than the old, but the school had lost another physical link with the heady days of the early 1840s.[11]

The incorporation of the University of Louisville in 1846 resulted from the coincidence of time, place, and leadership. During the 1830s the city fathers looked toward a prosperous future as the crossroads of trade and travel in the trans-Appalachian West. No one saw this vision with greater clarity than James Guthrie, the school's dominant figure during the middle decades of the nineteenth century. In 1837 he had persuaded the city council to open both the Medical Institute and the Collegiate Institute. Beginning in 1847, Guthrie served as president for twenty-two years, the longest term in the university's long history. He assembled the board of trustees annually to approve candidates for medical and law degrees, but otherwise the trustees met only in response to a crisis. They lacked either the will or the ability to resolve disagreements over the purpose of the university.[12]

The same was true of the other local leaders who had helped establish the university and its predecessors. Both John Rowan and William Garvin served, for a time, as presidents of the Louisville Medical Institute. Like Guthrie, they were respected figures in the community. They also owed their living to other

James Guthrie (1792–1869), third president, Louisville Medical Institute, 1843–1846; second president, University of Louisville, 1847–1869. His leadership of the city council was a major factor in the founding of the University of Louisville.

pursuits and showed little interest in the school's daily affairs. Samuel Smith Nicholas, the first president of the University of Louisville in 1846-1847, was equally respected, but uninterested in the details of running an institution of higher education. The Louisville College, meanwhile, operated so sporadically that those associated with it never had a chance to assert themselves as educational leaders. Furthermore, they did not command the respect that men such as Guthrie, Rowan, Garvin, and Nicholas enjoyed.[13]

These men provided no more leadership than the faculty wanted. Even the dean of the medical school, probably the most powerful administrative figure in the university's early history, exercised little authority. His duties consisted of collecting fees, keeping records, advertising, and maintaining the building and grounds. Like the medical school, the law school lacked strong leadership, and undoubtedly needed none as long as the university consisted of independent units which owed little allegiance to the president and trustees.

During this period, the board's primary authority consisted of approving candidates for degrees submitted by the medical and law faculties. Under this arrangement, the city could not establish a unified school. Of course, leadership and organization in a nineteenth-century institution of higher education should not be held to a twentieth-century model, but the founders of the University of Louisville undoubtedly fell short of their ambitious goals.[14]

The Academic Department remained dormant until early in the twentieth century. Nevertheless, the university's early years were by no means a story of failure. The medical and law schools remained in more or less continuous operation. The latter attracted few students, but during the coming decades Louisville's reputation as a medical center grew. For the remainder of the nineteenth century, the University of Louisville consisted of a medical and a law school held together tenuously by a common board of trustees.

The vision of a comprehensive university belonged to those who saw it as but one component of the city's overall public school system. As such, it had to teach the liberal arts. The medical faculty had no objection to this, provided it did not come at their expense. The local physicians who attacked the medical school may or may not have sympathized with public education, but they were undoubtedly jealous of the medical faculty. This fractious mixture made compromise unlikely.

In their own minds all three factions had justifiable positions. The advocates of public education were part of a growing national movement in that direction. The medical faculty wanted nothing more than what was typical of medical schools during this period. Finally, local physicians were understandably threatened by interlopers who undercut their status and income. The medical faculty won in principle, but in the process exhausted itself bickering and feuding. The city opened its own liberal arts school and swore off further support of the University of Louisville. While adherents of all of these factions shared a common interest in the university, the institution that had been cobbled together in 1846 satisfied none of them.

FIVE

CIVIL WAR TRAVAILS

LOUISVILLE VOTERS seemed reasonably unified in their thinking about the issues that divided the nation in the 1860 presidential election. They cast the majority of their ballots for John Bell of Tennessee and Stephen A. Douglas of Illinois, the two moderate candidates. Abraham Lincoln of Illinois and John C. Breckinridge of Kentucky, candidates strongly identified with the North and the South, respectively, received relatively few votes. Most local voters apparently shared the views of Samuel Smith Nicholas, the university's first president, who attributed the Civil War to extremists of both South and North, and who decried "all bastard allegiance to a section, to a party, or to a policy." Though a slave owner, Judge Nicholas favored gradual emancipation, opposed secession, and worked successfully to keep Kentucky in the Union.[1]

James Guthrie, president of the University of Louisville at the outbreak of the war, held similar views. A slave owner and states' rights Democrat, he also opposed secession. In 1860 Guthrie had even been considered a compromise presidential candidate, and the next year he represented Kentucky at the Virginia Peace Convention. As president of the Louisville & Nashville Railroad, Guthrie also controlled a vital supply line. After an initial period of indecision, he placed the L&N at the disposal of the United States Army.[2]

Others held more extreme views. Professor David W. Yandell of the U of L medical school answered the South's call to arms. As a military surgeon, he was baptized by fire at Shiloh, where he served as medical director of General Albert Sidney Johnston's army. James Speed, who had taught in the law school before the war, moved to Washington in 1864 to join President Abraham Lincoln's cabinet. As early as 1849, Speed had spoken out against slavery. As a result of this position, he lost a bid to serve as a delegate to Kentucky's 1850 constitutional convention. This opposition to slavery also hampered his political career until the outbreak of the war, during which he served first as Lincoln's principal advisor on Kentucky affairs and then as attorney general. He continued for a time as attorney general under Andrew Johnson. Like many Kentuckians, Speed had opposed secession, and worked to preserve the Union without resorting to force. As a cabinet member, Speed favored the president's policy of moderation toward the South and won Lincoln's praise for honesty, poise, and levelheadedness.[3]

The Civil War and subsequent readjustment disrupted affairs in Louisville, which was occupied and held by United States soldiers, and further diminished the University of Louisville, which already had lost much of its vigor through political wrangling in the late 1840s and 1850s. During the war, university classes dwindled, and the remaining faculty members became involved in local military and political activities. Falling enrollments closed the medical school for the 1862-1863 session. The next term resumed with the announcement that the faculty would devote spe-

This earliest photograph in U of L's Kornhauser Library depicts medical school graduate Thomas Sutton in 1862.

cial attention to military surgery and surgical anatomy "in view of their present importance." Professor Theodore S. Bell served on the United States Sanitary Commission during the conflict, and the city's military hospitals were filled with physicians who remained to teach in the U of L medical school and rival schools that came into being following the war.[4]

To make matters worse, in 1863 the medical school dean, Joseph W. Benson, a Southern sympathizer, was convicted by a United States court-martial for fraud and negligence on a contract to supply feed for government horses. The faculty supported his innocence, but he was imprisoned for a time. In September 1864, after Benson had been incarcerated almost a year, he offered his resignation, which the faculty refused to accept.[5]

Benson returned to the medical faculty following his release from prison, and in 1866 resumed his deanship for a session. Wartime passions were rekindled when Benson supposedly tampered with affairs at the local Freedman's Bureau hospital. According to some witnesses, Benson stole whiskey, performed needless surgery, and sold the corpses of black infants to medical schools for dissection. One of Benson's enemies even charged that babies were murdered so that their bodies would be available for medical study. Early in 1868, a local Republican newspaper claimed that some rural blacks stayed away from Louisville for fear of meeting the same fate.[6]

Meanwhile, U of L's law school continued to hold classes. With the recent demise of Transylvania's law school, it was now the oldest and most respected in Kentucky. The graduating classes, once it became clear that the war would be prolonged, dropped from twenty-seven in 1861 to eight the following year. Law classes remained small in 1863. Nevertheless, the University of Louisville and the University of Virginia were the only southern schools that offered law classes throughout the war.[7]

At the close of hostilities, the medical school was reportedly destitute and its property about to revert to the city. One faculty member volunteered to sow grass on the school's bald lot, provided that he could pasture stock there. In 1866 low enrollments forced the university's medical school and the Kentucky School of Medicine to merge for one stormy term. A local newspaper commented that the combined school first formed a faculty of Southern sympathies and then reorganized with men of "just the opposite character."[8]

Returning veterans brought their wartime experiences back to school. A former Confederate officer who enrolled in the law course reported that Louisville was swarming with more rebels than he had seen since the demise of the Confederate States. Before long, the same young man found himself under suspicion for his imprudent reply to a U.S. soldier who had advocated the execution of Confederate president Jefferson Davis. On July 4, 1865, a penniless David W. Yandell returned to Louisville, convinced that the nation suffered from an abundance of ill-trained physicians. He reopened his practice and was soon reappointed to the U of L medical faculty. In the fall of 1865 the medical school faculty allowed at least one destitute Southern applicant to pledge his honor in lieu of immediate payment of fees.[9]

The Civil War's most lasting impact on the University of Louisville probably came in the form of lessons and experiences gained by physicians such as Yandell, who returned from their military careers to staff Louisville's medical schools and hospitals. These doctors had gained intensive experience in surgery, the treatment of wounds, the importance of sanitation, the administration of hospitals, and a host of other medical lessons that were the inevitable by-products of a war. They brought these experiences back to civilian life and applied them in consolidating and reforming the medical profession. Not surprisingly, it was this branch of higher learning that, in many ways, led the transition from the nineteenth-century college to the twentieth-century university. While difficult to measure, the impact of the war on medicine and medical education seems profound. The war also settled, in its own way—on the battlefield—a legal question that undoubtedly challenged antebellum law faculty and students: the constitutionality of secession.

SIX

COMPETITION, CONSOLIDATION, AND REFORM

A T THE END of the Civil War the University of Louisville consisted of a weakened medical school and a part-time law school, loosely bound by one board of trustees. The issue of the establishment and nourishment of a strong, permanent liberal arts college, which had been so dominant in the life of the university and its predecessor schools for two generations, was dead, not to be resurrected for more than forty years. Meanwhile, new medical schools continued to open in Louisville, and their histories eventually became intertwined with that of the university.

By 1910, when Abraham Flexner published his landmark report on medical education in the United States and Canada, the U of L medical school had initiated changes which foreshadowed developments university-wide. Including the revival of the Academic Department in 1907, these changes ushered in a new era in the university's development.

After the war, competition among medical schools not only resumed, but quickened its pace. Louisville was well located on river and rail routes that still drew students from throughout the region. Furthermore, medical schools remained relatively inexpensive to open. They required a minimum of equipment and, in the 1860s, the curriculum still consisted mainly of lectures. Finally, the profession failed to regulate itself. In the absence of outside control, standards for medical school admission and graduation remained low. The faculties of rival schools engaged in open competition for students, whose fees constituted the only source of institutional income. A large enrollment indicated a successful school.[1]

The situation was already tense when, in 1869, a third medical school opened in the city—the Louisville Medical College. The University of Louisville faculty charged that the name was designed to confuse prospective students, which was undoubtedly true. The founder and dean of the new school was Edwin Samuel Gaillard, a one-armed Confederate veteran, who used his *Richmond and Louisville Medical Journal* as the vehicle for a series of hyperbolic attacks upon the Medical Department of the University of Louisville. Gaillard's charges and the subsequent response pushed competition farther toward its peak.[2]

The university's president through the entire Civil War era, James Guthrie, died in 1869, many years before his dream of a truly comprehensive educational institution would be realized. Guthrie's successor, Isaac Caldwell, a prominent local attorney, continued the line of distinguished leaders who used their business and professional ties to boost both city and university. Born in Adair County, Kentucky, near Columbia, he attended Georgetown College, practiced law in Columbia, then moved to Louisville in 1852. After assuming the presidency in 1869, Caldwell supported Louisville commercial interests and the Louisville & Nashville Railroad in 1870 when the state legislature debated a central Kentucky right-

Edwin Samuel Gaillard (1827–1885) led the Louisville Medical College attack on the University of Louisville. (Annals of Medical History [1940].)

Isaac Caldwell (1824–1885) third president, University of Louisville, 1869–1885, opposed the intervention of federal authority in Kentucky civil rights matters when he argued the case of Blyew v. United States *before the U.S. Supreme Court in 1872.*

of-way for the Cincinnati Southern line, a potential rival of the L&N for the Southern trade.

Friends considered Caldwell a likely candidate for the United States Senate in 1875, but he withdrew from the contest. During his term as U of L president, Caldwell was described as "a man of fine social qualities, of great physical and mental vigor, and yet . . . all the ardor of youth." His devotion to the university never faltered; fatally ill in 1885, he continued to call meetings of the board of trustees until his death in November of that year.[3]

In 1874 the Hospital College of Medicine opened, further complicating the situation by creating still more competition for the university's Medical Department. The University of Louisville attempted to join forces with this new school, with one offering a spring and the other a winter session. This would have allowed students to complete the two required terms in one calendar year, giving the cooperating schools a competitive advantage. The plan failed, but shortly thereafter the Kentucky School of Medicine and the

Louisville Medical College, the most frequent violators of accepted standards, reached just such an agreement. Furthermore, they cut fees under the guise of tuition scholarships.[4]

The University of Louisville fought back by establishing the *Louisville Medical News*. As the title indicated, this was less a scientific journal than a medical newspaper. It covered a variety of topics, but specialized in bashing the Louisville Medical College and the Kentucky School of Medicine. At the same time, L.R. Sale sued the Louisville Medical College, charging that the school solicited students under false pretenses. The *Medical News* covered the Sale case with perverse delight. In 1877 the Louisville Medical College agreed to reduce the number of tuition scholarships offered. While the harshest hostilities among Louisville medical schools then subsided, an uneasy detente at best prevailed among them.[5]

Between 1860 and 1910, the University of Louisville alone produced four thousand medical doctors. The city's boast of being the nursery of Western physicians was no exaggeration. As before the war, most students came from the trans-Appalachian region. Most were Kentuckians, but many others arrived by steamboat or railroad from Indiana, Tennessee, Mississippi, and even Texas. Because U of L's Medical Department was the oldest and best-established medical school in the city, it enjoyed a slight edge over the Kentucky School of Medicine and the Louisville Medical College in attracting students. The Hospital College of Medicine ran a poor fourth.[6]

One observer wrote that "crude boys thronged from the plantations" to attend these schools. Contemporary accounts indicated that the city's medical schools accepted many students who wrote poorly and read with great difficulty. One student claimed that any white man who paid his fees could graduate from U of L's medical school. Another U of L student remembered Louisville as "a riverboat town of prostitutes and saloons," not a stimulating center for intellectual activity. Presumably, some students took full advantage of the city's opportunities.[7]

The townspeople had no reason to like medical students, except for the money they brought into the local economy. Contemporary accounts reported that students drank, gambled, and engaged in public brawls. Some even carried firearms. One would-be physician left his wife and eight children and came to Louisville under the pretext of studying medicine. Rather than enroll in school, he passed himself off as a wealthy mine owner, married a local belle, and lived "in a random fashion" supported by an allowance from his first wife. Furthermore, most students probably smelled of the anatomy laboratory; those willing to pay $6 per week for room and board enjoyed the luxury of a common bath, while others sacrificed this extravagance and paid as little as $3 per week.[8]

During the 1880s, medical students at the University of Louisville attended classes that began at 8 A.M. on Monday and ran through Saturday morning. Simon Flexner, an 1887 U of L graduate who later achieved distinction as a pathologist and medical administrator, recalled that lectures followed one an-

School of Medicine catalogs for the early 1870s list Simon Kracht as janitor, but as a "resurrectionist" he also made late-night forays with spade and sack to local cemeteries to rob graves. Such trips to the cemetery were vital to the training of physicians in the days before cadavers for dissection were legally procured. This is the earliest known photograph of a U of L staff member.

other "in a bewildering sequence through a succession of long days." Louis Frank long remembered the first amputation he observed as a medical student. The patient lost his leg and died shortly after the procedure. A horsehair pad covered the operating table, which was in regular use for a variety of purposes. Both Flexner and Frank lived to witness revolutionary changes in medical education, which undoubtedly colored their recollections of student life.[9]

Although the by-laws of the medical school threatened expulsion for any student who participated in the acquisition of cadavers without faculty authorization, at least some medical students continued to engage in the illegal procurement of corpses. Frank was part of a group that in the 1880s bribed the night watchman at the city morgue, climbed through the back window, and absconded with the body of a black man.[10]

Later, Frank took part in a grave-robbing expedition. He and his companions removed half the dirt used to fill the grave, split the top of the casket with a spade, ran a rope under the shoulders, and raised the body while the remaining dirt steadied the coffin. As late as the 1890s, irate Hoosiers gunned down one member of a University of Louisville grave-robbing excursion into southern Indiana. In 1894 the Kentucky statutes set the maximum penalty for disinterring bodies at a $1,000 fine and six months in jail, which provided some indication of the risks medical educators and students were willing to take.[11]

Reform efforts appeared earlier and took root sooner in the medical school than they did in the law school. As early as 1866, the medical faculty showed an interest in cooperative efforts to standardize fees and raise academic requirements. Over the next decade, several initiatives failed to produce results. In 1874 the medical faculty called for a regional meeting on these matters, but warned that unilateral changes were unrealistic. Two years later, a University of Louisville representative attended the organizational meeting of the American Medical College Association. The medical school endorsed the association's standard of a three-year course, but the AMCA failed to gain a wide following. In 1884 the medical school canceled its membership because the organization was "virtually nonexistent."[12]

More than any other medical faculty member of the late nineteenth century, David W. Yandell provided a model of professional behavior for students and colleagues alike. The son of Lunsford P. Yandell, one of the original Louisville Medical Institute professors, he squeaked through his studies, received his M.D. degree from the Louisville Medical Institute in 1846, continued his education in Europe, and served a brief term on the U of L faculty before the Civil War. During the war he served in the Confederate Army as a physician and medical administrator. Yandell returned

David W. Yandell (1826–1898), an LMI graduate, provided a model of professional behavior for medical students and faculty alike during the second half of the nineteenth century, when he taught at U of L.

to Louisville following the war, rejoined the university medical faculty, and became an outspoken advocate of more intense clinical training. Early in the 1870s he worked with the Sisters of Charity to erect a hospital for use as a teaching facility by the University of Louisville. In 1888, largely due to Yandell's persistence, the medical school opened a new dispensary. He also edited the *American Practitioner* and served as president of the American Medical Association. Though the frequent target of attacks by rival doctors and competing schools, Yandell exercised restraint in his replies to criticism.[13]

No faculty member devoted more energy to the U of L medical school during the late nineteenth century than James Morrison Bodine, who served as dean from 1867 until 1907. The dean's job remained one of relatively little authority, but according to one account required close attention to the school's receipts and expenditures, "excellent administrative ability,"

During the 1880s, the Louisville Medical College introduced lantern slides as instructional aids. (Louisville Medical College, Catalogue, 1884.)

and, undoubtedly, a saintly toleration for eccentric behavior. After fourteen years on the job, Professor Bodine begged for release from "the cares and labors of office," but was reelected by unanimous vote. In the words of one observer, he never joined "angry factions," a record which, if accurate, probably still stands.[14]

Theodore S. Bell had also been associated with the medical school before the war, but like Yandell became more prominent after the conflict. Known as "a wise and genial Christian," Bell was also considered an expert on malarial diseases, and his contemporaries credited him with saving many lives through timely warnings of impending pestilence. Actually,

Bell died on the verge of the bacteriological revolution, and never learned the origins of cholera, yellow fever, malaria, and other contagious diseases common in nineteenth-century Louisville. Like many of his contemporaries, he believed that heat, moisture, and vegetable decomposition combined to produce a morbid vapor that led to summer and autumn "fevers." He prescribed sleeping on the upper levels of dwelling houses where patients were further removed from such effluvia (as well as the mosquitoes that actually carried malaria). Bell believed that an isothermic line limited the extent of great epidemics and that Louisville's daily mean temperature kept the city out of frequent danger.[15]

Another U of L physician, Richard Oswald Cowling, founded the *Louisville Medical News* and devoted much of his career to attacking wrongs in medical education and practice. In addition to using the *News* to criticize competing schools, he strived to improve conditions in the state's prisons and to eliminate public executions. A practical man, Cowling considered hunting and fishing better therapy than many other contemporary treatments. He also preached against the "abominations of piqué dresses and flannel bellybands" when worn during Louisville's sultry summers.[16]

Like Yandell, many other Louisville medical professors had experience as military surgeons. John A. Ouchterlony came to the city as a U.S. Army doctor during the war and remained to teach in the Louisville Medical College, the Kentucky School of Medicine, and the University of Louisville. Edward Rush Palmer, an 1864 graduate of the University of Louisville, served in one of the city's military hospitals during the last year of the conflict. Lunsford P. Yandell Jr., the brother of David W. Yandell, was also a veteran of the Confederate medical corps who later taught at the University of Louisville, although he died at a relatively early age. The Civil War, during which many more soldiers died of disease and infection than from battle wounds, must have provided a terrible and unforgettable experience for these young physicians.[17]

By the late nineteenth century, Louisville's medical schools claimed a respectable array of specialists in various fields. Notable examples included Dudley Sharpe Reynolds in ophthalmology; H.A. Cottell on diseases of the nerves; Joseph M. Mathews, called "the father of proctology"; and Theophilus Parvin, a specialist in the medical and surgical diseases of women. Edward Rush Palmer, who joined the U of L faculty after the war, specialized in urology. His annual sex education lecture was given in a room crowded by medical students and students from local theological seminaries. The growth of specialists indicated Louisville's status as an urban center, where there was a large enough clientele to support the varying branches of medical practice.[18]

Although by 1880 Louisville had slipped to six-teenth in size among American cities, it was enjoying an increase in its population and a boom in its post-war manufacturing industries. The rising strength of its homegrown L&N Railroad Company, chartered in 1850, was eclipsing the steamboat trade and nourishing Louisville's meat packing, hemp rope and bag production, and other businesses. A national magazine hailed it as "one of the four great cities of the West," along with Chicago, St. Louis, and Cincinnati. Steam engines, boilers, agricultural implements, cement, and other products were made in the Falls City's factories and shipped to market by river and rail. As rail routes expanded exponentially after the Civil War, the L&N captured a generous portion of the southern trade. In 1883 the city put on an elaborate Southern Exposition to show off its industrial, agricultural, and artistic prowess and housed the exhibits in elaborate new buildings erected south of what became Central Park. These large structures were bathed in the glow of thousands of the new incandescent light bulbs invented by Thomas Edison, who returned to Louisville for the occasion. He had worked there briefly as a telegraph operator just after the Civil War. U.S. president Chester A. Arthur opened the exposition, which proved so popular it was held for each of the next four years.[19]

For a time during these heady days of Louisville's Gilded Age, the duration of study for the M.D. degree remained as it had been before the war, i.e., attendance at two years of lectures, the second a repeat of the first. Until 1876 the U of L faculty still required students to submit a thesis. The requirement was then dropped, purportedly to encourage more clinical and laboratory work. Students still underwent a final oral examination by the faculty. Originally, these tests were administered at times set by the school, but eventually problems arose because of "the want of promptness" by some faculty members. The professors were later allowed to schedule finals at their own convenience. Some also administered daily quizzes, which supposedly encouraged independent thought, rapid induction, and "kindly intimacy" between the faculty and students.[20]

Local medical professors taught a course of lectures and limited laboratory work that took up the student's entire day when school was in session. In 1880-1881, the University of Louisville medical faculty probably averaged about $2,000 each from lecture fees alone, to which was added remuneration from their private practices. During that session, Professor Bell lectured from Tuesday through Friday from 10 A.M. to 11 A.M. and held quiz sessions from 3 P.M. to 4 P.M. on Thursday. Professor Bodine lectured on Wednesday, Thursday, and Friday from 11 A.M. until noon, met a clinical class on Saturday from 9 A.M. until 10 A.M., and held an evening quiz session on Wednesday. Professor David W. Yandell had no lectures or quizzes that term, but met a surgical clinic on Tuesday and Friday mornings.[21]

Graduation ceremonies took place during the late winter or early spring. They were festive social occasions. In 1887, for example, when the university celebrated its fiftieth anniversary, members of the medical class received their diplomas at Macauley Theater in a program "graced with flowers in profusion, music, and eloquence in due measure." The ceremony opened with prayer and continued with the dean's presentation of candidates to the president. Following the distribution of diplomas, school officials recognized honor students and awarded books, medals, and medical instruments to those who had distinguished themselves. Faculty and student addresses followed the awards. Some of the 1887 graduates undoubtedly joined the medical school alumni association, which had been organized three years earlier to cultivate good feelings, strengthen ties with the university, and advance science.[22]

Halting moves toward higher standards were detectable by the late 1870s and early 1880s. As noted earlier, part of the impetus may have come from the American Medical College Association, formed in 1876 with the participation of the University of Louisville. The AMCA stipulated that all member schools require a three-year course for the M.D. degree, and in 1877 the university complied, but the plan failed to gain national acceptance. During the early 1880s, the U of L Medical Department introduced optional courses in the use of ophthalmoscopes, laryngoscopes, and microscopes, but students still studied obstetrics and gynecology with an "inge-

nious manikin." Upon graduation they probably knew less about childbirth than most mothers and all midwives.[23]

Despite improvements, Louisville's medical schools, designed for the mass production of physicians, were still subject to few regulations. By 1887 the city supported four medical schools, two pharmacy colleges, a nurses' training school, and a dental school. During the following decade, Louisville added a medical school for blacks, a homeopathic medical college, and another medical school for whites, the Kentucky University Medical Department.[24]

University officials, as well as those of the other medical schools, still advertised the city as an unparalleled educational center. Their promotional literature extolled the town's ideal climate, fine location, and the moral fiber of the local population. Louisville's medical schools boasted magnificent equipment, well-stocked libraries filled with rare and costly volumes, and even tried to entice students with descriptions of comfortable seats in the lecture halls. Before the Civil War, medical literature had described the city as a Western metropolis, but after 1865 promotional material touted Louisville as the crown jewel of the New South.[25]

In 1890 the founding of the Association of American Medical Colleges, a revival of the AMCA, brought lasting changes to the U of L Medical Department. The medical school did not apply for AAMC membership initially, but pledged to lobby other southern schools for cooperation with the association's requirement of a three-year course of study. In 1891 the faculty urged Dean Bodine to attend the organization's meeting "at whatever sacrifice," but instructed him to move no faster than other southern schools on the three-year course requirement. In 1895 and 1896 the medical school raised its entrance and graduation requirements in conformity with AAMC standards; in the latter year Bodine served as president of that organization. By this time, the curriculum reflected the impact of developments in bacteriology, which were revolutionizing medical education and practice. At the same time, the state asserted its control over professional conduct among physicians, largely through the state board of health.

From 1890 through 1894, the medical school awarded 858 M.D. degrees. During the next five years, following the introduction of higher standards for admission and graduation, the number of graduates dropped to 276. In 1899 the four-year course became a requirement.[26]

Despite these changes in graduation requirements, the Council on Medical Education of the American Medical Association described Louisville in 1907 as one of "five especially rotten spots" responsible for most of the abuses in the nation's medical education. That fall some local officials reportedly warned an AMA inspection team that they would not be welcome in the city. In that same year, however, in part because of the negative publicity, four local schools merged into two. The Hospital College of Medicine and the Louisville Medical College united to form the Louisville and Hospital College of Medicine. Furthermore, the University of Louisville absorbed the Kentucky University Medical Department, which had been founded in 1898 as part of what had been and would again become known as Transylvania University. It was becoming clear that the days of U of L's rivals were numbered.[27]

In 1908 the General Assembly provided legal authority to open a medical school at State University in Lexington, the immediate predecessor institution of the University of Kentucky, which took its current name in 1916. Later in 1908, representatives of several Louisville schools met with officials of State University. The Kentucky School of Medicine and the Louisville and Hospital College of Medicine proposed affiliation with State University, provided that the new school remain in Louisville. Not to be outdone by its rivals, the University of Louisville offered a combination with State University under the same terms, but both offers were declined. In July 1908, the University of Louisville absorbed the Kentucky School of Medicine and the Louisville and Hospital College of Medicine. The era of medical school competition in Louisville had ended. For the next half century the University of Louisville would operate the only medical school in the state. Not until 1960 did a medical school open at the University of Kentucky.[28]

SEVEN

THE LATE
NINETEENTH-CENTURY
LAW SCHOOL

U OF L'S LAW SCHOOL during the late nineteenth century had a weaker corporate identity than its counterpart in medicine. Consequently, it left a weaker documentary record. The professors bickered less, probably because they had less to bicker about. As late as the 1870s, the school still supported a faculty of only three professors, each of whom met classes two days per week for four hours. In 1872 students still attended two courses of lectures for the degree and paid a $5 matriculation fee, a $20 fee to each professor, and a $10 diploma fee.[1]

During the following decade the law faculty made a feeble but notable attempt to raise its standards. Perhaps they were spurred by the American Bar Association, which had been founded in 1878, or inspired by developments at Harvard University, where changes that would dramatically alter American legal education were already underway. At least for the time being, however, standards imported from the East were more than the Louisville market would bear. Enrollments dropped significantly during the brief, unsuccessful experiment to elevate local standards in legal education.[2]

The law school showed even less tendency toward change during the last decade of the century. Louisvillians apparently remained satisfied with the school's informal arrangements, rented quarters, and late afternoon classes, which allowed students to keep daytime jobs as law clerks. The faculty encouraged students to visit local courts and offered optional mock court sessions, but continued to ignore the case method of instruction being used at Harvard. They also apparently saw no need to hire full-time teachers. In fact, school literature even boasted that the faculty consisted of "practical lawyers" and not professional educators. Admission required "sufficient mental development," but prospective students of "fair ability" were also encouraged to enroll. The University of Louisville Law Department paid little heed in 1893 when the American Bar Association established a section on legal education. Even a volume designed to tout the state's bench and bar admitted that Kentucky's law schools, including the University of Louisville, compared unfavorably with those in newer states to the north.[3]

James Speed, who had left his law school post during the Civil War to serve as Lincoln's attorney general, returned to his teaching position following the war. He was undoubtedly the best-known member of the faculty, though his reputation was built upon politics and government service, not teaching or scholarship. After the war, Speed favored the constitutional amendment granting former slaves full rights of citizenship and assistance to freed slaves, and he argued that blacks should be allowed to vote. While continuing as attorney general under President Andrew Johnson, however, Speed swung his support toward the "radical" congressional program for Reconstruction. He resigned in 1866 be-

James Speed (1812–1887) taught in the U of L law department before and after the Civil War.

Kentucky before coming to Louisville. Another teacher, Bland Ballard, a native of Shelby County, who taught at Louisville from 1871 until 1873, held a law degree from Transylvania University. William Overton Harris had acquired a law degree at the University of Virginia before coming to Kentucky. In Louisville he served as dean of the law school for two decades and was remembered for his "kindly sympathy" toward students.

During the 1880s, Professor William Chenault, the school's first administrator to hold the title of dean, led a campaign to raise admission standards, lengthen sessions, and hire some full-time professors. While this endeavor reflected national trends in legal education, for the moment it failed in Louisville. Of all the university's law faculty, Chenault demonstrated the greatest dedication to teaching as a profession.[5]

Almost all the law faculty had been influenced, in one way or another, by the Civil War. Bruce had served as a Kentucky delegate to the Confederate Congress; Ballard had served on the United States district court, where he handed down a number of treason and conspiracy convictions; and Harris had marched with the Virginia Military Institute cadets at the Battle of New Market in 1864. Thomas E. Bramlette, who taught law at Louisville in 1872 and 1873, had served as a colonel in the U.S. Army during the war before being elected governor in 1863. Henry J. Stites, who taught in the law school from 1868 until 1872, had attempted to remain neutral during the conflict, but had been so harassed that he had sat out much of the war in Canada.[6]

A number of the law school's graduates left a record of accomplishments. Rozel Weissinger, for example, served on the faculty of his alma mater. He also represented Jefferson County in the state legislature and in 1896 published a book on monetary policy, in which he upheld the conservative platform of the gold Democrats. John A. Logan, a Civil War general and longtime U.S. representative and senator from Illinois who ran for vice president in 1884 on the Republican ticket with James G. Blaine, also had graduated from the Louisville law school. Albert Shelby Willis served as President Grover Cleveland's ambassador to Hawaii during a tense period of provi-

cause of increasing disagreements with the new chief executive.[4]

The university's postwar law faculty members were too involved in practice or public service to give much time to teaching. Peter B. Muir, for example, who taught from 1862 until 1868, even resigned from the bench because its rewards could not compare with his "large and highly remunerative" private practice. Some of the professors, such as Horatio W. Bruce, who taught from 1873 to 1880, had begun to leave courtroom advocacy and take up corporate law, a growing field during the late nineteenth century.

Most of the law faculty, like the students, were native Kentuckians, although some had come to Louisville from other parts of the state. In the late nineteenth century, the school also boasted more professors who had formal law degrees. Professor Muir, for example, came to Louisville from Nelson County, where he had studied law privately. Bruce had also studied privately and practiced in his native eastern

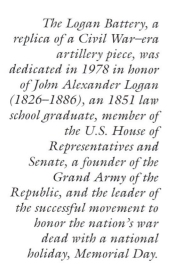

The Logan Battery, a replica of a Civil War–era artillery piece, was dedicated in 1978 in honor of John Alexander Logan (1826–1886), an 1851 law school graduate, member of the U.S. House of Representatives and Senate, a founder of the Grand Army of the Republic, and the leader of the successful movement to honor the nation's war dead with a national holiday, Memorial Day.

sional government. Reuben T. Durrett made a fortune in local law practice, after which he retired to amass a magnificent collection of books, manuscripts, and other material on regional history. Norman J. Coleman, who in 1889 became the first secretary of the new U.S. Department of Agriculture, was also a graduate of the U of L law school.[7]

Law students spent relatively little time in class and never developed the *esprit de corps* found in the medical school, but some feeling of comradeship sur-

faced. At one point, a group of students substituted beer for the brownish Ohio River water Professor Charles B. Seymour used to quench his thirst during lectures. The victim of the prank, who claimed never to consume liquor in any form, took one sip of the brew, spewed the beer toward the class, and launched into a temperance lecture.[8]

Students apparently competed for top marks on the school's final examination, because in 1883 one group charged that the honor roll had been falsified.

After a tense investigation, the faculty decided that the accusation was merely malicious, but bad feelings lingered. Eleven years later, the faculty discovered remarkable similarities in two examination papers, but following a thorough investigation the university's trustees concluded that the likenesses were coincidental. The law school also boasted the Henry Clay Club, organized in 1846, which reportedly gave the embryonic attorneys a forum to develop oratorical talent, self-assurance, judicial discretion, and administrative ability.[9]

If U of L law students felt a sense of clubbiness, it was of the exclusive sort, because they did not want females in the lecture hall. When some young women from the community of Anchorage, several miles to the northeast, applied, the men made sure class meeting times would not accommodate their transportation schedules. In 1892 the law dean and faculty flatly refused admission to several female applicants. Nearly twenty years would pass before a woman received a U of L law school diploma.[10]

Even though formal legal education gained popularity during the late nineteenth century, a law degree remained less important to a practitioner than the M.D. degree was in medicine. Until late in this period, most law practice consisted of courtroom advocacy. Trials often were social occasions drawing onlookers, and the attorney's talents were on display before the entire community. In this fashion, a lawyer was informally certified by potential clients, public opinion, and his adversaries, or judged to be a poor ally in court and denied legal business. Physicians, unlike attorneys, practiced their profession in the relative privacy of the sickroom and were less subject to direct public scrutiny. The M.D. degree was a more valuable badge of certification, which helped account for the larger medical school enrollments.

Furthermore, the legendary frontier lad who studied law by the firelight continued to exert a strong hold on the legal imagination. Finally, the law lent itself to study in informal solitude more than did medicine. As the field of corporate law became more common, however, the law degree took on added importance, but this trend was not fully evidenced in Louisville until the twentieth century. Louisville's

James Speed Pirtle (1840–1917), fourth president, University of Louisville, 1886–1905, was a founder of the American Bar Association in 1878 and the Filson Club in 1884.

emergence as an urban center accounted for the city's thriving legal community, which in turn led to much of whatever success the law school achieved during the nineteenth century.[11]

Physicians recognized earlier the need for self-reform, which accounted for still more differences between medical and legal education. By the 1880s scientific discoveries in pathology, bacteriology, and physiology, plus the opening of an excellent school at Johns Hopkins University, made medical education more expensive, demonstrated the need for higher standards, and eventually improved the quality of instruction and research. Leaders in the profession soon realized that their best interests were not served by an educational system that produced an overabundance of poorly trained physicians. By the 1890s, national medical associations had taken an assertive role in enforcing standards, which did not go unnoticed in Louisville. While legal education underwent changes at the same time, law schools remained much less obliged to heed standards other than those imposed within their own states, where most of the students would practice. Harvard University's case system of legal education, which was not adopted in Louisville until the twentieth century, claimed to present the law in a scientific fashion, but much of the practicing attorney's success still depended on verbal agility, knowledge of the local bench and the opponent's weaknesses, and a commanding presence and unshakable self-confidence that never considered the possibility of defeat.[12]

The makeup of the university's central administration also demonstrated the school's slow-footed response to national trends in higher education. The professional academic administrator had become a permanent fixture on many campuses, but not yet in Louisville. U of L's presidents remained local businessmen and attorneys interested in promoting the school as a component of the city's economic and cultural life. Their claims about the city and the university were sometimes exaggerated and foolishly optimistic, much in the vein of the New South philosophy advocated by Henry Watterson's *Courier-Journal*. The University of Louisville, despite its defects, was one of many civic assets that local leaders considered an essential part of their city's regional leadership.[13]

Judge James Speed Pirtle, the university's fourth president, was a good example. Chosen by the trustees to succeed Isaac Caldwell, who died in 1885, Pirtle himself served as a trustee for thirty-five years, from 1880 until 1915. For two decades he was president; for most of the rest of the time he was the board's secretary. A native Louisvillian, Pirtle was a member of the first class graduated from Louisville Male High School in 1859. In 1861 he graduated from the U of L law school, which was directed at that time by his father Henry. When Henry Pirtle retired from the university in 1873, James Speed Pirtle took over his professorship. An influential attorney, Pirtle was a judge on the chancery court, represented the Illinois Central Railroad, was president of the Louisville Bar Association, and was also a founder of the American Bar Association.[14]

The period of Pirtle's presidency, which bridged the turn of the nineteenth century to the twentieth, coincided with the beginning of the South's slow response to trends in higher and professional education that had already been implemented in other sections of the country. Furthermore, many of Louisville's medical and law professors were aware of the inadequacies under which they operated. Early in the twentieth century the need to conform to national standards in medical, legal, and pre-professional training became increasingly apparent. The growth of an academic bureaucracy went hand-in-hand with these developments.[15]

EIGHT

THE REBIRTH OF THE LIBERAL ARTS COLLEGE

A S THE UNIVERSITY OF LOUISVILLE'S medical and law schools responded to educational changes, the Louisville Commercial Club began arguing for a liberal arts college to fill the gap between the city's high schools and its various professional schools. They were aided by Judge Theodore L. Burnett, who in 1905 succeeded Judge James Speed Pirtle as president of the university. Burnett, the university's fifth president and the first who received a salary, graduated from the Transylvania University Law Department in 1846, practiced law in his native Spencer County, and served in the Mexican War. With the outbreak of the Civil War, he joined the Confederate Army and served briefly under General Albert Sidney Johnston, but soon left to become a Kentucky representative to the Confederate Congress. Following the war he returned to Taylorsville, then moved to Louisville in 1866. In 1870 he became city attorney. A "stalwart figure, almost statuesque in proportion," Burnett lived to be the last surviving member of the Confederate Congress.[1]

Inspired in part by what they considered Louisville's glowing commercial prospects, Judge Burnett and other civic-minded reformers shared a vision not only of abandoning political "bossism," but of changing the educational system as well. U of L law school alumnus Robert Worth Bingham, who as county attorney and mayor epitomized the city's response to progressivism, was one of the leaders of

Theodore L. Burnett (1829–1917), fifth president, University of Louisville, 1905–1911, was the oldest man appointed to the U of L presidency, and the oldest when he left it.

the movement to open the liberal arts college and thus satisfy the demand for pre-professional training.[2]

Soon after taking office, Burnett engaged John Calvin Willis as chancellor and assigned to him the responsibility of raising money for the proposed col-

The Silas Miller Mansion, home of the College of Liberal Arts, 1907–1925. (CSC.)

lege. Willis spent the latter part of 1906 on the road and returned to Louisville claiming that industrialists Andrew Carnegie and John D. Rockefeller, two of America's richest men, were contemplating substantial gifts to the University of Louisville. Later, reports surfaced that the new college would be affiliated with the Methodist Church, which was also considering a sizable pledge, and possibly other churches as well. There was even talk of an appropriation from the city. The *Courier-Journal* exaltedly predicted that the school would eclipse "any institution of its kind in the South."[3]

The grand expectations raised by Willis came to nothing. Just as it appeared plans for the college were about to fail, however, a half dozen local benefactors contributed enough money in a "Founders' Fund" for classes to open as scheduled. Willis, who had been appointed the first dean of the college, left in 1908 under suspicion of misusing funds. He died in 1922 in the Cook County, Illinois, jail, having been convicted of check-writing fraud.[4]

In September 1907 the long-awaited College of Liberal Arts opened. The first students, 104 in number, attended classes in a converted residence at 119 West Broadway. Built for Silas Miller, a steamboat captain, the three-story, limestone-front mansion was known for its stately design, pier mirrors, marble mantles, and carved woodwork. Most recently the building had been occupied by the former Kentucky University Medical Department. Two smaller structures in the rear of the property also were used for classroom, office, and library space. According to its catalog, the school offered instruction in more than a dozen classical, scientific, and philosophical departments; awarded bachelor's, master's, and doctor's degrees; and admitted "both ladies and gentlemen."[5]

The latter claim was the only one that resembled the truth. In fact, females were very much in evidence at the new college. The first graduating class, in 1908, was comprised of ten women and eight men. The *Colonel*, the college's first student yearbook, and the "Courses and Rules," its catalog, listed Grace A.

John Letcher Patterson (1861–1937), acting president, University of Louisville, 1928–1929. The College of Arts and Sciences owes much of its early success to Patterson's prestige as a scholar and educator. He served as dean (1908–1922), chancellor (1922–1926), and director of the Graduate School (1926–1937). A classicist, Patterson published several volumes on ancient languages and literature, plus a book entitled Universities of the United States *(1916). His physician contended that the educator's second stroke —the third a month later was fatal—came as a result of excitement brought about by the 1937 flooding of the Ohio River. One observer called Patterson "the greatest friend the university ever had." The library's Patterson Rare Book Room was named for him, as was Patterson Hall.*

Kennedy as a Latin teacher and Edna Dolfinger in art. They taught part-time, as did virtually all of the faculty during the college's first year or two.[6]

The effort to revive the dream of a liberal arts college as the keystone of a true university survived the Willis debacle. John Letcher Patterson, who had come to the new college as a professor of ancient languages in 1907, followed Willis as dean. By the end of Judge Burnett's presidency in 1911, the school had added art, drama, and athletic programs, and had established a library. The university finally had a liberal arts college on a permanent footing. It was the best thing that had happened in the life of the institution since the founding of the medical institute seventy years earlier.

John L. Patterson's career at the University of Louisville was as distinguished as Willis's was inglorious, and under his leadership the college not only survived but also grew in strength and stature. Though slight of frame, Dean Patterson commanded respect through firm but fair policies, unfailing courtesy, and his reputation as a classicist. According to one observer, he personified "the scholarly southern gentleman."[7]

What respect Patterson had he certainly owed to his character and demeanor, rather than his entourage, perquisites, or the college facilities. His office, for example, was a converted parlor, furnished with a double knee-hole desk that accommodated the dean on one side and his office staff on the other. Somehow the college building at Second and Broadway took on an antique charm over the years. It housed a small, convivial group and resembled a family residence, rather than "the cold austerity" of a large, impersonal university.[8]

Patterson worked quietly and informally to accomplish what he could with meager resources. The college library, for example, supposedly originated in 1911 when Patterson himself and his servant, Harry, constructed the first shelves and placed them, along with some of Patterson's private book collection, in the basement of the building. Within four years the collection had grown to two thousand volumes. In 1918 the library was moved to a large room in a separate rear building, and soon it contained more than four thousand books.[9]

Before the decade's end Dean Patterson conducted an informal, one-person search for a college librarian by observing the progress of graduate student Evelyn Schneider, who had demonstrated an interest in research. Convinced that she possessed the necessary qualities to replace the outgoing librarian, Patterson in 1919 offered Schneider the position,

The music room of the liberal arts college at 119 West Broadway.

Evelyn J. Schneider (1896–1996) began her career at U of L in 1919 when she became librarian for the College of Arts and Sciences. The library then had three thousand volumes and was in a large room at 119 West Broadway. In 1925 the collection, now ten thousand volumes, was moved into what is now Ford Hall on the Belknap Campus, and from there to the new Administration Building on the Belknap Campus in 1927. By the end of World War II the library had grown to almost one hundred thousand volumes and was in desperate need of a larger facility. Schneider then oversaw the construction of the new library building, which opened in 1956. Following her retirement in 1965, Schneider lived to see the library expand even farther with its move into the William F. Ekstrom Library in 1981, to witness the naming of Schneider Hall, now home of the fine arts department and art library, and to celebrate her one hundredth birthday.

provided that she begin work that summer on a library science degree.[10]

The early College of Liberal Arts had no more interesting faculty member than Eber C. Perrow in English. A Tennessee mountaineer who had earned his doctorate from Harvard University, Perrow came to Louisville shortly after the liberal arts college opened. Peculiar in habit and appearance, he lived in a home with a dirt floor, wore a long red beard, and farmed on the outskirts of town. On his way to class, farmer Perrow would step off the streetcar at the busiest corner in the city, remove his work boots, and don his dress shoes. Eventually, the hectic pace of big city life forced the early retirement of this woolly backwoodsman. Suffering from overwork, Professor Perrow resigned, moved to northern Georgia, and lived in a cabin several miles removed from civilization. In retirement, Perrow taught morning Sunday school at the Baptist church, afternoon Sunday school at the Methodist church, and demonstrated that his family could subsist on little cash, provided they had no rent to pay and owned "ten acres of land, twenty chickens, and a cow."[11]

Other colorful members of the early college faculty included Austin R. Middleton in biology, a man of boundless energy in the promotion of his own cause. Professor Middleton made a career of sending a steady stream of feckless memoranda to presidents, deans, and anyone else in authority. He requested everything from "a radiator for the rat room" to a vivarium. At one point, with ninety new microscopes, twenty-three journal subscriptions, and the possibility of two students, Middleton decided to offer the M.S. degree in biology and wondered if such a course required "official sanction." From time to time, Middleton also preached at Fourth Avenue Methodist Church and took attendance from the pulpit. His classes were large, however, apparently because he showed great liberality in grading. Later in his career, Middleton attempted to establish "the University of the Americas," based on his biological expeditions to Honduras arranged through the United Fruit Company. One colleague affectionately recalled that Middleton's plans frequently went beyond the realm of dreams and bordered on hallucinations.[12]

Eber C. Perrow and his mountain home.

Some members of the college faculty established programs of true quality, even in the absence of sufficient resources. By the 1920s, for example, the school boasted a small but fine group of historians, including Robert S. Cotterill, Louis R. Gottschalk, and Norman J. Ware. Cotterill had already begun to establish his reputation with a book on pioneer Kentucky and several major journal articles on antebellum and Civil War railroads. Though fresh from graduate school, Gottschalk was soon to publish his biography of Jean Paul Marat, and had a textbook on the era of the French Revolution underway while in Louisville. Ware, whose appointment was in sociology, had published a serviceable history of the American industrial worker before the Civil War, and was at work on a study of the labor movement during the late nineteenth century. In 1926 the university's history department took part in establishing a quarterly journal published in conjunction with the Filson Club, a local historical society, with Cotterill as managing editor. These professors attracted a respectable number of graduate students interested in research. In 1924-1925, for example, Cotterill offered a year-long seminar on the Civil War in Kentucky, which led to master's theses on the commonwealth's relationship to the Confederate States, Kentucky railroads during the war, and the state's decision to remain neutral.[13]

Intercollegiate athletics came with the revival of the college. Shortly after the new division opened, one observer confidently asserted that since the university led the South in scholarship, it should also assert its dominance on the athletic playing field. Within a few years the school had fielded its first intercollegiate men's football, basketball, track, and baseball teams. From the beginning, the teams sported the colors of red, or crimson, and black. In 1913, at the suggestion of Ellen Patterson, the dean's wife, a student-faculty athletic board adopted cardinal and black as the official colors. Soon teams were referred to as the "Cardinals" or "Fighting Cardinals."[14]

U of L's first track team was anchored by captain William Hamilton, who achieved extraordinary distinction as a sprinter. Following a successful 1907-1908 season, Hamilton, a student in the medical school, captured a spot on the U.S. Olympic team. At the Olympic Games in London in July 1908, he won a gold medal for his relay team's victory. Later in the year Hamilton won other races in Europe and in the United States, setting world records in the 100-, 150-, and 300-yard dashes. The 1909 student yearbook took justifiable pride in calling the University of Louisville "the home of America's greatest dash man."[15]

Forty-eight students, many of them from the medical and law schools, tried out for the 1909 baseball team. Coach John Ray, whom the yearbook called "the best baseball authority in the state," chose seventeen—two catchers, five pitchers, five outfielders, and five infielders, including captain Thomas Walker, "a man who knows the game." The squad won ten of its fifteen games that year against high schools and colleges in the region. Six hundred fans attended the second game, played in a cold April drizzle. This Cardinal baseball team was deemed "the greatest team that ever wore the U of L colors" in the 1910 yearbook.[16]

The school fielded basketball teams beginning in 1908, but during the first few years its teams competed only against local clubs, mostly YMCA and

U of L's 1927 track team was crowned "Kentucky Champions of Track" after winning the Kentucky Intercollegiate Track and Field Meet. The 1950 track season was highlighted by Herb Kebschull's 1:57.3 half mile and Chuck Jett's 50–second quarter mile performance.

The 1909 varsity base-ball squad played an exhibition game with the All-Professionals, a team made up of minor league men wintering in Louisville. This game at once proved there had been no mistake in the selection of the varsity, as they put it on the "Cracks" by the score of 8–6.

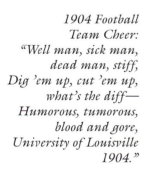

1904 Football Team Cheer: "Well man, sick man, dead man, stiff, Dig 'em up, cut 'em up, what's the diff— Humorous, tumorous, blood and gore, University of Louisville 1904."

YMHA squads. U of L's first intercollegiate men's basketball team played, and lost, a total of three games in 1911-1912. The season must have produced some enthusiasm, however, because there was talk of winning the state championship the following year. The 1912-1913 team went 2-3. Early Louisville roundball contests gave no hint of the school's later glories on the hardwood. The first team with a winning record went 8-3 in 1915-1916. More often than not, however, one losing season followed another until after World War II.[17]

Although there was no organized football team prior to the opening of the college, informal pick-up games were played throughout the early years of the century. The opposing teams were not always other colleges; some represented communities or community organizations. Most of U of L's football players at this time were medical students.

Organized football came to the university in 1912, when two students, Stanley Walker and Roy Daniel, approached the faculty about starting a team. The young men convinced Dean Patterson that scholarship money could encourage good high school players to come to the University of Louisville, arguing athletics was an essential ingredient in a classical Greek education. The university responded with an allocation of $625. More than half of this first official squad consisted of medical students. Their coach was Lester Larson, a local typewriter salesman who had played at the University of Chicago under football pioneer Amos Alonzo Stagg. Professor Eckart Von Walther of the history department, who in 1911 became the equivalent of U of L's first athletic director, served as the team's manager, and Stanley Walker was its captain. The first game of that initial season, played on October 11, 1912, at High School Park at Brook and Breckinridge Streets, was a 32–0 victory over Transylvania. Coach Larson's teams went 3–1 that year and in 1913 enjoyed a 5–1 record.[18]

During the early years of the college, the women's basketball team was at least as active as the men's. (The school's first female team, in 1909, like the men's, played only local clubs. According to the yearbook, only two of the fifteen "girls" who showed up for the first practice had ever played the game.) In

In 1922, the U of L women's basketball team won the "Girls' Intercollegiate Basketball Championship of Kentucky."

1913-1914, for example, the women's basketball team fielded a small but scrappy squad "marked by considerable speed." During this era the women were neatly uniformed in cardigan-type sweatshirts, discreet black bloomers caught below the knee, and matching opaque stockings. In 1917 both the men's and women's basketball teams won their respective state championships.[19]

Gradually, students in the College of Arts and Sciences—the name was changed in 1912—developed social, cultural, and intellectual interests that provided a common bond and identity. Some student activities were humorous in retrospect. In October 1909, for example, Ellen Patterson sponsored a tea for women students in the college, which provided some indication of the type of skills school authorities thought young ladies should acquire as part of their higher

Women's League, 1909.

Helen McClure Hodges, first recipient of the Woodcock Medal.

education. "Miss Ward" poured, "Miss Catlin" served the frappé, and "everybody went and met everybody else, and all had a good time." Before long, the college included such organizations as the Current Events Club, whose members discussed such timely topics as tariff reciprocity; the Glee Club, whose combined voices were supposedly sweeter than Apollo's lyre; and a women's organization that met each Friday to forget "all else except the joy of being together."[20]

In 1910 the college first awarded the Woodcock Medal to recognize high academic achievement. Bishop Charles Edward Woodcock of the Episcopal Diocese of Kentucky established the award as a memorial to his son. Originally given to a student other than a senior—the first recipient was Helen McClure Hodges, a junior in 1910—the honor eventually was reserved for members of the graduating class. In 1920 the first ten recipients formed the Woodcock Society, with the intention of creating the nucleus of a Phi Beta Kappa chapter.[21]

At first, Dean Patterson opposed social fraternities and sororities because he considered them undemocratic, but eventually these organizations became

Graduating class of 1916.

an important part of undergraduate life. College students also debated the merits of the honor system, whereby the faculty left them alone during examinations and assumed that any cheaters would become social outcasts. Before long, it became evident that no steps were taken to ostracize the dishonest, and the dean directed faculty members to proctor all examinations.[22]

In 1909 Abraham Flexner, a Louisville native, visited the university in preparing his report on medical education in the United States and Canada for the Carnegie Foundation. The fact that his brother, Simon Flexner, was a graduate of the U of L medical school and a distinguished physician did not deflect his disapproval. He found classes unmanageably large, laboratories crowded and understaffed, and clinical facilities poor. Flexner praised the recent medical school mergers, but concluded that the University of Louisville, which still relied largely on tuition and fees, simply lacked the resources to fund a modern medical school. In his recommendations for the future of medical education in the South, Flexner called for six four-year schools in the region, but recommended none for Kentucky. Furthermore, he labeled U of L's

new liberal arts college "a people's institute," unworthy of its name and incapable of providing academic leadership for the university.[23]

It is an understatement to observe that the Flexner report, published in 1910, gave the university's medical and liberal arts departments a poor rating. "We have indeed progressed too far in our social and educational development to use the word 'university' for an enterprise of this kind," he wrote. The fact that Flexner lambasted virtually every medical school save Johns Hopkins probably gave little comfort to U of L leaders. Rather than being defeated by this criticism, however, they learned from it. It served as a stimulus to Patterson, who began a campaign to improve the quality of liberal arts education at the university. By 1914 the college had awarded 101 degrees at the undergraduate and master's levels and employed a full- and part-time faculty of twenty. Six members held doctoral degrees. By 1915 Patterson had organized the Graduate School of Arts and Sciences and had added courses in economics, art, and sociology.[24]

In that year the dean's efforts were rewarded in a most impressive manner: the university achieved ac-

Created by U of L medical school alumnus Harold F. Berg
and Murray State University art professor Joseph Rigsby
and dedicated in 1978, this mosaic features a larger than
life likeness of Abraham Flexner (1866–1959) in the center.
Depicted on the left side is medical education before this
native Louisvillian's landmark report; to the right, the
higher standards of medical schools thereafter, which led to
changes at U of L and elsewhere.

David William Fairleigh (1853–1924), sixth president, University of Louisville, 1911–1914. An 1874
graduate of the University of Louisville law school,
Fairleigh practiced law in Brandenburg, Kentucky,
until 1887, when he returned to Louisville and, with
partner Frank P. Strauss, formed a prestigious law
firm that represented several powerful interests. A longtime trustee of the university and a local Republican
politician, Fairleigh represented Governor William S.
Taylor before the state election commission in the vio-
lently contested 1899 Kentucky governor's race. The
dispute concluded with the assassination of Taylor's
opponent, William Goebel, and the awarding of the
election to Goebel on his deathbed.

Medical students aboard the U of L Medical Special *for a field trip to the Eli Lilly Company plant in Indianapolis about 1911.*

creditation by the Association of Colleges and Secondary Schools of the Southern States. Patterson became the university's chancellor in 1922. In this capacity he had overall responsibility for academic affairs, although he had limited authority outside the College of Arts and Sciences, where he directed much of his energy toward the advancement of graduate studies.[25]

The medical school had undergone substantial changes prior to the Flexner report. Following the elimination of local competitors, admission and graduation requirements had been raised, and the number of degrees awarded had been reduced. This was the local response to a national trend which emphasized cooperation rather than competition in medical education. As noted previously, to some extent, the bacteriological revolution generated these changes, but they also reflected the medical profession's efforts to raise standards and limit access. During the early nineteenth century, the number of

medical schools had increased along with the geographic expansion of the United States.

In some respects, of course, this trend had harmed the interests of the medical profession and the public. A solution that severely reduced the number of medical schools in the South, however, posed additional problems. If medical education was to become more expensive and exclusive, it could limit enrollment of students from rural and economically depressed areas, thereby reducing the supply of practitioners to those places.[26]

Simultaneously, significant changes were underway in higher education. The old-time college had emphasized discipline and piety, whereas the new higher learning prepared young men and women to enter the professional workforce. A new generation of university presidents, called "the captains of erudition" by one pundit, had appeared on the scene. This new vision of higher education was reflected in the ambitious aspirations of the revived College of Arts and Sciences. Unfortunately, the University of Louisville at this point still lacked the resources needed for even moderate success in this area.[27]

While the Flexner report did not result in sudden or dramatic changes, it did create a stir, renewing the city's interest in financial support for the university. The Louisville Board of Trade feared the possible loss of the medical school might diminish the city's reputation as an educational and business center. After a city investigation of the entire university, beginning in 1910, the city council made an appropriation of $10,000. When David W. Fairleigh became the sixth president of the university in 1911,

succeeding Judge Burnett, he and Dean Patterson negotiated continuing annual appropriations from the city of Louisville.[28]

Changes in medical education and higher education reflected what one historian called the emergence of "a new middle class." Generally, this group stressed formal academic training, identified with their professions, and believed that scientific principles could be applied to the management of business, government, and education. In so doing, they sought to produce a more orderly society. By 1914 the University of Louisville had moved in that direction, but still lacked the leadership needed for wholehearted change.[29]

NINE

CAMPUS AND ACADEMIC EXPANSION

URING THE TWO DECADES that followed the Flexner report in 1910, the
University of Louisville took on the administrative structure of a modern institution of higher
education. It acquired a full-time president who
served as the executive agent of the board of trustees.
It also held middle managers, called deans, accountable for their schools. The board, president, and deans
concerned themselves with accreditation standards,
financial affairs, and lines of authority. As a result,
academic purpose and command came into sharper
focus, but this process produced strains which eventually resulted in sharp conflict.

In 1914 Arthur Younger Ford became president
of the University of Louisville. Previously, he had been
managing editor of the *Courier-Journal* and had
gained respect in local and statewide circles. A.Y. Ford
resembled earlier presidents in that he was a local
leader, rather than a professional educator. On the
other hand, he saw the need for a president to do
more than convene the board and serve as a part-
time problem solver, and under his leadership the
office became full time. As the first president to assert any real control over the formerly autonomous
medical and law departments, Ford generated more
administrative momentum than the university had
ever seen. During the boom years of the 1920s he
raised money, improved facilities, established enduring academic programs, and in general turned the
University of Louisville to face the future.[1]

*Arthur Younger Ford (1861–1926), seventh president,
University of Louisville. Ford's twelve-year presidency
proved to be one of the most successful in U of L's history.
A graduate of Brown University, Ford was a banker
and journalist before coming to the university as a part-
time, but salaried, president. His first move was to
establish a central administrative office, the first in the
history of the university. He then embarked on a
$1,500,000 program of physical expansion and aca-
demic improvement, financed in part by city taxes.
Ford also had a reflective, contemplative side, and
throughout his life cultivated an interest in poetry and
reading for enjoyment.*

Ford Hall, shown here in 1926, was erected in 1904 and named in honor of President Ford in 1982.

A law student in the 1920s recalled that the school's rented home was so filthy it resembled "King Tut's tomb when they broke into it." (CSC.)

When Ford took office, the law school still operated with a part-time dean overseeing a part-time faculty teaching part-time students who attended classes between four and six o'clock in the afternoon. Even though the school had adopted the case system of instruction in 1909, its acceptance of emerging national standards in legal education was slow in coming. Finally, though, it had ended its resistance to women students. N. Almee Courtright was graduated in 1911, followed by Marguerite T. Dravo, Elizabeth W. Marshall, and Laura L. Wehner in 1914. Enrollment fell off during World War I, and the school struggled to hold classes during the 1918-1919 year.[2]

In 1923 the Law Department officially became the School of Law and hired one full-time professor, who also performed routine administrative duties such as managing records, taking care of correspondence, and working on publicity. The following year President Ford insisted on requiring students to have some college courses before they could be admitted to the law school. The faculty resisted, resenting the president's growing power and his willingness to dictate policy. But they knew accrediting agencies could "advertise broadcast" the names of schools that failed to comply with their standards. The president found a reform-minded ally in Leon P. Lewis, who in 1925 became dean, but the vision of a daytime law school with a full-time faculty remained elusive.[3]

In many ways, the law school facility epitomized its problems. One student recalled an interior so filthy it resembled "an ancient ruin" that looked like "King Tut's tomb when they broke into it." Another observer remarked that the school's rented building, located downtown on Armory Place, was "a dark, dingy place, where students threw tomes at wandering rats in crowded classrooms." Ford realized the school's accreditation was threatened by its inadequate facilities, but at the same time he was also

Benjamin F. Washer was associated with the Jefferson School of Law throughout its forty-five-year history. Attending what they sometimes called "the Washer School," his students produced a yearbook, organized a debating society and other social groups, and in 1925 established an alumni association. Wilson W. Wyatt, one of the school's many prominent graduates, taught there in the 1930s.

obliged to consider the wishes of his law students and professors, who preferred a downtown location close to courts and law offices. The central site encouraged the use of part-time faculty and the enrollment of part-time students who worked as law clerks, which ran against national trends in legal education. Dean Lewis showed more than the usual appreciation for national accreditation standards. On the other hand, the popularity of a less formal approach to legal education was underscored by the success of a local rival, the Jefferson School of Law, which had been opened in 1905 to offer night classes.[4]

By the end of the 1920s, the Jefferson School of Law had provided a successful alternative to U of L's law school for a quarter of a century. A proprietary school, it was organized by several prominent local attorneys, among whom were Shackelford Miller Sr.,

Thomas R. Gordon, and Benjamin F. Washer. Its part-time instructors dunned students directly for tuition, from which they drew their own fees and rented classroom space. Like U of L's law school, the Jefferson School moved from place to place, always within walking distance of the courthouse. Unlike U of L, it offered courses during the evening.[5]

In 1925 U.S. Supreme Court Justice Louis D. Brandeis, a Louisville native, pledged $10,000 per year for ten years to the U of L law school, provided a matching amount could be raised locally. Brandeis had already demonstrated an interest in developing the university's library collections. President Ford rejected the offer, fearing it might divert attention from a general endowment campaign then on the drawing board. The president's concern was legitimate, but he may have erred in declining the justice's

U.S. Supreme Court Justice Louis Dembitz
Brandeis (1856–1941) was a great supporter of the
University of Louisville, first showing his interest in
the early 1920s. A native Louisvillian, Brandeis
proposed to his brother Alfred, also of Louisville, a
plan to make the university a major center of
academic research by creating specialized library
and archival collections in such areas as sociology,
art, music, and labor. To back up this plan,
Brandeis donated his personal papers, books, and
pamphlets. He encouraged the university to acquire
additional archival materials, made suggestions for
book purchases, and donated funds to catalog, bind,
and shelve them. After his death, U of L benefitted
from his estate. His ashes and those of his wife,
Alice, are buried under the law school portico.

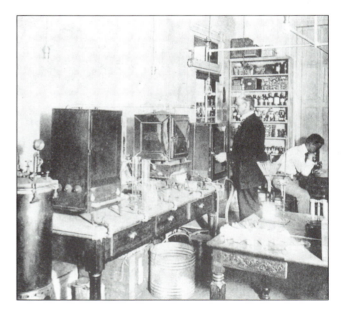

After absorbing the Louisville Medical College, the
U of L medical department occupied its former
rival's facilities at First and Chestnut Streets,
shown here in 1912. (CSC.)

City Hospital in 1929. (CSC.)

generosity. The proposal certainly would have benefitted the law school and might have given momentum to the general campaign. Furthermore, Ford's decline of a special offer for the law school contradicted his acceptance of a special gift at about the same time for an engineering school.[6]

Brandeis nonetheless continued his support of the law school through gifts and frequent advice. He had U.S. Supreme Court briefs deposited in the library, gave sums of money for special law school projects, and communicated his hopes for the school in eloquent letters to his relatives and to Louisville friends. The attention of such a distinguished jurist was undoubtedly an inspiration to university officials.[7]

While the medical school continued to suffer from problems not unlike those identified in the Flexner report, its physical facilities improved. In 1909, for example, the school abandoned its original property on University Square and moved seven blocks east to First and Chestnut Streets, where it occupied the building of the former Louisville Medical College, one of the schools absorbed in the merger a year earlier. Built in the 1890s, this relatively new facility provided a well-appointed interior, modern laboratories, and more classroom space than had been previously available.

Shortly thereafter, construction began on a new City Hospital building on the site of the original Louisville Marine Hospital, located within walking dis-

tance of the medical school. Opened in 1914, this "Million Dollar Hospital," which the university used for teaching purposes, became an immediate source of controversy. Local physicians resented use of the facility by medical professors and their "non-resident, non-taxpaying students." Furthermore, the faculty failed to work well with hospital officials. At one point, President Ford declared university-city hospital relations were "in a state of demoralization." Eventually, in 1922, Ford and city officials reorganized the university's hospital affairs around salaried heads of various departments. Meanwhile, in 1921, an accreditation inspector reported that the medical school suffered from outdated equipment, a meager budget, and grade inflation. President Ford, who renamed the Medical Department the School of Medicine in 1923, paid serious attention to the medical school and thus strengthened his authority over it.[8]

Shortly after the new hospital opened, the University of Louisville also expanded its offerings in the health sciences. In 1919, supported by the Rockefeller Foundation and the state board of health, the university established a School of Public Health, which was soon absorbed into the medical school. Arthur T. McCormack, who had led the state's public health movement, served as the first and only dean of the short-lived school, which claimed to offer courses through the doctoral level.[9]

A year earlier, the university took over the Louisville College of Dentistry, by then a proprietary school, but which in 1887 had opened as the dental department of the Hospital College of Medicine. The Hospital College in turn was affiliated with Central University, a Southern Presbyterian school in Richmond, Kentucky. James Lewis Howe served as dean of both medicine and dentistry. Although entering students were supposedly required to have "a very good English education," some lacked even high school diplomas. They attended one twenty-two week session a year for two years, taught mostly by experienced practitioners such as Francis Peabody, president of the dental faculty in the 1890s, and Edward Henry Hubbuch, whose affiliation with the school spanned the years 1898 to 1936. In 1895 the dental department acted in conformity with changing national standards by adding a third year to the curriculum. By century's end students were taking courses in embryology and bacteriology and using x-ray technology.[10]

In 1900 the dental department faculty withdrew from the Hospital College of Medicine, reorganized as a for-profit corporation under the name Louisville College of Dentistry, and occupied a new building at 129 East Broadway. William Edward Grant served as dean and eventually became the school's sole owner. In 1901 Aimee L. Jones became the first female graduate. The school's inability to meet rising standards, coupled with Grant's failing health, led to the takeover by the University of Louisville in 1918. The university paid rent to Grant until 1923, when it purchased the building. Henry B. Tileston, who had been associated with the school for twenty-two years, became its first dean under the university's administration.[11]

A grant from the American Dental Association enabled U of L's dental school to set up a research laboratory in 1922 under the supervision of bacteriologist Theodore Beust, a member of the dental faculty from 1917 until his death in 1937. In 1923 the school received the Dental Education Council's class A rating. By the end of the decade it had broadened its science curriculum, changed its entrance requirements to include two years of college work, and enlarged its library collections, placing them under a full-time librarian.[12]

In 1918 the University of Louisville took over the independent Louisville College of Dentistry (shown here in 1912), which had originated in 1886 as the dental department of the Hospital College of Medicine. (CSC.)

Medical students entered the twentieth century with an *esprit de corps* which still eclipsed that of all others in the university. Most of them were in a strange city, where they lived in "cheap boarding houses," shared meals and leisure time activities, and through other common experiences were bound together as a group. Some students held informal gatherings each Saturday night, where they discussed medical and other topics and swilled refreshments that flowed "as free as the sparkling water from the mountain." For those less given to secular distractions, the school boasted the world's largest Bible class made up exclusively of medical students. At the new City Hospital, aspiring physicians gained clinical experience by treating a variety of indigent patients, ranging from victims of frostbite to drug addicts. After graduation, many practiced in rural areas and small towns throughout the region. One medical school graduate enjoyed the distinction of opening "the first Rexall store" in King City, Missouri. Some alumni even consulted their former professors in difficult

In 1923 Marie Biehl (1895–1976), pictured here, became the first woman to complete the entire U of L medical course. The first woman to receive her M.D. from U of L was Estelle Sederberg, a transfer student, in 1905.

cases, as in the instance of death from alcoholic poly-neuritis, in which a gallon of "hooch" was sent to the medical school, presumably for laboratory analysis.[13]

The medical school remained largely a man's world throughout this period, as the faculty apparently remained comfortable with the 1870 stance of Professor Theophilus Parvin. He argued that association of the sexes in clinic and classroom worked against "the modesty and delicacy which are so essential to womanly character." The school did finally admit a woman in the 1890s, but she was promptly hooted out of the lecture hall. In 1891 the august professor D.W. Yandell had posed the question, "Should Women Practice Medicine?" He thought not.[14]

In 1905, however, Estelle Sederberg, apparently after transferring from another school, received her M.D. from the University of Louisville. The first

woman to earn the M.D. after completing the entire course at the university was Marie E. Biehl, in 1923. Some other local medical schools were more welcoming. Katerina J. Rohrer, probably the first woman in the state to receive a medical degree, graduated from the Hospital College of Medicine in 1887, and Sarah Helen Fitzbutler, the first black woman to receive her M.D. in Kentucky, graduated from the Louisville National Medical College in 1892.[15]

With schools across the nation, the University of Louisville was swept into the patriotic enthusiasm that followed America's entry into World War I. By the fall of 1917, more than half of the Arts and Sciences upperclassmen had volunteered for, or been drafted into, the armed forces. The next spring Dean Patterson published a plan calling for colleges and universities to aid in the war effort. Patterson's plan for colleges to help train military officers received national press coverage, and the War Department subsequently adopted a similar plan for a national Student Army Training Corps. In the fall of 1918, the University of Louisville opened a unit of the corps, complete with a mess hall and barracks. Uniforms were in short supply, so the cadets wore khaki arm bands. Meanwhile, Eckart von Walther, a German citizen and "perfect gentleman" who had served the college since the early days of the school, resigned from the faculty. Although the reasons for his resignation remain unclear, the move may have been forced by the professor's nationality. The ugly cloud of anti-German sentiment that enveloped the country for a time did not spare Louisville or its university.[16]

At the same time, commencement programs stressed patriotic themes and the school added a course entitled "Europe and the Great War," which traced the causes of the conflict. At one point, the college faculty resolved that the school stood for "the high value of true citizenship," a worthy but vague goal which in this instance meant that enlistees were eligible for leaves of absence from their academic pursuits. Later, the world-wide influenza epidemic caused suspension of classes at the university.[17]

The war took its toll on all the departments of the university, although Arts and Sciences, with its

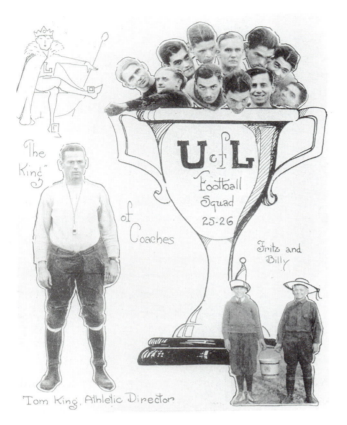

The undefeated 1925 U of L football team.

large number of female students, in some ways fared better than others. Low enrollments left the medical school unable to meet its expenses. Having made a commitment to put that unit and its facilities at the disposal of the Council of National Defense, the board of trustees on more than one occasion mortgaged university property to finance medicine's continued operations. When conditions in the law school reached a low point in the fall of 1918, that school's faculty received the board's approval to cancel classes for the upcoming 1918-1919 year. It was not until the 1920-1921 academic year that law regained income and enrollments close to its pre-war levels.[18]

After the war, student life in the College of Arts and Sciences took on a new glimmer of excitement, helped in part by the success of the football team. While no teams were fielded during the four-year period from 1917 through 1920 because of the war and lack of funding, the program was well-established

by 1925. In that year, under the leadership of Coach Tom King and star running back Fred Koster, the football squad won eight games, lost none, and allowed only two points to be scored against it. In the late 1920s the Louisville eleven included Lawrence "Chink" Wetherby, who later became governor of the commonwealth, a player described as "not endowed by nature with a football carriage," but "a mighty nice little end."[19]

One of President Ford's first initiatives was to seek increases in the city's appropriations for the university. When the city council reacted unfavorably to this request, Mayor John G. Buschemeyer and Ford took the matter of the university's financial needs public, and in 1916 the state legislature approved a special city tax. In 1917 the city council began levying this tax, which, with state approval, was increased from one and three-quarter mills to five mills by 1920. By then the university was receiving more than $50,000 per year in operating funds from this tax. The problem of the university's inadequate physical facilities, however, remained.[20]

Just as city financial support for the university was increasing, so were enrollments in the College of Arts and Sciences. By the fall of 1920 the student body exceeded six hundred. Without question the college had outgrown its home at Second and Broadway. Soon after Ford had taken office in 1914 the university had offered $30,000 for the Norris property, a large, undeveloped tract in Louisville's Highlands neighborhood. After this offer was refused, the family of William R. Belknap, a local hardware dealer who had recently died, donated funds sufficient for the school to acquire the seventy-nine acre Gaertner tract for $61,000. Referred to—prematurely, as it turned out—as the Belknap Campus, it was adjacent to and twice the size of the Norris property.[21]

In 1920 the university submitted a $1 million municipal bond issue to develop this Highlands campus, but the proposal was defeated at the polls. Some moderate black leaders, wanting to avoid the disfavor of whites who had supported black causes, counseled passage. Large numbers of blacks, however, who paid city taxes but were prevented by state law from attending the university, cast the deciding votes against

Dean Patterson and faculty at the undeveloped Highlands campus in 1922. (Louisville Courier-Journal.)

the measure. Awareness of the growing political and economic strength of African Americans during and after World War I had eluded U of L officials. Just as they had not reckoned with this black renaissance, they also had failed to take account of the rise of a new generation of black leaders, who relied on fellow blacks, rather than influential whites, for support.[22]

After this defeat, President Ford assured black opponents that if the issue were passed on a future ballot, a portion of the money would be set aside to support higher education for African Americans. Unfortunately, even though the bond issue passed in 1925, Ford's promise went unkept for the remainder of the decade. The best the university could do was to approve a $2,000 annual appropriation beginning in 1924 for the provision of extension classes for blacks. Offered on the Simmons University campus at Seventh and Kentucky Streets, the classes were taught by Simmons faculty and adjunct instructors from the community, all of them black.[23]

Discouraged by their defeat at the ballot box, university officials in 1923 sold the Highlands property acquired through the Belknap family. Wakefield-Davis, a real estate firm, bought it for $125,000, giving the university a good return on the sale. It was quickly developed as University Park, a residential area with streets named Princeton, Harvard, Yale, and Sewanee. The university immediately purchased the former Louisville and Jefferson County Children's Home at Third and Shipp Streets for $325,000. Just under two miles south of the downtown business district, this site occupied a central location in the community. As early as 1916, evidently, Mayor Buschemeyer and others had promoted it as "ideal" for the university. This turn of events disappointed the Belknaps, but President Ford believed he lacked the resources to develop a completely new campus, even if the bond issue were to be resubmitted and approved.[24]

Lying within one of the early tracts identified in the Fincastle surveys of 1774, which rewarded Virginia veterans of the French and Indian Wars, the land that became this new Third Street site eventually was owned by Ewell Shipp. His heirs sold the land to Thomas Browne, who in turn sold 82.5 acres to the city of Louisville for about $10,000 in 1850. It was specified by Browne that the land was to be used for the benefit of the public. This property was occasionally referred to as the "Southern Cemetery" and was known legally as the Oakland Cemetery, although there is no evidence anyone was ever buried there. Shipp Street, for many years the northern border of the campus, was named for Ewell Shipp.[25]

In 1854 the city of Louisville granted a charter to the Louisville House of Refuge for the care of the city's wayward and delinquent children. This development was a local manifestation of the nationwide reform school movement, begun earlier in the century. In 1859 the city appropriated $60,000 for construction and site improvements, and in the following year conveyed the deed of the property to the organization, with the restriction that at least forty

Gardiner Hall, shown here in 1926, had been erected in 1872 and later was named in honor of benefactor Clarence R. Gardiner. (CSC.)

acres be set aside and maintained for the public as Southern Park. The removal of this restriction in 1866 freed up all sixty-seven acres for the institution's use.[26]

The Louisville House of Refuge's first and "most refined" building was completed in 1861 and named for the president of the institution, John G. Baxter, later mayor of Louisville. Before it could be used for its intended purpose, however, the building served as a Union hospital during the Civil War. Located just southwest of Fort McPherson and the Brown Hospital, also a federal hospital during the war, the entire site was given over to the military. Troops paraded on the grounds and were quartered in barracks built there. Soon after the war's end, federal authorities turned the site back over to the institution, which

"with commendable haste," according to Baxter, "prepared for the reception of inmates," the first of whom was admitted in July 1865. The Baxter Building was damaged by a fire and was torn down in 1925 to make way for the Speed Museum.[27]

Other structures, such as the current Gardiner Hall, Ford Hall, Jouett Hall, and Gottschalk Hall, were added from 1868 through 1896. Gardiner Hall, built in 1872, is the oldest surviving building on the original campus site at Third and Shipp Streets. In 1886 the House of Refuge was renamed the Louisville Industrial School of Reform. In 1920 school officials changed its name to the Louisville and Jefferson County Children's Home and began laying plans to move to what became known as Ormsby Village near Anchorage in far eastern Jefferson County.[28]

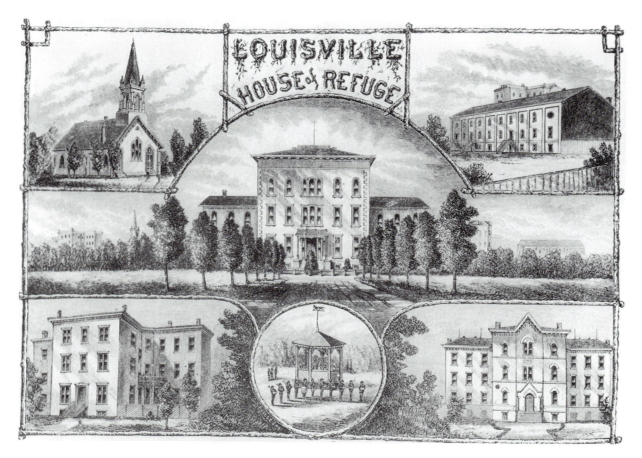

The city's "wayward and delinquent children" were cared for in the House of Refuge, which occupied what became the site of the university's main campus. Union troops paraded on its grounds during the Civil War.

The forty-seven-acre Children's Home property provided several buildings adaptable for immediate use, and in the fall of 1925 the College of Liberal Arts began classes in its new residence, called "University Campus." Renamed Belknap Campus in 1927, the area was nicely wooded and had a pastoral charm, although the original buildings—dormitories and shops for delinquent and truant youth, both male and female, black and white—reflected the "fiscal and moral economy" of their previous tenants. The university immediately sold eight acres on the southeast edge of its new property to the "Louisville Base Ball Company," which built Parkway Field there for the Louisville Colonels baseball team. In 1927 the J.B. Speed Art Museum opened on the northwest corner, where the Baxter Building had stood. Ready street-

Many students commuted to the Belknap Campus by streetcar.

The Playhouse, shown here in 1926, was built in the Carpenter Gothic style in 1874 as an interdenominational chapel on the grounds of the old House of Refuge. One of the oldest buildings on the Belknap Campus, it was moved to the triangle formed by Cardinal Boulevard and Second and Third Streets in 1980. (CSC.)

car access enhanced the value of the site to students, virtually all of whom were commuters.[29]

The buildings taken over by the university included a charming frame chapel, which was remodeled as the Playhouse. The college already had a thriving dramatic organization, directed by Boyd Martin, who also served as drama critic for the *Courier-Journal*. In 1921 the Dramatic Club became the University Players, who now blossomed in their new quarters. After modification, the Playhouse included seating for over five hundred, a $2,000 light board, and "toilet facilities for the comfort of the guests." In 1927 Martin staged a $3,500 production of *Romeo and Juliet*. According to a regional publication, this represented "the high water mark for Southern players." Articles on the Little Theater movement in the South placed the University of Louisville and the University of North Carolina student repertory companies in the same distinguished category.[30]

Pleased with its new home, the university contracted for a master development plan, which was drawn up by Frederick L. Morgan of the Allied Ar-

chitects Association of Kentucky. Morgan envisioned a campus that, if completed, would provide "one of the most beautiful groupings of collegiate buildings in the South." He called for "broad, grassy courts" surrounded by structures that would be "famous the world over for the simple beauty of their shining colonnades and lofty white portals." While envisioned in grand scale, with the old buildings torn down to make way for the new, the campus changed little in fact. The 1927 Administration Building was the only structure occupied under the Allied plan. Designed to resemble Thomas Jefferson's rotunda at the University of Virginia, it originally housed the president's office, the library, classrooms, the registrar, the admissions office, storerooms, and the bookstore.[31]

Under President Ford's leadership, the university also acquired a $250,000 donation to establish an engineering school. The gift came in 1924 from William S. Speed and his sister, Olive Speed Sackett, in honor of their father, cement magnate James Breckinridge Speed, who had died in 1912. Before the actual donation, Ford had asked Bennett M.

Founded in 1911 and directed by local theatrical legend Boyd Martin (1887–1963) from 1914 until 1955, the University of Louisville Players were noted for the quality of their theatrical productions. U of L alumnus and famed Broadway set designer Rollo Wayne (1889–1954) assisted with many productions. From humble beginnings in a small room at 119 West Broadway, the University Players went on to perform at the University Playhouse and all around the city of Louisville. They are shown here in a 1927 production of Romeo and Juliet.

CAMPUS AND ACADEMIC EXPANSION

The Allied Architects plan included an administration building designed to resemble Thomas Jefferson's famous rotunda at the University of Virginia.

The Administration Building, shown here in 1927, was under construction when President George Colvin took office in 1926. It was renamed Grawemeyer Hall in 1988. (CSC.)

Shown here in 1926, this building was erected in 1893. Once called the Leathers Building, it was later named in honor of Dean Bennett M. Brigman. Born in Louisville in 1881, Brigman obtained a master's degree from U of L and in 1918 began teaching engineering and drawing at the College of Arts and Sciences, which offered a two-year program for engineering training. Brigman became the first dean of the Speed Scientific School at its inception in 1925.

Brigman, an Arts and Sciences professor, to investigate the possibility of opening an engineering school. Brigman favored the cooperative system of education, whereby students combined classroom and industrial work. This approach was adopted and Brigman became the first dean of the Speed Scientific School, which opened in 1925 in two buildings on the southwest corner of U of L's brand new campus.[32]

Dean Brigman guided the school with a paternal hand. He saw that his "boys"—Speed had no female students until the 1930s—learned not only engineering, but also professional pride, loyalty to their employers, and even personal grooming. An early Speed School faculty member recalled that the students "affectionately" called Brigman "Dad." By the time they finished, many Speed School graduates considered themselves "rugged individualists," whose education had imparted not only technical knowledge, but also devotion to accurate detail and rigorous analysis.[33]

College social life quickened following World War I. In part, the school was simply growing up, although

students undoubtedly reflected the characteristics associated with "the lost generation," a common description of 1920s youth. On September 24, 1926, the first weekly student newspaper, the *Cardinal News,* appeared, coming out thirty-one times until it ceased publication on June 3, 1927. Graduate and undergraduate students edited the newspaper, which sold for a nickel and was self-supporting. The staff covered a variety of local, national, and university issues. The death of American socialist and labor leader Eugene V. Debs and the collapse of the Florida real estate boom drew comments from the editor, Samuel E. Hyman. Significant university topics included construction bids for the Administration Building; the heyday of U of L football under coach Tom King; theatrical productions under drama coach Boyd Martin; U.S. Supreme Court Justice Louis D. Brandeis and his growing interest in the School of Law; and the beginning of an endowment campaign.[34]

The *U of L News* followed the *Cardinal News* with its first issue on February 24, 1928. The new Faculty Committee on Student Publications exercised final control over the student paper, which was free.

Greek Houses in 1930.

In May 1930 the editors complained that they had not received the amount of support hoped for and the paper was discontinued the next year. The present *Cardinal* first appeared in 1932 and has been published continuously since that time. The new paper operated under a Board of Student Publications, which originally included three faculty members and the editor and business manager of each student publication. Although the *Cardinal* was distributed free of charge, it was financially solvent through advertising sales.[35]

Campus elections were hard-fought contests often dominated by Greek organizations, as social fraternities and sororities assumed an even greater importance in the college. As noted previously, Dean Patterson frowned on these groups and successfully resisted them until after World War I. In the medical school, however, one fraternity, Phi Chi, had appeared in the 1890s. It remained the only Greek organization there until 1905, when a chapter of Pi Mu was established. By 1920 there were four more medical fraternities as well as three dental fraternities. Following the war some liberal arts students, risking discipline by the faculty, formed clubs in secret, with the hope that they would be recognized in time. Soon they overcame the resistance, and the administration set rules for the establishment and deportment of fraternities and sororities.[36]

Delta Sigma, which lays claim to being U of L's first undergraduate social fraternity, was organized in 1921. By 1925 it had its own house on South Third Street. Not surprisingly, the 1920s comprised an active period for Greek life at U of L. During the decade another medical and another dental fraternity

Established in honor of U of L music instructor Agnes Moore Fryberger (1868–1939), the annual all-campus music event known as the Fryberger Sing was first held on May 18, 1938. After a brief lapse the competition was revived in 1941. For more than half a century the Fryberger Sing has been held in various locations on campus, including indoors in the Playhouse and outdoors on the oval in front of the Administration Building. Performing groups representing fraternities, sororities, and other campus organizations are judged on tone, intonation, interpretation and artistic effect, diction, selection, and appearance. Contestants are shown here in 1958.

were organized; two engineering fraternities were founded; and ten fraternities and seventeen sororities (some honor societies, some social organizations) also were recognized on campus. U of L graduates during the 1920s were overwhelmingly members of Greek societies, sometimes more than one. Observers went so far as to report that the rush for freshman pledges became so intense that each chapter bagged "several misfits every year." Meanwhile, critics of the Greek system attacked fraternity men as "well dressed young loafers." Caught up in the intellectual trends of the decade, some student writers delivered nihilistic attacks upon revival meetings, big business, social climbers, and anything else that, in the minds of their targets, may have smacked of purposefulness.[37]

At the same time, the college developed social affairs of its own, the biggest of which was the Spring Carnival, held in such local night spots as the Eagles Hall, Rainbow Gardens, and the Henry Clay Hotel. The *U of L News* claimed that women students sometimes obtained higher grades by "vamping" men professors, which, according to the newspaper, demonstrated that there was more to college than "book larnin'." One student recalled that his parents considered automobiles "portable seduction platforms," although his memory was that the models of the period were too small to serve that purpose comfortably. During the noble experiment of Prohibition, one student and faculty member shared a drink prepared on cold winter nights, when a bathtub filled with wine was left outside. Most of the liquid froze. That which did not was dubbed by those who drank it as "leopard sweat."[38]

In 1928 Laurence Lee Howe, law school editor for the *U of L News*, published an endorsement of New York governor Alfred E. Smith, the Democratic candidate in the presidential race. According to Howe, Smith's opponent, Secretary of Commerce Herbert Hoover, and his fellow Republicans wanted to run the United States like "a big corporation" instead of a political entity. He found Hoover's public pronouncements "a maze of circumlocution," while Smith issued "fearless and outspoken" statements based upon the democratic principles of the founding fathers. Finally, Howe condemned Hoover by his association with the administrations of Republican predecessors Warren G. Harding and Calvin Coolidge. Despite Howe's endorsement of Smith, Kentucky voters supported Hoover by an overwhelming margin.[39]

When A.Y. Ford became president in 1914, the University of Louisville largely resembled the school that it had been throughout the nineteenth century. When he died, in 1926, the university had begun to resemble the institution it would become during much of the twentieth. He added new academic programs, improved old ones, initiated a coordinated effort to increase public and private financial support, and strengthened the president's office. The latter occurred without incident, mostly because Ford reacted promptly and wisely to obvious crises, seized opportunities to develop new programs, and took the initiatives necessary to increase funding. His successor sought to consolidate these gains, particularly in the College of Liberal Arts, not in an effort to meet a crisis, raise money, or expand programs, but to define the role and scope of that division and assert his ultimate authority over it. He met with stubborn resistance, much of it in response to his own inability to control the situation.[40]

TEN

PRESIDENT VS. FACULTY

PRESIDENT A.Y. FORD died in June 1926, and the board wasted no time in seeking a replacement. The trustees wanted someone who could continue the momentum generated during Ford's administration, including fund-raising and the expanding role of the president's office. Within a few weeks they had chosen George Colvin, a Kentucky native who had been elected state superintendent of public instruction in 1919. He had also been an unsuccessful candidate for governor in the Republican primary in 1923, and for the past three years had been superintendent of the Louisville and Jefferson County Children's Home.

Colvin was the first U of L president who began his service in the office in a full-time capacity. Like Ford—indeed, like all of his predecessors—Colvin had no experience as a scholar or university administrator, but he had devoted much of his life to education. Upon learning of the appointment, Frank L. McVey, president of the University of Kentucky, told Colvin that the University of Louisville presidency would present many obstacles. Colvin confided to McVey that he faced bewildering problems created by policies that had evolved without careful planning.[1]

Colvin and the trustees had as a goal what was already reality in many American colleges and universities: a powerful president who served as executive agent of the board. At the same time, a successful academic administrator needed to retain the confidence of several other groups: alumni, students,

deans, and, most emphatically, faculty. Colvin began his administration with the board's confidence. His lack of experience in higher education, coupled with his background in state politics, meant he would have to earn the trust of the faculty. The board wanted Colvin to focus his attention on the College of Liberal Arts—the name had just been changed again—and he did.[2]

By the end of the fall 1926 semester, his first as president, Colvin had alienated several members of the liberal arts faculty. His critics complained that the president misunderstood the purpose of a university. Consequently, they argued, his policies endangered academic standards. The controversy centered around the administration's decision to concentrate resources on undergraduate rather than graduate instruction. This policy arose from financial necessity and civic obligation. The president and trustees argued that the university could not support a strong graduate program. Because much of their budget came from municipal resources, they felt an obligation to apply funds where they would benefit the greatest number of students. As a corollary to this argument, the administration intended to establish a minimum enrollment for undergraduate classes and to divert library gifts away from resources for graduate study. The president and the board asserted that they had ultimate responsibility for such policies and the power to carry them out.[3]

In response, reports circulated of angry ex-

George Colvin (1875–1928), eighth president of the University of Louisville, 1926–1928, has been the school's most controversial president. An 1895 graduate of Centre College, Colvin held honorary degrees from Centre and the University of Kentucky. Colvin's views on education emphasized instruction and service rather than scholarship and research, and he considered many university faculty members to be cloistered academicians with little knowledge of practical affairs. He informed historians that the purpose of history was to build character, and advised economists that their discipline should avoid "contentious questions." Colvin was not the first U of L president who came to the university as a former local or statewide political office-holder, but for the next seventy years, at least, he would be the last.

changes in committee meetings, as well as private disagreements between the president and faculty members. Some of the more heated encounters involved historian Louis R. Gottschalk and his roommate, Hill Shine, who taught English. Many believed Colvin intended to dismiss Gottschalk and other vocal opponents of his policies. In December, Louis Siff, head of the mathematics department since the beginning

of the college, committed suicide. Friends believed he was depressed over the possible loss of his position. In January 1927, anonymous letters to the editor began to appear in local newspapers, expressing unhappiness with the Colvin administration. These epistles brought several charges against the president and the board of trustees.[4]

Warwick Anderson, who in 1922 had followed Patterson as dean, resisted presidential encroachments on his power. In defiance of Colvin, he continued to make appointments without board approval. In retaliation, Anderson was stripped of the power to recommend appointments. On several occasions, Colvin urged Anderson to resign and return to teaching. Eventually, Anderson was dismissed. Gottschalk and his history colleague Robert S. Cotterill were perhaps the most vocal advocates of graduate education and research in the college, which naturally put them at odds with the board's policies and the president's implementation of them.[5]

All of these issues surfaced during Colvin's first semester in office, and he compounded his problems by issuing one-year contracts during the second semester. This was not intended, he claimed, to purge the faculty, but to provide the board an opportunity to study and revise its personnel procedures. Colvin contended that, because of poorly kept records, he could not determine what mutual obligations existed between the faculty and administration. Liberal arts faculty members charged that one-year contracts broke the unwritten tradition established under Dean Patterson: permanent appointment following a one-year trial period.[6]

In February 1927, both Gottschalk and another history colleague, Rolf Johannesen, received the standard appointment contract to sign and return to the president. At the time, both were exploring employment possibilities with other universities. Johannesen was promoted in rank from assistant to associate professor, but without an increase in salary. He protested to the president, and Colvin replied that a raise was impossible. Johannesen delayed for almost two weeks as he continued to negotiate for a job elsewhere. Colvin construed his silence as a rejection of the proffered terms and dismissed him. Gottschalk, mean-

In 1896 the building now known as Gottschalk Hall, after Louis R. Gottschalk, was erected as the "Colored Girls' Building" for the reform school at what was then First and Shipp Streets. The firm of Clark and Loomis designed the new building, which cost about $15,000.

while, had requested a leave of absence for the coming year to accept a temporary appointment at the University of Chicago. When he learned of Johannesen's plight, he resigned, effective the end of the semester, and issued a press release critical of the Colvin administration.[7]

The trustees accepted Gottschalk's resignation, making it effective immediately, although they would pay his salary through the end of the spring semester. They also issued a statement blaming Gottschalk, in large part, for unrest within the faculty. Eventually, they withdrew this charge, but refused to reinstate Gottschalk for the remainder of the semester. Furthermore, the board reconsidered Johannesen's situation. Concluding that Colvin had misinterpreted the professor's silence, the trustees reinstated Johannesen.

Meanwhile, Gottschalk asked the American Association of University Professors (AAUP) to investigate the situation.[8]

The events surrounding Gottschalk and Johannesen led the liberal arts faculty to call for an internal investigation as well. Later that spring, the president, trustees, and faculty convened for a joint meeting. Press coverage was forbidden. The conferees accumulated more than five hundred pages of charges and countercharges, but the hearings produced little in the way of positive results. Instead, they stimulated speculation, aggravated animosities, and, according to faculty members, resulted in administrative reprisals. Following the conference, thirty-nine of the forty-seven members of the liberal arts faculty called for the president's resignation. A group of disaffected students even read a "Declaration of Independence" condemning "King George Colvin" for his "educational crimes." Meanwhile, the endowment campaign planned under Ford—the first university-wide fund-raising effort in U of L's history—was wounded beyond recovery. Several who had promised significant contributions withdrew their pledges.[9]

Following the internal investigation, Professor Simeon E. Leland of the University of Kentucky visited Louisville to gather preliminary information for the AAUP. He found Colvin friendly and willing to have the AAUP help improve faculty-administration relations, though he opposed a formal investigation. The president attributed most of his problems to the laxity of former administrations. Leland also noted that, from the beginning, some members of the faculty had considered Colvin a poor choice as president.[10]

During the summer of 1927 the AAUP undertook a full investigation. Local chapter members believed that a negative report would bring down the Colvin administration. The committee interviewed the president, board members, faculty, alumni, and students, and early in the fall of 1927 wrote and circulated a draft report. Most of the readers supported the committee's damning criticism of both the president and the board of trustees, though one committee member recommended major revisions.[11]

The dissenter, Arthur O. Lovejoy, a Johns Hopkins University philosophy professor who had written much of the AAUP's landmark 1915 report on academic freedom and tenure, defended the trustees and focused blame on the president. The trustees had acted on what they properly considered reliable information from their chief executive officer. Furthermore, the board had done "some unusually decent things," including reversal of their ruling on Johannesen's dismissal and partial retraction of their statement on Gottschalk. Lovejoy argued that the draft report implied that a university faculty was beyond administrative control, which was not only incorrect, but also indefensible to the layman. He recommended that the final report emphasize problems created by the lack of a faculty voice in university governance, for he knew that in many instances others exercised ultimate authority.[12]

The AAUP censured the University of Louisville, but the committee's published report may have made less of an impact than two studies commissioned by the board of trustees before Colvin took office. The first, submitted in 1927 by Dean Frederick J. Kelly of the University of Minnesota and referred to as the Kelly Report, became a planning document for the College of Liberal Arts, which upheld the policy of de-emphasizing graduate instruction. The second, prepared by President McVey of the University of Kentucky in 1927, recommended changes in the organization and administration of the University of Louisville. In effect, the McVey report clarified the boundaries of presidential, decanal, and faculty authority. Entitled "Organization of the University of Louisville" and referred to as the "Blue Book" because of its cover, it became the university's first governing document after its adoption in 1928.[13]

Colvin continued in office until the summer of 1928, when he died following a delayed appendectomy. Even from his hospital bed, the president was working to "break up opposition" to his administration. Colvin was heartened, no doubt, by the trustees' publication in the local newspapers and in pamphlet form of a series of statements supporting his actions. The student newspaper, the *U of L News*, which unlike its predecessor, the *Cardinal News*, had stayed away from the Colvin controversy, criticized "those few hoodlum fools on the faculty" who reportedly "gathered for a celebration upon hearing of the death." Yancy Altsheler, a board member, concluded that Colvin had been the wrong man for a difficult assignment.[14]

The Colvin years at the University of Louisville were marked by rancor and public embarrassment. His administration destroyed the endowment campaign planned by President Ford. Ford's sincere promise to direct some of the 1925 bond issue revenue to black higher education also remained unkept. The faculty lost several distinguished members, including Gottschalk and Cotterill in history and Ware in sociology. Still, by strengthening the central authority of the president and board of trustees, the combative president continued a process begun under Ford. With the support of the board, he prevailed over the liberal arts faculty, Dean Warwick Anderson, and the AAUP.

A more skilled leader might have done the same with less bloodshed, but Colvin's goal was in line with national developments in higher education. The trustees supported him—for too long, perhaps—because he represented them in a struggle for control of the College of Liberal Arts and ultimately the university itself. Disagreements between faculty and administration would occur periodically, of course, but never since have they reached the level of animosity prevalent during the Colvin years.[15]

Upon Colvin's death in 1928 the trustees appointed the esteemed John Letcher Patterson acting president of the university. Although Justice Brandeis feared that the university would be unable to attract a qualified replacement to succeed Colvin, Patterson's year of service in the president's office undoubtedly helped ease the tension between those who set university policy and those who taught its students. The institution's next president inherited an office stronger than that occupied by either Ford or Colvin.[16]

ELEVEN

ACADEMIC
RESPECTABILITY

T HE NEXT PRESIDENT of the University of Louisville was neither a Kentuckian nor a politician. For the first time in the institution's history, the board of trustees selected someone other than a resident of the commonwealth. Raymond A. Kent, dean of the College of Arts and Sciences at Northwestern University, took office in the summer of 1929. He was the first professional educator to hold the office since the chartering of the university in 1846. During his fourteen-year presidency, the university recovered from the Colvin administration, weathered the Great Depression and the charged political atmosphere of the 1930s, and saw its academic divisions move into the mainstream of accreditation standards. Kent also fulfilled Ford's earlier pledge to provide higher education for African Americans by establishing the Louisville Municipal College for Negroes in 1931.[1]

Late in the 1930s Kent turned his attention toward fund raising. Unfortunately, the advent of World War II interfered with those efforts, and at the end of his administration the university still lacked the resources necessary to match the level of the region's strongest institutions of higher education. Nevertheless, under his skillful leadership the university achieved a solid measure of academic respectability.

Kent even looked like a university president. At forty-six, the new chief had iron gray hair and keen, alert eyes. He spoke with ease and authority. Though somewhat austere, he had the sort of level-eyed cour-

Raymond Asa Kent (1883–1943), ninth president of the University of Louisville, 1929–1943, and the first who had devoted his entire career to higher education. Shown here in 1939, Kent was the son of English immigrants. He was educated at Cornell College (A.B. 1903), Drew Theological Seminary, and Columbia University (Ph.D. 1917). Kent's address to the 1935 graduating class, "An Open Season for Youth," helped set the tone for academic freedom and excellence at the university.

tesy that commanded respect. One dean recalled that Kent seldom gave direct commands. Generally, he asked, "Do you think that you would have time to do this?" The son of an Iowa farmer who had fought in the Civil War, Kent at one time had studied for the ministry. Shortly after taking office, he noted the deficiencies of the University of Louisville and determined what should be done to correct them. Most of all, he wanted each academic division to meet the requirements for full accreditation.[2]

Kent assembled an able group of deans. In medicine, John Walker Moore took over the same year the new president entered office. As dean of the school and staff executive at Louisville City Hospital, Moore demonstrated leadership ability, enthusiasm for teaching, and uncanny diagnostic powers. In 1930 the School of Law and the College of Liberal Arts came under the direction of Neville Miller and Julius J. Oppenheimer, respectively. Miller's leadership kept the law school's accreditation intact. Later, as mayor, he led the city through the traumatic period of the devastating 1937 Ohio River flood. Under Oppenheimer the College of Liberal Arts achieved a stimulating intellectual atmosphere recalled years later by students and faculty alike.

Neville Miller practiced law in Louisville with his father, Shackelford Miller Sr., and his brother, Shackelford Miller Jr., before becoming the U of L law school's dean, then the city's mayor.

The law school building, shown here shortly after it was built in 1939 for $200,000, was one of only two buildings that followed the magnificent plan for the Belknap Campus designed by Jens Fredrick Larson. Larson's original drawing had the word "Brandeis" emblazoned on the facade, but it was not until 1997 that the school was named in his honor. Also in 1997 the building was named Wilson W. Wyatt Hall.

LAW

The university's efforts to conform with national educational standards encountered no test more severe than that facing the School of Law. When Kent took office, the law school was little more than "the meanest most inefficient night . . . school." In addition to falling short of accepted standards for the number of full-time faculty and the extent of library holdings, it held classes in downtown quarters the president termed "disgracefully dirty" and which one inspector called "cramped and dingy." Ten years later in 1939, however, the school finally took occupancy of a spacious new building on the Belknap Campus, constructed with federal WPA funds and private contributions. By that time, the law school also met national standards set by the American Bar Association and the American Association of Law Schools for the number of full-time faculty and the size of its library. During this process, accreditation reports provided the ammunition law school officials needed to justify increased financial support.[3]

To some extent, the progress made in the professionalization of legal education outpaced changes in the requirements of the daily practice of law. By the end of the Kent administration, Louisville law professors accepted the need for a full-time faculty, but still insisted upon applied as well as theoretical training. Professors, students, and practitioners alike conceded that reading and discussing cases taught fundamental principles, legal reasoning, and verbal agility, but offered little instruction in client relationships, the mechanics of litigation, and drafting legal documents. To some extent, mock court sessions, a legal aid society, and a law school briefing service compensated for the practical elements many found missing in formal instruction. Part-time work as clerks for local attorneys also remained a popular activity for law students.[4]

MEDICINE

A smoother amalgamation of formal instruction and applied training took place in medicine. During their first two years, students took pre-clinical work in anatomy, pathology, physiology, and pharmacology. By this time such courses were frequently offered by full-time professional teachers with Ph.D. rather than M.D. degrees. Professor Sidney Isaac Kornhauser, for example, reigned over the anatomy laboratory with a firm but fair hand, insuring that each student had "an adequate supply of well injected material." Kornhauser, a leader in the field of histology, even designed his own cadaver cabinets, which kept the subjects "in proper condition."[5]

Third- and fourth-year students completed clinical training in internal medicine, pediatrics, obstetrics, psychiatry, and surgery, with Louisville City Hospital as their training ground. One student recalled that, during this period, the hospital was "clean, crowded, and busy." Medical students and interns who trained there learned painful but valuable lessons: never to grimace in the face of a patient, no matter what the condition; the wisdom that experienced nurses could offer to brash young physicians; and, in the days before air conditioning, that flies in the operating room were swatted *away* from the patient.[6]

Spafford Ackerly, who in 1932 came to the Department of Psychiatry, brought major innovations to the hospital's treatment of mental illness. Psychiatry had become part of the medical school curriculum five years earlier. Furthermore, with the help of the *Courier-Journal*, Ackerly successfully campaigned for reforms in all of the state's mental institutions.[7]

DENTISTRY

By the 1930s, officials of the School of Dentistry were struggling with the question of whether to train students as skilled technicians or scientists. On the one hand, "restoration and replacement" occupied much of the practitioner's day. Investigators discovered that students borrowed few books from the library and spent little time studying outside the classroom and laboratory. Furthermore, some feared that overemphasis of pure science could make dentistry an adjunct to medicine. Others argued that the future of the profession lay in emphasizing diseases and infections of the oral cavity and their overall relationship

The dental clinic, shown here in 1926, provided hands-on experience in the "restoration and replacement" that occupied much of the practitioner's day. (CSC.)

to good health. The two views were not mutually exclusive, but the trend was toward the latter, the modern dentist as scientist rather than technician. In 1939 the school changed its terminal degree from the D.D.S. to the D.M.D.[8]

ENGINEERING

Accreditation was also an issue for the Speed Scientific School, which in 1938 became the first engineering school south of the Ohio River to receive the highest possible rating in all its departments from the Engineers' Council for Professional Development. The Speed School boasted no more energetic faculty member than Robert Craig Ernst, known to some as "the big boss," who later served as dean. During his early years on the faculty, Ernst led the movement to establish the Division of Industrial Research, which opened in 1938 and signaled the school's offer to apply its scientific expertise to the solution of industrial problems. Ernst and others viewed their profes-

Robert C. Ernst, who had joined the school's chemical engineering faculty two decades earlier, succeeded Ford Wilkinson as dean and served until 1969. In 1975, the Chemical Engineering Building, built in 1967, was renamed Ernst Hall.

In 1936, in a small wooden structure on the site now occupied by the Ekstrom Library, math professor Walter Lee Moore, shown here in the physics workshop in 1978, helped create what was probably U of L's first observatory, equipped with telescopes furnished by the Louisville Astronomical Society. It was torn down in the mid-1950s and the equipment moved to a dome on the roof of the new Natural Sciences Building. In 1978 U of L dedicated the new Walter Lee Moore Observatory on the 200–acre Horner Bird and Wildlife Sanctuary in Oldham County, a 1960 gift to the university.

sion as the ideal combination of applied scientific expertise and business acumen.

The Division of Industrial Research carried out a variety of contracts with local businesses and government agencies, including the citrus industry's need to find use for its waste. In this case, graduate student Howard Bumstead determined that grapefruit rinds and pulp contained a high sugar and cellulose content and could be converted into breakfast cereal. Bumstead's "grapefruit flakes" were "disagreeable to the taste" and even with artificial flavoring remained difficult to chew. On the other hand, Bumstead averred, they contained more nutritional value than Purina Complete Rabbit Chow.[9]

Prior to Dean Brigman's death in 1938, this forward-thinking educator envisioned the extension of the campus southward. When the city straightened Eastern Parkway east of Third Street in 1930 and created an underpass for Third Street traffic under the Southern Railroad crossing, it included plans for a pedestrian tunnel negotiated by Brigman. Under his replacement, Ford L. Wilkinson Jr., the university hired Jens Fredrick Larson, architect of the new law

school building, to design a new facility south of Eastern Parkway. The James Breckinridge Speed Building was made possible by another gift from the Speed family, this one in the amount of $130,000, plus $70,000 in WPA funds. Occupied in 1941, it marked the advance of the Belknap Campus across its original boundary lines. Four years later another new building, one for the Institute of Industrial Research, was completed just south of "Main Speed," as students referred to it for many years.[10]

LIBERAL ARTS

During the 1930s, the College of Liberal Arts underwent a major reorganization. Generally, it began to follow the model developed by Robert M. Hutchins of the University of Chicago, who advocated a curriculum centered around independent study and the world's great literature. At the University of Louisville, the liberal arts program was divided into three divisions: humanities, social sciences, and natural sciences. Traditional departments still existed, but were de-emphasized during the first two years of study, when the students fulfilled common requirements and passed sophomore comprehensive examinations. In their junior year, students selected a departmental major. The junior college sought to integrate various academic disciplines and provide a broad background, while the senior college curriculum encouraged independent thought and research.[11]

This program proved especially effective in the Division of Humanities, owing in large part to the division head, Professor Ernest Hassold. As a Ph.D. in English, Hassold had been trained in the traditional canons of literary criticism, but he also had a seminary education and a broad appreciation of philosophy, art, and music, and their relationship to literature. In the English department, Hassold encouraged reading the work of contemporary authors such as William Faulkner, rather than ending the survey of literature with the Victorian masters. Most of all, Hassold was a dedicated leader. His devotion to the divisional concept won and kept converts among the faculty and students.[12]

MUSIC

The early liberal arts college offered a few music courses, and in 1929 it created a music department headed by Edward J. Wotawa, who had been brought over from Male High School. Soon he was directing the U of L orchestra, chorus, and string ensemble. Wotawa and a few other instructors taught harmony, music history, and sight-singing. Students of music appreciation attended class in a small ivy-covered brick building set in a grove of trees north of the Playhouse. Formerly the reform school's Catholic Chapel (the Playhouse had served as the Protestant chapel), it was sometimes called "the Temple of Apollo" by its denizens. For the most part, however, serious area music students relied on the Louisville Conservatory of Music, which had begun in 1913, for their instruction.[13]

In 1931 the privately-owned Louisville Conservatory of Music, located on Brook Street a dozen blocks north of the Belknap Campus, declared bankruptcy. Some wanted the University of Louisville to take over operation of this music school, but Kent

"A music school is no more and no less essential to a community than any other school maintained within its border. Music can be studied elsewhere, just as engineering, or medicine, or the liberal arts. Music can be imported for those to whom it is essential; music can be pursued abroad. But the community that fails to support the fine arts on a sound and dignified basis cannot hope for the cultural progress that is needed to balance industrial and civic expansion." —Dwight Anderson, Dean, School of Music, 1937–1956.

resisted the added financial responsibility. Eventually, he agreed to operate a School of Music for three years on an experimental basis. Occupying the conservatory building and employing some of its faculty, the new U of L school opened in 1932 under Dean Jacques Jolas, a pianist on loan from the Julliard School of Music in New York. Music education enjoyed the support of influential local citizens, but Kent thought Jolas incurred too many unplanned expenses by overemphasizing "public propaganda through formal concerts." In 1935 Fanny Brandeis, a niece of Justice Louis D. Brandeis, begged the president to keep the music school, but feared he would not. The

School of Music was retained, but Kent insisted upon a new dean.[14]

Kent's choice was Dwight Anderson, a pianist who had come over from the conservatory faculty. The school moved to a house at Fifth and Ormsby Streets formerly occupied by Hattie Bishop Speed, who paid the rent. In the late 1930s it moved to Patterson Hall on the Belknap Campus. Anderson served as the music school's chief administrator for two decades, where he reportedly trained over one thousand piano students, including Lee Luvisi, who joined the faculty in 1962 and continued his highly acclaimed career. Anderson recruited such noted faculty members as Gerhard Herz, in music history; Moritz Bomhard, for three decades director of the Kentucky Opera Association; and Ernest Lyon, band director. In 1938 Anderson organized the Chamber Music Society. Among the music school's early graduates was organist William J. Schwann (1913-1998), class of 1935, who gained prominence as the publisher of an invaluable catalogue of musical recordings.[15]

SOCIAL WORK

In 1936 the University of Louisville opened the Graduate Division of Social Administration (predecessor of the Kent School of Social Work), which grew out of classes in applied sociology offered since the 1910s. The demand for professional social workers, coupled with the need of local agencies for post-appointment training, led to the establishment of the division. Classes emphasized relief administration, case work, community organization, and social research. Students submitted a thesis, frequently based on local fieldwork, as part of their degree requirements. One studied life in a new public housing project which he thought had the potential to become a model community. Apparently, the residents considered this a more remote possibility than did the author and his faculty advisors.[16]

Classes in social work had been available in Louisville since 1918, offered by the Louisville Conference of Social Workers and the city's Welfare League, a forerunner of today's Metro United Way. In 1923 the Welfare League created the Louisville School of

Margaret Kirkpatrick Strong (1883–1971).

Social Work. U of L students could enroll in the school and use the courses to count for their degree requirements. Norman J. Ware, the U of L sociology professor and historian, had served as an advisor to the independent school. Ware had worked at Chicago's famous Hull House under its founder, Jane Addams, whom he listed as a reference. The Louisville school closed in 1926 and Ware, disturbed by President George Colvin's policies, left for a position elsewhere, but the university continued to offer courses in social work.[17]

In 1930 Professor Margaret Strong joined the sociology department and from 1931 until 1936 served as its head. Like Ware, she was a Canadian with a doctorate from the University of Chicago and ties to Hull House. In 1936 Strong became the first director of the new U of L Graduate Division of Social Administration and provided able leadership for the growth and promotion of social work education. She was the first woman in U of L history to be appointed to the rank of full professor and the first to head a separate U of L graduate division or school.[18]

THE GRADUATE SCHOOL

Graduate studies and library resources were weak links in any hope the university had of achieving broad regional leadership in higher education during the 1930s. The Graduate School attracted mostly local students. On the other hand, the program did train many capable people, such as those who produced a valuable series of history master's theses on local topics, primarily under the direction of Professor William C. Mallalieu.

When the university opened its new campus, the library was first housed in the Home Economics Building, then was moved to the north wing of the Administration Building. There it continued to suffer from major deficiencies throughout the period. President Kent's efforts to win membership in the Association of American Universities met continued failure, owing in large part to defects in graduate education and the library.[19]

Kent's emphasis on academics influenced his view toward athletics. The president frowned on intercollegiate and intramural sports. He publicly scorned alumni who measured the university's qual-ity by the success of its athletic teams and bluntly declared that they should have learned better while students. Kent's advice was not well-received, especially when the football team suffered humiliating losses, such as a 105-0 drubbing by Murray State University during the 1932 season, when the squad lost all nine of its games. One graduate complained that the president's athletic policies made the University of Louisville "the laughing stock of the South."[20]

By the end of the Kent administration, all academic units of the University of Louisville were accredited by their respective agencies, a goal the president had established upon taking office. Most remarkably, Kent achieved this end in the midst of one of the worst economic depressions in the nation's history. In some ways, however, the University of Louisville retained vestiges of the nineteenth century. The medical and law schools maintained their traditional dominance of academic resources. Furthermore, most of the noteworthy academic expansion took place in professional programs for engineering, music, and social work. Graduate programs and library resources, traditional measurements of university status, remained embarrassingly weak, despite the president's good intentions.

TWELVE

A DREAM DEFERRED

THE LOUISVILLE MUNICIPAL COLLEGE for Negroes (LMC) grew out of the increasing political and economic strength of American blacks following World War I. This was the period of the Harlem Renaissance and Marcus Garvey's Universal Negro Improvement Association as well as the mass migration of blacks out of the rural South. In urban areas, African Americans formed a political base that gave their leaders a new degree of independence from white supporters. As noted previously, black opposition to the 1920 U of L bond issue, subsequent support of an improved version, and lobbying for action constituted evidence of this trend in Louisville.[1]

Black Louisvillians had refused to support an institution they could not attend. Their repudiation of the $1 million U of L bond issue of 1920 had led to its defeat at the polls. (Unlike other southern states, Kentucky had not passed laws disenfranchising African Americans.) But after President A.Y. Ford's assurances, a similar bond issue, this time with black support, passed in 1925. Ford then earmarked $100,000 to be used for black higher education. It was a major victory for both the black community and the university. Seven months later, however, Ford died, and his heartfelt promise went unfulfilled during the stormy two-year Colvin era and beyond. For six years, higher education for African Americans at the University of Louisville would remain a dream deferred.[2]

By this time school segregation had been burned into Kentucky law. In 1904 the state legislature had overwhelmingly passed the Day Law, which prohibited the teaching of both whites and blacks in the same school. Its intent, in the words of its sponsor, was "to prevent the contamination of the white children of Kentucky." The law was aimed at Berea College, an integrated private school in the eastern part of the state, which had admitted black students since 1866. The Day Law survived an appeal to the U.S. Supreme Court in 1908, despite the eloquent dissent of Justice John Marshall Harlan, himself a Kentuckian.[3]

The Day Law had effectively and devastatingly ended black higher education in Kentucky, save for two African American schools, one in Frankfort and the other in Louisville. The State Normal School for Colored Persons had opened in Frankfort in 1887, but for years it had suffered from political patronage and inadequate funding, with its curriculum falling short of minimal standards. The school did not become fully accredited until 1939, shortly after its name was changed to Kentucky State College for Negroes.[4]

In Louisville a black institution named Simmons University offered a college department, a normal school, and a theological school, as well as primary and secondary programs. Established by the General Association of Colored Baptists of Kentucky, the school had opened in 1879 as the Kentucky Normal and Theological Institute. Soon it was headed by

Parrish Hall.

William J. Simmons, president from 1880 until 1890, who in 1884 changed its name to State Colored Baptist University. The institution also offered training in medicine and law through the Louisville National Medical College (1888-1912) and Central Law School (1890-1941), proprietary institutions holding affiliation agreements with State University. Charles H. Parrish Sr. became president in 1918, and the following year the school was renamed in honor of Simmons.[5]

While the State Normal School for Colored Persons (in 1902 its name had been changed to Kentucky Normal and Industrial Institute for Colored Persons, and in 1926 to Kentucky State Industrial College for Colored Persons) in Frankfort and Simmons University in Louisville had struggled valiantly to offer programs of high quality to their students, after the turn of the century neither school came close to securing the funds necessary to meet accreditation standards. In Louisville, black leaders met with U of L officials in 1926 and 1927 and urged them to make good on the university's promise to provide higher education for African Americans. The university continued to do nothing, and in the summer of 1929 several exasperated black leaders implored newly arrived U of L president Raymond A. Kent to act. With the founding of Louisville Municipal College, he did.[6]

Like U of L's whites-only liberal arts college, which just six years earlier had moved to its new Belknap Campus a mile and half to the south, Louisville Municipal College for Negroes opened classes in 1931 on a ready-made campus. The university had purchased the site at Seventh and Kentucky Streets from Simmons University in August 1930, and had moved quickly to prepare it for student use. A three-story brick women's dormitory was converted to classrooms and science laboratories and subsequently renamed Parrish Hall. Another building, formerly the Simmons chapel, now housed administrative offices and the library. Five years later the university acquired the four-story brick Simmons theological building, and renovated it for classrooms and other uses. The school named it Steward Hall in honor of William H. Steward, a prominent black leader who, as chairman of their boards, had been a constant driving force behind State and Simmons Universities.[7]

The property and renovations cost $145,000, most of which came from the funds set aside from the 1925 bond issue, plus accrued interest. Northern philanthropic organizations also helped. The Rockefeller Foundation's General Education Board supplied $25,000, and the Rosenwald Fund provided $1,000 for library books. The city increased its appropriation to the university to cover LMC salaries and operating expenses.[8]

Because of financial difficulties, Simmons University had struggled to maintain the breadth of its offerings in the years since World War I. The terms of the U of L purchase allowed Simmons to offer only theological instruction in one building on the grounds

Steward Hall was named for local civic leader William H. Steward (1847–1935). It was designed by African American architect Samuel M. Plato for Simmons University, whose property the University of Louisville purchased in 1930 for the new Louisville Municipal College.

for a few years. In 1935, when the University of Louisville bought the remaining building from Simmons University, Simmons moved to Eighteenth and Dumesnil Streets, where it continued to operate under its new name, Simmons Bible College. By April 1936 Louisville Municipal College for Negroes occupied the entire block bounded by Seventh Street on the east, Kentucky Street on the north, Eighth Street on the west, and Zane Street on the south. The site had been devoted continuously to higher education for blacks since 1879.[9]

The University of Louisville complied with the prevailing legal doctrine of segregation, but it also paid lip service, at least, to the spirit of the "equal" portion of the U.S. Supreme Court's 1896 ruling in *Plessy v. Ferguson*, that states could provide "separate but equal" educational and other facilities for blacks. School officials and black community leaders were united in their determination that the Louisville Municipal College for Negroes would offer a sound four-year undergraduate pre-professional liberal arts program. In 1932 the university employed Rufus E. Clement as the first dean of the new school. He held a doctorate in history from Northwestern

Rufus Early Clement, Dean, Louisville Municipal College, 1931–1937. "Dean Clement made history so clear that I wanted to visit all the places we studied," recalled Bessie Russell Stone, LMC Class of 1936, years later after she had retired from her career as a librarian. When Clement lectured, she said, he "would put his hand up to his forehead, close his eyes and make history come alive."

Louisville Municipal College faculty, 1931.

David A. Lane, Dean, LMC, 1937–1942.

Bertram W. Doyle, Dean, LMC, 1942–1950.

University and proved himself an effective administrator and educator. Faculty members included outstanding male and female educators such as Henry S. Wilson in chemistry, George D. Wilson in education, Charles H. Parrish Jr. in sociology, William M. Bright in biology, and Nancy B. Woolridge in English, all of whom held Ph.D. degrees from distinguished institutions.[10]

On February 9, 1931, the first students, eighty-three in number, enrolled in the Louisville Municipal College for Negroes. Functioning as "a separate institution under the administration of the board of trustees of the University of Louisville," it was the only full-fledged black liberal arts college in Kentucky and the only one in the nation supported by city funds. The following fall semester saw LMC's enrollment grow to 153, typical of student body size through most of the school's history. Not until after World War II did the enrollment exceed 200. For two decades it would remain a segregated undergraduate division of the University of Louisville. Florence Johnson, who received her bachelor's degree in chemistry in 1932, was the school's first graduate. Before it closed in 1951, the institution had enrolled

2,649 students, 512 of whom graduated with degrees in a broad array of academic disciplines. Many more women than men attended.[11]

Although U of L president Raymond A. Kent subscribed to the separation of the races, he insisted on a high-quality educational program. He assumed that Louisville Municipal College should have a black rather than a white dean; told the dean to report directly to him (albeit privately, not with the other deans) as did deans of the other U of L schools; rejected the inclusion of nonacademic courses in the curriculum; and opened the school in the midst of one of the worst depressions in the nation's history. In 1936 Louisville Municipal College for Negroes was accorded full accreditation by the Southern Association of Colleges and Secondary Schools.[12]

After building a solid foundation for the school, Rufus E. Clement left the LMC deanship in 1937 to assume the presidency of Atlanta University. He was replaced by David A. Lane, who believed the municipal college should be closed and the University of Louisville desegregated. Kent disagreed, which may have led to Lane's eventual departure. In 1942, the final year of the five-year Lane administration, how-

Student life at Louisville Municipal College.

ever, the U of L board of trustees removed the words "for Negroes" from the school's name after LMC students had petitioned for the revision. Furthermore, at that point the wording on students' diplomas became "University of Louisville" rather than "Louisville Municipal College for Negroes." In that year Lane was succeeded by the more conservative Bertram W. Doyle, author of a well-known study entitled *The Etiquette of Race Relations in the South* (1937), who served as dean until 1950.[13]

Comparable to other colleges of the period, "Municipal," as students often called it, offered a four-year undergraduate course of study leading to the bachelor's of arts and bachelor's of science degrees. Not surprisingly, most LMC students were graduates of Central High School, the only high school in Lou-

isville available to African Americans. One was James Shively, who later recalled how he graduated from Central in 1940, entered Louisville Municipal College the same year, interrupted his education to serve in the army during World War II, and eventually completed his bachelor's degree in chemistry in 1949.[14]

Student activities at Louisville Municipal College were similar to those found at other American colleges in the 1930s and 1940s. The student center on the campus's southern edge was a gathering place for playing cards, checkers, chess, ping-pong, badminton, horseshoes, and the like. Students could sign up for such intramural activities as basketball, softball, track, tennis, and volleyball. The school newspaper, the *Bantam*, carried advertisements for the College Pilch Tea Room, the Royal Café, the Drip

Members of the Varsity Club in the "L" formation around Miss Municipal of 1947.

Coffee Cup, and Charlie Moore's Café, as well as for several nearby nightclubs.[15]

Fraternities and sororities sponsored dances, parties, teas, banquets, fashion shows, recitals, issues forums, poetry readings, plays, and concerts. Athletes who had earned letters in their sports could join the "L Club." The college had a representative student council, and each class elected its own officers. There was a journalism club, an international relations club, and departmental clubs devoted to biology, chemistry, sociology, French, German, and English. An active, successful drama club performed before appreciative audiences, as did members of the Frederick Douglass Debate Society. Students sang in the glee club, quartet, or double sextet. The college choir was recognized regionally, once performing with the popular Broadway actress and singer Ethel Waters.[16]

Homecoming was an important annual event, bringing the college closer to the community it served. The occasion was marked by a dance, bonfire, parade, and crowning of a homecoming queen, "Miss Municipal." Baccalaureate and commencement services were held at Quinn Chapel AME Church and were accompanied by banquets, receptions, dances, and concerts. The *Bantam* covered all these activities, and, of course, organized sports.[17]

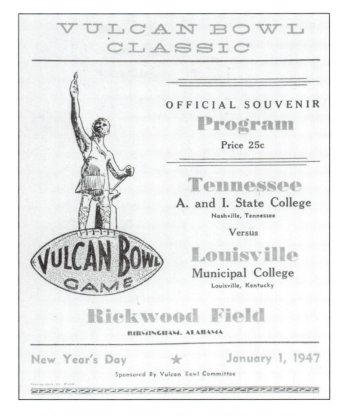

Vulcan Bowl program and team. The Louisville Municipal College fielded the Bantams (facing page), who wore purple and white and played their home football games at Central High School.

School spirit doubtless was enlivened by LMC's athletic teams, though coaches and players received little financial support from the university's budget. Only in the school's last few years were funds earmarked for intercollegiate athletics. Prior to 1946 interested student athletes and a few professors who volunteered as their coaches created basketball and football squads which played a few games against other black schools. After World War II, however, the program was organized along more modern lines and added track and tennis.[18]

Members of the Mid-Western Athletic Conference, LMC's Bantams, as they were known, played their home games at Central High School. The football team opened its 1946 season under coach Dwight Reed with a 13–7 upset win over Morristown College, the 1945 South Atlantic Conference champion, and went on to post a 5–1 record. On New Year's Day, 1947, Louisville Municipal College played in its first college bowl game. For that matter, it was the first bowl game played by any U of L squad. The Vulcan Bowl, the oldest of the bowls matching squads from historically black schools, was held in Birmingham, Alabama, where the Bantams lost to Tennessee A&I (now Tennessee State University) by the score of 32–0.[19]

LMC basketball teams in the postwar era played full home and away schedules against schools from Ohio, Tennessee, Alabama, and elsewhere. One of their toughest rivals, year in and year out, was the Kentucky State College Thorobreds. Led first by head coach Dwight Reed, then by John Crowe, and finally by Willie Lewis, the Bantams were described in news reports as "aggressive," "scrappy," and adept at "ball hawking." In January 1948, LMC defeated the Seagram Sportsmen 58-44 in the first game played in LMC's new gym at Eighth and Zane Streets. Earlier the games were held at the Madison Rink at Ninth and Madison Streets. Sometimes the men's game was preceded by a women's contest, such as in December 1949 when the Fort Knox Wacs beat the Municipal Bantamettes by the score of 24-11.[20]

Occasionally events brought LMC students in association with their counterparts in the College of Arts and Sciences, notably activities sponsored by the YMCA and the YWCA. In 1948 LMC students for the first time were invited to the Belknap Campus for an informal gathering and a panel discussion on promoting good relations among students. At one point members of an LMC sorority contacted students on Belknap Campus about opposing discrimination in area hospitals. The *Louisville Defender* and the *Leader*, the two local African American newspapers, covered these and other LMC events.[21]

In 1946 the *Courier-Journal* described Louisville Municipal College as having "a well-rounded faculty made up of high-grade people with good educational backgrounds" and "a general student esprit de corps that better than matches . . . that of the

university as a whole." The writer also noted, however, that the school "fell far, far short of meeting the needs of the Negro community it is designed to serve," pointing to deficiencies in science laboratory equipment and the library. Somewhat larger budget appropriations provided by the U of L administration may have improved LMC's financial situation in its last few years, but clearly the school's requirements were never sufficiently met.[22]

Louisville's blacks were proud of their college campus at Seventh and Kentucky, but understandably they did not consider it the answer to all their educational needs. Even before the end of World War II, local rumblings had called for the desegregation of the University of Louisville, some blacks viewing the establishment of Louisville Municipal College as one step toward U of L's complete integration. After all, the other U of L schools, such as arts and sciences, medicine, dentistry, engineering, and law, remained inaccessible to African Americans. Blacks seeking admission to graduate school, or wishing to pursue professional studies in medicine, law, or social work, for example, could not attend such programs in the Commonwealth of Kentucky. In 1949 they could not achieve those goals at the University of Louisville.

Following World War II, several factors led to the closing of Louisville Municipal College and the integration of all U of L academic units in 1950 and 1951. The high cost of running two separate liberal arts colleges was a factor; legal barriers to integration were being challenged successfully in the courts; local private colleges were integrating; and some U of L deans believed black students might be welcomed in their units.[23]

For several years the Louisville chapter of the National Association for the Advancement of Colored Persons (NAACP) had been weighing plans to fight segregation at the University of Louisville and the University of Kentucky. After the end of World War II, and in the context of federal court challenges to the segregation of post-graduate education in public universities in Maryland, Missouri, Texas, West Virginia, and Oklahoma, local NAACP leaders pressed the University of Louisville to open its graduate and

Lyman T. Johnson.

professional schools to blacks. After the university responded that it was a private institution, receiving only about 15 percent of its budget from public funds, the NAACP turned its attention toward the University of Kentucky, clearly a public institution.

Lyman T. Johnson, a Louisville school teacher and president of the Louisville branch of the NAACP, then applied to UK's graduate school. When his admission was denied, he brought suit against the University of Kentucky. The federal district court ruled in Johnson's favor on March 30, 1949, and that summer Johnson was among thirty blacks who entered UK's graduate school.[24]

The court's 1949 ruling, which was restricted only to the University of Kentucky, did not affect the Day Law, although a year earlier the Kentucky legislature had changed the statute slightly to permit black physicians and nurses to receive in-service and postgraduate instruction in Louisville's public hospitals. Black students were still barred from undergraduate programs at all traditionally white schools in the commonwealth, and from all graduate and professional

programs save those at the University of Kentucky. In Louisville throughout the spring and summer of 1949, U of L president John W. Taylor and the trustees were divided in their opinions concerning how they should respond. Taylor had spoken favorably of integration, even before the courts had ruled against the University of Kentucky. The summer passed, however, without positive action from the president and trustees.[25]

Still, a noteworthy measure of student sentiment had been taken that spring. On March 25, 1949, the *Cardinal* carried a report of several "interested groups" which pointed to the existence of discriminatory clauses in the constitutions of some campus student organizations. The Independent Women, the Newman Club, the Religious Council, and others hoped the nation's colleges and universities would take the lead in desegregation. After they called for a student referendum on racial discrimination, the Student Council agreed to permit such a vote. The matter would be attached to the ballot for the upcoming student council elections, to be held on April 8.[26]

Morris Edward, representing the Louisville Municipal College, proposed the following three questions be added to the ballot: "1. Do you favor permitting new organizations to come onto the campus only if they have no discriminating clauses in their constitutions? 2. Do you favor removal from the campus of those organizations which have not removed constitutional discriminating clauses by 1955? 3. Are you in favor of the U. of L. administration discontinuing its discriminating policies regarding race, creed, or color?" While Edward indicated he did not believe the second question would pass in a studentwide election, the three questions gained approval by the U of L student council itself. The votes were 16-3, 11-8, and 17-2, respectively.[27]

A total of 2,136 out of 5,000 eligible students voted, the largest number ever in a campus election to that point. With the wording changed only slightly, but the meaning consistent with the original proposal, the students voted no to all three questions. The first lost 991 to 1,143; the second lost 879 to 1,261; and the third lost 1,025 to 1,116. The third, and possibly the most significant, would have carried had forty-six votes gone the other way. Student council president Max Spicker observed that members of fraternities and sororities pushed up the tallies against the questions, "since they are the ones who would be affected."[28]

The *Cardinal* clearly supported all three questions, offering editorials on fairness and Jeffersonian ideals of equality. The *Courier-Journal* was positive about the results, stating, "It does confirm that prejudices are breaking down. One can hardly imagine such a poll having been conducted even a few years ago." This was also the first time the U of L student council recognized representatives from the Louisville Municipal College. Nonetheless, despite signs of softening in the opposition to integration, segregation had not yet ended at the University of Louisville.[29]

University officials knew they were especially vulnerable to any court test of admission to U of L's medical and dental schools, since the University of Louisville offered the only such programs in the state. When the university denied Kentucky State College graduate Richard L. Dawson's application for admission to its medical school, local NAACP attorney James Crumlin, in a letter to Taylor and the trustees dated September 30, 1949, implied that the NAACP would file suit against the university. While the NAACP raised funds to support its threatened action, the university conducted a poll of Louisville citizens which demonstrated that white opposition to the desegregation of the university appeared to be weaker than many had anticipated. When the board of trustees continued to delay, the NAACP announced in late November 1949 that it would definitely file suit if the University of Louisville did not admit Dawson to its medical school.[30]

Looking forward to the biennial meeting of Kentucky's General Assembly early in 1950, U of L trustees favorable to the integration of the university prevailed on local legislators to offer an amendment to the Day Law. With the support of Governor Earle C. Clements and Lieutenant Governor Lawrence Wetherby, the latter a U of L alumnus who would become governor in November, the legislation carried on March 2, 1950. Henceforth, blacks could attend any Kentucky college with whites if the

Sociologist Charles H. Parrish Jr. was the only Louisville Municipal College faculty member who continued as a U of L professor after LMC's closing.

institution's trustees approved. U of L's trustees polled faculty and administrators, who, with the exception of those at the dental school, supported integration. Dental school dean Raymond Myers responded that "the inclusion of Negro students and Negro patients in the dental clinic would present very serious problems."[31]

Thus by the spring of 1950, legal pressure from the black community, court rulings, legislative actions, the financial burden of running two separate liberal arts colleges, and the good will of white leaders such as U of L trustee and former mayor Wilson W. Wyatt and black leaders such as school administrator Albert E. Meyzeek and newspaper publisher I. Willis Cole had signaled the end of U of L's separate college for African Americans, the Louisville Municipal College. In April 1950, the trustees approved a schedule for the desegregation of the university. U of L graduate and professional schools would integrate in the fall of 1950, the Municipal College would close in the spring

Henry S. Wilson.

George D. Wilson.

of 1951, and the College of Arts and Sciences would enroll its first black students in September of that year. Shortly thereafter, a report issued by the president's office claimed that while some other traditionally white southern schools had earlier admitted black students to professional programs, the University of Louisville was "the first in the South to open all of its facilities to Negroes." The *Cardinal* called the action "both wise and courageous," conceding that this was "only one step, albeit a long one, in the right direction."[32]

Louisville Municipal College entered the last year of its life without its dean, Bertram W. Doyle, who resigned to accept a bishopric in the Colored Methodist Episcopal Church. The trustees formed a committee of LMC faculty to administer the school. The group's members were Charles H. Parrish Jr., George D. Wilson, Henry S. Wilson, William H. Wiggins, and Howard R. Barksdale. The board also promptly arranged to sell the LMC campus to the Louisville Board of Education, effective June 1951.

In contrast to the school's beginning, which had occurred after several years of unkept promises, its end came quickly.[33]

While the desegregation of the university went smoothly, the fate of the Municipal College faculty became embroiled in controversy and bitterness. Several LMC professors with doctoral degrees, tenure, and many years' service sought to continue their careers with the University of Louisville, but on October 20, 1950, President Taylor informed them in writing that they would be released at the end of the school year with two months' severance pay. Still, Taylor was regarded as more supportive of the LMC faculty's position than board chairman Eli H. Brown III and some other members of the board. The entire university community was surprised when the president suddenly resigned in November. His departure was for personal reasons having nothing to do with LMC matters. Brown was left as acting president for most of the 1950-1951 academic year.[34]

At its meeting of May 18, 1951, the first attended by newly named president Philip G. Davidson, the board, in what it believed was a spirit of compromise, voted to bring one LMC faculty member, sociologist Charles H. Parrish Jr., to the College of Arts and Sciences. The trustees also promised to assist other LMC faculty in obtaining Ford Foundation fellowships, or offer them one semester's salary as severance pay. Thus, only Parrish continued his employment with the university at LMC's closure and became U of L's first black faculty member after LMC's closing. At one point in the spring of 1951, LMC students and faculty had been asked who among the faculty should be chosen if the University of Louisville fulfilled its promise to employ an LMC faculty member. Parrish was the clear choice, possibly because more of his sociology students could be expected to enroll in arts and sciences and because the sociology department had expressed interest in employing him.[35]

Thereafter the University of Louisville claimed the distinction of being the first historically white university in the South to have a black faculty member. Parrish continued his distinguished career at the university, in 1959 becoming head of its sociology department. For years after his retirement in 1964, he kept an office on campus and remained accessible to students and colleagues.[36]

Shamefully, all of the other LMC faculty members, victims of the transition from segregation to integration, lost their jobs. Professors George D. Wilson and Henry S. Wilson rejected the trustees' May 18 offer, and the university subsequently settled by granting them more than one year's salary and offering to help them find comparable positions elsewhere. In the fall of 1951 G.D. Wilson, with the aid of Wilson Wyatt and Governor Lawrence Wetherby, became head of the education department at Kentucky State College in Frankfort. H.S. Wilson, after working for a time as an executive for the city's Mammoth Life Insurance Company, joined the Bellarmine College faculty in Louisville.[37]

Professor George D. Wilson cited a failure of faculty and administrative leadership as the cause of the unjust treatment of LMC faculty, although he believed that if President Philip G. Davidson, who

Whitney M. Young Sr. (1895–1975) was among nationally prominent LMC graduates. He was president of the Lincoln Institute in neighboring Shelby County, Kentucky's foremost college preparatory school for African Americans, and a member of a committee appointed by President Lyndon B. Johnson to implement the Civil Rights Act of 1964. Young's three children achieved distinction in their own fields: Arnita Young Boswell, a social work professor at the University of Chicago; Whitney M. Young Jr., head of the National Urban League; and Eleanor Young Love, an education professor at the University of Louisville and, as assistant dean of University College (1969–1970), the first African American dean in a U of L division other than LMC.

did not arrive in Louisville to commence a daily routine until the fall of 1951, had been in place earlier, the episode would have reached a happier conclusion. As William F. Ekstrom, then head of the English department, later noted, "It wasn't much of an integration, but it was a beginning."[38]

Louisville blacks clearly hailed the integration of the University of Louisville, as did whites who sympathized with their cause. Furthermore, the university administration reaped an economic benefit, as it no longer had to fund a separate liberal arts college.

It also received some favorable publicity nationally. Nonetheless, the sudden absence of the Louisville Municipal College was a source of feelings of loss and sadness, especially among many of its students. Years later Lillie Gilliam, a member of the class of 1950, spoke touchingly of the "camaraderie" among students there. "The teachers gave of their best, and the students gave their best in return. . . . It was a heartbreak when it closed down," she recalled. "I felt a sense of loss."[39]

The Louisville Municipal College closed at mid-century, but its spirit and influence have endured. Parrish Court, named in honor of Charles H. Parrish Jr. in 1977, is a Belknap Campus landmark. Groups of LMC alumni have continued to meet regularly and have remained active in the community. Graduates of Louisville Municipal College were not discouraged by segregation, limited resources, and overwhelming odds. They went on to make contributions regionally and nationally to their communities and professions.[40]

THIRTEEN

FAMINE, FLOOD, AND WAR

PRESIDENT RAYMOND A. KENT emphasized the achievement of academic respectability, a significant challenge in itself, but at the same time he faced social and economic issues unparalleled in the history of the university and the nation. He took office in the wake of the disastrous Colvin presidency, and a few months later Wall Street crashed and the United States plummeted into a financial depression that lasted until the outbreak of World War II. This severely limited the potential for increased public revenue and private giving to support Kent's academic ambitions. The depression at home and the threat of war in Europe and the Far East stood in the close background of his entire administration. As if that were not enough, in 1937 Louisville experienced the worst natural disaster in its history in the form of a flood of the Ohio River. Kent provided steady, reliable leadership throughout this period.

President Kent and his successors also allowed university personnel to work hand in hand with city officials during these crises. U of L law school dean Neville Miller was elected mayor of Louisville in 1933, and he recruited political science professor Kenneth P. Vinsel to head the city's work relief program and U of L physician Hugh Rodman Leavell to serve as public welfare director. Vinsel returned to the classroom in 1935, but a few years later, following America's entry into World War II, another Louisville mayor with U of L ties, Wilson Wyatt, brought him back to head the new Louisville Area Development Association and direct city planning efforts. A writer for a national magazine credited Vinsel for his role in laying the groundwork for Louisville's "intelligent postwar expansion."[1]

The Great Depression of the 1930s exerted a sobering effect on students across the United States and, at the University of Louisville as elsewhere, it focused student attention on public policy. In a straw poll conducted in November 1932, U of L students expressed overwhelming confidence in the Democratic presidential nominee, Franklin D. Roosevelt, although Socialist candidate Norman Thomas won a small following in the College of Liberal Arts. Republican incumbent Herbert Hoover, himself an engineer, had considerable support in the Speed School. Some students blamed unbridled capitalism for the horrors of World War I and the harshness of the economic depression. The student newspaper issued shrill criticisms of American nationalism and warned that capitalist warmongers lurked behind the Italian-Ethiopian conflict. The national student peace movement gained a foothold in Louisville, where local pacifists denounced war, preparedness, and mandatory military training, and espoused pacifism as the solution for national and international problems. The university's first student handbook, published in 1933, listed among its student organizations a Socialist Club for those "interested in the study of Marxian theory of economics." One campus militant criticized the pseudo-radicals who merely played "in the fish-

bowl of frustrated individualism," flirting with left-wing ideologies only to preserve the existing order.[2]

No division of the university experienced the effects of the depression sooner than the Speed Scientific School, where the cooperative curriculum depended on finding industrial jobs for students. The impact of the crisis even caused the administration to consider broadening the curriculum to include "courses on the current economic order." At one point, the dean suggested adding a class entitled "the evolution of civilization," where students would study "the meaning and object of life" and "the relationship of engineering to the whole picture." By the end of the decade, one administrator speculated that the engineering school may have confined students to "a circumscribed environment" that limited their versatility following graduation.[3]

President Kent opposed political extremism in any form. In 1935, he publicly denounced those who enticed the nation's youth with simplistic ideologies such as pacifism, militarism, communism, and rugged individualism. He refused to support participation in a national peace strike because it endorsed a special interest. On the other hand, he upheld the university's duty to offer academic instruction regarding any ideology. In 1938 the president privately confessed his belief that "the older order certainly cannot continue," by which he meant that unregulated capitalism was not in the nation's interest. Kent's experience in dealing with political situations led him to the conclusion that few people attempted to understand or exercise genuine toleration of opposing points of view.[4]

Reports of radical and unruly undergraduates appeared from time to time, but for the most part U of L students seem to have engaged in relatively innocent diversions. In 1931 Kent hired two detectives to investigate suspicious activities at the Cardinal Inn, a student eatery on the edge of campus. After extensive undercover work, the detectives found that undergraduates met there to eat, smoke, and play cards. Gossip was probably the most dangerous activity on the premises.[5]

The Cardinal Inn had opened on Shipp Street at the northwest corner of the Belknap Campus about five years earlier. There students could buy hot lunches for thirty cents, drink Oertel's ginger ale, play pinball, and even buy clothes. For many years, under changing ownership, it served as a popular off-campus gathering place. Kent's gumshoes suggested, to no effect, that the nearby College Club Sandwich Shop offered more proper surroundings.

From its beginning in 1932 the student newspaper, the *Cardinal*, successor to the *Cardinal News* and the *U of L News* of the late 1920s, reflected a variety of student opinions. In its first year, for example, it became involved in a controversy surrounding men's varsity football. Several letters to the editor signed "Agnes" criticized those who argued for a good football program to promote the school, but a reply called the anonymous writer "a lightweight from the neck up." In December 1932 the *Cardinal* announced new rules for fraternity and sorority dances, posted by Dean Hilda Threlkeld. Not only did the rules limit the number of stags (four men to each woman), but also stated that "drunkenness or disorderly conduct" were "forbidden at future dances."[6]

The next year the editors of the *Cardinal* complained that some young men became disagreeably drunk at school dances, but this was hardly a new development. The University Women's League warned female students that, for dignity's sake, they should avoid smoking or lounging on the campus lawn. Conversely, some women students remained so shy that they even refused examination by the school physician.[7]

The annual *Cardinal* joke edition became a regular item during the 1930s. On February 10, 1933, the editors announced the upcoming comic issue and encouraged readers not to take offense. The special issue appeared the next week, printed in red ink. Gag articles included parodies of how the editors imagined various American authors would describe Belknap Campus. Sinclair Lewis, for example, wrote that "Elmer Gantry surveyed the ugly red brick buildings which raised their drab shapes into a grey, winter sky." Later, the Louisville *Herald-Post* ran an editorial criticizing undergraduate newspapers, but did not mention the *Cardinal* by name.

The early *Cardinal* was a vigorous student weekly with editorial opinions on local, national, and international issues. In 1936, for example, editor Lewis M. Cohen wrote that during his term he had

On January 9, 1938, University of Louisville student George Lighton (b. 1910) was killed in action while fighting on the Loyalist side in the Spanish Civil War.

tried to arouse "a lasting social consciousness." The newspaper promoted isolationism and argued against military preparedness during the 1930s. Generally, the administration upheld the *Cardinal*'s right to take unpopular positions on controversial issues, although in 1937 President Kent did censor the paper for what he called factual inaccuracies in a story.

George Lighton exemplified the militant student intellectual of the 1930s. In class he displayed contempt for anyone or anything that smacked of bourgeois values. When time allowed, Lighton took hobo trips throughout the United States, Canada, and Mexico, gathering material for novels of social criticism and poetry. He graduated with honors in humanities and sociology and wrote a senior thesis on the Industrial Workers of the World organization as reflected in literature. Following graduation, Lighton joined the Loyalist side in the Spanish Civil War, which he considered a great battle between fascism and socialism. After eleven weeks overseas, Lighton decided to return to the United States to resume his education and prepare a graduate thesis using material gathered in Spain. On January 9, 1938, however, Lighton, a Loyalist army private, left a shallow entrenchment to carry a message to his squad leader. He was spotted by a sniper, shot, and killed.[8]

A few others besides Lighton were drawn to leftist ideologies in reaction to fascist aggression in Spain or the seemingly hopeless domestic economic situation. One such convert, Harvey Curtis Webster, had come to the U of L English faculty in 1936 and for several years was active in a local Communist organization. Though he never accepted all of the party's teachings, Webster enjoyed his role as a writer for its publications. Eventually, however, he became disgusted when the editors encouraged him to give favorable reviews to any books by Communist authors, without regard for the true quality of their work. Webster finally broke with the group in 1939, when Germany and the Soviet Union signed a mutual nonaggression pact.[9]

Ellis Freeman, of the Department of Psychology, became the university's best-known faculty activist of the decade. An enthusiastic researcher and inspiring teacher, Freeman made frequent public appearances before local groups, where he discussed his psychological research and political philosophy. A local attorney complained that at a meeting of B'nai B'rith, the local chapter of a national Jewish service organization, Professor Freeman advocated abolition of the profit motive. A parent who heard him speak at a public school reported that the professor was "distinctly red." In truth, Professor Freeman opposed unrestricted capitalism and believed that the state should provide jobs paying enough to fulfill basic needs for those ready to work.[10]

President Kent defended the professor's freedom of speech under the First Amendment, as well as the importance of free thought in an academic environment, but he had little confidence in Freeman's judgment. Furthermore, Freeman carried on a running salary feud with Kent, which undoubtedly hindered communication between the two. Later Freeman became embroiled in a controversy with the

Harvey Curtis Webster (1906–1988) taught English at U of L from 1936 until 1972.

American Legion when he attempted to scuttle a right-wing youth conference. Finally, a bank employee's revelation that the professor had a small investment in Soviet gold bonds created an uproar that was aggravated by Freeman's decision to sue the bank. Eventually, Freeman left the University of Louisville, perhaps unwillingly, with a year's salary.[11]

During the 1930s, the university proudly trumpeted its relationship with Justice Louis D. Brandeis, one of the best-known American Jews of his day. President Kent even noted that some individuals "not wholly friendly to Jews" spoke favorably to him of Brandeis. The university also provided faculty positions for refugee Jewish scholars and tuition remission for refugee students. At the same time, however, a local physician charged that the medical school allowed a maximum Jewish enrollment of ten percent in each entering class and that Kent, who opposed the quota in principle, believed efforts to abolish it would be counterproductive.[12]

Completed in 1962, the Rauch Planetarium honored Dr. Joseph Rauch, for forty-five years rabbi of Temple Adath Israel, Kentucky's oldest Jewish congregation, and for twelve years a U of L trustee. It was razed in 1998 to allow expansion of the Speed Museum, and plans were made to replace it with a bigger and better structure to continue this memorial to one of Louisville's most influential twentieth-century civic leaders.

The university experienced at least one other incident that raised eyebrows in the local Jewish community and illustrated that prejudicial remarks by faculty members were not unknown. Henry G. Hodges, who taught political science during the 1930s, was an expert on contemporary Europe. Hodges's travels and research in Germany placed him in demand as a public speaker. In September 1934 he told one group that World War I left the Germans with a national inferiority complex; that Adolf Hitler was "a master of mob psychology;" and that anti-Semitism existed in the United States as well as overseas. He also attributed Hitler's political success, in part, to Jewish domination of the professions. Hearing this, local civic leader Morris Waldman, a Jew, referred to Hodges as "an innocent abroad" and recommended that Joseph Rauch, rabbi of Temple Adath Israel and a U of L trustee, "have a heart to heart talk with the boy" about the implications of his remark.[13]

Among the many unresolved problems faced by the university throughout this period was the quality of its facilities. In the early 1930s, Kent asked Bennett M. Brigman, dean of the Speed School, to accept for a time the additional post of buildings and grounds director. Brigman took the assignment seriously and repeatedly warned the president that campus buildings needed major repairs. According to one report, the dean even included some of the deteriorating structures in his prayers. The school's buildings and grounds budget was so low that "a new set of harness for the campus mule" (the university did use a mule for work on the grounds) required presidential approval.[14]

During the late 1930s, the university adopted a master plan developed by architect Jens Fredrick Larson. Although it was elaborate in scope, few of the plan's projections reached the stage of bricks and mortar. Larson's grand vision of a Georgian style campus was ultimately confined to two new buildings, one each for the law and engineering schools. Shortly after World War II, a consultant reported that the university's facilities remained in poor condition.[15]

In addition to having facility problems, the university also suffered from an ambiguous legal status. A nineteenth-century court ruling had declared the school a private corporation, but in 1937 a judicial decision termed it "a public institution supported by taxation." In fact, school officials wore both public and private "hats." During the 1930s, furthermore,

The extravagant campus plan prepared by Jens Fredrick Larson included the new law school, but remained largely unfulfilled. (CSC.)

the danger of competition from the University of Kentucky in Lexington, the major state-supported institution of higher education, became increasingly evident. From time to time, sparks flew between Louisville and Lexington over the issue of UK extension courses offered in the Falls City. Proponents of the University of Kentucky also wanted to establish a medical school, which U of L officials considered a duplication of effort. Moreover, U of L's education department competed with the Louisville Normal School, which existed to train teachers for the city system.[16]

The 1930s also was a time of financial hardship. During the decade municipal support for the univer-sity suffered a relative decline while at the same time private giving decreased. Approximately one half of the institution's overall operating revenue came from tuition and fees, approximately one third from the city, and the remainder from endowment and other money-making enterprises. Beginning with the 1937 centennial celebration, Kent devoted greater atten-tion to fund raising. He appointed a publicity com-mittee and even predicted that a wealthy benefactor would "give the university a sum large enough to guarantee its leadership for an indefinite number of years." Kent may have had in mind a donation by Justice Louis D. Brandeis, who had demonstrated a keen and consistent interest in the school and had offered a substantial gift for the law school a dozen years earlier, but no such gift materialized.[17]

In the late summer of 1941 the university formally recognized as U of L alumni the 2,400 graduates of the medical schools and the dental school it had absorbed earlier in the century. Although President Kent disclaimed any connection between this action and his nascent development program, U of L officials probably hoped the doctors and dentists receiving the impressive diploma-like certificates would express their appreciation in tangible ways. Soon, though, World War II diverted the president's attention from private fund raising.[18]

Justice Brandeis did devote considerable effort, however, in developing special library collections at the University of Louisville, including books on World War I, railroading, Palestine, and Judaism. A Louisville native, Brandeis also advised the school to become a repository for manuscripts and other primary material relating to Kentucky history in order to sustain the research programs necessary for a true university. Ultimately Brandeis named the university the repository of his own papers, and he and his wife chose the law school portico as the burial place for their ashes.[19]

In the midst of these financial and other problems at the university, the city of Louisville experienced a natural disaster without parallel in its past. Ohio River floods have plagued Louisville many times, but none was more destructive than the "superflood" of 1937. In the wake of a wet December, extraordinarily heavy rains began to fall in the Ohio Valley soon after the beginning of the year. The river reached flood stage at Louisville on January 16, 1937, crested at forty feet above normal on January 27, and finally receded to below flood stage on February 7. Many Louisvillians probably agreed with one observer's description of the long, watery nightmare: "Rare meteorological conditions had created this calamitous inundation of almost Biblical proportions."[20]

The waters flooded about three-fourths of Louisville. More than 200,000 people had to flee their homes, and perhaps as many as two hundred lost their lives. Property losses totaled $50 million. Martial law was declared as troops patrolled the city, with all of

The 1937 flood surrounded the Belknap Campus, where a rowboat is seen from the south and water laps against the Shipp Street wall near the Confederate Monument. Downtown, boaters row west on Broadway past the School of Dentistry.

this occurring during the dead of winter. U of L's President Kent, a man not given to exaggeration, put the matter in stark terms: "The greatest catastrophe struck Louisville that she has ever known."[21]

In anticipation of loss of generating capacity, Louisville Gas and Electric Company officials asked the university to close its campuses on Friday, January 22, 1937. Soon the Belknap Campus was completely surrounded by water, as was the Louisville Municipal College for Negroes at Seventh and Kentucky Streets. Water poured into the downtown law, dental, and medical school buildings. U of L buildings and grounds staff manned rowboats and stood watch around the clock to protect the Belknap Campus during the two weeks it was closed. Two employees actually circumnavigated the campus in a rowboat.[22]

Students were preparing for final exams when the university shut down. Some faithful scholars completed term paper assignments by candlelight. Final exams in the College of Liberal Arts were waived, and, according to Dean J.J. Oppenheimer, "leniency was the keynote in grading, failures being allotted only in flagrant cases."

Instead of boning up for finals in the library, students helped move library books from lower to upper floors of the various buildings housing them. According to one report, "not a book was damaged." Oppenheimer boasted of additional accomplishments of students: they "made rescues, ran soup kitchens, sewed, typed, bandaged, filtered water, drove relief cars." They also operated a short wave station, served as guards, and drove powerboats. Melzar Lowe, captain of the football team, "was one of the most requested boat operators." Medical students worked tirelessly at City Hospital and at relief stations.[23]

Other U of L facilities were pressed into service. Beginning on Sunday, January 24, the Louisville Municipal College housed and fed hundreds of area residents. A few "refugees" took shelter on the Belknap Campus. The law school building served as a barracks for 140 soldiers.[24]

Belknap Campus offices reopened on Monday, February 8. When the new semester's classes resumed two days later, enrollment was down somewhat. The

James Morgan Read (1908–1985) taught history at U of L from 1935 until 1943, when he was sent to a conscientious objector camp in Tennessee for refusing military service during World War II. After the war he served as foreign secretary of the American Friends Service Committee. He then joined the United Nations in 1950 and was the deputy high commissioner in the United Nations Office of the High Commissioner for Refugees from 1952 until 1960. In 1954 he and his office were awarded the Nobel Peace Prize.

Cardinal's "Flood Edition" of February 11, 1937, reported that although two basketball players failed to return to class, the team would be ready for its next game; that the next two productions in the Playhouse would be postponed; and that the planned "Valentine Sweetheart" contest would be canceled: "Girls whose names were entered in the competition and who supplied photographs for publication purposes may claim them by calling at the office of the University News Bureau, in Gardiner hall basement across from the League Room."[25]

All in all, the university escaped heavy property damage. Kent put the loss at $8,765, principally in injury to basements, boilers, and electrical wiring. The

Termed "Lady Engineer" in the 1934 Speed Scientific School yearbook, Margaret Mattingly was that unit's first female graduate, in 1937.

bookstore reported the loss of cigarettes, soft drinks, and candy, a fact that probably did not surprise hungry student workers who helped clean up during and after the flood.[26]

Hardly had the flood debris been cleared away when attention turned to the threat of another world war. Prior to December 7, 1941, the university community was more isolationist than interventionist in its attitude toward war in Europe and the Far East. Liberal arts dean Oppenheimer warned against militarism and war hysteria. Editors of the *Cardinal* urged that the United States remain neutral. Furthermore, they argued that Britain, in light of her history as a colonial power, hardly represented democracy in a struggle against totalitarianism. Shortly before the United States entered World War II, James Morgan Read of the history department published a study of World War I propaganda, in which he argued that both sides had been guilty of atrocities and that each had exaggerated the crimes of the other.[27]

By the summer of 1941, however, the university had taken on a wartime aura, even though the country remained at peace. Oppenheimer noted an enrollment drop, which he attributed to the uncer-

tain times. Many engineering upperclassmen had quit school, often to take well-paid jobs in defense industries. The law dean, Jack Neal Lott, complained that he could not predict enrollment for the coming year because many of his students had already been called into military service. The growth of defense industries created a local housing shortage, and many medical students were turned out of their apartments. On September 19, 1941, the *Cardinal* noted that women outnumbered men two to one in the entering freshman class. The dean of women, Hilda Threlkeld, observed that personnel shortages had created new opportunities for females in industry and the professions, but cautioned her charges that the woman's most important role remained in the home.[28]

The Japanese attack on Pearl Harbor in December 1941 ended hope that the nation could avoid war. Shortly thereafter, the *Cardinal* reported that the old days of American isolationism were past. Early in 1942 a poll of formerly peace-loving students found that only six percent opposed the bombing of Japanese cities. By this time, proposals surfaced for special, accelerated programs to produce graduates who would be "absorbed into the war effort." According to one

Wartime women professionals.

count, 5,358 students who had attended the University of Louisville, 130 faculty members, 2 deans, and 1 trustee served in World War II, for a total of 5,491. Of this number 195 were women. One hundred eleven U of L students lost their lives. One survivor, Edward R. Hagemann, a U of L student in the 1940s who later joined the school's English faculty, fought in the Pacific theater as a Marine Corps officer. Of island-hopping and hand-to-hand fighting, he recalled that once ashore "there were you and the Japanese." Neither side could leave and somebody eventually won. Years later, he claimed he could recognize anyone who had seen combat in the South Pacific by studying his eyes.[29]

The University of Louisville did not escape the hardships accompanying America's entry into World War II. Its enrollment and budgets declined severely. In 1945 dental school enrollment was only fourteen, instead of the usual sixty-two. The College of Liberal Arts and the Louisville Municipal College were hit especially hard. By the spring of 1943 the *Courier-Journal* had declared that the institution faced "virtual extinction."[30]

Kent's efforts just before his death in February of that year, however, helped the university win a United States Navy officer training unit. Beginning in July 1943 and lasting for three years, the V-12 program boosted the school's fortunes by replenishing the male student population and bringing in much-needed revenue. To prepare for its new resident students, in May 1943 the university, heretofore sometimes referred to as a "streetcar college," built its first dormitories. They were four barracks-style structures named for graduates who had died earlier in the war, Otter Hall, White Hall, Leopold Hall, and Menges Hall. Financed with contributions from the city, county, and local businesses, each building accommodated 125 students packed four to a room. A cafeteria was added, and in the summer of 1943, 475 young enlistees from around the nation began their war-accelerated training to become naval officers. By August the Belknap Campus resembled a naval base more than it did the site of an institution of higher education.[31]

The V-12 program helped make basketball a major U of L sport. Before then it had been "more of

The "temporary" barracks buildings constructed for the Navy V-12 program during World War II, as illustrated in this 1948 Navy ROTC photograph, were used by U of L from 1943 until they were torn down in 1979. In 1955 they were moved from their original site, now occupied by Schneider Hall, to the area where the Chemistry Building now sits. (CSC.)

a gesture than a pastime," according to a local newspaper writer. "We had high-school basketball stars from all over the country," noted Samuel V. Bell Jr., who later became a professor in the Speed School. The 1943-1944 team, with only one civilian in its starting lineup, was referred to as the "Sea Cardinals." The next year's team, the first under Coach Bernard "Peck" Hickman, set a new U of L record: 16 wins and 3 losses.[32]

From time to time, tension arose between civilian university employees and Navy personnel. One faculty member complained that frequent inspections by Navy "specialists" generally resulted in contradictory recommendations. A local man was "burned up" when he saw newspaper photographs of white-clad cadets marching around the campus, flirting with coeds, and getting a college education while his son took Army basic training "on a hot desert in the southwest."[33]

During the V-12 program's final year the Navy established a unit of the Naval Reserve Officers Train-

On August 22, 1943, the Courier-Journal *featured campus life during World War II with this caption: "Classwork over for the day, V-12's and co-eds at the University of Louisville do a bit of cramming on 'campusology.'"*

ing Corps (NROTC) at the University of Louisville. The first students entered the NROTC program in the fall of 1946, making the University of Louisville one of fifty-two universities in the country to develop future officers of the Navy and Marine Corps as a part of Public Law 729. The Naval Science Building was dedicated in June 1947. The first officers through the program were commissioned in June 1950. Over the next three decades more than five hundred officers were commissioned through U of L's NROTC. Blaming military reductions, the Navy informed U of L in 1976 that its NROTC unit would end with the class of 1979.[34]

In 1949 an Air Force ROTC unit was established at the university. It trained officers who received a baccalaureate degree along with their commission in either active, reserve, or National Guard service. In 1981, two years after the Air Force ROTC moved into the Naval Science Building, that structure was renamed Dougherty Hall, after U of L law school alumnus Gen. Russell E. Dougherty, who until his retirement in 1977 had headed the U.S. Strategic Air Command. The Army ROTC was a presence on campus (as an extension center of Western Kentucky University) for many years prior to the establishment of the U of L unit in 1984. Through the years, U of L ROTC units published their own newsletters, sponsored various social functions, furnished color guards for football and basketball games, and provided instructors for some regular university classes. More important, they provided education and training for hundreds of military officers.

Kent died in February 1943, the third U of L president in a row to die in office. He had attended a Washington meeting of a Navy advisory council planning the national V-12 program, and suffered a fatal heart attack on his train ride home. Kent left the university with a much larger measure of academic prestige than his predecessor. Unfortunately, time and circumstances never allowed the full application of his talents to fund raising. Under the right conditions, he might have made an equally significant contribution in this area. Raymond A. Kent's untimely death marked the end of a long and respected presidency and the beginning of an eight-year period during

Einar Jacobsen (1893–1967), tenth president, University of Louisville, 1943–1946. Prior to his career as an educator and his brief term at U of L, Jacobsen had been an actor, Marine Corps officer, lecturer, and movie director. In 1946 Jacobsen visited England to study the progress of public education in that country following World War II.

which the university was headed by four different men, two of whom were acting presidents.[35]

Kent's successor, Einar Jacobsen, served as president from 1943 until 1946. Having come to U of L from the deanship of the School of Education at the University of Pittsburgh, he responded to the trustees' call with a confident assertion: "The big job is to win the war and the University of Louisville has its program under way." (Continuing a tradition rooted in the Civil War era and developed during World War I, the University was preparing to train military personnel.) Jacobsen recognized the problems that would accompany postwar adjustment, and while at the university he served on the federal commission which helped plan what became the G.I. Bill.

Under Jacobsen's presidency in 1944 the Division of Social Administration became the Kent School of Social Work, designed to deal with potential social problems in postwar America. A group of interested citizens led by Annie Ainslie Halleck raised $50,000 for new faculty positions to help strengthen this effort, which was a memorial to President Kent, who had worked to place professional social work education under the province of the university.[36]

Jacobsen did not leave the university under completely happy circumstances, as some faculty members were alienated by his rightist political views. Moreover, some even charged that Jacobsen was openly anti-Semitic. Jacobsen's attitudes offended many people connected with the university and undoubtedly contributed to his short term in the president's office. He left Louisville in 1946 to head the City College of Los Angeles and later served as superintendent of the public schools of Santa Barbara, California.[37]

During 1946 and 1947 Professor Frederick W. Stamm served as acting president, highlighting a long and distinguished career with the institution. In 1921 and 1923 Stamm had taken bachelor's and master's degrees at the University of Michigan, where he majored in economics and finance. He worked at several accounting and teaching jobs until 1929, when he enrolled at Harvard University, where he completed an M.B.A. in 1931. Stamm then came to the University of Louisville to lecture on economics and finance, and in 1937 became head of the Division of Adult Education. At the time of his interim presidency he was the university's controller. For a time he held the jobs of president, controller, and business manager simultaneously, spending his "mornings in one office and afternoons in another."

President Raymond A. Kent's achievements in academics seem all the more remarkable in light of the social and economic challenges he faced. His decision to support an undergraduate division for African American students illustrated either his sense of justice or his sense of reality in the face of black voters, or a combination of the two. He led the university through a period when Americans' confidence in their

Frederick Walden Stamm (1899–1992) was controller when asked to serve as acting president, University of Louisville, 1946–1947. In 1946 he was elected president of the Association of University Evening Colleges, an organization designed to study the role of evening colleges in the urban university. Stamm wrote a syndicated newspaper column, "Money Talks."

political and economic institutions came to a severe test and their willingness to tolerate left-leaning criticism from college students and professors reached its limits. He cultivated the university's relationship with Justice Brandeis, not only for the intellectual prestige it bestowed upon the school, but for the possibility of more tangible benefits. When the university's centennial year, and the lessening of depression-related problems, provided an opportunity, he sought to devote increased attention to raising financial resources. The coming of World War II slowed this effort and the president's death ended it, but Kent had surely kept the faith.

FOURTEEN

THE "GOLDEN AGE"?

THE UNIVERSITY OF LOUISVILLE faced many of the same problems that confronted the rest of postwar America. White officials contended with the burgeoning civil rights movement, as African Americans in Louisville contested discriminatory laws and customs, such as being denied access to the mainstream of public education. By the late 1960s, college and university campuses had become centers of an increasingly militant counterculture that questioned postwar ideals of suburban tranquility at home and the containment of Communist aggression abroad. Meanwhile, the flight of tax-paying citizens to the suburbs helped bring the University of Louisville to a critical point in its history—entrance into the state system of higher education.

As World War II ended, however, the United States seemed poised on the verge of a bountiful, powerful future. No group better illustrated this confident outlook than the veterans who entered college under Title II of the Servicemen's Readjustment Act of 1944, commonly known as the G.I. Bill. At the University of Louisville and across the United States, veterans swelled college enrollments, turned in above-average classroom performances, and brought needed revenue to the nation's institutions of higher learning. Even veterans who before their military service had been on academic probation and who now had returned to the university improved their grade point standings.[1]

The G.I. Bill not only minimized postwar unemployment, which was the primary motive for its passage, but also touched off a period of educational expansion. At the University of Louisville the 1946-1947 school year enrollment included 3,633 veterans out of a total of 7,996. The next year there were 4,746 veterans among 9,790 students; in 1948-1949, it was 4,183 out of 9,408; and in 1949-1950, the number was 3,800 out of 9,758. U of L Dean of Men Morton Walker had the difficult task of helping the returnees find off-campus housing.[2]

From 1947 until 1950, the University of Louisville even had a former soldier, John W. Taylor, in the president's office. Taylor believed America's world leadership and economic prosperity should be backed by educational innovation. His administration introduced "College-by-Radio" classes, a "Neighborhood College Program," which held classes at branch libraries, and other ideas that brought the benefits of the campus to many who otherwise would have been without them. These programs, along with U of L's sesquicentennial celebration, attracted national publicity to the school as well. In 1948 Taylor and the trustees established the board of overseers to advise the trustees, improve town-gown relations, and promote financial gifts to the university. The president also found a colorful and resourceful ally in Louisville mayor Charles P. Farnsley.[3]

The Neighborhood College Program began in 1947 in the Division of Adult Education, lasted for a

John Wilkinson Taylor (1906–), eleventh president, University of Louisville, 1947–1950. Neighborhood College programs and the Southern Police Institute were developed during Taylor's presidency, and he brought national press coverage to the university with a college-by-radio experiment. In 1950 Taylor went to the United Nations as Director General of UNESCO.

branch libraries were included, with others added as time went on.[4]

From the program's beginning, its teachers from the university ranged from well-known full professors like music historian Gerhard Herz to little-known English instructors like Mona Van Duyn and even the occasional student like Stuart B. Flexner. In 1949 Van Duyn taught English composition at the Iroquois library and Flexner, along with fellow student Robert L. White, gave an "experimental course for high school students in creative writing" at the Highland branch. All three practiced what they preached. In 1991 Van Duyn received the Pulitzer Prize in American poetry for her book *Near Changes*; in 1992 she became the nation's first female poet laureate. Flexner was a noted lexicographer, and White taught literature at universities in the U.S. and Canada.[5]

In 1948 the university teamed up with the National Broadcasting Corporation to use radio as another method for taking higher education to people, whether in their homes or in the jails (Mayor Farnsley wanted prisoners to receive college-level courses, too). The chairman of the Federal Communication Commission grandly predicted that "college-by-radio" would put "American education 25 years ahead." Local residents could pay U of L tuition, receive study materials in the mail, and listen to classroom discussions on the radio. The university offered "radio-assisted correspondence courses" entitled "Problems of Modern Society" and "Contemporary American Literature" in the fall semester of 1948, with WHAS and WRXW each handling student discussions two days a week. WAVE presented dramatizations of novels one day a week. NBC won a Peabody Award in drama for its NBC University Theater, which originated from and was developed with the U of L program.[6]

Both the mayor and the president boosted the university as a vital community asset. Indeed, Louisville stood to gain from any investment in the Belknap Campus. A newly arrived faculty member saw it in 1947 as "a rather nondescript medley of faintly prisonlike old brick structures with a bit of new Colonial Georgian, upon which had been superimposed the temporary frame structures of a Wartime Navy

quarter century, and served ten thousand students. Working from the premise that the public library had available space in the community and that the university had the faculty, Taylor and Farnsley suggested that by combining these two assets, college level instruction could be brought to the masses. Individuals could sign up for the courses at no charge, unless they wanted to earn college credit. The response to the announcement was overwhelming. More than 275 persons registered for the first classes, taught at the Highlands and Eastern library branches. Phone lines were swamped with requests for information. Newspaper articles told readers to "Lay Off!" or "Just Give Up!" but also called for more sites to be found for the classes. Soon the Shawnee and Crescent Hill

Post." (These "temporary" barracks would provide much-needed office, classroom, laboratory, and dormitory space for decades. The last one, which served as the core of what became the Fine Arts Building, was not torn down until 1993.) At one point Farnsley suggested that the city purchase the privately owned Louisville Railway Company, which operated the community's bus lines, and add its profits to the university's underfunded budget. Charges of socialism helped squelch the deal, though, and the city's appropriation remained at about ten percent of U of L's total budget.[7]

By the end of Taylor's brief administration, however, some believed he devoted too much attention to external aspects of higher education. William F. Ekstrom, who came to U of L at the same time as Taylor, recalled him as "a flamboyant public relations man with a strong interest in intercollegiate athletics" who came "under a cloud for quite other reasons, most of which have long since been forgotten." A contemporary attributed the president's abrupt resignation to certain unpublicized family difficulties.[8]

Taylor's unexpected departure in November 1950 left the University of Louisville with little immediate prospect for locating a permanent replacement. Falling back on a nineteenth-century tradition, the board of trustees persuaded its chairman, attorney Eli Huston Brown III, to serve as acting president. A Louisville native, Brown was a graduate of Princeton University and Harvard Law School. Returning to Louisville, he served as United States district attorney and as attorney for the Federal Land Bank, and also began to cultivate a successful private practice with his firm of Brown, Greenebaum and Eldred. In addition to his work for the arts in Louisville, Brown headed the real estate firm of Eli Brown and Sons, and worked for the renovation and restoration of St. James and Belgravia Courts in the Old Louisville neighborhood. He also worked for Louisville's Riverfront Plaza project, and his real estate connections proved helpful in the university's building program.

Assisted by temporary vice president, trustee, and physician Oscar O. Miller, both working without salary, Brown saw to it that his presidency was "no

Eli Huston Brown III (1906–1974), acting president, University of Louisville, 1950–1951.

left-hand operation by an extremely busy man." Brown did not profess to be a scholar, but thought his permanent replacement should be. During his administration, Brown stressed the importance of a liberal arts education, worked for closer relations between the trustees and the university community, presided over the desegregation of the university by means of the closing of the Louisville Municipal College, balanced the university's budget, and raised salaries as well as tuition.

In the spring of 1951, well before the new president moved to town, Brown and the board asked three veteran U of L administrators to assume responsibility for the university's daily affairs, thus initiating for a few months "a novel experiment with a triumvirate" of adult education division head Woodrow Strickler, engineering school dean Robert Ernst, and graduate school dean Guy Stevenson. These three men oversaw the daily operations of the university until the new president's arrival that fall.[9]

Philip Grant Davidson (1902–), twelfth president, University of Louisville, 1951–1968, believed that educational advancement and community welfare were inseparable, worked to improve town-gown relations, and "built new quality into an old institution." Under Davidson's guidance, the university began its first doctoral programs, more than tripled its annual budget, planned and began work on a new health sciences complex, and established the schools of business and education. Davidson Hall (below) was named in his honor and that of his wife, Jane.

As Taylor's replacement, the trustees selected Philip G. Davidson, then provost and dean of the graduate school at Vanderbilt University. They made an excellent choice. After earning his doctorate in American history at the University of Chicago, Davidson had taught at Agnes Scott College in Atlanta. His book *Propaganda and the American Revolution* (1941) established his reputation as a scholar. In 1942 Davidson moved to Vanderbilt, where his amiable ways helped make him a successful administrator. After taking office in Louisville, he quickly earned the respect of the faculty, students, trustees, and civic leaders. Woodrow M. Strickler, who had been at the university since 1938, served as Davidson's executive vice president and followed him as the chief officer. Together, with a small staff coordinated by longtime assistant Eleanor Turner, they provided two decades of stable, enlightened leadership, which carried the university through one of the more challenging periods in its history.[10]

Davidson knew U of L's strengths and weaknesses before he took office. In 1948 he had visited the campus with a Phi Beta Kappa inspection team. The group turned down the university's application for a chapter of the scholastic honor society because it found an overtaxed library and crowded laboratories. Its members also wondered whether the College of Arts and Sciences was the heart of the university or an appendage of the professional schools. Shortly after moving to Louisville in the fall of 1951, Davidson again noted some of the same defects. He further pointed out that the Graduate School attracted too many local students and that the undergraduate program needed to enroll more of the best products of area high schools. The new president cautiously termed the University of Louisville "a good institution with a good staff and faculty." He believed the base existed for building "a first class institution."[11]

The Department of English well illustrated the academic quality achieved during the Davidson administration. Its faculty included David W. Maurer, an authority on the language of criminal subcultures, who conducted studies of moonshiners, drug addicts, bookmakers, and prostitutes. In one of his books Maurer analyzed and described the language and techniques of big-time "confidence men," a study so popular that movie makers allegedly used it to produce a box office success entitled *The Sting* in 1973.[12]

Maurer's English department colleague Harvey Curtis Webster wrote a standard biography of Thomas Hardy, as well as a thoughtful column for the *Louisville Defender*, an African American newspaper. Richard Kain specialized in Irish literature, published extensively on the literary revival that paralleled the growth of Irish nationalism, and taught one of the first graduate seminars in the United States dealing with the controversial work of James Joyce. Finally, Mary E. Burton, who in 1950 became only the third woman in the history of the College of Arts and Sciences to attain the rank of full professor and the first in the humanities, wrote books on William Wordsworth and his wife Mary. In 1965 the university established a doctoral program in English, its first in the humanities.[13]

The Division of Humanities also boasted fine scholars in other departments. In music history, for example, Professor Gerhard Herz became one of the nation's prominent authorities on the life and work of Johann Sebastian Bach. Herz portrayed his subject as an orthodox Lutheran composer, troubled by the pietistic movement of the eighteenth century. Furthermore Herz stressed the importance of performing Bach's work in the charming Baroque style of the composer, not with the massed choirs and booming organs popularized during the nineteenth century.[14]

Robert S. Whitney, conductor of the Louisville Orchestra (1937-1967) and dean of the School of Music (1956-1971), symbolized the symbiotic relationship between these two cultural institutions. Not only did Whitney serve simultaneously as dean and conductor, but many other members of the music school faculty also performed with the orchestra. Led by Whitney and inspired by Mayor Farnsley, the orchestra rose from relative obscurity and financial distress to become the leading component of the arts renaissance that took place in the city following World War II. On the advice of Farnsley, Whitney revived the eighteenth-century tradition of presenting new compositions at each concert. These works were com-

Robert S. Whitney (1904–1986).

missioned by the orchestra, prepared by outstanding contemporary composers, and recorded and distributed on long-playing records. The success of the project, which began during the late 1940s and continued into the next decade, brought financial support from the Rockefeller Foundation and earned critical acclaim from listeners in the cultural capitals of the world.[15]

Professor Justus Bier, who taught art history, won scholarly distinction for his multi-volume study of Tilman Riemenschneider, a German sculptor who worked during the late fifteenth and early sixteenth centuries. He also demonstrated a refreshing interest in Kentucky artists, including Carl C. Brenner, a nineteenth-century German immigrant who had followed the Hudson River School of landscape painters. Bier brought culture into the homes of thousands of Kentuckians by serving as an art critic for the *Courier-Journal.*[16]

The Department of History claimed the university's resident cynic—Professor Laurence Lee Howe, who showed a well-honed sense of human frailty. In a book on the Roman office of pretorian prefect during the third century A.D., the professor found that what had been the emperor's bodyguard evolved into a position of broad military, judicial, and administrative power. The prefects unsuccessfully sought to reconcile the empire's conflict between justice and despotism. Not having succeeded, they presided over "the most disastrous failure in the history of man's efforts to build a reasonably just and stable society." In a shorter piece, Howe decried those historians whose work was influenced more by current events than by evidence of the past. He believed that members of his craft should heed Leopold von Ranke's injunction to study what actually happened and why, not relate their subjects to contemporary social and political concerns.[17]

No overview can mention every noteworthy faculty member of this era, but any list would be incomplete without psychology professor Ray Birdwhistell, a cultural anthropologist. Birdwhistell achieved distinction not only as a teacher, but also as a scholarly proponent of kinesics, a field devoted to the study of

Belknap Campus's famous white squirrels are among the university's most colorless and colorful characters.

human gestures and their hidden social meanings. According to the *New York Times*, his 1952 manual on the subject initiated the first sustained, systematic research into what later came to be called "body language." Among other things, Birdwhistell found that residents of Louisville, Atlanta, Nashville, and Memphis smiled more than people in northern and eastern cities. He warned, however, that this was not necessarily a sign of happiness.[18]

At the beginning of the postwar period, university publications stressed the material benefits a college degree offered. Incoming freshmen were told that education was a financial investment, with dividends that depended less upon inventory size than marketing skills. Undergraduates were advised that church attendance often led to success in life, while backsliders risked failure. If they followed the precepts of their freshman handbook, engineering students must have epitomized "the organization man" described in the popular book of that title by *Fortune* magazine editor William H. Whyte. Strongly worded statements urged them to dress and behave properly and to cultivate the qualities that insured future success— "scholarship, practicality, and sociability."[19]

The 1949 student handbook noted the "atmo-

U of L flags.

life, to make it even "more congenial." In 1957 a gift from Rachel M. Bigelow, whose later bequest made possible the construction of the University Center, enabled Creese to design a new flag for the university. Creese wanted his creation to "harmonize" with the city flag. It replaced the handsome "L" flag, created by student Charles Dorn and his mother in 1915. Interestingly, neither is U of L's official flag. In 1961 the board of trustees resolved "that the University of Louisville has never adopted a University flag; that the red flag with gold sunburst now displayed on the Campus, and all duplicates thereof, is not, and never has been, the flag of the University."[21]

Adding still more color to the university in the years after World War II was the U of L marching band. President Taylor took a personal interest in the band, which had its beginnings in the late 1920s under E.J. Wotawa, freshly arrived at the music school. By the fall of 1933 the band was performing at football games outfitted in uniforms provided by newspaper publisher Robert Worth Bingham. Later in the decade Ernest Lyon, also of the music school faculty, directed its efforts. Taylor created a separate Department of Bands in the music school. During the fall of 1947 the band secured its first complete set of uniforms in over ten years and gained the sobriquet "The Best-Dressed Band in Dixie" by a local broadcaster. (When it was discovered that another Southern school used that description for its band, the U of L band, in 1949 numbering nearly one hundred, became simply the "Marching Cardinals.") During the late 1940s and early 1950s, the university's football fans were treated to highly entertaining halftime shows choreographed by student director Charles Hammond.[22]

Budget difficulties plagued the band in the 1960s. The Marching Cardinals performed their last show for nearly a decade at the final home football game of the 1970 season. For most of the 1970s, a pep band played at the games. In 1979, however, a full-fledged marching band returned to the university, complete with new uniforms. In addition to its customary place at home football games, the band has served as the official band of the Kentucky Derby (1937-1954, 1956-1969, and 1980 to the present). When television viewers around the world hear the

sphere of friendliness" marking the campus, where "everyone speaks to everyone else," especially along "Howdy Walk," the sidewalk connecting Gardiner Hall and the Administration Building. A sense of affability seemed to pervade the campus, and its park-like surroundings drew students outdoors. So did Belknap's legendary white squirrels, which, along with their gray counterparts, have delighted and pestered students and faculty of this and every generation.[20]

One faculty member who was taken with Belknap Campus's "shaded walks with well-shaped and heavy old trees of an amazing variety" and its old buildings "quaint and human in scale" was art historian Walter L. Creese, who pictured its overall effect as "straight out of 19th Century novels about Old Siwash." Creese called for more benches, fountains, flowers, flags, and festivals to add color to campus

The well-dressed Marching Cardinals playing for the Kentucky Derby in 1948. Hilda Gay Mayberry, pictured here with her many awards, was named the best majorette in the United States in 1952.

strains of "My Old Kentucky Home" on the first Saturday of May each year, they are listening to U of L's Cardinal Marching Band.

During the 1950s, the dean of men and the dean of women enforced a well-defined code of student conduct. Adult chaperones attended all undergraduate social functions, where they were supposed to be treated as guests, not "snoopervisors." At one point, the university hired a doorman for fraternity and sorority parties. According to the dean of men, this reduced drinking and disorder, but evictees could always retreat to nearby Sherman's Tavern, where underage drinkers were served. In 1955 the dean of women, Hilda Threlkeld, reported that female enrollment had declined because women married early or obtained satisfactory jobs without a college degree. She also feared that some parents did not want their daughters to socialize with blacks. As late as 1967, women students were not supposed to wear slacks in class or the library.[23]

Pat King and Marie Graves were pro and con on the slacks vs. skirts discussion at the University of Louisville in 1944. (Louisville Courier-Journal.)

The Cardinal *staff cleaned up after the Student Union building burned.*

A full-service student cafeteria had opened on campus in 1945 in the Student Union, a barracks structure located on the site of Schneider Hall, but the building was destroyed by fire in 1951. After the fire, the cafeteria was moved to the former Navy V-12 mess hall, where it stayed until 1959. That building later became the Fine Arts Building before being razed in 1993. In 1959, the University Center, a multi-purpose facility for students, opened on campus, amid a flourish of publicity. The new building, nicknamed the "hula hoop" building because of the circles affixed to its roof line, had a cafeteria, a snack bar (the SUB), and a faculty dining room, along with meeting rooms, game rooms, lounges, and offices, offering a large, on-campus gathering place.[24]

The opening of Stevenson Hall north of Shipp Street in 1959 marked the appearance of U of L's first modern dormitory. That year's catalog carried this announcement: "All unmarried, non-resident freshman male students of the university are required to live in one of the university-supervised dormitories for one year. Students will be assigned, two to each room, to the new air-conditioned dormitory adjacent to the campus, until all rooms have been allocated." Those registering too late for Stevenson Hall were forced to settle for one of the barracks, which had served as dorms since the end of the V-12 program. Students paid $310 per semester, includ-

U of L's annual Turkey Trot was a brainchild of the L Club intramural committee. The L Club was organized in 1928 by fifteen varsity lettermen to promote school spirit and provide opportunities for all students to participate in sports. The first homecoming event of the intramural program was billed as a mile and a half inter-fraternity cross-country race, named by Ellis Mendelsohn after he became head of intramural sports in 1953. Participants literally ran for the birds. First, second, and third place finishers won a live turkey, a goose, and a chicken, respectively. The last place finisher received a goose egg. In 1970, a women's race, the Hen Waggle, was added.

ing meals. It was the first cost increase since 1947. Stevenson provided "gracious living," according to the *Cardinal,* which termed the old dorms "Black Holes of Calcutta."[25]

Following World War II some women students were housed on campus in Robbins Hall, and later others lived in the barracks. Threlkeld Hall, built in 1962, was U of L's first "coed" dormitory. A wall separated the 126 women in the north end of the building from the 136 men in the south end. "As far as I'm concerned," the dorm director said, "it's the Berlin Wall."[26]

The University of Louisville achieved a renewed sense of self-esteem during the 1950s. Several factors contributed to this feeling. First, the university shared in the national sense of self-confidence that followed World War II. Second, the school had some genuine

centers of traditional academic excellence, such as the Department of English. Third, successful athletic teams, particularly in basketball, created a positive common identity. Fourth, Davidson was an amiable, accessible leader who inspired confidence. One faculty member spoke admiringly of Davidson's "benevolent paternalism."[27] Fifth, fissures in the social structure, particularly in race relations, had not yet attracted the attention they later did within the white community. Sixth, in addition to tuition and other sources of revenue, for the time being the city of Louisville provided basic financial support for the school and the prospects seemed good for private giving. As a corollary to this, the president and the board operated with a freedom they would not have had as a wholly public entity. Finally, the University of Louisville was relatively small. Professor met president on the sidewalk with a level-eyed courtesy which would have been more difficult in a larger organization. It was a combination that proved transitory.

As the postwar period wore on, students showed an increasing dissatisfaction with assumptions that the American social order rested upon a secure consensus. By the late 1950s, for example, the university harbored some disciples of the "Beat" movement, originally a literary genre that celebrated jazz, drugs, and street life. The university's beatniks hung out in the cafeteria, drank large quantities of black coffee, and quoted the works of Jack Kerouac, whose novel *On the Road* (1957) helped lay the basis for the late 1960s counterculture. One unfriendly observer said they resembled refugees from a Russian novel and wanted to "stand up and be battered about by life."[28]

Students became more assertive during the early 1960s, as young men and women reared after World War II, inspired by the civil rights movement, and unfamiliar with wartime sacrifices entered the university. In 1963, for example, some students protested the inspection of off-campus housing, curfews that discriminated against women, and the principle of *in loco parentis*, the notion that the school should promote and enforce parent-like rules of conduct. A defiant editorial in the *Cardinal* quoted Joseph Heller, author of the anti-military novel *Catch-22*: "Anyone can do anything that you can't stop them from doing."[29]

While many U of L students may have been inspired in the classroom, they found fewer opportunities for enthusiasm on the gridiron. The school lacked the resources to produce big-time football contenders, but despite inadequate finances Coach Frank Camp compiled a respectable record (118 wins, 95 losses, and 2 ties) over a career that spanned twenty-three seasons. Camp came to the university in 1946, following a three-year period during the war when no games were scheduled. In only his second year, Camp led the Cardinals to their second undefeated season, with a record of 7-0-1. John Unitas, a U of L quarterback in the early 1950s who later became a stellar player in the National Football League, credited his college coach with providing invaluable instruction in the game's basics.[30]

Frank Camp (1905–1986), U of L head football coach, 1946–1969, compiled a record of 118–95–2. One of his players, John Unitas, said, "I learned more football from Coach Camp than from anyone."

Other standouts during the Camp era included running back Leonard Lyles, kickoff return specialist George Cain, and center Andy Walker, three of U of L's first black athletes after the closing of Louisville Municipal College and the integration of the university. They joined the squad in 1954. (The university's first African American athlete after LMC was Laurence Simmons, a lineman from Central High School who was a member of Camp's 1952 football squad for a short time.) Nicknamed "the fastest man in football," Lyles set school records for the most touchdowns per season, most points per season, highest average gain per carry, most career points, and most career touchdowns. Like Unitas, Lyles also went on to professional glory. Camp's best team was the 1957 squad, which went 9 and 1 before capping the season with a New Year's Day win over Drake in the Sun Bowl at El Paso, Texas. It was U of L's first bowl

During his college career, U of L quarterback Johnny Unitas completed 247 of 502 passes for 2,912 yards and 27 touchdowns, setting a school record as a freshman with 4 TD passes in one game. He went on to become, in the eyes of many, the greatest professional quarterback of all time. Unitas Tower, a Belknap Campus residence hall, was named for him (below left).

"The fastest man in football," Lenny Lyles was named the national rushing leader of 1957. Lyles still holds the school record in scoring with an amazing three hundred career points. A first-round draft choice of the Baltimore Colts in 1958, Lyles had a distinguished eleven-year professional career.

Peck Hickman, who became U of L head basketball coach in 1944 and athletic director in 1953, compiled a lifetime record of 443 wins and 183 losses. As his assistant, John Dromo recruited All-Americans Charlie Tyra, Wes Unseld, Butch Beard, John Turner, and Don Goldstein, among other standouts, to the U of L basketball program. He also coached the U of L golf team for thirty-seven years.

game since the end of segregation, the first ever by an integrated U of L squad, and the university's first bowl victory.[31]

The Cardinals fared better in basketball than in football, in part because the hardwood sport required fewer players and was less expensive. The talents of Coach Bernard "Peck" Hickman and his able assistant, John Dromo, also accounted for much of this success. In a career that spanned twenty-three seasons, from 1944 through 1967, Hickman won 443 games and lost 183. The University of Louisville won the National Association of Intercollegiate Basketball (NAIB) championship in 1948 and the National Invitational Tournament (NIT) crown in 1956. Hickman's teams also were frequent contenders for the National Collegiate Athletic Association (NCAA) champion-

ship. His 1958-1959 squad was the first U of L team to reach the NCAA tournament's Final Four.[32]

An even more important basketball breakthrough occurred shortly after these events. In 1962 Hickman and Dromo recruited three African American players and broke three historic color barriers. Sam Smith, Wade Houston, and Eddie Whitehead became the first black basketball players at U of L (in the post-LMC era), the first at any traditionally white Kentucky university, and probably the first such players in the Southeast. They competed on U of L's freshman team their first season, and on the varsity after that.[33]

During Hickman's last year, 1966-1967, his team was led by All-American Westley Unseld, a rugged pivot man who became a professional star, then a

A consensus All-American, Westley Unseld ranks seventh on the university's all-time scoring list, with only three varsity seasons, 1965–1968. In average point totals per season he ranks second. Unseld's forty-five-point effort against Georgetown College in 1967 stands as the highest single-game point total in Cardinal basketball history. Following his stellar professional career, Unseld was elected to the Basketball Hall of Fame in 1988.

National Basketball Association head coach. Hickman was followed as coach for four years by Dromo, a master at charming high school students into Cardinal uniforms. Joining Unseld on Dromo's 1967-1968 squad was Alfred "Butch" Beard Jr., another African American recruit who attained national stature in both college and professional ranks. Dromo even alleged that Adolph Rupp, the legendary coach at the University of Kentucky, promoted him for out-of-state jobs in order to soften the recruiting competition.[34]

U of L's early basketball teams competed in the Southern Intercollegiate Athletic Association from 1912 until 1924; in 1925 the school joined the Kentucky Intercollegiate Athletic Conference. During the late 1940s, the University of Louisville took part in organizing the Ohio Valley Athletic Conference, but its membership in the OVC was brief and controversial. In 1949 a football player at Western Kentucky University left the Hilltoppers' program and shortly thereafter appeared on the roster at Louisville. Western charged that the University of Louisville lured the young man away; Louisville officials replied that he had left Bowling Green voluntarily and later enrolled in their program. The conference judiciary committee ruled the player ineligible, but the Cardinals used him anyway and then withdrew from the OVC, shortly before being ejected. For some years thereafter, Western and Louisville did not schedule each other in football or basketball.[35]

For most of their history the U of L basketball Cardinals did not have a gym of their own. From 1912 until 1930 U of L's "home court" was one of many facilities in the city, including St. Xavier High School and the YMCA. For part of the 1924-1925 season the team played in a Brown Hotel dance hall.[36]

In 1931 the Cards moved into Belknap Gym, built on campus for $50,000. At one end of the court, the basket was mounted directly to the wall, occasionally causing knee injuries and reportedly even blackouts to some of the players who ran into it. The six-hundred-seat gym was consistently filled with standing-room-only crowds. Parking on campus was a problem even then; games were often delayed for up to an hour to allow fans time to park.

In 1945 the Cardinals began playing their games in the newly renovated downtown Armory, later renamed Louisville Gardens. Belknap Gym continued as a practice facility. During sell-out games at the Armory, a closed-circuit television with a three-by-four-foot screen was installed at the campus gym to accommodate even more fans.

The solution to U of L's basketball facilities problem finally came in 1956 when the state opened its new fairgrounds facility in Louisville, complete with 16,600-seat Freedom Hall. In 1984, a $13.7 million renovation added nearly three thousand seats, a new scoreboard, a better floor, new lighting, and other improvements. The site has hosted six NCAA Final Four championships. In 1995 the *ESPN College Basketball Magazine* touted Freedom Hall as America's "Best Playing Floor."[37]

The 1963 retirement of baseball coach John Heldman Jr. called attention to one of the university's oldest organized sports. Though seldom heralded, it had also been one of the most successful. Teams in the early years of the century often included students from the schools of medicine, law, and, for a time after 1918, dentistry. Sometimes the team members had to purchase their own uniforms and equipment. Squads coached by Tom King in the 1920s and by C.V. "Red" Money in the early 1930s were particularly successful. In 1937, following a three-year period when no teams were fielded, Heldman began his twenty-six year coaching career, which at the time of his retirement was by far the longest of any head coach in any U of L sport. No member of any Heldman team ever experienced a losing season. His 1957 team went undefeated.[38]

Although the university received some national publicity from its athletic successes during the Davidson years, all of it may have been overshadowed, at least for a few weeks, by a glorious series of performances by several U of L students in a much different intercollegiate competition. The *GE College Bowl*, a popular television show sponsored by General Electric, ran on network TV—first NBC, then CBS—in the late 1950s and 1960s. Every week two college teams of four students each were pitted against each other, with the winner returning the next week to take on a new challenger. If a team won five consecutive contests, it was retired. By the spring of 1963, only ten teams had remained undefeated for five weeks.[39]

The questions thrown at the contestants—each team's members sat behind a long desk—were brainwrackers from the liberal arts: literature, history, mathematics, music, art, and science. Contestants tried to be the first to push a buzzer to answer a "tossup" question. A correct response earned the whole team the right to try for "bonus points" by answering several additional questions. A scoreboard recorded the tally while a clock marked the time left

Anne Groves, Frank Krull, Evelyn Feltner, and Giles Kotcher, shown on television as they competed in the 1963 GE College Bowl.

on the thirty-minute program. Members of the studio audience cheered and groaned throughout the fast-paced contests, which were presented live on Sunday evenings.

In early 1963 Martin Stevens, associate professor of English, assembled a U of L team by holding tryouts for eighty students. Team members chosen included Evelyn Feltner, Anne Groves, Giles Kotcher, and Frank Krull. The contingent was rounded out by J. Daryll Powell, who served as alternate and team manager. The team was first pitted against a veteran Kenyon College squad. Having knocked off four consecutive opponents, the heavily favored Ohio team needed only a victory over the untested U of L foursome to retire undefeated.

Kenyon proved no match for the Louisvillians. Nor could the University of Idaho combat U of L's brilliant onslaught in round two. Against its third opponent, the University of Delaware, on April 28, 1963, U of L scored 370 points, the second highest in the history of the game to that point. By that time the entire city of Louisville was ablaze with Cardinal pride. The *Courier-Journal* editorialized about the "weeks of national glory." A Chicago columnist in town for the Kentucky Derby returned home to write a tongue-in-cheek column about the Louisville university that was "overemphasizing education." He came to see a horse race but all the attention seemed to be turned on "a team of young people competing in the 'College Bowl.'"

The fourth opponent, Iona, was a formidable challenger. Just before the program went on the air, "one Louisville team member turned green and threw up," according to Powell, who thought he would have to stand in. "Should have gotten 10 points for a tossup," he joked. Not even Stevens was unaffected by the pressure. One week Feltner's sunglasses fell victim to the tension. "She'd asked me to hold them for her, and when I looked down, there they were in pieces."

But Iona tumbled, and the University of Louisville joined an elite group of only sixteen other schools that had ever won four consecutive contests out of the 174 that had made the attempt. Alas, the fifth victory and accompanying silver cup were not to be. "They lost to a team of brilliant buzz-saws from Yeshiva University, before a loudly partisan audience that ended by disturbing both teams with the outbursts of enthusiasm," a *Courier-Journal* editor wrote. The studio audience of three hundred was dominated by Yeshiva's "thunderous cheering section," though there "was some energetic cheering from a palpably small group when Louisville scored."

The crowd of two hundred well-wishers who welcomed home the team at Standiford Field on May 13, 1963, according to the newspaper, "couldn't possibly have been more enthusiastic if the team had beaten Yeshiva." The U of L band played "Hail, Hail, the Gang's All Here," and the crowd, led by Kentucky governor Bert Combs along with other city, county, and state officials, sent up "a deafening roar of applause."

The festivities continued at a convocation in Bigelow Hall, where President Davidson told the audience, "In all my years at the University, I have never seen anything that captured the imagination of the community and endeared the University to the people more than this team. Everybody has identified with us." Basketball coach Peck Hickman presented the team with trophies inscribed with the words "College Bowl Champs." Stevens received a

standing ovation when he responded, "Thanks from all of us to the best fans any College Bowl team could possibly have."

Doubtless the university's academic reputation was enhanced by these events. The *Courier-Journal* boasted that the students on the team "brought national recognition to their school, with practical results already apparent in the flow of enquiries and applications from superior students all over the country." Furthermore, according to the *Cardinal*, it opened Louisvillians' "eyes to the academic standing of the university." Finally, the school's "sterling performances on the air" secured $13,000 in scholarship funds for the university, half from GE and half from appreciative local businesses.[40]

While these enthusiasms may have been infused with hyperbole, it seems certain that under Davidson the university projected an image of community involvement, moderate growth, and academic respectability. Some observers even hoped the president might build "a Vanderbilt on the Ohio." The school fell short of this goal, but it did expand and strengthen its programs during the postwar years. One national survey reported that nearly half of the university's entering freshmen ranked in the top fifth of their high school classes. During the 1950s and 1960s, the university also added its first doctoral programs, although some faculty members charged that doctoral studies drained funds from undergraduate instruction, catered to narrow departmentalism, and came about through political maneuvering.[41]

The university's physical facilities also improved dramatically during the Davidson era. At the beginning of the period, one report noted that railroads, homes, and businesses hemmed in Belknap Campus and formed unattractive surroundings. The author even quipped that if the university acquired a new building, the president would have to hold it over his head while someone else looked for a spot to put it down. Eventually, aided by the passage in 1952 of a $4 million bond issue, Belknap Campus grew in acreage and added a respectable number of new buildings, including a library, a student center, dormitories, a gymnasium, and classroom structures. As he

In 1956 U of L's main library moved to this new building, featured in a 1963 Encyclopedia Britannica *article as a notable example of modular library architecture.*

Belknap Campus, 1953.

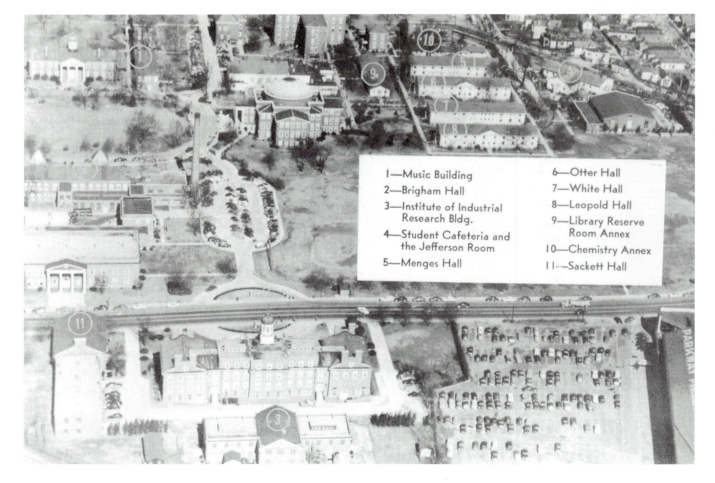

1—Music Building
2—Brigham Hall
3—Institute of Industrial Research Bldg.
4—Student Cafeteria and the Jefferson Room
5—Menges Hall
6—Otter Hall
7—White Hall
8—Leopold Hall
9—Library Reserve Room Annex
10—Chemistry Annex
11—Sackett Hall

observed the growth, historian Laurence Lee Howe complained that federal "urban renewal," which provided much of the new space, was "a soulless & mindless power" recklessly demolishing "poor people's homes & honest men's business places."[42]

Just north of the Belknap Campus lay Old Louisville, a residential section that had grown up during the late nineteenth century. This neighborhood boasted many of the city's finest examples of Victorian architecture, but its prestige declined following World War II. Old Louisville reached a low ebb some time around 1960, as more middle-class families moved to the suburbs. At the same time, however, J. Douglas Nunn, urban affairs editor for the *Courier-Journal*, published a series of articles comparing Old Louisville to Boston's Beacon Hill, Washington's Georgetown, and other renovated residential districts. Davidson and other community leaders also took up the cause of the university's northern neighbors. A high point in the campaign came when U of L art historian Theodore Brown and art librarian Margaret Bridwell published an illustrated booklet on the history of Old Louisville, which depicted it as one of the city's few architectural areas that survived, more or less intact, from the nineteenth century. As the decade progressed, so did the renovation of Old Louisville homes and the area's revival as a residential district.[43]

From its first days on the Belknap Campus, the university was separated from its neighboring community to the north by Shipp Street. There was a time when the university gave its address as "Third and Shipp, Louisville 8, Ky." Shipp ran diagonally from Brook and Warnock Streets, on the southeast, past the Confederate Monument at Third Street, on the northwest. Another section ended at Seventh Street. Streetcars maneuvered down Shipp carrying U of L students to class via the loop encircling the Loop Hole Restaurant where the west wing of the Life Sciences Building now stands, and baseball fans to Parkway Field via a second loop near the present Chemistry Building.[44]

Although Robbins Hall, given to the university in 1944, was the first U of L property across Shipp Street, for all practical purposes the northward march

Shipp Street Wall, 1952.

of campus buildings began with the construction of Stevenson Hall in the late 1950s, forcing students to dodge cars on Shipp Street to get to class. In 1971 the last portion of the Belknap Campus section of Shipp Street was renamed Intramural Place, as construction of the Humanities Building began.[45]

An attractive low stone wall bordered the south side of Shipp Street. So popular was it as a gathering place for students that it once captured the concern of the U of L Women's League. In 1934 that group, "to aid the University in preservation of the dignity of co-eds," urged that the young ladies not be allowed to smoke, sit on the Shipp Street wall, or lounge on the grass.[46]

The removal of most of the wall in the early 1970s was met first with resistance, then sadness, from many people who remembered it as a favorite resting and meeting place. At that time two U of L biology professors called it "a tangible reminder and physical link between the University Belknap Campus and Old Louisville, and the older generations of Louisvillians who established the University." The small section of the Shipp Street wall running just north of the Speed Museum and Ekstrom Library is the only portion of the wall near its original location. Dismantled stones

Parkway Field, shown here in 1954, became the home of the U of L baseball team in 1952. (Louisville Courier-Journal.)

have been used at various places on the Health Sciences and Belknap Campuses, most notably the enclosure of the north end of Parrish Court between Gottschalk and Gardiner Halls.[47]

Parkway Field, at the southeast corner of the campus, sat on eight acres of land sold by the university to the "Louisville Base Ball Company" in 1923 for use by the Louisville Colonels. That team's field, Eclipse Park at Seventh and Kentucky, had burned the year before. A new stadium at Parkway Field opened on May 1, 1923, complete with a grandstand to accommodate a reported eighteen thousand fans. Almost thirty-one years later, on December 31, 1953, U of L bought Parkway Field back, agreeing to lease it to the club for ten years. The Colonels played there until the 1956 season, when they moved to Fairgrounds Stadium. The stands, which had deteriorated, were removed in 1961. Several star major leaguers played at Parkway Field, including Babe Ruth in 1924, 1928, and 1932, and Jackie Robinson in 1946. Gridiron star Johnny Unitas played there when it

served as home for the Cardinal football team in the early 1950s.[48]

The extremes of Cold War ideology provided an intangible threat no less real than the problems of urban decay. During the early 1950s, disciples of Wisconsin senator Joseph McCarthy stirred up a moderate amount of dust at the University of Louisville. One informed the Jefferson County Grand Jury that several university faculty members preached subversive doctrines in the classroom. The anti-Communist crusaders lacked enough evidence for an indictment, but a suspicious observer wrote that a shadow of doubt still hung over the school. Around the same time, a national magazine reported that six U of L faculty members required Communist-inspired textbooks published by the Cornell University Press. One U of L professor, troubled by his youthful flirtation with Communism during the 1930s, appeared anonymously on a television program to renounce his former activities. Another faculty member, as vigor-

international center building on belknap campus

The International Center is housed in a building named for longtime director George L. Brodschi, a Romanian who moved to the United States in 1947. Brodschi worked to increase enrollment of foreign students, encourage students to travel abroad, and interest Louisville in international affairs. He also served as U of L's Fulbright and foreign student adviser, and taught international law.

ous a Cold Warrior as McCarthy, dismissed the senator as a Republican partisan engaged in a campaign to discredit prominent Democrats. There were apparently no internal efforts to penalize or intimidate U of L professors who were accused of having Communist sympathies. President Davidson admonished Louisvillians to exercise caution in casting aspersions upon their neighbors.[49]

The McCarthy scare passed, but during the 1950s and early 1960s university groups debated such grim topics as whether South America would side with the Soviet Union in World War III. The *Cardinal* carried macabre advice on how to survive a nuclear war, and university officials discussed the location of fallout shelters on campus. Shortly after World War II, the University of Louisville established an International Center, which reflected the United States' more active involvement in world affairs, including power struggles between the United States and the Soviet Union. In 1955 the center attracted Eleanor Roosevelt, widow of the wartime president and former U.S. delegate to the United Nations, who gave an address on the UN at the Playhouse. Within four years of the center's founding, the enrollment of foreign students at the university had grown from two to more than one hundred.[50]

Relations between the races presented problems closer to home. In 1951, the year the university closed the Louisville Municipal College and integrated all of its programs, it opened the Southern Police Institute (SPI). U of L's action was inspired in part by Swedish sociologist and economist Gunnar Myrdal, who advised that professionally trained law enforcement officials might improve race relations in the American South. David A. McCandless, then the city's director of public safety, became the institute's first director (and later the first dean of the School of Police Administration). Funding was provided initially by the Carnegie Corporation and the Rockefeller Foundation's General Education Board.[51]

The Southern Police Institute reportedly was the first such organization in the United States, after the Federal Bureau of Investigation's National Academy (founded in 1935), to offer training for law enforcement executives, and the first based at a university. The institute conducted intensive seminars in homicide and sex crime investigations and other topics. In its first twenty years it enrolled officers from the federal government, from nearly one thousand cities and towns, all fifty states, and thirty foreign countries. After McCandless's death a colleague described him as "a world influence and pioneer in the police education field."[52]

Even though now legally integrated, the university still operated in a segregated city. Rising tuition rates probably discouraged some potential black students, and the school retained obvious legacies of Jim Crow. Fraternities and sororities excluded applicants on the grounds of race and religion; nearby restaurants refused service to black students; and some physical education and botany classes used off-campus facilities having discriminatory policies. On the other hand, the university's enrollment of black students helped encourage the desegregation of some other municipal facilities, such as the city's parks and public schools.[53]

In 1960 Professor Ray H. Bixler of the Department of Psychology directed a group of students in conducting an opinion poll concerning desegregation. It found that a little more than half of the white Louisvillians questioned would attend movies with blacks. Slightly fewer than half would eat at restaurants that served blacks. Because of the prevalence of these attitudes locally, Professor Charles C. Parrish Jr. felt "right at home" two years later while traveling in Rhodesia, where policies of racial separation prevailed. The discriminatory policies of two restaurants adjacent to campus drew students' objections in 1961, and President Davidson spoke with their owners "in an effort to get them to admit *all* University students." In 1963 the Louisville Board of Aldermen passed a public accommodations law, banning discrimination of services on account of race. By the mid-1960s, local civil rights activists, including some members of the university community, called on the city to enact an effective open housing ordinance. While supporting the measure in principle, the *Cardinal* called open housing marches counterproductive.[54]

All of these events affected the health sciences, but the medical and dental schools, more than the other university units, also had their own significant influences. In part, these distinctions resulted from the rapidly rising expense of medical and dental education, making these programs a large portion of the university's budget. As early as 1948, the skyrocketing costs of medical education brought the first regular state support to the University of Louisville: grants for medical research. The state exercised no control over the university, but some legislators reasoned that Kentucky's only medical school deserved their financial support. Despite opposition from the University

Dr. Martin Luther King Jr. spoke on open housing legislation to an overflow crowd in the Allen Court Room of the School of Law in 1967.

of Kentucky, the General Assembly narrowly approved SB 105, the funding measure for these appropriations. Later, the dental school also received financial assistance from the state.[55]

This action came amidst controversy. On July 22, 1948, Sidney I. Kornhauser, head of the anatomy department and a member of the medical school's admissions committee, reported he had been offered bribes to try to influence the application procedure for prospective students with low scholastic standings. Some of this pressure supposedly came from prominent Louisvillians. Kornhauser stated that several students were accepted, that they did meet the minimum standards, and that this problem occurred at medical schools around the country. Following denial of these charges from President Taylor and medical school dean John Walker Moore, reports surfaced that support for the 1948 legislative allocation may well have been traded for a dozen slots in the freshman medical class. Moore stated that the scholarships were awarded since money was made available for a program to alleviate the shortage of doctors in rural areas and added that there was no political pressure at work. Kornhauser resigned from the admissions

committee, but both he and Taylor denied this action was precipitated by the dispute.[56]

Even with additional funding, the medical and dental schools faced an uncertain future. Both occupied buildings dating from the turn of the century. The medical school's teaching hospital, Louisville General, had been constructed prior to World War I, remained under the Jefferson County Board of Health's administrative control, and served primarily as an indigent care facility. By the early 1960s, Davidson feared that both the medical and dental schools faced loss of accreditation unless they found new homes. At the same time, however, plans existed for a new health sciences complex, which would form part of a larger aggregation of hospitals, doctors' offices, and other health care facilities. Gradually, the medical center just east of downtown Louisville took shape. From the university's perspective, a high point came in 1970 with the occupation of new medical and dental buildings, but the problem of the teaching hospital remained.[57]

Meanwhile, many believed that the state needed a medical school in Lexington at the University of Kentucky, and in 1955 both gubernatorial candidates promised to create one. The winner, A.B. "Happy" Chandler, did just that. The governor also promised to increase support for U of L's medical school, provided that President Davidson would not oppose a second medical school at the University of Kentucky. Officially, Davidson remained neutral, but privately he remarked that Louisville could accommodate all the qualified medical school candidates from within the state. UK's first medical school class entered in 1960. Around the same time, the Lexington institution began planning a dental school, which opened in 1962. U of L's medical school, begun in 1837, had outlasted Transylvania's and all of its other competitor schools, and for the last half-century had been the only medical school in the commonwealth. Now once again it would have a formidable competitor in Lexington.[58]

The university's financial struggles had become apparent earlier in facing the high costs of its medical and dental schools, but they were not limited to those areas. By the early 1960s, Davidson had exhausted the likely prospects for additional private and municipal support. Local leaders held out little hope that individual and corporate giving could meet the university's financial needs. At one point the board considered purchasing nearby Churchill Downs, home of horse racing's famous Kentucky Derby, in hope of assuring a steady revenue stream. This plan, labeled "shameful and godless" by a local minister, proved impractical. In 1960 city voters soundly rejected a U of L bond issue that had reluctant backing from city government and outright opposition from fire fighters, police officers, and other city employees who feared passage would threaten their hoped-for pay raises.[59]

The institution's worsening financial condition during the 1960s was especially hard on Buildings and Grounds, as that unit was forced to maintain the school's physical plant on the proverbial shoestring. Longtime superintendent Kelly Lewis, and then his successor Wade Woods, demonstrated great ingenuity with their skeleton crews. According to one of his staff members, Woods "squeezed every penny he got," on more than one occasion buying coal on credit to heat campus buildings.[60]

In 1965 Mayor Kenneth Schmied warned university officials that he could not fund higher education at increasing levels. He recommended that the school seek more state support. Beset by similar funding problems, the municipal universities of Cincinnati, Pittsburgh, and Houston were also seeking increased state funding. Davidson, who preferred the relative independence of the university's semi-private status, turned reluctantly toward state affiliation.[61]

Controversies centering on the fate of U of L's football program during the Davidson era provide examples of declining budgets, charges of political interference, faculty and student discord, and presidential leadership. Faced with a projected budget deficit for 1955-1956, the board of trustees considered two alternatives: eliminate football or merit raises. Ten years later, following two disastrous seasons on the gridiron and amidst mounting deficits in football budgets, the university again considered abandoning the sport.[62]

Faculty sentiment leaned toward abolition, as reflected in a senate vote of sixty-eight in favor of dropping football and sixty-two opposed. On the next day, February 10, 1965, setting off "storms of controversy," Marlow Cook, Jefferson County judge and a member of the U of L board of trustees, and Louisville mayor William O. Cowger, who had appointed Cook to the board, issued statements suggesting "employees" had no business determining university policy. The two political leaders advocated a community fund-raising effort to move the football program toward "big-time" status.[63]

The faculty promptly censured Cook and Cowger, asserting that "a university in which the faculties do not make academic policy is a mockery of the idea of a free university." U of L faculty were members of "a time-honored and noble profession," they said, not "merely employees." Enraged, faculty spokesperson William Furnish, a biology professor, and his colleagues called on Cook to resign from the board or retract his "offending remarks."[64]

The board met on February 11 and approved a statement issued by chairman Eli Brown stressing "the importance of the faculty of this institution." On the day of the decisive board meeting, a group of 150 student demonstrators stood in the pouring rain to show support for football. Wearing black armbands, they chanted "Give us football / We will stay. / We won't go / To U of K."[65]

Davidson himself quickly jumped to the defense of the faculty. He gave a statement strongly supporting the right of faculty to make recommendations to the board about football or any other university matter. The student senate praised both Davidson and the board. The faculty, meeting in a closed session, proclaimed their confidence in the president, who chaired the meeting, and ended it by giving him a standing ovation. At the same time Davidson undoubtedly was at work behind the scenes to avoid giving unnecessary offense to Cook and Cowger, who controlled the allocation of local public funds to the university. It can also be safely assumed that he was not about to oversee the abolition of football. The trustees decided to continue the program at its current level for the time being and appealed to the community for greater support. Again football survived, faculty prerogatives were preserved, the president was praised by all sides, the students were happy, and the teams continued their mediocre seasons.[66]

One faculty member, historian Laurence Lee Howe, characterized the period from the early 1950s through the mid-1960s as the "golden age" of the University of Louisville. By this he meant that faculty and administrative cooperation, the absence of great social turmoil, and enlightened leadership combined to produce an unusually harmonious academic community. This equilibrium was shaken by racial conflict and student unrest during the late 1960s. It would be disturbed even more by entrance into the state system of higher education. In retrospect, this so-called "golden age" comprised a deceptive tranquility, actually producing many portents of the more turbulent late 1960s and early 1970s. During later, more uncertain years, these times, in memory, took on a rose-colored tint that Davidson, whose responsibility it was to anticipate problems, probably never saw.[67]

FIFTEEN

STATEHOOD

B Y THE EARLY 1960s, President Philip G. Davidson was well aware that the University of Louisville could not maintain the breadth and quality of programs for its students or the level of services to its community in the absence of major increases in revenue. The city's support had been reduced to the point where it was supplying only 10 percent of the school's budget. For years, county support had not exceeded one percent. For more than a decade, state funds, limited to medical and dental education, had not gone beyond eleven percent. Furthermore, the city's population was in decline; within ten years more people in Jefferson County would live outside of Louisville than in the city itself.[1]

In 1961 a state commission appointed by Governor Bert T. Combs to study Kentucky higher education received a proposal from the University of Louisville offering to lower tuition in return for increases in state funding. The commission recommended that the commonwealth consider boosting its U of L subsidy or bringing the institution into its system of higher education. In order to fund necessary budget increases during a period of rapid growth, however, the university continued to raise tuition. In 1966 a U of L student's tuition bill was three and a half times what a University of Kentucky student paid. By then Davidson had decided that the University of Louisville needed either to cut programs or to pursue state affiliation. He chose the latter course, which

became the university administration's primary goal for the remainder of the decade.[2]

Another higher education study commission was created in 1965 by Governor Edward T. Breathitt. On the eve of the biennial meeting of the state legislature in 1966, commission members strongly suggested the possibility of state affiliation for the University of Louisville. In February 1966 a house resolution called upon the University of Kentucky and University of Louisville presidents to establish a committee to study U of L's entry into the state system of higher education and to make recommendations prior to the 1968 meeting of the legislature. Davidson and UK president John W. Oswald then created their joint committee, chaired by Lisle Baker, executive vice president of the Courier-Journal and Louisville Times Company, to conduct the study.[3]

The Baker committee contracted with a New York educational consulting firm, Heald, Hobsen and Associates, which proposed six options for U of L's financial future: (1) becoming totally private, which would require intensive U of L fund-raising efforts and obligate the state to create a new, separate university in Louisville; (2) receiving some state support and coming under limited state control; (3) becoming an independent state university; (4) having each institution administered by its own president, each reporting to a common board of trustees; (5) having a single University of Kentucky on two campuses, each with a chancellor reporting to a single president and

"No wonder tears were shed as a small group gathered at Standiford Field to bid goodbyes to the Davidsons in January [1968]. The future was extremely uncertain, and some form of state affiliation loomed ahead. There was the strong sense of the end of an era which, though not really golden in any budgetary sense, was nevertheless a period of growth and excitement and relative stability. What lay ahead was a vast uncertainty in a very worrisome future." —William F. Ekstrom, Recollection. *The Davidsons are shown here near the beginning of his presidency in the early 1950s.*

board of trustees; or (6) becoming a branch of, and subordinate to, the University of Kentucky.[4]

In its "confidential draft" issued in March 1967 and published immediately in the *Courier-Journal*, the consultants recommended option five, that the universities of Louisville and Kentucky become "sister" schools under one board and one president. The Baker committee endorsed this recommendation. The boards of the two universities would be combined during an initial period of transition, and the merged institution would be known as the "Commonwealth University of Kentucky."[5]

Davidson was not opposed to a merger of equals, but he preferred preserving as much of the university's independence as possible. Publicly, both he and Oswald favored a combination of the two schools— not an absorption of one by the other—although the exact terms were yet to be worked out. Apparently Oswald and Davidson worked well together. Soon after his arrival in Lexington Oswald received a U of L honorary degree; years later he recalled his "very close relationship" with the University of Louisville.[6]

On August 7, 1967, officials of both institutions attended a dinner meeting at UK's Spindletop Hall, where the two presidents expressed mutual admiration and indicated their support, in principle, for some sort of combination. The meeting ended with a bombshell, however, when U of L trustee John Tarrant declared that his school should be absorbed by the University of Kentucky. Other board members assured Davidson that they disagreed with Tarrant, but some feared that UK officials did not. Eight days later Davidson announced his retirement, citing his age and his belief that the University of Louisville stood on the verge of a new era and needed fresh leadership. The president noted he would take a leave of absence effective February 1, 1968, and retire effective June 20, 1968. The trustees accepted his recommendation that executive vice president Woodrow Strickler succeed him in office.[7]

For most of Kentucky's history, the state legislature had largely overlooked Louisville in its appropriation of money for higher education. It had funded four-year teachers' colleges in Frankfort, Richmond, Bowling Green, Morehead, and Murray, and a liberal arts college in Highland Heights, and was turning them into "regional" universities. The General Assembly had created a comprehensive university in

Woodrow M. Strickler (1912–1975), thirteenth president of the University of Louisville, 1968–1972, coped with student activists during the late 1960s and in 1970 led the University of Louisville into the state system of higher education. Known by many as "Woodie," Strickler was one of the most popular of the university's presidents. Strickler Hall was named in his honor in 1975. In 1996 the name was changed to Woodrow M. and Florence Strickler Hall in recognition of the contributions of the president's wife to the life of the university.

Lexington in 1916, and in the early 1960s had duplicated at that institution costly medical and dental education programs long in existence at the University of Louisville. During the 1960s the legislature had begun sprinkling more than a dozen two-year community colleges, administered by the University of Kentucky, all over the state. Jefferson County, the state's only large metropolitan area, with over twenty-one percent of the Commonwealth's population and a third of its tax base, had received only nominal appropriations for U of L's medical and dental schools and lately, in 1968, the opening of a UK community college in downtown Louisville. "Of course," noted longtime administrator William F. Ekstrom, "the University was partly responsible, for it loved its independence and did not seek state affiliation in the fifties when the state's largess to higher education was at its peak."[8]

Woodrow Mann Strickler had served ably as executive vice president under Philip G. Davidson since 1958, but after a heart attack in the fall of 1967, he was in precarious health. He was on a leave of absence from September 1967 until February 1968. At first Strickler agreed only to serve briefly in an acting capacity as president while the trustees searched for a permanent successor to Davidson, but then in March 1968, in Ekstrom's words, he "made an agonizing decision which may have shortened his life but which demonstrated a sacrificial devotion to the institution of the highest order. He agreed to accept the presidency on a permanent basis and the search for a new president was very quietly aborted."[9]

Strickler was perhaps uniquely qualified to provide stability and continuity of purpose during the university's movement toward state affiliation. A 1934 graduate of Bucknell University, Strickler took an M.B.A. degree from the University of Pennsylvania in 1935. Before entering the field of higher education, he worked with the Illinois Commerce Commission and a Chicago advertising firm. In 1937 and 1938 he lectured at Northwestern University in the Department of Business Organization and Industrial Management. Strickler came to the University of Louisville in 1938 as an instructor in economics. For the dozen years prior to his appointment as executive

vice president he headed the Division of Adult Education. That unit had been created in 1935 to expand the university's offerings for working students who could take courses only in the evenings.

Following Tarrant's bombshell at the Spindletop meeting, University of Louisville officials became more methodical in their pursuit of state affiliation. In the fall of 1967 they toured the commonwealth and visited alumni who were members of the General Assembly. They also discussed state affiliation with both gubernatorial candidates. Louie Nunn, the Republican, promised his support for increased state funding for the University of Louisville. He recommended that the university enter the state system as an independent institution, a strategy less likely to draw opposition from the regional universities. The Democratic nominee, Henry Ward, also expressed his support for increased state aid. Like Nunn, he indicated that a UK-U of L combination would threaten the regionals. Ward suggested that the regional universities, acting in concert, had more legislative strength than the University of Kentucky.[10]

Meanwhile, the universities of Kentucky and Louisville continued their work on a merger plan for presentation to the 1968 General Assembly. After they failed to agree, Louisville acted alone, fearing further delay. Strickler's representative on the scene in Frankfort was Dee Ashley Akers, a politically savvy Kentuckian who in 1965 had joined U of L's law faculty. Akers "lived and breathed politics and well understood the psychology of rural legislators," recollected Ekstrom, and "spent most of his time in lobbying" them. U of L's success in Frankfort was something entirely new. "We didn't even know how to deal with legislators in our own backyard at that time," Ekstrom recalled.[11]

Following a "strenuous ordeal," on March 13, 1968, the university received unanimous legislative support for HR 91, a joint resolution that called for U of L's entrance into the state system in 1970, regardless of progress in the merger talks. U of L vice president for planning and development William McGlothlin, who sat in the gallery when the proposal passed the Senate, wrote that tears came to his eyes "as the votes piled up." The *Courier-Journal* subsequently criticized the University of Louisville for acting alone, which the editors claimed undermined the chance for a merger with the University of Kentucky.[12]

Any remaining hope for merger slipped away following the 1968 meeting of the General Assembly. Later that year, Oswald, who may have overestimated his trustees' enthusiasm for merger, left the University of Kentucky. Five years earlier, when Oswald had arrived in Lexington, he had been "flabbergasted" to find that the presidents of the regional institutions had such strong political connections. One had been speaker of the house, he noted, and another a member of the governor's cabinet. Ultimately, Oswald's lack of support from the governor helped lead to his departure. Early in 1969, the boards of the two schools established a joint committee that endorsed the 1967 consultant's plan for combination, but shortly thereafter the state's Council on Public Higher Education called for a new look at U of L's entering the state system as an independent institution. In August 1969, Otis A. Singletary, Oswald's successor as UK president, took office amid general feelings that much had been accomplished in the merger talks, but he found little agreement on details. U of L officials who attended a dinner meeting at the Singletary home in September left with the impression that the two schools were unlikely to agree on the specific terms of a combination.[13]

Shortly thereafter, Singletary wrote to Strickler that before continuing the merger discussions he wanted a thorough examination of the University of Louisville's indebtedness, operating budget, and future financial needs. He recommended that the merged institutions have one president, chancellors at the Louisville and Lexington campuses, and be known as the University of Kentucky. Furthermore, he proposed that the merged school retain only the existing University of Kentucky board of trustees, with the addition of three nonvoting members from Louisville. Finally, he recommended that financial support for the University of Louisville be based on "the availability of additional funds."[14]

Strickler considered the proposed composition of the board inequitable. He also pointed out that the University of Louisville's case for increased funding had already been made. Finally, Strickler noted that concessions to all of Singletary's recommendations would compromise U of L's institutional integrity. Overall, Singletary's proposals seemed more like absorption than merger, including the proposed name for the merged institution. Perhaps Singletary's points were negotiable, but Strickler obviously thought further discussion useless and believed he had the strength to act alone. On November 7, 1969, shortly after receiving Strickler's reply, Singletary announced their deadlock to the press. The universities of Louisville and Kentucky were too far apart on too many issues to negotiate a merger.[15]

With merger no longer an issue, the University of Louisville approached the 1970 General Assembly with plans to enter the state system as an independent institution. Friction between a Republican governor—Louie Nunn was the only Republican to hold the office in the second half of the twentieth century—and a Democratic legislature made the process less than smooth, but the passage of Senate Bill 117 and its approval by the governor on March 30, 1970, ensured that the university would enter the state system on July 1, 1970. Furthermore, all of the school's undergraduate, graduate, and professional programs remained intact.[16]

The underlying conflict between the University of Kentucky and the University of Louisville was apparent throughout the legislative session. The state would now have two universities with graduate programs through the doctoral level and an array of professional schools. Representatives of the other state institutions of higher education feared the worst, that additional funds for the University of Louisville would come at their expense. Further adding to their fears was Governor Nunn's support for the creation in 1968 of what became Northern Kentucky University, which soon absorbed Cincinnati's Salmon P. Chase College of Law.[17]

Upon its entrance into the state system the University of Louisville instantly became the commonwealth's second largest university. In its first biennial budget, however, the institution was disappointed to receive a state appropriation of only $13.2

million, much less than the $34.5 million it had requested, far less than that allocated to the other schools. It was barely more than the state's allocation for the school's final year as a semi-private, municipal institution. Still, the amount was $5 million more than Nunn had stipulated. The governor, a graduate of the U of L law school, later recalled that he had overcome the opposition of the regional schools by providing generous increases in their budgets. He also noted his belief that subsequent legislative sessions would result in more satisfactory appropriations for the University of Louisville.[18]

During the days leading up to July 1, 1970, when Senate Bill 117 was to take effect, the University of Louisville continued to suffer from internal dissent regarding the wisdom of state affiliation. Trustee Charles P. Farnsley, who had returned to the board in January 1970 after a fourteen-year absence, believed relinquishing local control was "the most disastrous thing that will ever happen to the city of Louisville." He considered state affiliation the first step in making the University of Louisville a regional satellite of the University of Kentucky. Many undoubtedly shared the former mayor's fears, but saw no alternative other than the curtailment of programs. More disturbing were the objections of trustee John Tarrant, who considered state affiliation unconstitutional, blamed the University of Louisville for the breakdown of the merger discussions, and accused the institution's officials of fiscal mismanagement. Frequently, trustees' meetings became protracted ordeals that accomplished little and ended in frustration. Long-suffering chairman Edwin G. Middleton must have breathed a sigh of relief on June 29, 1970,

when he adjourned the outgoing board *sine die*, signaling the end of the University of Louisville as a semi-private, semi-municipal institution, and its beginning as a full-fledged member of the state system.[19]

At the point of state affiliation, appointments to the U of L board were made by the governor, not by the mayor and county judge, though for a time these two officials retained an important role in the nomination process. Governor Nunn was not happy with this compromise measure, but acceded to it in deference to the wishes of local interests. When city and county support declined, the mayor and county judge lost their ability to control some appointments to the board. Only two members continued after July 1, 1970: Middleton, who was elected chairman, and Woodford R. Porter, elected vice-chairman.[20]

In retrospect, it could be argued that some form of greater cooperation between the University of Louisville and the University of Kentucky would have served the commonwealth better, but neither school could agree on terms of merger that suited the other. Neither fully appreciated the other's position: the University of Kentucky's struggle to build a state university in the continuing absence of adequate resources or the University of Louisville's long service to the commonwealth without the benefit of comparable public support. Apparently, neither school had enough political strength to force significant concessions from the other. Furthermore, no state authority seemed willing or able to serve as an effective mediator. The University of Louisville scored a significant victory by retaining all of its programs upon entrance into the state system, but the question of future funding remained unsettled.

SIXTEEN

STUDENT UNREST

PRESIDENT WOODROW STRICKLER provided seasoned leadership as the university entered the state system. He also had an understanding ear for student protestors during the late 1960s and early 1970s. These factors, amid a fairly conservative social climate coupled with the lack of a sizable on-campus student population, helped account for the university's relative stability during one of the stormier periods in the history of American higher education. In retrospect, the counterculture and racial tensions that confronted the university's leadership in the late 1960s were not a sudden, unpredictable outburst. Evidence of social and political conflict, rather than consensus, appeared throughout the period, although differences became more pronounced during Strickler's presidency.

During the quarter century following World War II, the University of Louisville had enjoyed administrative stability, a good faculty, and a respectable semi-private tradition. In spite of financial limitations, the school made notable contributions to the community and to scholarship, although its impact was generally confined to the state and local area. During this period, the school possessed an atmosphere of small town informality, which was characteristic of a city that had not grown too large to maintain an air of unstudied familiarity.

Opinions surrounding civil rights issues became more polarized in America in the late 1960s. Civil rights activists who favored compromise and nonvio-

lence were sometimes overshadowed by advocates of stronger measures. At the University of Louisville, those who focused attention on evidence of the historical and lingering oppression of blacks locally and nationally sometimes found organized protests more fruitful than individual speeches. In April 1968 U of L black student protesters urged the university to do much more than highlight its few African American faculty members and its high-profile black athletes.[1]

On March 4, 1969, the Black Student Union submitted a plan calling for more intense efforts to recruit minority students and teachers, increased financial aid for black students, and new course offerings in black history and literature. After the university failed to meet all of the BSU demands, on April 30, 1969, a group of students and other sympathizers occupied Strickler's office for a few hours, then quietly left. The next day twenty-one black students took over the Arts and Sciences dean's building. (Ironically the dean, Richard Barber, was out of town studying student unrest on other campuses.) They were forcibly removed by police, and some were arrested.[2]

J. Blaine Hudson III, one of the black student leaders, later recalled that Strickler honestly wanted to remedy past injustices, but could not fully appreciate the black students' position. The president believed that the black students had legitimate complaints, but expected unrealistically quick results. Strickler praised the campus ministers for their leadership during the

U of L students at a protest rally in 1969. The poster warned that the University of Kentucky would be the next target of black student groups that presented U of L officials a twelve-page set of demands. A compromise between the U of L administration and the black students was announced at the end of the rally.

Police escort a demonstrator away from the Arts and Sciences dean's building on May 1, 1969. (Louisville Courier-Journal.)

crisis, but complained that the faculty responded too slowly. At the time of the confrontation, trustee Woodford R. Porter Sr., the university's first African American board member, warned that if moderate protestors were denied victories, more militant leaders would seize control of the civil rights movement. One direct result was the creation of the Office of Black Affairs to assist in the recruitment of more black students and faculty, create tutoring programs, and coordinate black studies in the curriculum.[3]

Opposition to the Vietnam War took root slowly at the University of Louisville. In 1965, when a small group of students gathered to criticize penalties for burning draft cards, a rival faction drove speakers from the platform with volleys of tomatoes and eggs. As late as January 1967, the *Cardinal* and some student organizations still supported United States military involvement in Southeast Asia, although within a few months the student newspaper changed its stance. At the height of anti-war activity, Dean of Students Dave Lawrence described events at the University of Louisville as relatively mild compared with those at other institutions.[4]

The University of Louisville's version of student activism exhibited strong religious overtones, expressed through the newsletters of various campus ministries. In 1968, for example, a writer for one of

Woodford R. Porter Sr., a Louisville businessman, was the first African American appointed to U of L's board of trustees. Beginning in 1968, he served in that position for twenty-four years, serving as chair for four terms. The university's Porter Scholarship was named for him. He is pictured here in 1980 receiving U of L's coveted Minerva Award of Merit.

these sheets attacked the United States for its arrogant abuse of power and endorsed the presidential campaign of Eugene McCarthy, a peace candidate. In the spring of 1969, Arthur Blessitt, "the hippie evangelist," arrived on campus under the auspices of the Baptist Student Union to bring his message of "peace, love, and change." Meanwhile, Roman Catholic students questioned internal issues such as papal authority and the value of confession. While conservatives decried the growth of religious radicalism, the campus ministries probably provided an outlet for ideas that could have taken more militant forms.[5]

At the same time, the university retained a strident conservative voice through the local chapter of Young Americans for Freedom (YAF), a right-wing youth organization. Spokesmen for this group considered the university's Newman Center "about as Catholic as Mao Tse-Tung" and charged that the faculty ranged from pro-Communist to "knee-jerk" liberal. Not surprisingly, the YAF vigorously espoused the Cold War doctrine of containment, the belief that, unless contested at every point, Communist aggressors would engulf the free world.[6]

Charles Westerman took this picture of fellow U of L students collecting donations after four Kent State University students were killed by the Ohio National Guard in May 1970.

In the 1970s U of L students opposed building a nuclear power plant at Marble Hill and rallied in support of Earth Day.

The peace movement and counterculture appeared in other aspects of student life. One nearby restaurant, Masterson's, refused service to long-haired university students. Drugs were not uncommon on campus. According to one report, students bought drugs on trips home for the holidays, from soldiers stationed at nearby Fort Knox, and from local dealers. The grove of trees on the western edge of Belknap Campus became a meeting place where students circulated joints. One undergraduate reported that, when high, he swam nude in the lake at Cherokee Park. An older faculty member complained that "slobbishness" had become a way of life.[7]

Political moderates had little room to maneuver in this atmosphere. Strickler illustrated their dilemma when he called upon local residents to view student dissent as an expression of concern by a legitimate segment of society, but warned that any protest should remain within rational limits. In 1969 the president concluded that the student newspaper's April Fool edition overstepped the bounds of rationality by using what the *Courier-Journal* called "a couple of poverty-stricken four-letter words." Strickler briefly halted publication of the *Cardinal*, which some labeled an attack on free expression. Caught in the middle, the president also received heated comments from some who considered his stand on dissident behavior too lenient. A *Louisville Times* editorial, however, averred that the university had exercised "grace and good sense" in the matter.[8]

Strickler's four-year presidency, which constituted a watershed in the history of the university, was marked by other notable accomplishments. Under his guidance the university occupied the new Health Sciences complex, began work on new life sciences and humanities buildings, and established the School of Police Administration (which incorporated the Southern Police Institute and National Crime Prevention Institute and which later became the School of Justice Administration). Strickler also helped establish the Kentuckiana Metroversity, a consortium of colleges, universities, and seminaries in the greater Louisville area. With his approval, in 1968 a student-run radio station, WLCV, began its life in a dormitory room with a "carrier current" transmitter, making its signal available for the most part only in the residence halls. (A new AM transmitter was installed in 1995, enabling the station, then located in the Student Activities Center, to be received anywhere on Belknap Campus.) It typically responded to students' requests in its musical selections.[9]

Another important issue confronting Strickler early in his presidency tested his diplomacy skills. Kentucky Southern College, opened in 1962 by the Long Run Baptist Association, soon occupied a 238-acre tract along Shelbyville Road in the city's eastern suburbs. During the decade the school built a classroom and administration building, dormitories, a student center, and a president's home, attracted a student body of over 850 at its peak in 1966, a faculty of nearly 50, and a staff of about the same size. By 1967

*Kentucky Southern College in 1968 on the verge of closing. It had been "loved into existence" by its president, Rollin S. Burhans. (*Louisville Courier-Journal.)

it had also acquired a $5 million debt and soon was financially insolvent. Its officials discussed possible merger with Western Kentucky University and the University of Kentucky. Despite a spirited "Save Our School" campaign conceived and led by its students, the college closed. In the end, KSC officials accepted U of L's offer to absorb the school, admit its students, acquire its property, assume its debt, and fund faculty and staff salaries through August 1969.[10]

Strickler came under some criticism for taking on a large financial burden at the very time he was seeking state affiliation. The president believed, however, that the acquisition of this prime real estate would be of enormous future use to the university. Furthermore, he feared that if he did nothing, another state university would establish a branch campus on the site and compete for state funds the University of Louisville desperately needed and for students it wished to serve. School officials named the former Kentucky Southern grounds Shelby Campus, in honor of

Kentucky's first governor, Isaac Shelby, and thereafter considered KSC students U of L alumni.[11]

While U of L students of the late 1960s and early 1970s were neither immune to nor unsympathetic about the concerns of student activists elsewhere in the United States, their forms of protest usually bore little resemblance to those of their counterparts at such places as Columbia University and the University of California at Berkeley. Civil rights and the war in Vietnam certainly occupied U of L students' attention, but so did such issues as high prices in the campus bookstore, the "weekday curfew for sophomore girls," and the lack of a procedure for the student evaluation of professors and their courses. At one point a group known as the Students for Social Action (SSA) pressed for changes in these and other matters. In February 1968, SSA gained eleven hundred signatures on a student petition. Under the leadership of senior political science major Mark Alter, who sported "a reddish-brown beard a la Hemingway," the group met regularly with Strickler to lobby for its causes.[12]

In a feature story about "activism on the campus," a *Courier-Journal* writer chose the words "tranquillity" and "calm" to characterize U of L's campus. In contrast to the "unrest and violence" marking student protest in some other states, U of L students displayed "activism in its mildest form." Alter said that on the Belknap Campus "you have about one anarchist and about three guys who have read enough to sincerely believe they are Marxian economists," far too few radicals to support major disturbances. Walter Porter, in his second year as a law student, believed that the campus's calm was attributable to its homogeneous student body, with most students hailing from Louisville and still living at home. The newspaper writer attributed U of L's "placidity" to students who were "cautious, even conservative," and "fairly contented with their lot."

Strickler probably would have agreed. He approved reductions in some bookstore prices, permitted changes in the dress code, increased library hours, extended the curfew for women, and allowed for Arts and Sciences students to evaluate their professors from "superior" ("really 'tops' among instructors") to "in-

adequate" ("ranks among the worst of instructors"). The evaluations would also seek judgments about professors' class preparation, exam frequency and difficulty, and "any personal idiosyncrasies such as 'annoying mannerisms,' 'personal appearance,' or punctuality in coming to class."

Woodrow M. Strickler remained a symbol of stability as his presidency bridged the era of state affiliation. One observer noted that he represented the university's interests quietly and calmly in what frequently were heated meetings of the state's Council on Public Higher Education. Strickler continued to suffer from heart disease, however, and in the spring of 1972, after seeing the university through its first experience with the General Assembly as a state institution, he announced his retirement, effective August 31, 1972. Looking back on the administration, Strickler's vice president for academic affairs, William F. Ekstrom, had great praise for the outgoing president:

> It is difficult to imagine a more stressful situation than the four and a half years of the Strickler Administration. The hopeless budgetary crises, the anxious uncertainty about our status in the state's system, the wrenching and costly requirements when we did get in, the tremendous expansion of enrollments without adequate resources to manage it, the taxing loads of faculty and staff, and the unsettling experience of student unrest were more than any one president should ever be called upon to endure. Without Dr. Strickler's patience and thoughtfulness, his terrific people skills, his managerial ability, and his resources of credibility and good will which at times were drained almost to the diminishing point, I sometimes wonder whether we could have made it with status and programs intact. From my point of view the University's debt to his unflagging leadership was incalculable.[13]

When Strickler stepped down as president, the board appointed William F. Ekstrom, then vice president for academic affairs, as acting president. Like Strickler, Ekstrom was a familiar face long associated with the university. Years earlier he had attended the University of Illinois for his undergraduate and graduate work. During World War II he was attached to

U of L president Woodrow M. Strickler, standing behind Kentucky governor Louie B. Nunn, hoped for a much larger appropriation when the university joined the state system of higher education in 1970.

the Chinese Air Force as an interpreter. In 1946 he returned to Illinois as an instructor in English, and received his Ph.D. degree in 1947. That year he moved to the University of Louisville, where he became an assistant professor of English and later head of the department.

Declaring he had "no intentions of allowing the University to drift" during this crucial period of "preparation," Ekstrom worked for the equalization of male and female salary scales, opened an Affirmative Action Office, increased benefits for retired faculty and staff members, established the University Archives and a Legal Affairs Office, stepped up black recruitment and general enrollment, and started a Pan-African studies department and other interdisciplinary areas. In 1973 the university celebrated its "triquartiquentennial," the 175th anniversary of its founding, complete with a special logo. Under Ekstrom's direction, the University's first state-financed construction package was approved, an event which was a milestone in the University's history. The result was the building of Davidson and Strickler

Halls, both of which were constructed quickly using a "fast track" method.[14]

To no one's surprise, membership in the state system did not offer an immediate solution to the university's financial woes. Although at the beginning of the decade the Carnegie Commission on Higher Education indicated that Louisville and Jefferson County suffered a deficiency of higher educational opportunities, other universities in the state system were determined not to sacrifice their budgets for the University of Louisville. One state university administrator wrote that the University of Louisville re-

William Ferdinand Ekstrom (1912–), acting president, University of Louisville, 1972–1973 and 1980–1981, is shown at the dedication of the Ekstrom Library in 1981.

minded him of "the big, black grackle" that had invaded his backyard and wanted all the birdseed for himself. For their part, U of L officials contended that other members of the state system were determined to relegate their university to as small a role as possible, without due recognition of its established graduate and professional programs. At least one U of L faculty member abhorred the very idea of "being under the boot of some cloddish Kentucky gook in Frankfort" and vowed to resign.[15]

By 1973 the total years of service to the University of Louisville provided by Davidson, Strickler, and Ekstrom approached eighty. The twenty-three year era they oversaw from the institution's central administrative offices was associated with the modernizing and strengthening of academic programs and the coming of more rigorous academic standards. It also evoked, in the minds of many who looked back to the 1950s and 1960s from the vantage point of later years, the mostly happy memories associated with the paternalistic leadership of a smaller, more cozy, semi-private university.

Having come through a period of some student unrest, the University of Louisville entered the 1970s somewhat unsure of its new position in the state system of higher education. The next decade would be one of the more dramatic, and in some ways eventful, periods in its history.

SEVENTEEN

GROWING PAINS

UNIVERSITY OF LOUISVILLE officials knew their choice of a successor to Woodrow Strickler, who had been at the school since 1938, would be crucial to the institution's future. It was clear the trustees thought it best to look outside the university, probably outside the state, and surely outside the Kentucky political arena for a new president. They announced their selection in February 1973.[1]

James Grier Miller came to the university with a distinguished scholarly background and a notable record as an academic administrator. Having taken four degrees at Harvard University (A.B., M.A., M.D., and Ph.D.), at the age of thirty-two he was named head of the Department of Psychology at the University of Chicago. In 1955, when Miller was thirty-nine, he became professor of psychiatry and director of the Mental Health Research Institute at the University of Michigan. In 1967 he was appointed vice president for academic affairs, and later provost, at Cleveland State University.

Miller began his day-to-day work at the university in September 1973 and was the subject of an "Introduction to the Community" ceremony on campus in October. Shortly after that inauguration, former president Philip G. Davidson declared that the new chief was a man of "first class intellect" and "blunt impatience" who would "really shake" the University of Louisville. Miller, who may have been regarded by some as an abrupt change from two de-

cades of avuncular leadership, wisely appointed William F. Ekstrom as his executive vice president.[2]

During the Miller administration, the University of Louisville's state appropriation increased by more than four hundred percent, from $16.7 million in 1973-1974 to $68.2 million in 1980-1981. Edwin G. Middleton, a prominent local leader and former chairman of the board of trustees, believed Miller guided the school through a difficult period during which it made "more progress than any comparable university in the country." Former governor Bert T. Combs also praised Miller's performance, noting that he "handled himself very well" in the difficult negotiations for state dollars. Ekstrom later recalled that his former boss enjoyed an excellent working relationship with Julian Carroll, governor from late 1974 through late 1979, which accounted, in part, for the university's financial success. Of course, other schools argued that every dollar going to the University of Louisville came out of their pockets.[3]

Miller's success in winning a larger share of the state budget was nowhere better illustrated than in the fire he drew from opponents. In fact, rivalries within the state system of higher education caused some of the commonwealth's most spirited political debates of the mid-1970s. Miller and University of Kentucky president Otis A. Singletary became central figures in the fracas, primarily because their schools had the most comprehensive graduate and professional programs in the state and, therefore, the

James Grier Miller (1916–), fourteenth president, University of Louisville, 1973–1980. Both a psychologist and a psychiatrist, Miller was author or co-author of 140 articles and nine books, including the 1102–page Living Systems, *published by McGraw-Hill during his tenure at the university. Miller was a founder and first head of EDUCOM. For seventeen years he served as editor of the journal* Behavioral Science. *In 1995 the James Grier and Jessie Louise Miller Information Technology Center was named in the Millers' honor.*

most to gain or lose. Singletary contended that the state had the money to build only "one REAL university" and that one should be the University of Kentucky, the senior member of the state system of higher education. He also argued that the University of Louisville should be stripped of doctoral offerings that duplicated those at UK. Miller replied that the same programs at different schools should be funded equally, and argued that the state needed more rather than fewer intellectual leaders trained at the doctoral level. At one point, the *Louisville Times* complained that the battle between the two universities had become "bloodier than the siege of Leningrad."[4]

The debate peaked in 1977 when the Council on Higher Education approved mission statements for all of the state's universities. These documents recognized the University of Kentucky as "the" major state university, with broad responsibilities for professional programs, graduate education, and research. Louisville was deemed "a" major state university, sharing with UK statewide responsibilities in medical, dental, and legal education, and having a special mission in urban affairs. Although mission statements assumed the need for coordination and cooperation between the two schools, throughout the decade both adhered to self-serving arguments, each accusing the other of playing politics.[5]

In order to differentiate itself from the University of Kentucky and to carve out its own niche in the state's higher education realm, the University of Louisville began especially to underscore its urban mission, both in Kentucky's largest city and throughout the commonwealth. This emphasis did not spring forth full blown in the mid-1970s, however. In 1966 Davidson and the board of trustees had established the Urban Studies Center (USC) "to develop ways by which the University can be of greater service to the community" through interdisciplinary research and services. Joseph F. Maloney, a political scientist, was brought from Massachusetts to direct the center, which was funded chiefly through contracts and grants from private and governmental agencies.[6]

In the fall of 1968 the Urban Studies Center launched a two-year master of science degree in community development via the graduate school. That program stressed the need for finding solutions to problems of contemporary urban life. The next year J. Douglas Nunn, urban affairs editor for the *Courier-Journal*, became Maloney's assistant, and the center moved to Gardencourt, ironically a sylvan setting in the city's eastern suburbs. In 1971 the Institute of Community Development (ICD) began as an outgrowth of the USC to house the degree program. The ICD and the USC soon separated, with Nunn as director of USC and Maloney of ICD, which moved from Gardencourt to the Belknap Campus.[7]

Throughout the decade the university highlighted the work of these divisions. The Urban Stud-

John Houchens, longtime registrar, near the pendulum in the rotunda of the Administration Building in 1978. (Louisville Courier-Journal.)

ies Center focused on the impact of rural migration to the cities, conducted public opinion surveys, studied housing and social service needs, and estimated population changes. In 1980 it helped create the Kentucky State Data Center (KSDC) which, with state and federal support, became the common-wealth's official clearinghouse for U.S. Census data. Meanwhile the Institute of Community Development's graduate program was experiencing rapid growth. Beginning in 1987, the center housed the editorial offices of the *Journal of Urban Affairs*.[8]

Closely tied to increased funding was the unprecedented expansion of physical facilities that took place during Miller's "bricks and mortar" presidency. Major construction projects were begun, new land acquired, and older buildings remodeled. At the same time, most of the Belknap Campus was placed on the National Register of Historic Places. An especially pleasing addition to the Administration Building, whose rotunda was opened up to resemble more closely its original design, was a seventy-three-foot-long Foucault pendulum, which captivated visitors. The idea for the pendulum came from academic affairs vice president John A. Dillon and retired registrar John M. Houchens. The apparatus itself was designed, created, and installed in the late 1970s by retired U of L mathematician Walter Lee Moore and physicist Roger E. Mills, with assistance from Speed School electrical engineering faculty and students, facilities management and physical plant department staff, and others.[9]

More than once, however, local interest in the preservation of historic buildings clashed with the university's intentions for campus development. The most publicized case came as the university planned a new library on the site of the Playhouse, the nineteenth-century frame building that had served the school for over half a century as a theater and concert hall. In 1977 the Playhouse was dismantled and three years later reconstructed on another site, but to some critics this apparently casual willingness to demolish the structure was evidence that the university had grown increasingly impersonal. William Morgan, a professor in the fine arts department and architecture critic for the *Courier-Journal*, complained that too few of the many new buildings possessed genuine architectural distinction and that some looked as if they belonged in a suburban office park.[10]

Belknap Campus expansion also brought complaints from neighboring business establishments, which were sometimes forced to sacrifice their locations to the university's plans for development. At the same time, Norbert F. Elbert, the school's vice president for financial affairs, who had several decades of experience in campus development at U of L, believed that membership in the state system, because of inefficiency, patronage, or other factors, caused the cost of new buildings to jump by at least one third.[11]

One of the most interesting buildings added during this period was the Ecumenical Center, located to the east of the Life Sciences Building. Aris-

ing out of discussions occurring late in the Davidson administration, this structure was funded through the cooperative efforts of area Protestant, Roman Catholic, and Jewish organizations and was completed in 1974. It sponsored various student activities and housed the offices of the United Campus Ministry, the Newman Center, and Hillel. In 1991 it was renamed the Interfaith Center. Shortly after that structure was dedicated, the Baptist Center, located just north of it, was completed. It was financed by the Southern Baptist Convention.[12]

One can cite other examples of the university's more human face during this period. After Miller found himself wading ankle deep in rainwater covering low-lying campus walkways, he made long-needed drainage improvements and built new sidewalks. And although the new library building project displaced the Playhouse, it was designed with a concave section

The designers of the Ekstrom Library, opened in 1981, spared the huge tulip poplar on the building's west side.

to accommodate the massive tulip poplar at the structure's west face. That tree was identified as perhaps Belknap Campus's oldest by Louis F. Muller, superintendent of grounds. For nearly three decades Muller, who earned his bachelor's degree in horticulture from the University of Kentucky, took special pride in the campus's landscape, multiplied its flowerbeds, and added many varieties of shrubs and trees to an already park-like setting.[13]

Among the major facility problems successfully addressed by Miller were those related to the education and music divisions. From its beginning in 1907 the liberal arts college had offered education courses to U of L students interested in teaching as a career. From 1914 until 1935 those who wished to teach at the elementary school level could attend the college for two years. After working two additional years in the programs offered by the Louisville Normal School, which was administered by the city board of education, they could receive their bachelor of science degrees in education from the University of Louisville. Secondary education majors took all their work in the college.

In 1930 Julius J. Oppenheimer had become both head of the education department and dean of the liberal arts college. Serving for the next thirty years as department head and twenty-seven years as dean, Oppenheimer oversaw the gradual growth of the department and nurtured its students' grounding in the liberal arts. He also questioned the need for the city's normal school, which closed in 1935. In 1960 Frank Stallings succeeded Oppenheimer as department head and managed the unit's transition, begun under President Davidson, as it achieved the status of a separate school in 1968. That year F. Randall Powers was appointed first dean of the School of Education. In the first year of his administration the school's faculty grew from fifteen to twenty-four, and by 1978, when Powers retired, the number had increased to sixty-four with the help of federal grants and new state dollars following the university's entrance into the state system. By that time planning for the school's new $4.5 million building had begun. Heretofore scattered among a half dozen buildings, education faculty and programs would soon be brought to-

gether. Ground was broken in March 1979, a few months after Raphael O. Nystrand succeeded Powers as dean.[14]

The School of Music had moved from Belknap Campus to Gardencourt in 1947. A beautiful estate with an elegant Georgian mansion and gardens located five miles east of the campus overlooking Cherokee Park, Gardencourt had just been bequeathed to the university by Mattie Norton, who had lived there. While it provided an inspirational setting for music instruction, the forty-year-old building suffered from poor temperature and noise controls. More importantly, its remoteness was a hardship on students, who had to travel to Belknap for some of their classes. School officials tried to address this problem in part by holding some music classes in the Reynolds Building from 1963 until 1969. That facility at Third and Eastern Parkway, originally a Ford Motor Company plant, had been donated to the university by the Reynolds Aluminum Company. One observer described it as a large "dingy" building "ill-suited for student instruction or practice."[15]

The music school's facilities woes were a counterpoint to its successes in other areas. Dean Dwight Anderson, who had recruited a superb faculty, was succeeded in 1956 by Robert Whitney, conductor of the Louisville Orchestra. From 1956 until 1967 Whitney served simultaneously as dean of the music school and conductor of the orchestra. By 1956 the orchestra had become known internationally for its performing and recording contemporary compositions. Among the notable faculty members of the 1950s were violinist Sidney Harth and trumpeter Leon Rapier. By the late 1960s, however, facilities problems were threatening the school's accreditation. At one point a National Association of Schools of Music inspection team noted that "the School of Music exists under conditions that defy description, but which give indisputable proof of the quality of the instructional program."[16]

In 1969 the school left Gardencourt for the just-acquired Shelby Campus, solving one problem—the improved facilities resulted in re-accreditation—and making another even worse—distance. Eight years later Miller and the trustees secured approval for a new music school building on Belknap Campus. In 1980 under Dean Jerry Ball, who closely oversaw its design and construction, students and faculty moved into their new $9.75 million building, complete with the three-floor Dwight Anderson Memorial Library and an impressive main recital hall.[17]

Associated with the music school in the eyes of many in the community was WUOL, U of L's classical music radio station at 90.5 FM. With Miller's support, WUOL began broadcasting out of Strickler Hall on December 20, 1976, as the city's first stereo, full-power classical public radio station. From time to time it featured performances by pianist Lee Luvisi, soprano Edith Davis, violinist Peter McHugh and his accompanist Naomi Oliphant, and other U of L music school faculty members who have achieved national prominence.

By the mid-1970s, the only classical station in Louisville was WFPK 91.9 FM, which was low power, non-stereo, with only one day a week of totally new programming. The university station picked up where WFPK's previous competition, WHAS 97.5 FM, part of the Bingham media conglomerate, left off. WHAS had operated from 1966 through 1975 as a classical music station, then had moved to a more commercially profitable format of all news and information, and later to country music. WHAS gave its entire collection of records and tapes, along with its automated tape-playing system, to the new U of L station, along with a cash grant and rent-free space at its television tower for the transmitting equipment. The university also won a grant from the U.S. Department of Health, Education, and Welfare to purchase needed equipment.[18]

In 1995 WUOL added a new digital microwave system to link the studio to its new transmitter at Floyd Knob, Indiana. Two years earlier, WUOL had joined with the city's public library–sponsored stations, WFPL 89.3 FM and WFPK 91.9 FM, to form the Public Radio Partnership. WUOL continued as the partnership's classical music arm, while WFPL offered news and information and WFPK provided jazz and alternative music.[19]

Also during this era the expansion of the Health Sciences Center included the revival of the School of Nursing. The University of Louisville had first established a nursing school in 1952. Its 1952-1953 *Bulletin*, published in March 1952, described a four-year program of courses leading to the B.S. degree in nursing. The names of seventeen faculty members were listed, including Anne D. Taylor, dean and professor of nursing. The new school, which had been authorized by the board of trustees on February 29, 1952, opened in September of that year, under an arrangement wherein the city-county board of health agreed to absorb any financial losses to the university. Only eight freshmen students enrolled that fall, however, and the board of health could not promise to sustain its support.[20]

While President Philip G. Davidson and officials of the School of Medicine urged the school's survival, the U of L board was unwilling to continue the school if a deficit appeared likely. The board disestablished the school effective July 1, 1953. Apparently no other bulletins were issued and no degrees were awarded.[21]

Over a quarter of a century later, in 1979, the university created the present School of Nursing. It was an outgrowth of a two-year nursing program begun in 1974 and housed in the medical school. In 1975 it had been expanded to a four-year curriculum. The new school offered the B.S. and M.S. in nursing degrees, both of which were accredited by the National League for Nursing, as well as the two-year associate degree.[22]

Despite solid achievements in state funding and physical expansion, Miller's administration suffered from an unsettling degree of internal criticism. Attacks were particularly strong from his academic deans, who resented the president's tendency to bypass middle management and what they saw as his failure to delegate authority appropriately. They also believed he relied too heavily on administrative theories. This internal discord became public in the summer of 1976, when a confidential report was leaked to the press. Twelve of thirteen deans approved the document, which faulted the president for failure to delegate authority outside the central administration, not consulting with academic deans during budget preparation, and interference with issues beyond his immediate jurisdiction. While they were sometimes critical of the president's administrative style, Arts and Sciences Dean A. Joseph Slavin and Academic Vice President John A. Dillon both insisted that Miller possessed a worthy vision of what a true university should be and the will to strive toward that goal.[23]

Most of Miller's critics undoubtedly had the University of Louisville's best interests at heart, but Alan A. Johnson's attacks upon the administration assumed an extremely bitter tone. Called to the deanship of the Graduate School in 1975, Johnson was dismissed from that position the following year, shortly after the deans' confidential report on President Miller's administrative style was made public. By this time Johnson was also embroiled in the defense of a doctoral student in psychology who had been dismissed from the degree program, allegedly because he was not suited for clinical work. This crusade pitted Johnson not only against the Department of Psychology, but also against his superiors in the administration, who had upheld the department's decision.

Eventually, Johnson sued the university on a variety of counts, including the charge that he had been falsely enticed to the position of Graduate School dean, which he said lacked any real authority. In connection with his legal actions, the former dean tested, again and again, the university's compliance with the Kentucky Open Records Act, a law governing access to public documents. He also issued a series of memoranda to the faculty senate and the graduate faculty, calling for votes of no confidence upon various administrators, claiming to be "the rightful dean" of the Graduate School, and even offering to "move in as president and restructure the administration." Eventually the former dean's suit was thrown out of court. Johnson was assessed costs, and the court indicated it was not prepared to entertain any further litigation concerning his deanship.[24]

The mid-1970s was also a period of faculty discontent, much of which focused on the university's leadership. The faculty, like the deans, saw an erosion of academic influence in running the university. Some complained that the school was top heavy with over-

In 1976 Mary K. Tachau, professor of history, was sworn in to begin the first of two terms as faculty representative to the U of L board of trustees, becoming only the second woman trustee in U of L history. She was also the first female to serve as university ombudsman, as chair of the history department, and as chair of the faculty senate. An authority on the U.S. Constitution, Tachau served as historical advisor to the Select Committee on Presidential Campaign Activities (the Watergate Committee).

paid administrators, while faculty salaries remained low. At one point, officials from the local chapter of the American Association of University Professors reported strong sentiment for unionization. According to an outgoing chair of the faculty senate, Professor Mary K. Tachau, the university's board of trustees had too little appreciation for the academic purpose of the institution and too much regard for the business end of its operation. Most of the trustees' university associations were with administrators absorbed in the day-to-day operation of the institution. Tachau complained that the board usually heard from the faculty only during grievances, law suits, and other instances when standard procedures had broken down.[25]

Tachau also found the title "chairman" an uncomfortable fit. A few years after she joined the faculty in the early 1960s, the title of department "head" began to give way to department "chairman," especially in the College of Arts and Sciences, where the dean began to confirm such an appointment only after an election by the department's faculty members. Then as women began occupying more U of L leadership positions amidst the feminist movement of the 1970s, the title gradually was termed "chairperson" or just "chair," which Tachau and others preferred over the more cumbersome "chairwoman."

The staff was no less assertive than the faculty. Staff members formed their own senate, criticized the employee benefits program, and warned administrators not to call them "non-academic personnel." A survey in the mid-1970s found that half the staff who responded favored some form of unionization, slightly more than half claimed morale was low, and two-thirds believed they had suffered a loss in real wages during recent years. Around the same time, the university adopted a system of "point factor analysis," which some critics considered a white-collar form of the time and motion studies used to rate assembly line workers. Even the head of the Affirmative Action office complained her duties only multiplied the red tape. Despite the university's efforts to place more minority applicants in better jobs, a local newspaper noted blacks still held a disproportionate share of menial positions at the school.[26]

President Miller also had to contend with disagreements at the Health Sciences Center. The center had grown rapidly during the 1970s, in part through the efforts of Harold E. Boyer, a persuasive, dedicated, and effective administrator who had originally come to the university as a member of the dental school faculty. In 1972, the year before Miller's arrival, Boyer had become vice president for health

affairs. Boyer controlled more than half of the university's budget and oversaw a campus that not only was physically separate from other branches of the institution, but historically also had enjoyed a large degree of autonomy. Boyer wanted more independence than Miller, who was ultimately responsible for the university's efforts in the health field, was willing to allow, leading to conflicts between the two. Further exacerbating this situation, Boyer and Dean Arthur H. Keeney of the medical school failed to mesh. Keeney believed Boyer's background in dentistry did not qualify him to oversee a medical school. He also contended his school suffered under Boyer's view of coordinated health care, which emphasized a "team" approach among physicians, dentists, nurses, and technicians. Keeney, a native Louisvillian who commanded wide respect in the medical community, was not opposed to cooperation, but believed patient welfare was ultimately the physician's responsibility. Despite such controversies, which were not uncommon in medical schools elsewhere in the nation, the U of L School of Medicine maintained a respectable national ranking. One report placed it forty-second out of 121 medical schools in the United States.[27]

The School of Law was somewhat weaker than its counterpart in medicine. The same report ranked it eighty-ninth out of 166 law schools in the nation. During the early 1970s, a local study criticized the school for poor facilities and relatively low faculty salaries, but still called it "alive and well." By the end of the period, the school's space problems had been lessened by the addition of new classrooms, offices, and library facilities.

To law students, the final measure of the school's quality was their success on the bar examination. One year, when an unusually high number failed the test, the administration initiated a study which found that students who held jobs while in school, often as law clerks with local firms, performed better than those who supposedly devoted full time to their studies. One official also cited poor writing as a reason why some students failed to gain admission to the bar. Nationally, critics of the bar examination charged that, while it tested memory, it did little to measure an aspiring attorney's ability to interview clients, conduct legal research, or perform in court. The examination's most severe critics contended that it was merely a cynical means to limit entrance into an overcrowded profession.[28]

In the late twentieth century the law school boasted that it was the nation's fifth oldest in continuous operation. Prior to the opening of the University of Kentucky law school in 1908, it had long outlived virtually all of its rivals in the city and the state. Its most serious competitor was the Jefferson School of Law. Unable to meet stiffer national requirements in legal education, which called for day classes, a full-time faculty, and adequate physical facilities and library holdings, this proprietary school merged with the U of L law school in 1950.[29]

The university absorbed Jefferson's 1,513 graduates, including such luminaries as Wilson Wyatt (c. 1927) and Carl Perkins (c. 1935), both of whom played important roles on the state and national scenes, into its alumni organization. These and other graduates embodied a statement from the school's namesake appearing in the front of each year's bulletin: "The study of law qualifies a man to be useful to himself, to his neighbors, and to the public." Many accepted U of L's offer of diplomas reporting their graduation from the U of L School of Law. Thereafter the school began offering evening law classes, as the Jefferson school had done since its founding forty-five years earlier. The school granted its first J.D. (Juris Doctor) degree in June 1966, thereby joining many other law schools in replacing the LL.B.[30]

Among other changes and additions to the law school during the second half of the twentieth century was the publication of the *Law Review*, begun in 1961 and later renamed the *Journal of Family Law*. In 1971 the *Journal of Law and Education* appeared, in collaboration with the University of South Carolina's law school. The *Louisville Law Examiner*, now named the *Brandeis Brief*, was first published in 1974, the same year a new library wing was completed. A new classroom wing was added in 1982.

A major contribution to the academic life of the university of Louisville came in 1981 with the completion of another new building, the William F. Ekstrom

Library. At the same time, however, the university still ranked near the bottom of the Association of Southeastern Research Libraries in the number of volumes and periodical titles per student. For much of the period, the library system also suffered from a lack of central authority. One study found too little coordination in acquisitions, cataloging, and other areas, a problem which was created by the autonomy of various special libraries scattered around the campuses. Eventually, with Miller's support, the system was consolidated under one administrative head, which promised greater efficiency but threatened the close relationship professional school librarians had developed with the divisions they served.[31]

John Demos, who headed the library system during this period, contended that librarians at the University of Louisville enjoyed more respect than many of their counterparts at other universities. He attributed this to the awarding of faculty status to professional librarians, thus giving them an active role in university governance. He believed that academic librarians could further enhance their status by keeping more abreast of cultural, scientific, social, and other developments.[32]

In the 1970s a growing strength in archival, manuscript, and rare book resources enhanced the library system's research value and gave the general collection a unique personality. This development also added to the stature of the university as a research institution. Some of these major holdings included the magnificent Farm Security Administration photographs from the 1930s; the archives of the Louisville & Nashville Railroad, which had been a strong political and economic force in the South and Midwest since before the Civil War; the papers of Supreme Court Justice Louis D. Brandeis and of several prominent Kentucky political figures, such as Senator Mitch McConnell and Romano Mazzoli, twelve-term member of the U.S. House of Representatives (1971-1995); a splendid collection of material on the golden age of Irish literature; valuable holdings on the history of American medical education and practice during the nineteenth and early twentieth centuries; the archives of the Louisville Orchestra; a series of photographs commissioned by the Standard Oil Com-

Three of the main library's facilities through the years: the Administration Building, the building now called Schneider Hall, and the Ekstrom Library.

pany to document American life during the late 1940s; an African American book collection and manuscript resources of Kentucky's major ethnic minority; and an outstanding collection of material on the career of novelist Edgar Rice Burroughs, the creator of Tarzan.

The presence of nationally significant historical materials helped channel the work of the Oral History Center, which began in 1968. Within three decades thirteen hundred tape-recorded iterviews supplemented the written records. These developments constituted a belated acknowledgment of the wisdom of Justice Brandeis, who, over fifty years earlier, had encouraged school officials to collect the primary resource documents that would support significant original research by scholars at the University of Louisville and elsewhere in the humanities and social sciences.[33]

The Miller years were marked by an increased emphasis on research, publication, and other forms of creative activity in virtually all academic areas at the University of Louisville. In his 1978 and 1979 annual reports, the president recognized a number of senior and junior faculty members who had made welcome contributions to their fields. Their works ranged from subjects that must have seemed esoteric to the layman to topics that had an obvious impact on daily life. The university's scientists had made advances in environmental engineering, fetal blood transfusion, microsurgery, cancer research, and the tracing of the relationship between physical and mental illness. Researchers in the Louisville Twin Study, reportedly the world's oldest such investigation, continued to make contributions comparing the effects of genetics and the environment on human behavior. Other scholars produced books, articles, and professional papers on criminal justice, labor arbitration, and the preservation of ancient stone monuments. Potters, concert pianists, historians, and astronomers at the University of Louisville had all achieved recognition for their work.

Under Dean A. Joseph Slavin, the College of Arts and Sciences upgraded its requirements for promotion and tenure, although some charged that the university callously applied the principle of "publish

U of L "streakers" posed on the tops of cars, scaled Unitas Tower, and, here, performed wheelies on motorcycles.

or perish" without regard for the faculty members who had been hired before its adoption. Slavin, who had sometimes been critical of the Miller administration, conceded that the president lent a sympathetic ear to proposals for hiring senior scholars to serve as leaders in growing departments.[34]

The University of Louisville entered the 1970s riding the crest of student activism from the previous decade, but before long the earlier spirit waned and then disappeared. An editorial in the student newspaper attributed the growing mood of campus conservatism to an increased anxiety over employment opportunities and disillusionment with plans for perfecting the human condition. On the national level, even friends of the New Left student movement admitted that the earlier years of "hope, expectancy, and change" were forgotten, at least for the time being. Some observers considered the 1974 "streaking" fad an outgrowth of the free-spirited counterculture of the 1960s, but one local psychiatrist believed the University of Louisville's nude runners had more in common with the goldfish swallowers and telephone booth stuffers of an earlier era. In 1977, when Iranian students at the University of Louisville

Students created a highly visible protest against the Shah of Iran in 1977 outside the Humanities Building.

demonstrated against the repressive regime of Shah Mohammad Reza Pahlavi, they met outright hostility from their American counterparts, who only a decade before were attacking United States imperialism in the Third World. By the late 1970s, one study found that entering freshmen at the University of Louisville leaned more toward the political right than the average first-year college student in the United States. Well over one-third of the same group considered themselves "born again Christians."[35]

True to its heritage, however, the student newspaper managed to raise hackles on campus during the late 1970s. The *Cardinal*'s April Fool issue in 1977 startled the university community with its realistic announcement of the death of President James Grier Miller. Two years later the paper's joke issue created an uproar by reporting the outbreak of World War III, displaying a photograph supposedly portraying diplomats as nudists frolicking on a beach, and splash-

ing its headlines with four-letter words. The issue lambasted university police, student government leaders, and some faculty and administrators, among others. An advertisement promised a free chicken dinner for each "proof-of-voting seal" for John Y. Brown, a gubernatorial candidate who had made his fortune as head of the Kentucky Fried Chicken Corporation. After *Cardinal* editors Thomas Murray III and Donald Floyd Jr. were fired, they sued for reinstatement and received partial vindication in court. Several school officials then helped the newspaper establish itself as a nonprofit corporation separate from the university, supported by grants from U of L endowment funds. This separation of the *Cardinal* from the university administration helped ease tensions between the two. For whatever reason, the newspaper's resulting independence marked the beginning of a long period of relative calm in campus journalism.[36]

After the election of Ronald Reagan as president of the United States in 1980, a student publication with financial backing from a national conservative political organization appeared on campus. The editors of the *Louisville Scholar* endorsed the philosophy of the former movie star and California governor: increased defense spending, cutbacks in social welfare programs, and tax policies that seemed to favor the relatively well-to-do. They sought to model their journalistic efforts after conservative pundit William F. Buckley Jr., and in 1983 they chose Phyllis Schlafly as Woman of the Year for her work in defeating the proposed Equal Rights Amendment to the U.S. Constitution. One faculty critic of the *Scholar* accused the staff of employing character assassination, innuendo, and guilt by association. The editor replied that other Communists had made similar accusations about his newspaper.[37]

One characteristic of U of L students changed little during the decade: the majority (82 percent in 1979) were residents of Louisville and Jefferson County. According to a popular guide to student life in American colleges and universities, the large U of L commuter population made the school a dull place to spend one's undergraduate days. At the same time, however, the university stepped up its efforts to make the campus an interesting place for activities outside

The Black Diamond Choir was organized in 1969 by students Beatrice Brown and Joetta Harrington to promote fellowship and the value of cultural diversity. In the almost thirty years of its existence the choir has sung at churches all around Kentucky; gone to national festivals; participated in countless community civic and cultural events; performed with such noted individuals as Jessye Norman, Charlton Heston, and Lily Tomlin; sponsored an outreach project to serve the needy; appeared on local television; and made recordings.

the classroom. In 1976 the school's first vice president for student affairs, Edward H. Hammond, entered the office with the promise to develop "a highly coordinated delivery system" for student services. Meanwhile, by the end of the decade, lower tuition rates had more than doubled U of L's enrollment from the 9,668 students who had matriculated in the fall of 1970, the university's first semester in the state system of higher education. The student body now included a higher proportion of blacks (9.4 percent in 1976) than most universities in the state system, but these minority students also suffered from a relatively high attrition rate. Thirty years after desegregation, observers noted that black and white students still often kept to themselves at the University of Louisville.[38]

U of L's main student yearbook, which began soon after the revival of the liberal arts college early in the century and had appeared more or less continually for decades, was published only sporadically in the 1970s. By 1984 it was gone. Under several names, however, the yearbook provided generations of students with a record of their time on campus. Many issues were ordinary, some were remarkable, all were memorable.

The first of these reminiscences of school years past was called the *Colonel*, published from 1909 through 1912. In 1922 and 1923 the annuals came out under the name *Kentucky Cardinal* and were special issues of a student literary magazine. From 1924 through 1972, the yearbook was known as the *Thoroughbred*. No issues were published in 1932, 1934-1938, 1943, 1945-1946, or 1970-1971. During and just after World War II, much smaller alternative annuals appeared: the *Key*, issued by the "war babies" of 1943 who saw classmates leave for the armed forces, and *Class Cards* in 1946. In 1970 and 1971, the *Thoroughbred Magazine*, full of campus news articles, short stories, plays, poems, and photographic essays, as well as senior pictures, was published in six issues in lieu of the *Thoroughbred*. In 1974 and for the two years following, the yearbook was called *Deja-Vu*. The name was changed to *Minerva* in 1979; it last appeared in 1982. No yearbook appeared in 1973, 1977-1978, or 1981. In 1983 a slim publication, *Bird's Eye View*, ended this phase of the annual, which for seventy-five years had portrayed campus life at the University of Louisville.[39]

During some years the main yearbook's studio portraits of students included those enrolled in the

Ruth Wilson Cogshall prepared this 1925 cover of the Satyr, *a U of L student literary magazine that succeeded the* Kentucky Cardinal *magazine.*

medical, law, and other schools. At other times some of these schools published their own annuals, often light-hearted and cleverly titled. The 1919 dental school yearbook was *The Plugger*. Its 1968 and 1969 versions were called *The Remake*. Later, seemingly inevitably, it became *Impressions*. Taken together, U of L's yearbooks provide an important pictorial chronicle of U of L social clubs, honorary and religious societies, musical and dramatic performances, intramural and intercollegiate sports, and other activities. In some years, the turbulence of the times comes through. In others, campus life appears serene. Virtually all the yearbooks succeed in drawing alumni memories back to important watershed eras of their own lives as students at the University of Louisville.[40]

A hallmark of one's college life, and an activity often pictured in yearbooks, is the time spent at tables with friends, food, and drink, whether on campus or adjacent to it. Throughout its history, the Belknap Campus has attracted only a few student hangouts to its periphery. For years the Masterson family operated a popular restaurant and bar on Third Street north of the Confederate Monument. Opening in the mid-1940s as the Hollywood Steak House, it was renamed Masterson's in 1962. Although Masterson's did offer meal plans to students and was open all night, seldom did it raise (or perhaps lower) itself to the status of a typical student eatery.

One alternative near-campus dining spot was The Scene, a coffeehouse located on Barbee Street, about where the Interfaith Center now stands. Run by Stuart Jay and Wendell Cherry, The Scene was billed as a place where students could meet, sip coffee, and listen to music. Another hangout, The Cellar, at Third and Brandeis Streets, advertised dinner and dancing in a "pleasant European atmosphere."[41]

For many years after its opening in the mid-1920s the Cardinal Inn, at First and Shipp Streets, was probably the area's best remembered off-campus student gathering spot. When its building was demolished in 1967, to make way for the construction of the Humanities Building, its owners, the George brothers, reopened in an unpretentious structure on Brook Street. There from early morning until night its popular steam table drew students to its Lebanese and American specials. At the same time its back hallway pay telephones sometimes found students and faculty busily, if not somewhat furtively, placing their bets on the day's sporting events at Churchill Downs and elsewhere. In the face of further campus expansion, the Cardinal Inn closed in 1978.

Campus expansion had also threatened the existence of the Red Barn, located across the street from the Cardinal Inn. For decades this large brick building had served as a metal fabrication and welding shop for the Caldwell Tank Company, but that property was acquired by the university through urban renewal in 1969 and the structure was scheduled for eventual destruction. Its five thousand square feet of floor space proved enticing to a group of enterprising students, however. Louis Bornwasser and others begged a small amount of money from the university and turned a drafty, leaky building into a passable concert hall, dance hall, and movie theater. A few U of L officials, notably newly arrived student activities head George Howe and housing director Harold Adams, encouraged these efforts. The campus had never seen anything quite like it. A few years later the Miller administration responded to a "Save the Red Barn" campaign by approving a $500,000 renovation. This added a new stage, new lighting and sound equipment, a new roof, and even an addition to house the student activities office.[42]

Before long the Red Barn began providing an outlet for student causes, and at the same time developing a reputation for quirky fun. Comedian and social activist Dick Gregory spoke there, and benefit performances were held for environmental campaigns marked by such slogans as "Save the Gorge" and "Fight Marble Hill." In April 1970 attorney William Kunstler was scheduled to speak. A year earlier he had gained notoriety with his courtroom defense of the "Chicago Seven," leaders of demonstrations held at the 1968 Democratic national convention. On the day before Kunstler's appearance the city fire marshal made an unexpected visit, found the building one exit short of acceptable, and forbade the students to use the facility. A maintenance crew worked around the clock to frame a new doorway, breaking through three layers of brick in the process. University administrators may not have been enamored of Kunstler, but they liked censorship even less. During his address to a full house, a bomb threat forced the evacuation of the building. After a search found nothing amiss, eleven hundred students, reportedly nearly twice as many as were there earlier, "filed back in" or watched through the open doors.[43]

At one of the Red Barn's traditional "Derby Eve" parties, in 1980, ABC television broadcast "Friday Night Live from the Kentucky Derby," which was staged at the facility. Singer Dan Fogelberg premiered his hit song "Run for the Roses," and the program featured interviews with members of U of L's NCAA champion basketball team. Actor and horseman Jack Klugman was wedged into the audience, and at one point he reacted to the noise, the crowds, and the stifling heat by looking into the camera and declar-

ing, "If my horse wins the Derby, I'm going to buy this garage and then I'm going to burn it to the ground." The students booed him roundly and commemorated the event by dedicating the Red Barn's bathrooms to "Jack" and his horse "Jaklin."[44]

By the mid-1970s at least one University of Louisville division had developed an especially broad appeal to many students, both black and white, young and old. This was the unit known as University College, which offered late afternoon, evening, and weekend classes taught by both full-time U of L professors and part-time instructors. In 1972 it began to offer its own degrees. Persons unable to attend U of L classes offered through the College of Arts and Sciences and some other units during the daytime, Monday through Friday, could attend a broad range of course offerings at other times. Over the years thousands of Louisvillians, most of them attending the university as "part-time" students, received associate's or bachelor's degrees through University College.[45]

"UC," as it was universally called, also offered scores of noncredit courses in such diverse areas as wine-tasting, speed-reading, calligraphy, and hot air ballooning, and continuing education courses in real estate, computer languages, and many other fields. For two decades it was overseen by Dean William Huffman, who in 1957 had shepherded its transition from its earlier incarnation, the Division of Adult Education, which had been established in 1935.[46]

As tuition fees decreased following state affiliation, UC enrollments increased. Soon, in sheer numbers, it was rivaling the College of Arts and Sciences as U of L's largest academic division. As University College became U of L's "open enrollment" unit, students unable to meet the criteria necessary for admission to another undergraduate school also found UC more inviting. In 1974 Wendell G. Rayburn became dean, the first African American to head a U of L school or college. In 1975 University College established the West Louisville Educational Program (WLEP). Designed to appeal especially to academically underprepared students from Louisville's black community, the program's services were made available to all students.[47]

In the mid-1970s, under the auspices of University College, the university began offering classes at Fort Knox, located thirty-seven miles south of Louisville. Soldiers and civilians in the area of the military base could take arts and sciences, business, education, and other courses at what became known as the Fort Knox Center. In a similar fashion, workers in the city's central business district could attend classes offered at U of L's Downtown Center at Fifth and Muhammad Ali Boulevard. This experiment, begun in 1985, lasted just under three years, but the Fort Knox Center remained strong.[48]

Just as U of L's student body was beginning a period of rapid growth in numbers, the school achieved a few fleeting moments of gridiron glory under Coach Lee Corso, who from 1969 through 1972 compiled a record of twenty-eight wins, eleven losses, and three ties; won two conference championships; and brought the Cardinals into the upper levels of the national standings. His 1972 squad finished eighteenth in the final Associated Press poll. Fans liked the coach almost as much for his flamboyance as for his winning record. In 1970, for example, Corso revealed a plan to stop Long Beach State star Leon "Superman" Burns in the Pasadena Bowl. The coach boarded the plane for California with a box supposedly containing the mythical element kryptonite, which in comic book fiction had been the nemesis of "the Man of Steel." The game ended in a 24-24 tie.

After Corso's departure to become head coach at Indiana University, the Louisville team slipped back into the doldrums. One local sportswriter complained that in trying to establish a big-time program the university merely played strong opponents and chalked up embarrassing losses. Amid faculty cries to abolish the sport, President James G. Miller warned that such a course might cost the university more in public favor and alumni support than could be gained by eliminating the program.[49]

What the Cardinals lacked in gridiron prowess was more than regained on the hardwood. During his first nine seasons, from 1971-1972 through 1979-1980, Coach Denzel "Denny" Crum led the team to a record of 219 wins and 56 losses. During this pe-

Lee Corso, head football coach from 1969 until 1972, led his last team to a number-eighteen ranking in the final AP poll.

riod, the Cardinals won more than twenty games each season; appeared twice in the National Invitational Tournament; took seven trips to the National Collegiate Athletic Association tournament; made three appearances in the Final Four of the NCAA; and won the NCAA title in 1980, with a squad led by senior guard Darrell Griffith, recruited from Louisville Male High School. When U of L added the 1980 NCAA basketball title to its 1948 NAIB and 1956 NIT crowns, it became the only school to have won all three national championships. The basketball team also continued to hold the NCAA record for consecutive winning seasons.[50]

Critics, meanwhile, posed vexing questions about the purpose of college athletics. One newspaper editorial charged that student athletes in major

Coach Denny Crum led the U of L basketball Cardinals to two NCAA championships, in 1980 and 1986, and in 1994 he was inducted into the Naismith Memorial Basketball Hall of Fame.

financial support for men's versus women's sports. Men's basketball, for example, generated large amounts of ticket and television revenue, while women's intercollegiate basketball, which had been re-established in 1975 after a nearly fifty-year absence, was not self-supporting. It grew in popularity, however, as did the women's volleyball program, begun in 1977. Gradually through the 1980s, the university added more women's sports and made other necessary adjustments.[52]

Although continuing disparities in the funding of men's and women's sports comprised a dilemma, much of the imbalance in gender equity, especially as it related to the number of women's intercollegiate sports and women participants therein, was eventually overcome. Overall, Hudson's complaint and similar pressures, as well as increased fan support, resulted in the placement of women's athletics on a better footing. In 1998 the university added three new women's sports teams (softball, golf, and rowing) to the existing nine (basketball, cross country, field hockey, soccer, swimming and diving, tennis, indoor track, outdoor track, and volleyball), for a total of twelve. This action equalized the numbers of men and women athletes. Still, these problems pointed to the truth of writings by social critics who charged that American sports had become a form of show business.[53]

men's sports, such as basketball, were exploited for their ability on the court, while relatively little concern was shown for their academic progress, provided they remained eligible to play. In 1980 another critic of the system, U of L's assistant athletic director for women's sports, Rebecca S. Hudson, filed a complaint with the U.S. Office of Civil Rights accusing the university of failure to comply with Title IX regulations requiring equal treatment for men and women athletes at schools receiving federal funds. Hudson acknowledged that strides had been made in equalizing financial support for men's and women's programs, but she feared that female athletes would suffer disproportionately in upcoming budget cuts.[51]

The solution to this problem was difficult because fans "voted with their feet" when it came to

When the university entered the state system it was operating under a set of internal rules that had changed little in more than four decades. The old McVey report, adopted in 1928, had given way to a 1936 "Organization" document that, like its predecessor, had a blue cover and was referred to as the "Bluebook." While this was by no means a carbon copy of the 1928 organization, it was laid out in similar fashion, so much so that it can be seen as an extension of the older document, not a thorough revision of it. The same was true of a 1956 revision, again with a blue cover, and a 1963 version, published with a red cover and subsequently referred to as the "Redbook." Even a 1971 printing, containing the appropriate language reflecting state affiliation, for the most part followed the structure of its predecessors. Soon, however, the university's new legal status and its unprecedented growth seemed to call for a substantive review of its bylaws as well. In 1976 the board established a committee to create a completely new governance document. The result was the *Redbook*, which was adopted by the board on October 17, 1977. Published in 1979, it underwent minor revisions over the next fifteen years. In the mid-1990s the paper copies gave way to an electronic version accessible via U of L's computer network.[54]

During the 1970s the University of Louisville assumed some of the trappings of a bureaucracy that had not been there before. To some extent, this was an inevitable by-product of both growth and burdensome red tape imposed by myriad state requirements new to the university. In any case, by the end of the period the school boasted a five-pound administrative handbook complete with an elaborate, fold-out organization chart festooned with lines and boxes. Much of the tome was filled with administrative memoranda, which covered everything from procedures for opening confidential mail to the university's "official abbreviation." (For a brief time Miller encouraged use of the abbreviation UL instead of U of L, and the local newspapers obliged, but tradition, euphony, and the objections of alumni could not be overcome. Soon the familiar U of L moniker was back in place.) The handbook contained more than its share of bureaucratic prose, including the description of the office providing "loss control services," entailing such tasks as "risk recognition." Another section of the handbook decried the school's lack of "a uniform image to present to the public," although some believed the administration already devoted too much attention to public relations.[55]

Ironically, even though the university spent more and more money interpreting its mission and services to the public, the 1970s was a time when the local press was filled with stories of internal squabbles at the University of Louisville, as well as accounts of a disturbing lack of common purpose within the state's system of higher education. The city's two daily newspapers, the *Courier-Journal* and the *Louisville Times*, for example, contained more negative coverage of the university than they had for decades. The university was receiving more public funds than it ever

The Courier-Journal's *publication of this photograph on page one was greeted with both grimaces and grins from the community and the university, and emulation from the tabloid* National Enquirer, *which also used it. Steven B. Bing, Vice President for University Relations, sat behind President James G. Miller, who was giving his State of the University Address in 1977.*

had before, making school officials increasingly accountable for their activities. At the same time, the post-Watergate era had produced a new breed of investigative reporters determined to expose corrupt or inept public officials.

To some old-timers, the 1970s brought into being a new, unfriendly institution, quite unlike the University of Louisville they had grown to know. William Furnish, who in the 1930s received his B.S. and M.D. degrees from the University of Louisville and for several decades taught in the Department of

Adele Brandeis is shown here on June 11, 1967, with President Philip Davidson and fellow board of trustees members Archibald Cochran and Baylor Landrum as they formally accepted the university mace, which would be carried for the first time in the commencement procession that day. Created by sculptor John Prangnell, assistant professor of fine arts, the mace has been at the head of all formal academic processions since that time. Brandeis, the first woman appointed to U of L's board, served from June 1949 until March 1970.

Biology, complained that by the mid-1970s the school lacked any sense of spontaneity. Faculty members no longer showed interest in the research of someone outside their department; busy scholars looked upon their dealings with students as burdensome chores; and a thicket of rules and regulations about promotion and tenure hampered creativity. Furnish believed that in theory the faculty had a stronger voice in university affairs, but noted that the cordial, informal relationship that once existed with the administration had been lost. He concluded, "I'm glad I'm not young anymore."[56]

Others disagreed. In a commencement address delivered shortly before his retirement, William F. Ekstrom succinctly expressed higher education's noblest goals. In clear and direct language, he told the graduates that a university should teach students to read, think, speak, and write critically and with discipline, imagination, and grace. Equipped with these tools, they were prepared to see life steadily and whole. Ekstrom, who throughout this tumultuous period remained widely respected, obviously believed that the University of Louisville was striving toward this end no less effectively than it had ever done.[57]

Miller retained the confidence of the board of trustees through the administration of Governor Julian Carroll. But the election of Governor John Y. Brown Jr. in November 1979 brought new board appointees who were less sympathetic to the president. Some of this change in feeling related to the building of the new University Hospital. In 1978 U of L had taken over the operation of the sixty-four-year-old Louisville General Hospital (in 1942 the name had been changed from Louisville City Hospital), and had initiated steps to replace it with a major new facility. In July of the next year the university assumed full ownership of Louisville General, renaming it University Hospital. Faced with soaring construction costs under Miller, the board "felt compelled to encourage his resignation." When Ekstrom once again became acting president in October 1980, he discovered to his "horror" that the hospital had become "a drain on the University's budget rising to the level of $1,000,000 a month."[58]

Perhaps the university could have adjusted to its new status as a state-supported university with less friction under someone other than Miller. On the other hand, things could have been worse. The well-worn grooves of municipal support and relative independence had been abandoned in favor of an unfamiliar relationship with the state. The growth of the university caused some to feel left out, powerless, and unappreciated. Attacked from within, the university's leadership also came under withering fire from other members of the state system, all of whom had many years of experience in the politics of Kentucky higher education. Miller, who, in Ekstrom's words, "did not have a vindictive bone in his body," demonstrated a high toleration for conflict. In fact, he weathered the tumultuous times better than many of his critics. During his administration, the university changed more than it had in any comparable period of its history.[59]

EIGHTEEN

AN AGENT
FOR CHANGE

IN JANUARY 1980, President James Grier Miller announced his retirement effective eighteen months later, on July 1, 1981, and the board of trustees set about to find his successor. In April, David A. Jones, who had just begun his second year of service on the board, was named search committee co-chair, along with trustee Mary Rudd. Jones was head of Humana, Inc., a nationally prominent chain of for-profit hospitals based in Louisville. He had been a critic of the university's handling of the hospital situation up to that point. The search schedule quickly changed when, on September 18, 1980, Miller suddenly announced he would leave for the West Coast in the next two weeks to head the Robert Maynard Hutchins Center for the Study of Democratic Institutions.[1] With Miller gone eight months earlier than expected, the board once again named William F. Ekstrom acting president until a successor arrived to take up his duties. Ekstrom dedicated the hospital's new ambulatory care building in November 1980, and communicated with the president-elect concerning sticky budget and hospital matters. He also rooted in vain for the basketball team in defense of its national championship won the year before; at the Midwest Regional in March 1981, an Arkansas player's astonishing game-winning shot nearly the length of the floor at the buzzer ended the team's season.[2]

Even more unexpected was an early morning telephone call Ekstrom received on Friday, February 13, 1981. The unidentified caller "announced hysterically that the campus was blowing up." Ekstrom arrived to find large holes in the streets and manhole covers on the roofs of university buildings. City officials immediately and correctly suspected a nearby industry's emptying of highly flammable chemicals into the sewer system, causing explosions that resulted in the collapse of some campus and neighborhood streets. Ekstrom closed the campus for the day, a student quickly marketed "Where were you when the sewers blew?" tee shirts, and the Ralston-Purina company ultimately provided monetary compensation to students and employees for their inconvenience.[3]

The person picked by Jones, Rudd, and their board colleagues to be the fifteenth president of the University of Louisville was Donald C. Swain, an Iowan who had spent his academic career in California. With a strong scholarly record as a historian at the University of California at Davis and impressive credentials as an academic administrator, Swain took office in April 1981, at the age of forty-nine. He had spent the previous six years as academic vice president for the entire nine-campus University of California system and was an award-winning author of two books on the history of the conservation movement in America. One of Swain's first official acts was to name Ekstrom his executive vice president, a position he held until his retirement at age seventy in 1982.[4]

In later years, Swain recalled that he took office with a mandate from the board of trustees to provide

Donald C. Swain (1931–), fifteenth president, University of Louisville, 1981–1995, introduced large-scale private fund raising, required the athletic program to become self-supporting, and won praise for U of L's rising confidence and power in the state's political arena.

"strong and decisive leadership," improve management, and address the difficult problems the school faced. The board also wanted better relations with the Louisville community, more political muscle in Frankfort, and increased private fund raising. Of course, the trustees would have desired such results from any president, but Swain was a fresh recruit, as yet unencumbered by the battle scars any leader eventually accumulates.[5]

Not since the days of Philip Davidson, who lived in the first "president's house," at 2230 Douglass Boulevard, had U of L's chief executive lived in a home acquired by the university for that purpose. Davidson's successor, Woodrow Strickler, owned his own home, and his successors for a time used a house located on Shelby Campus. Now, with a $250,000 gift provided by trustee David Jones, the university

purchased a large house on Longest Avenue in the Cherokee Triangle area, putting the president much closer to the Belknap and Health Sciences campuses.[6]

Cost overruns associated with U of L's management of the current hospital and its construction of the new university hospital threatened the institution's overall financial health and demanded the new president's immediate attention. Swain persuaded Governor John Y. Brown Jr. and the Council on Higher Education to delay a state plan to remove the hospital from university control. Instead, he proposed the creation of a private, nonprofit corporation to run the hospital, its members to be appointed by U of L's board of trustees. Furthermore, as part of a restructuring of the university's central administration, Swain and the board eliminated the position of vice president for health affairs, held by Harold Boyer, clearly, in the eyes of a local editorial writer, "one of the most powerful administrators at U of L." Boyer had been in charge of planning for the new hospital, scheduled to open in 1982, and he also oversaw the existing university hospital as well as medical, dental, and nursing academic programs. In Swain's opinion Boyer wanted too much independence for the Health Sciences Center. Boyer, a capable leader himself, undoubtedly thought he deserved it. Both may have been right, but Swain was president.[7]

In July 1981 the university awarded a two-year contract for the operation of the existing hospital to Hyatt Medical Management Services. The firm, based in California, agreed to maintain the hospital's role as U of L's teaching hospital for its medical, dental, and nursing programs, as well as its service as the principal indigent-care and emergency-treatment facility for Jefferson County and the entire western portion of the state. Subsequently, the university negotiated with local hospital company NKC, which proposed to lease the hospital for one dollar per year and treat indigent patients to the extent possible with public subsidies. Swain was troubled by the agreement, particularly by the provision to lease a publicly funded hospital for a dollar a year. He refused to agree without the concurrence of Governor Brown, which was not forthcoming. At that point university and state officials began discussions with Humana head David

Jones, who resigned from the U of L board of trustees in December 1981.[8]

On January 27, 1983, the contract crafted by university, city, county, state, and Humana officials was signed. Under the agreement, reportedly the first of its kind in the United States, Humana would manage the new $73 million U of L teaching hospital and would commit a portion of its profits in the form of substantial annual payments to the university for indigent patient care and for medical education. The company also provided $8 million for a hospital endowment fund and for additional equipment for the building. The university established a separate trust fund to administer city, county, and state government allocations for indigent care.[9]

Less than three months later, patients and staff were moved from the old hospital to its replacement, to be known as Humana Hospital University. Within a year, demolition of most of the old structure was complete. The central portion, into which the dean's offices moved, was renamed the Abell Administration Center, and the "K" wing, built in 1958, became the home of the School of Nursing. Donald R. Kmetz, who would continue as dean of the medical school, was named to the new position of vice president for hospital affairs in February 1983. Thereafter Kmetz would represent the president in dealing with Humana. A *Courier-Journal* editorial later proclaimed of Swain, "You have ensured that indigent people receive quality medical care by negotiating the takeover of University Hospital by Humana, Inc.," further asserting that this arrangement "may have also spared the university from financial disaster."[10]

While the Humana agreement happily ended the hospital management crisis with its crippling cost overruns, a series of state budget deficits during the 1980s and early 1990s forced the University of Louisville and other Kentucky public universities to reduce their spending plans and defined a long period of fiscal austerity. A few months in advance of Swain's arrival, the university had been told its 1981-1982 budget would be reduced by $2.6 million, which was in addition to the previous year's cut of $5.7 million. In July 1981 Swain announced a plan to cut the university's budget by five percent.[11]

In the spring of 1982 Swain responded to further reductions in state funding with a plan to cut $4.4 million over the next four years. Labeled by the *Louisville Times* "the most sweeping in the university's history," Swain's proposal, issued in the form of a report of the Steering Committee on Long Range Planning and Priorities, called for revising U of L's open admissions policy in University College and eliminating this academic unit entirely. (UC's dean, Wendell Rayburn, had left in the summer of 1980 to become president of Savannah State College in Georgia). The plan also created the new College of Urban and Public Affairs (CUPA), which in 1983 combined under one dean the Kent School of Social Work, the School of Justice Administration (including the Southern Police Institute and the National Crime Prevention Institute), the Urban Studies Center, and a new School of Urban Research and Development, comprising the Systems Science Institute and the Institute of Community Development. The plan's "vast changes" called further for an end to the two-year associate degree program in nursing, leaving only the four-year program and for reductions in the size of the entering classes in medicine, dentistry, and law.[12]

To replace University College, the president initially proposed the establishment of a "Basic College," essentially a community college. Instead, the Preparatory Division, an outgrowth of the West Louisville Educational Program, was created in July 1982 to receive students who needed what the press and public sometimes termed "remedial classes." In 1993 the "Prep Division," as it was often called, was renamed the Division of Transitional Studies. Swain viewed these actions as part of an overall plan to raise the university's admissions standards. With the support of the Council on Higher Education, he moved away from open admissions. At the same time the university maintained an avenue for disadvantaged students who demonstrated the potential to succeed. Although their preparatory courses did not reduce the number of units students needed for graduation, they could use them to improve their skills and work to qualify for admission to a regular degree program.[13]

By the end of his second year in office Swain had cut more than $6 million from the budget and

U of L's 1982 debate team, consisting of brothers Dave and Dan Sutherland, won first place in the National Debate Championship. They were coached by communications professor and later Arts and Sciences interim dean Tim Hynes.

H. Charles Grawemeyer (1912–1993), for whom the Administration Building was named in 1988, endowed five internationally known awards and several local ones as well.

had led the university through what the *Courier-Journal* termed "wrenching changes in academic programs." The newspaper also reported that the president's "honeymoon with the faculty ended long ago." Early in 1983 Swain, in a bold attempt to appeal to the community for private support to sustain U of L's quality in the face of severely declining state appropriations, launched a five-year fund-raising drive termed the "Quest for Excellence." Designed to raise $40 million, "the largest such campaign ever launched in Kentucky" actually raised $61 million. In retrospect, Swain was justifiably proud of his success in this area. He had demonstrated that large-scale private fund raising was possible at the University of Louisville.[14]

A local philanthropist's gift to the university in 1984 brought national and even international atten-

tion. H. Charles Grawemeyer, a friend of Swain and a 1934 graduate of the Speed School, had made his fortune as a local plastics industrialist, then had multiplied it through shrewd investments. Believing that other large academic prizes tended to overlook the humanities, he arranged for five "Grawemeyer Awards" of $150,000 each to be granted annually to individuals judged noteworthy for their contributions in the areas of music composition, ideas improving world order, education, psychology, and religion, the latter in cooperation with the Louisville Presbyterian Seminary. The most famous winner has been former Soviet president Mikhail Gorbachev, who came to Louisville in 1995 to receive the prize in the world order category.[15]

U of L's absorption of a local art school in 1983 called attention to another important endowment in

Art students in 1956.

the humanities, this one created years earlier and also especially influential. In 1947 a $1 million bequest from the estate of Marcia S. and Allen R. Hite had established the Allen R. Hite Art Institute at the university "for the furtherance of modern art in general and education by teaching, lecture and scholarship." A decade earlier, in 1936, the university had created its own fine arts department, which to some degree competed with the Art Center, a private school begun in 1929.[16]

The impetus for the university's progress in this area was provided in part by its first full-time professor of art, Richard Krautheimer, an exile from Hitler's Germany who was brought to Louisville in 1935 with the help of the Emergency Committee in Aid of Displaced German Scholars. Krautheimer left for a position at Vassar College in 1937 and was replaced by

Justus Bier, another German exile, who for years provided energetic leadership in the arts.[17]

In 1938, with the encouragement of U of L president Raymond A. Kent and the gift of a brick house at 2211 South First Street by Morris Belknap Jr., the Art Center moved within sight of the Belknap Campus. There for three decades the school provided instruction for U of L students majoring in art education, offered private art classes, and afforded studio space to local artists. In 1969, a year after the Art Center had changed its name to the Louisville School of Art, it moved out of its Belknap Campus site. It struggled financially, however, and in 1984, a year after it closed, the university awarded its first bachelor of fine arts degree, funded in part through the Hite Institute. The fine arts department's doctoral degree program in art history, authorized in 1990, also drew support from the Hite Institute, as did the Margaret M. Bridwell Art Library, the slide collection (called the Visual Resources Center), and scholarships for art majors.[18]

In addition to forcing U of L and the other state schools to trim their spending, national and state economic problems caused the commonwealth's educational leaders to reevaluate the need for cooperation and compromise. Swain quickly established a good working relationship with UK president Otis A. Singletary. Before long, they were discussing plans for combining programs at their schools, an initiative which, if not taken by the two university presidents, might well have fallen into other hands. Meanwhile, the Council on Higher Education had increased its influence, leaving less room for dispute among the state's universities.[19]

After additional state budget deficits forced sizable reductions in the university's spending later in the decade, Swain initiated a "restructuring and reallocation" process in the fall of 1990 designed to save $16.3 million over the next three years. Of course the state of Kentucky was not alone in this process, as most states were enforcing belt-tightening measures in public higher education. The president's basic premise was that by concentrating resources on stronger programs and reducing or eliminating weaker ones, the university would demonstrate accountability and ultimately be treated more favorably by donors, taxpayers, and state budget makers. Among other things, the plan called for an end to most of the undergraduate programs in the School of Education, making it a professional graduate school and offering, in the opinion of the education faculty, a better way to prepare teachers; eliminating the College of Urban and Public Affairs and moving many of its programs to other schools and colleges; and abolishing the geology department, which had been established twenty-five years earlier.[20]

Facing still another state budget reduction in the fall of 1991, Swain announced that $6.8 million would be sliced from the university's budget, necessitating faculty and staff layoffs and the elimination of some classes and the enlargement of others. In late 1991, the outgoing administration of Governor Wallace G. Wilkinson warned of even deeper cuts to come. In April 1992 the U of L board of trustees declared a "fiscal emergency" and approved staff layoffs and the elimination of unfilled faculty positions.[21]

In the fall of 1992, Governor Brereton Jones, Wilkinson's successor, announced additional state cuts, and the university prepared for a $2.15 million reduction in funding. Meanwhile the state's Council on Higher Education, under pressure from practicing dentists, announced it would study the possibility of reducing enrollments at the University of Louisville and University of Kentucky dental schools or eliminating one of them. Swain recalled that this resulted in "a tough political fight" between the two institutions. In the end, neither school was closed. By June 1993, the governor was warning of still more cuts in university budgets. However difficult these changes were for academic administrators, faculty, and staff, they seemed to be backed by widespread public pressure from the ultimate benefactors of public higher education, the taxpayers.[22]

Hit by wave after wave of state budget cuts, it is little wonder that faculty, staff, and student morale plummeted. Sagging expenditures prevented the hiring of more professors to meet rising enrollments—in 1990 the student population reached 23,610, for a time eclipsing that of the University of Kentucky and by that measure making the University of Louis-

ville the state's largest university. Students complained about large class sizes and the elimination of needed courses, and staff members, more vulnerable to layoffs than faculty, aired understandable worries as well.[23]

College of Arts and Sciences faculty tended to be the most critical, sometimes claiming the administration's limited budgetary largess favored schools such as business and engineering. After all, they reasoned, it was their unit that absorbed most of the growth in student enrollment that had been such a distinguishing feature in U of L's recent history. In the spring of 1970, the College of Arts and Sciences's final semester before state affiliation, it had enrolled 2,531 students. Within twenty years that number had grown to 11,732.

From time to time Arts and Sciences faculty indignation spilled over. At one point a member of the board of trustees said he understood why faculty research in the medical and engineering schools was important, but did not comprehend how it could be considered significant in the English department. Reminiscent of Governor Wilkinson's earlier criticism of state university faculty for "just doing research and writing letters to each other in . . . itty-bitty journals," the board member's comments drew the fire of some faculty members.[24]

Many faculty members throughout the university especially disliked Swain's plan to make department heads more accountable to the administration and less accountable to the faculty, intensify post-tenure review, and assert more administrative control over faculty rewards. At one point the faculty senate complained to the board of trustees that in the shaping of these major changes to the *Redbook* its "voice has been ignored." Two faculty assemblies met in the 1990s and communicated their protests of the governance changes directly to Swain. At one meeting of the Arts and Sciences faculty there was talk of the possibility of unionizing and calling for the president's dismissal.[25]

All of this, of course, was a continuation of the long-standing debate between faculty and administration regarding academic purpose and command. The president knew that the faculty enjoyed academic freedom in teaching and research. The faculty knew that the president had final responsibility in many administrative matters. Their disagreement lay in the definition of the boundaries of their respective realms.

Faced with too many students taught by too few faculty members in too few buildings, the University of Louisville initiated an enrollment management plan designed to reduce the number of undergraduates while increasing slightly the graduate student population. Swain later noted that the Council on Higher Education had encouraged U of L and UK to strengthen their graduate programs and research missions. In response he also created the position of vice president for research in 1990. But university budget cuts and a declining high school population contributed to a larger-than-expected drop in undergraduate enrollment over the next few years. The resulting loss of tuition revenue led to a renewed emphasis on recruitment and to efforts to retain existing students, especially those having completed their first year.[26]

As is the case in any university community, from time to time a student joins the staff of his or her alma mater and is thus "retained" for more than the usual four years at the school. "I came here as a freshman and I've never left," one sometimes hears. If any alumnus of any institution ever fit this description, it was Harry Bockman, who graduated with a bachelor's degree in biology in 1950, was hired in the registrar's office later that year, retired from that unit in 1992, and immediately signed on as a "temporary" employee so he could fill in during registration and other high-activity periods in the student services division. For thirty-three seasons Bockman held the down marker at U of L football games. For twenty-five years he zealously—some students surely thought overzealously—checked students' identification cards at the gates at basketball and football games. As a four-year member of the track team while an undergraduate, Bockman never lost a race, and he was later inducted into the U of L Athletic Hall of Fame. By 1968 he was already a fixture at the university. That spring's April Fool issue of the student newspaper announced that the board of trustees had named Bockman U of L president, replacing Woodrow Strickler. The *Cardinal* reported that his first order as president was to post guards at the door of each campus building. To gain entry, a student had to show his U of L ID, driver's license, birth certificate, social security card, draft card, credit card, checkbook, transcript, advisor's slip, car registration, and immunization record, among other things. "This should have been done long ago," the story reported Bockman as saying.[27]

Long before the arrival of President Swain, the University of Louisville had been criticized for trying to be all things to all people, a comprehensive university offering a very broad array of programs and facilities. It made the transition from a semi-private, municipally supported institution to a state-supported (in the late twentieth century the institution often used the term state-assisted, because of the small percentage of state funds as a total of its budget) university with all its undergraduate, graduate, and professional programs intact. Its motivation for seeking entry to the state system, however, was that it lacked sufficient revenue to fund its programs, and state affiliation was not accompanied by the kinds of budgetary infusions designed to change this. Swain spoke of making the University of Louisville one of the best of the nation's urban universities. But his attempts to structure the university in a way that would bring program definition and spending in line with available funds, which were being constantly reduced by the state, inevitably threatened some programs and helped create a sense of unease on campus.

Forced to make one budget cut after another, Swain approached these unpleasant but unavoidable tasks through strategic planning processes that originated in the business world but were becoming more commonplace in academic settings. Units were directed to identify goals and objectives consistent with the university's overall mission and to concentrate on the achievement of "priorities for action," or PFAs. Some faculty members charged that the president's style too closely resembled that of a corporation's chief executive officer, and complained that he planned "from the top down," ignoring or undervaluing their advice. Swain countered with the accurate observation that his planning initiatives found favor with the Council on Higher Education.[28]

The president's acceptance in 1991 of a salary

increase irritated many faculty and staff, for whom much smaller pay raises were budgeted. The board's chairman countered that Swain's resulting salary was consistent with that of presidents of comparable institutions; besides, the board was pleased with his achievements, wanted him to stay at the university, and believed his salary should be similar to that of the UK president. Swain also incurred faculty ire when he decided that individuals added to the library faculty would no longer be able to qualify for tenured positions; rather, they would be given term contracts, thus increasing the central administration's flexibility in budgetary matters. In addition, over the strenuous objections of the majority of medical school professors, who complained their opinions were ignored, the board of trustees approved Swain's plan to increase the amount of their private practice income used for the overall benefit of the medical school.[29]

The president's efforts to redirect resources to vital but underfunded areas saw dramatic results in the area of computing. The university had entered the computer era in 1958 when it installed its first mainframe, an IBM 610, in the Speed School's new Engineering Computing Laboratory (ECL). When the medical school acquired its own machine, an IBM 1130, in 1966, the university established the Computer Center to locate overall responsibility for computing in the central administration. The Computer Center leased an IBM 360/30 and began its operations on the ground floor of the Home Economics Building (now Ford Hall). Its director was John Sinai, a recently appointed physics professor. The center's first budget, for 1967-1968, was $156,365.[30]

Much of the work of the early Computer Center was confined to administrative areas such as payroll, student loans, alumni, and library serials. Discussions at advisory board meetings included such matters as whether or not the library should provide funds for its own key punch operator and how to support faculty members whose research required computing. In 1970 the center moved its operations to the Reynolds Building, where it installed a larger mainframe, an IBM 360/40. Affected by substantial budget problems associated with its transition to state affiliation, however, the university was then forced to contract with an outside firm to provide computing services. This arrangement lasted for three years.

In late 1978 Alfred T. Chen, an engineering professor in charge of the ECL, became head of the Computer Center, which at that point moved to the Standard Oil Building at the Belknap Campus's northwest corner. In 1978 the Computer Center and Management Information Systems (MIS) were combined to form the Office of Computing and Information Services (OCIS), which moved again, this time to the Ormsby Building several blocks north on Fourth Street. Following Chen's death in December 1983, a board of overseers study of OCIS recommended increased resources and services and placement at a high level in the administration. Chen's successor, Ronald L. Moore, joined the university in 1984. Three years later the unit was renamed Information Technology (IT) with Moore as vice president.

By the mid-1980s Information Technology was providing dial-in access to its IBM and DEC VAX computer systems and access to Bitnet, a national electronic mail (e-mail) network linking colleges and universities, which eventually gave way to the Internet. At that time it began working with the University Libraries to support an on-line catalog, and implemented PROFS, an IBM-based e-mail system for U of L faculty and staff. In 1991 the division moved its offices and equipment from the Ormsby Building back to the Belknap Campus, where it occupied the old University Center. That building, which had fondly been referred to as the "Hula Hoop Building" by generations of University College students, was completely renovated and renamed the Miller Information Technology Center (MITC), after former president James Grier Miller and his wife, Jessie.

During the 1990s IT continued to upgrade and add hardware and software, assigned e-mail accounts to students, provided voice-mail telephone services, supported computer labs scattered around the campuses, and implemented both a sophisticated on-campus data communication network and dial-in access, including the Internet and the World Wide Web. The unit administered U of L's imaging, media, television, and distance education services, as well as its copy centers, printing, and publications. Some faculty members decried the unit's growth, reach, influence, and enforcement of standardization, and argued instead for hiring many more professors and increasing salaries. At the same time, however, faculty lobbied for still more infrastructure and other improvements in computing services. By mid-1999 IT was managing forty-five thousand separate computer accounts and had an annual budget of $17 million.

While Swain's strong exercise of presidential authority sometimes raised faculty hackles on the campuses, it was often appreciated and praised out in the community. His presence on various boards and commissions placed him alongside the region's most influential community, business, and political leaders. In 1987 he was elected chair of the Louisville Chamber of Commerce, reportedly the first time in the nation's history a university president occupied such a position while in office. Three years later he was elected chair of the Greater Louisville Economic Development Partnership.[31]

In at least one instance the president's authoritative stances challenged a traditional center of power not internal to the university. In November 1988, the university announced it would soon implement a new policy banning smoking in all common areas of buildings, limiting it to specifically designated places, and resolving "irreconcilable differences" in favor of nonsmokers. Several legislators representing tobacco farming areas reacted strongly, some threatening budgetary repercussions for the University of Louisville if it persisted with this plan. "We might have to cut something out and put it somewhere else," the chairman of the House Agriculture Committee responded. Advisory group members who had written the policy's first draft reworked the document, making it slightly less offensive to tobacco interests, but under Swain's leadership the university found success in a policy area probably deemed too sensitive for action by other universities in the commonwealth. If the university took heat from rural legislators, symbolizing an ancient divide between Kentucky's largest urban area and the interests of much of the rest of the commonwealth, its progressive stance during the great smok-

ing flap of 1988 and 1989 also denoted the university's rising confidence and power in the state's political arena.[32]

In spite of friction on campus and grumbling from legislators, solidarity prevailed on at least one subject—basketball. Coach Denny Crum's Cardinals followed their 1980 NCAA national championship by appearing in the prestigious Final Four three times over the next six years, and in 1986 the team captured a second national title by defeating Duke University in Dallas, Texas. Nearly as memorable in the minds of U of L fans was the 1983 NCAA Mideast Regional championship game in Knoxville, Tennessee, which pitted U of L against UK. Much ballyhooed in the press as the "dream game," because UK had steadfastly refused to play U of L in a regularly scheduled game, this contest was won in overtime by U of L. That fall, following prodding by Governor John Y. Brown Jr. and additional pressure from fans and the media, the two schools began playing each other annually. To outsiders the issue of a match-up between the Cardinals and the Wildcats may have seemed trivial, but to Kentuckians few topics aroused deeper passions.[33]

Crum maintained a remarkably consistent demeanor throughout this period. He guarded his privacy and rarely moved into the spotlight, except of course during game time, when public attention was unavoidable. On the bench Crum could be seen chewing gum and holding a rolled-up program. Almost from the beginning of his U of L career, fans feared he would eventually move to UCLA, where he had been a player, then an assistant to celebrated coach John Wooden. When Crum received offers to return to his alma mater as head coach, however, he declined.[34]

For most residents of the state, the political and financial rivalry between UK and U of L in the 1980s and 1990s continued to place a distant second to basketball. Although the U of L team's successes after the 1986 NCAA championship season did not match the glories of Crum's earlier years, his squads attracted large, enthusiastic crowds to Freedom Hall, usually won more than twenty games per season, and

typically at season's end earned an invitation to the NCAA tournament. In 1994 Crum, who had spent his entire head coaching career at the University of Louisville, was inducted into the Naismith Memorial Basketball Hall of Fame. In January 1997 he won his six hundredth game. By the end of the 1998-1999 season, Crum's record had risen to 644 wins against 264 losses.[35]

Early in his presidency Donald Swain began stressing the need for the university's athletic program to become self-supporting. In 1981, his first year in office, he gave the football program four years to show it could succeed at the NCAA Division I-A level and pay its own way. Three years later the board of trustees created the University of Louisville Athletic Association, a separate foundation charged with managing U of L sports programs and their finances. To maintain institutional control, the president served as chair of the association's board. In 1985 the university ceased using general funds to support intercollegiate athletics, thus insulating academic budgets

In 1980 the University of Louisville defeated the University of California at Los Angeles to win its first NCAA championship in men's basketball. In 1986 the team captured a second national title by defeating Duke University in Dallas, Texas. In 1999 the Sporting News *named Louisville one of the nation's "elite eight" basketball programs.*

With Howard Schnellenberger's arrival, the University of Louisville became the only Division I-A school whose basketball and football coaches—Crum at U of L and Schellenberger at Miami—had each won the national championship in his sport.

from athletic expenditures. In short order, helped initially in large part by the success of its basketball teams and the guidance of William "Bill" Olsen, director of athletics, the university's intercollegiate sports program went from losing about $1 million a year to making approximately that much per year. This allowed U of L's athletic program subsequently to operate in the black, a rarity among the nation's universities. Significantly, the success of Swain's initiative constituted another step in the extension of the central authority of the president's office.[36]

While U of L football had enjoyed sporadic success in the post-Camp era, it had seldom made headlines outside Louisville. But in December 1984, under what some may have seen as a do-or-die effort to make the program profitable, Swain and Olsen signed Howard Schnellenberger as head football coach. Schnellenberger had won the national championship with his University of Miami squad just two years earlier, then had resigned to head a new professional team in the making in south Florida. When that

Orthopedic surgeon Rudy Ellis became the team physician for Cardinal sports in 1961. At the time of his death in 1997, he was still treating U of L athletes in all sports except football and baseball. A pioneer in sports medicine, he also served on the U of L board of trustees and board of overseers. John Tong, voice of the Louisville Cardinals for forty years, announced football games for twenty-five years and basketball for thirty-seven years. He retired at the end of the 1998-1999 season, shortly before his death. Both Ellis and Tong were inducted into the Kentucky Athletic Hall of Fame.

In 1996 The Tailgater's Handbook *named U of L the second best tailgating school in America. Papa John's Cardinal Stadium is shown here on opening day, September 5, 1998.*

effort stalled, the former Louisville Flaget High School star and University of Kentucky All-American accepted U of L's offer. Accompanied by an ever-present pipe and sonorous voice, Schnellenberger reportedly vowed to "take Cinderella to the ball twice."[37]

Under Schnellenberger the football program's achievements included schedules featuring more big-name opponents, a reasonable degree of success, and increased public support. "Our program is on a collision course with the national championship," Schnellenberger boasted prior to the 1990 season; "the only variable is time." That year the team won ten, lost one, and tied one. In October, *USA Today* contrasted the school's new gridiron program with the old, calling U of L football "a citadel of mediocrity for 72 autumns." At season's end the team accepted an invitation to play in the Fiesta Bowl. Their surprising 34-7 rout of traditional national powerhouse Alabama gave the school its first bowl victory since 1958.[38]

In 1957 the football Cardinals had begun playing their home games at a baseball park at the state fairgrounds. Although this facility, eventually named Cardinal Stadium, was renovated from time to time to make it more suitable as a gridiron, fans and city boosters often spoke of their wish for a stadium built expressly for football. The successes of Schnellenberger's teams were accompanied by increases in average attendance, from 27,663 in 1985 to 37,272 in 1994. The coach himself began lobbying for new quarters, and this led to a community-wide effort to identify funds for a new stadium. In January 1993 a committee of local government officials and business leaders headed by Malcolm Chancey, president of Liberty National Bank, recommended it be built on the old railroad yard just south of the Speed School, in effect making the stadium and its parking areas part of a greatly expanded Belknap Campus.[39]

By the end of the fall 1994 season, university officials had agreed to help form a new athletic conference, which became known as Conference USA. Schnellenberger was disgruntled at the prospect of having to conform to a conference schedule. This would remove the school from the list of "independents," those institutions not having conference affiliation, and make it more difficult for him to schedule certain teams. In December 1994 Schnellenberger abruptly left the University of Louisville to accept the head coaching position at the University of Oklahoma.

The coach's departure threatened plans for the new stadium. The hiring of Ron Cooper, then the youngest Division I-A head football coach in the country and one of only five African American head football coaches in NCAA Division I-A, and Chancey's dogged leadership, kept the project on track. The stadium was built mostly with private funds. Donations totaling $5 million from Papa John's Pizza and its CEO John Schnatter completed the necessary amount of $63.2 million.[40]

Construction began in 1996 with the first game in forty-two thousand-seat Papa John's Cardinal Stadium scheduled for the 1998 opener against the University of Kentucky. In his final U of L season Schnellenberger, who had pushed for an annual game with this in-state rival, saw his team lose in the inaugural contest. Under Cooper, his successor, the Cardinals won the next two annual games with the Wildcats, then lost the 1997 opener. A capacity crowd's jubilant inauguration of the new stadium in September 1998 was only slightly muffled by Kentucky's lopsided victory over Louisville.[41]

Student cheerleaders have been a part of U of L athletics since the beginning of intercollegiate competition. In the early years, one or two young women had the responsibility of encouraging the teams and exciting the crowds at the games. Newspaper articles frequently praised the efforts of these spirited early cheerleaders. By the late 1940s, young men had joined the women and the squads had increased in number. Over the years the uniforms changed, with short skirts for the women replacing long, full ones. The style of cheerleading also changed from fairly simple routines to complex ones requiring considerable athletic ability and agility. By century's end college cheerleaders had become skillful, well-conditioned athletes in their own right, enduring long practice sessions and developing their own teamwork and camaraderie.[42]

Furthermore, late in the century cheerleaders began to take part in challenging intercollegiate competitions of their own. The U of L squad proved to be one of the nation's most successful, winning the National Cheerleading Association Championship in 1985, 1986, 1989, 1992, 1994, 1996, 1998, and 1999. In 1996 the U of L team was part of a six-hundred-strong group of cheerleaders from around the country participating in a routine for the opening ceremonies of the Summer Olympics in Atlanta, Georgia.[43]

In a similar vein, the "Cardinal Bird" mascot became a familiar symbol of the school's athletic teams. Chosen probably because the cardinal was Kentucky's state bird, this image in the early part of the century appeared only in two-dimensional form. The first appearance of a "live" Cardinal Bird mascot was in the mid-1950s, when a student came to games dressed in a costume which was "thrown together." By the 1959 season the Cardinal Bird had taken a

somewhat more recognizable form. Still, the costume was a homemade affair whose head was created from a football helmet covered with chicken wire and papier-mâché. This representation of the Cardinal Bird continued through the early 1960s; for a time "he" was joined by a female companion known as Ladybird, outfitted in a similar costume complete with jaunty bow and long pipe cleaner eyelashes.

By the late 1970s the Cardinal Bird had evolved into the character known throughout the late twentieth century: padded body shell, furry red outer suit, large "hands," big, yellow feet with toes, and of course, the oversized head, complete with beak and teeth, at once menacing and lovable. The Cardinal Bird was played by both male and female students over the years, and developed a reputation and following of its own. In 1995, when the National Cheerleading Association judged college mascots independently for the first time, the U of L Cardinal Bird, a.k.a. Aaron Flaker, won first place in the national competition.[44] In 1982 a student dance team known as the Ladybirds began performing at basketball and football games. It won its first national championship in 1995, beating nine-time champion Memphis State University at the Universal Dance Association Collegiate National Dance Championship competition held in Orlando, Florida. The team, judged on choreography, synchronization, and crowd appeal,

Familiar sights at Louisville-area athletic, civic, and charitable events, the cheerleaders, the Ladybirds, and the very recognizable Cardinal Bird help raise school and community spirit.

According to Sydney Schultze, the women's studies program's first coordinator in the mid 1970s, "It is impossible to stress too strongly what this program meant to faculty and students. Feminism had opened our eyes and given us self-respect. Ours was not just an academic program, it was a cause. We were doing what had to be done." The women pictured here on the Belknap Campus are calling attention to Women's Week in 1978.

consistently placed in the top five, winning again in 1997.[45]

Despite achievements in athletics and other areas, the University of Louisville still suffered from vestiges of segregation. This became apparent following a series of court cases arising in Mississippi and elsewhere in the 1970s, referred to collectively as the *Adams* case, which focused public attention on an unfortunate facet of higher education. By 1981 the courts had found eighteen states, nearly all of them in the south, in violation of Title VI of the Civil Rights Act of 1964. Kentucky was among them. In January 1981 the U.S. Department of Education's Office of Civil Rights notified Governor Brown that Kentucky's public universities had to step up recruitment of black students, faculty, and staff, under threat of the loss of federal support.[46]

The state's Council on Higher Education (CHE) thereafter obligated the University of Louis-

ville and the other institutions to achieve appropriate recruitment and hiring goals. The schools made enough progress for the Office of Civil Rights to discontinue certain CHE reporting requirements in 1987, but the council and the university continued to use the 1981 "desegregation mandate," as it was sometimes called, to guide student, staff, and faculty recruitment efforts during the late 1980s and 1990s. When Kentucky was placed under the desegregation mandate in 1981, there were 1,701 African American students enrolled at the University of Louisville, 8.4 percent of the total. By the fall of 1995 the African American student enrollment had grown to 2,016, or 11.2 percent of the total. In addition, in the latter year, just after the end of the Swain administration, minority students made up 15.5 percent of the 21,218 total enrollment. At the same time 15.9 percent of the total of 1,154 permanent, full-time faculty were minority and 4.6 percent were African American.[47]

Women also sought to increase their visibility as a group with concerns unique to themselves. In 1973 English professor Lucy M. Freibert taught "Women in Literature," the first women's studies course given at the University of Louisville. Soon there were courses in other departments, some of which were interdisciplinary in nature. A student organization, Feminists on Campus at U of L (FOCUL), appeared in early 1975, and on February 17, 1975, Betty Friedan, founder of the National Organization for Women (NOW), spoke on campus. During that year the Women's Studies Program, headed by a coordinator and steering committee, began in the College of Arts and Sciences. The university began offering a minor in women's studies in 1981, and in 1995 it became the only Kentucky university and one of only a few in the South to offer a major in this field.[48]

An episode involving U of L's head football coach in 1975 illustrated the weakness of feminism at the university at that time and served as a catalyst for its subsequent achievements. Vince Gibson, newly hired and desirous of attracting better athletes, had sent out a call to the dormitories for female students to join the "Gibson Girls," an organization designed to present U of L's best face to prospective athletes during their recruiting visits to campus. These "girls" would give the athletes "campus tours," serve as their "dates," and assist "at various football functions." FOCUL members, including some female professors, were "outraged," thinking the coach's initiative "smacked of something close to prostitution." The "Gibson Girls" group soon faded away, but not before alerting many at U of L, both women and men, to the need for more understanding and activity in this area.[49]

In the late 1980s Freibert, with political science professor Mary E. Hawkesworth, began promoting the establishment of a Women's Center "to promote equality, to increase women's self-reliance, and to heighten the understanding of women's contributions to all cultures and societies" through public events. With Swain's blessing, former trustee Elaine "Cissy" Musselman joined the effort early in 1991 to help raise funds for the center, which began operating later that year under the direction of Judi Jennings.[50]

U of L's first school song was written in 1909 by music professor John Peter Grant and student W.T. Myers. Thereafter, alma maters and fight songs came and went through the years. In 1947 the university offered a $50 prize to the student who could write the best school song. The winning entry was written by two band members, James L. Powell, Speed School, 1947, and John Newton Young, an Arts and Sciences physics major. To everyone's surprise, an engineer and aspiring physicist defeated several music school students, who submitted every other song in the contest. The moving Powell and Young alma mater, premiered at the November 1947 homecoming, has endured for half a century, longer than any other U of L song.

Freibert also played the major role in changing the lyrics of U of L's alma mater. For years, while attending graduation exercises, she "had bristled, because the current version omitted women," who made up the majority of the student body. In the mid-

1980s she suggested changing the words "We thy loyal sons now stand" to "We thy sons and daughters stand." Others took up the cause, including Collette Murray, the university's first female vice president. Soon Swain authorized the change.[51]

For years female professors had asserted that they were paid less than men with similar qualifications and experience. In the early 1970s the U of L AAUP chapter's "Committee W," chaired by history professor Mary K. Tachau, found significant salary inequities. The university responded by increasing the salaries of several female professors at that time. In July 1994, the Task Force on the Status of Women, appointed by President Swain, issued a report asserting U of L women employees were victims of "subtle yet pervasive forms of discrimination." Women were underpaid throughout the university and underrepresented among executives, administrators, and the senior faculty ranks. Swain earmarked $200,000 to help implement the task force's recommendations and charged a commission to devise a comprehensive salary equity plan. In the spring of 1997 Swain's successor in office implemented the first phase of the commission's recommendations by awarding $1.1 million in salary adjustments to classified staff and promising that additional improvements in the pay of other women employees, including faculty, would be forthcoming.[52]

During an era marked by Kentucky's steady reduction of the percentage of its budget allocated to higher education, Swain strengthened U of L's endowment. Endowment funds, consisting of donations given to benefit the institution, were held in the University of Louisville Foundation. The foundation had been created in 1970 on the eve of U of L's becoming a state university. At that time its value was $11 million; by 1981, it had grown to $18 million. Relying more and more on private giving, the Swain presidency ended with his institution's endowment at the remarkable level of $183 million. The income was used to fund special professorships referred to as endowed chairs, academic scholarships, library collections, and similar needs. By mid-1998 the Foundation held $317 million, making U of L's the largest endowment among Kentucky's state universities and

Longtime Alumni director Rodney Williams (facing the camera) outside the University Club and Alumni Center. The U of L Alumni Association serves ninety thousand alumni and coordinates the activities of thirty-two clubs in the United States and five abroad.

the thirty-sixth largest among the nation's public universities.[53]

The new buildings added to the campuses during Swain's presidency reflect areas of university life he emphasized, one of which was the expansion of the alumni office. An alumni association had taken root soon after the move to the Belknap Campus in 1925. Supported by its members' dues, it operated somewhat independently of the university. By 1937 it had acquired a $7,500 debt. Early that year Leslie E. Shively became head of alumni relations, a position he held for most of the next thirty-five years. He repaid the debt, started an alumni magazine, and gradually restructured the organization. In 1945 even separate alumni groups such as those linked to the Speed School and the School of Medicine were centralized in Shively's office.[54]

Rodney Williams Jr. became director of alumni services in 1977. With the support of Steven Bing, Miller's vice president for university relations, he enlarged the board of directors, appended associations from each of the schools and colleges, and began publication of the modern alumni magazine. In the mid-1980s, with Swain's encouragement, he added thirty regional alumni clubs from around the country. One particularly successful innovation was Town and Gown Week, begun in 1983 at the suggestion of Lavinia Swain, the president's wife, which extended the traditional Homecoming weekend into a week of activities meant to appeal to the entire community.

For several years Williams and others had discussed the need for a "faculty club" containing dining areas, meeting rooms, and offices for alumni services. Gardencourt was an attractive possibility, but its distance from Belknap was a disadvantage. In 1987 Barry Bingham Sr., longtime publisher of the *Courier-Journal* and *Louisville Times* and a former member of the board of trustees, pledged $4 million for the construction of an on-campus University Club for this purpose, and for the club's endowment. To these funds were added $2.2 million from U of L's sale of Gardencourt in 1987, resulting in the addition of quarters to house the Alumni Office. In 1991 the University Club and Alumni Center, a handsome structure just east of the School of Education, was dedicated.

Williams's enthusiasm for alumni activities was matched by his devotion to Greek letter organizations and their role in the collegiate experience. In 1979 he was elected international president of Tau Kappa Epsilon; six years later he served as president of the National Interfraternity Conference. While the Greeks had been important in the life of the college since they had overcome faculty resistance following World War I, they were especially infused with enthusiasm and numbers by the veterans enrolling after World War II. Among new chapters formed then were

Phi Kappa Tau and Lambda Chi Alpha. Each soon grew to sixty members or more, and eventually approached one hundred. Greek membership declined during the era of the Vietnam War, as some students at the University of Louisville and other institutions equated these social organizations with the "establishment." By the late 1990s, one thousand students were active in the university's fourteen fraternities and nine sororities, a dozen of which leased houses on "Fraternity Row" along Confederate Place. Of these, three fraternities and three sororities were affiliated with the National Pan-Hellenic Council, an organization of historically black Greek-letter clubs. Large gatherings of the alumni of Tau Kappa Epsilon, Phi Kappa Tau, and Lambda Chi Alpha celebrated their societies' fiftieth anniversaries in the 1990s.[55]

The School of Business received more attention from the central administration during this period than it ever had. During the first half of the twentieth century, U of L students interested in economics and business administration could enroll in a smattering of appropriate courses in the College of Arts and Sciences, the Speed Scientific School, and the Division of Adult Education. After World War II, the college began offering a bachelor of science degree in commerce, and returning veterans made the Department of Economics and Commerce one of Arts and Sciences's most heavily enrolled units. In 1952 the board of trustees approved President Philip G. Davidson's proposal for the establishment of the School of Business.[56]

The new school opened in September 1953, with John R. Craf as dean. It was housed in Menges Hall. The first full-time faculty members included Frederick W. Stamm, William F. Thompson, Carl E. Abner, Robert W. Carney, Kathleen Drummond, Richard L. Hitchcock, and Fred W. Kniffin. Ninety-two undergraduate students and eighty-five M.B.A. candidates enrolled that fall. During the two decades following, the school moved first to Brigman Hall in 1958, then to Strickler Hall in 1974. Its enrollments showed large increases, especially in the 1970s. The school's undergraduate and graduate programs were accredited by the American Assembly of Collegiate Schools of Business in the 1980s. In 1985 its new

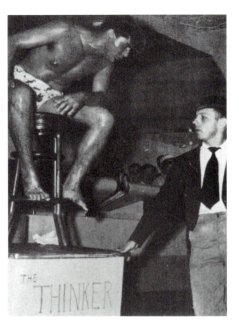

Fraternity frivolities during the 1940s and 1950s.

building at Second Street and Cardinal Boulevard was dedicated.[57]

In 1992 the school's name was changed to the College of Business and Public Administration. By the late 1990s it offered B.S. degrees in business administration (accountancy, computer information systems, equine administration, finance, management, and marketing) and in economics, as well as a master of accountancy degree. Through the Graduate School, the College of Business also offered the degrees of M.B.A. (Master of Business Administration), M.P.A. (Master of Public Administration), and Ph.D. in Urban and Public Affairs. The Urban Studies Center, which had been part of CUPA (where it was called

the Center for Urban and Economic Research), also moved to the business school under the name Urban Studies Institute (USI).[58]

The academic offerings of the old Institute of Community Development, which had ceased to exist, had been folded into CUPA. Now they too moved to the business school, which developed the doctoral program in urban and public affairs. In addition, the college housed the Executive-in-Residence Program, Small Business Development Center, and Telecommunications Research Center, the latter under the joint sponsorship of South Central Bell and the state. In 1995 the college eliminated its traditional departments, instead creating three "schools," those of business, accountancy, and economics and urban affairs. These initiatives occurred under the leadership of Robert L. Taylor, brought to U of L in 1984 by Swain, who considered him one of U of L's outstanding deans.[59]

For decades the university had portrayed itself as an indispensable provider of various essential services to the Louisville area, but in the late twentieth century many units expanded their public service roles. In 1990, for example, the law school reportedly became one of the first in the nation to require

On April 11, 1971, the University of Louisville dedicated a new health sciences center, which replaced medical and dental school buildings dating from the late nineteenth century.

pro bono service as a part of every law student's legal education. In 1997 the school was renamed the Louis D. Brandeis School of Law, in part, according to its catalog and other publications, to honor his vision of U of L's law school as "a national model in legal education emphasizing public service." It was a goal worthy of remembering by every person who walked through the law school's front door, thereby treading near the great justice's ashes.[60]

The dental school is another example. Under Raymond Myers, who served as dean from 1945 until his retirement in 1969, the school began enlarging its clinical and educational services to the public.

In the 1950s it sent its "Field Dental Unit," a clinic on wheels, to underserved areas throughout the state and provided free dental care to school children. In the 1960s it raised public awareness of tooth decay and promoted the benefits of fluoride. In 1970, the year after Harold E. Boyer became dean, the school moved into the new Health Sciences Center, the planning and construction of which Boyer had overseen, and further increased its clinical services.[61]

By the late 1990s the school, which continued to administer dental services for the Louisville and Jefferson County Board of Health, had added a biopsy service for a multi-state area, a dental oncology clinic in the J. Graham Brown Cancer Center, and student-led dental care in rural areas of the state. It also offered post-graduate programs in endodontics, periodontics, oral and maxillofacial surgery, prosthodontics, orthodontics, advanced education in general dentistry, general practice residency, and, through the Graduate School, an M.A. in oral biology.[62]

In 1952 the School of Dentistry launched its Dental Hygiene Program, the only such program in the state affiliated with a dental school. Its students could earn an associate degree or, through the College of Arts and Sciences, a B.S. in dental hygiene.

From the beginning of the Speed Scientific School in 1925, its students followed a cooperative program of education, working outside the classroom in business or industry for three-month periods throughout their university experience. During World War II the school's curriculum changed to a five-year program in which students worked at their co-op jobs during parts of their junior and "pre-senior" years. Thereafter students worked outside class for four quarters during their five years.[63]

For years the medical school had emphasized emergency services to benefit the community. In 1914 it helped equip and staff an "accident care" unit in the new City Hospital. In the 1930s the head of the school's surgery department, R. Arnold Griswold Sr., perfected important new procedures in the treatment of fractures, later helped Louisville develop innovative emergency vehicle services using trained personnel, and in the 1950s called for seat belts and other safety improvements in automobiles.[64]

One of Griswold's successors as head of the surgery department, Hiram C. Polk Jr., led community efforts to create a widely acclaimed trauma center at University Hospital. In his U of L career beginning in 1971 and stretching beyond a quarter century, Polk conducted important research in post-surgical infection control, acquired a reputation for being tough on resident surgeons, and built a widely acclaimed department. Moreover, by the 1970s the medical school had developed an internationally recognized program in microsurgery. In July 1998 the Kleinert, Kutz and Associates Hand Care Center, anchored by its two most highly acclaimed practitioners, Harold

E. Kleinert and Joseph Kutz, announced its intention to perform "the world's first successful hand transplant." Six months later, in January 1999, the Kleinert team of U of L surgeons, led by Dr. Warren C. Breidenbach, performed the first hand transplant in the United States, four months after physicians in France had performed a hand transplant there.[65]

In the College of Arts and Sciences, the political science department created the McConnell Center for Political Leadership in 1991. It was named for Senator Mitch McConnell, an Arts and Sciences alumnus, who raised funds for an endowment valued at $3.8 million by the summer of 1997. Located in Ford Hall, the center in 1992 began funding up to fifteen four-year scholarships a year for Kentucky high school students judged to have leadership ability. It also brought U.S. secretaries of state and other national and world leaders to the university for lectures and question-and-answer sessions with students, and it required the McConnell Scholars to complete public service internships.[66]

By the late 1960s, 66 percent of the members of the Louisville Orchestra were U of L music school faculty, students, or alumni, and during the closing decades of the century the school continued its equally strong ties with the Kentucky Opera Association orchestra, the Chamber Music Society, the Bach Society, and the Louisville Ballet orchestra. During this period the division forged close ties with local public school systems as well. In 1977, three years before the school moved to its new building on Belknap Campus, its dean, Jerry Ball, was named chair of the task force to plan the Kentucky Center for the Arts in downtown Louisville. After completion, that facility served as the Louisville Orchestra's new home. The music school's catalog during these years called attention to its "profound impact on the cultural life of Louisville and the state of Kentucky," a boast that to most observers probably seemed justified.[67]

From its beginnings as the Division of Social Administration in 1936 until it was placed under the College of Urban and Public Affairs in 1983, the Kent School of Social Work for all practical purposes had been a separate professional school, on par with U of L's other colleges and schools. Following the elimination of the College of Urban and Public Affairs, from 1992 until 1996 the Kent School and the School of Allied Health Sciences jointly comprised the College of Health and Social Services. Also in 1996 the post master's certificate program in family therapy became part of the Kent School, which once again became a separate professional school. That fall UK's College of Social Work and U of L's Kent School of Social Work began offering a joint Ph.D. program in social work.[68]

During the 1990s the School of Education expanded the number and size of its graduate offerings, made its doctoral program available on a cooperative basis to students at Western Kentucky University, and in general reshaped its curriculum in support of the Kentucky Education Reform Act of 1990 (KERA), a landmark in the state's checkered history of support for education. The school also phased out its undergraduate degrees in education (save that for vocational teacher education) and required teachers-to-be to earn an undergraduate degree in one of the traditional academic disciplines before acquiring a master's degree from the School of Education as a prerequisite to teacher certification. Many of these changes came in response to recommendations of the Holmes Partnership, a national organization of universities, schools, and other professional groups. In 1996, a visiting team from the National Council for Accreditation of Teacher Education (NCATE) gave the school high praise for its collaborative programs and for curriculum design and delivery. All of these achievements were made under the guidance of Raphael Nystrand, the school's dean since 1978. Swain credited Nystrand's leadership in making the school "one of U of L's strongest units."[69]

Beginning in 1962 students attending the Southern Police Institute could qualify for twelve semester hours of credit in the College of Arts and Sciences, reportedly making U of L's the first such program in the nation which gave college credit for in-service police education. In 1969, following the approval of the Southern Association of Colleges and Schools, the university established the School of Police Administration, making SPI part of that unit.

The new school, with SPI founder David A. McCandless as dean, offered the B.S. degree in either police administration or correctional administration, and later added the M.S. in the administration of justice. Ford Foundation grants provided substantial support for this effort.[70]

The National Crime Prevention Institute, founded in 1971, grew out of research conducted by police administration professor John C. Klotter in the late 1960s. Responding to the nation's rising crime rate and based on the Shelby Campus, it offered instructional programs in the new field of crime prevention methodology. Following McCandless's death in 1971, Klotter became dean. In 1979 the division was renamed the School of Justice Administration. Made part of CUPA in 1983 under Klotter's successor, J. Price Foster, justice administration became a department in the College of Arts and Sciences in 1992, where it continued to house the Southern Police Institute and the National Crime Prevention Institute.[71] In the second half of the twentieth century it was represented by an especially active alumni group begun by members of the first SPI class in 1951. For many years that association was shepherded by Dorothy Clore, longtime administrative assistant to the dean.[72]

U of L's Expressive Therapies program was reportedly the first art therapy program in the United States. It first appeared in 1957, lasted only a short time, then reappeared in 1969. In 1978 it became part of the Division of Allied Health. It offered a two-year graduate program leading to the M.A. in art therapy. Its graduates worked in psychiatric hospitals, mental health centers, drug and alcohol clinics, nursing homes, schools, and prisons.[73]

The Division of Allied Health began in 1977. In connection with Swain's strategic planning effort in 1992, the College of Health and Social Services was formed, combining Allied Health and the Kent School. Four years later, the Kent School again became a separate school and the School of Allied Health Sciences gained independent status. The latter school included degree programs in cytotechnology, radiologic technology, nuclear medicine technology, clinical laboratory science (medical technology), physical

In 1995 the University of Louisville dedicated a new symbol, the Alumni Clock Tower, part of the Student Activities Center completed in 1990.

therapy, and cardiopulmonary science (respiratory therapy), as well as graduate offerings in expressive therapies.[74]

More than a dozen buildings, many of them major in scope, arose during Swain's presidency. When completed in 1990, for example, the new Student Activities Center, spanning the railroad tracks between Brook and Floyd Streets, became the largest building on Belknap Campus. It housed, among other offerings, a cafeteria, several restaurants and fast-food eateries, a movie theater, a bookstore, meeting rooms, a ticket office, gymnasiums and other recreational facilities, and various student life and athletic department offices. Not only did the SAC, as it was called, supply much-needed services for the Belknap Campus's growing student body, it also exemplified the expansion of student services begun under stu-

dent affairs vice president Edward H. Hammond during the Miller administration. Finally, the structure was punctuated by a distinctive clock tower that soon competed with the *Thinker* on pictorial representations of the campus. The tower was topped with a carillon whose rich tones chimed the hour and played music apropos to the season. In a fitting tribute to Swain and his wife, Lavinia, the building was named for them in 1999.[75]

Swain retired in June 1995 at the age of sixty-three. His presidency had lasted over fourteen years, the fifth longest in U of L history and the second longest in the twentieth century. In a review of his administration, the editors of the *Courier-Journal* wrote that Swain had "led the renaissance of the institution at almost every level." His was an "era of good feeling" during which he "transformed" the university. Improved facilities resulted in a campus that "has never been more attractive or busier." Furthermore, Swain "built crucial ties between the business community and the campus." He "mastered" Kentucky politics, becoming "equally adroit as an administrator and politician."[76]

When the board of trustees hired Swain, they directed him to be a "change agent." Swain set out to find a solution to the hospital management crisis, improve relations with the University of Kentucky, involve himself and the university more fully in community affairs, and increase the administration's flexibility in managing faculty and other personnel and university budgets. His achievements in these and other endeavors sometimes brought him more praise from outside the university than from within. Not surprisingly, the president's admirers and critics viewed the situation from entirely different, and equally legitimate, points of view. Swain left the University of Louisville a measurably sturdier, more widely respected institution than he found it.[77]

NINETEEN

LOOKING AHEAD, LOOKING BACK

JOHN W. SHUMAKER, the sixteenth president of the University of Louisville, was chosen in April 1995 and began his administration on July 1 of that year, at age fifty-two. There was no interregnum; his predecessor, Donald C. Swain, had announced his decision to retire a year earlier, giving the board of trustees time to seek a successor.[1]

A native of Pittsburgh, Shumaker received his degrees in ancient Greek and classical studies from the University of Pittsburgh and the University of Pennsylvania. He began his teaching career at Ohio State University, where he soon received an administrative appointment. After a decade as dean and vice president at the State University of New York at Albany, he served for eight years as president of Central Connecticut State University.[2]

Swain had arrived in Louisville during a crisis involving the management of the U of L hospital fourteen years earlier, which was solved with the selection of Humana, Inc., to manage the facility. Now Shumaker was confronted by a somewhat related emergency. In 1992 Humana had spun off Galen Health Care, which became the corporation running the U of L hospital and other former Humana hospitals nationwide. In 1993 Galen was acquired by Columbia Hospital Corporation, which soon merged with Hospital Corporation of America. The new entity, Columbia/HCA Healthcare, was the nation's largest for-profit hospital chain. It located its headquarters in Louisville and, after protracted negotia-

John W. Shumaker (1942–), sixteenth president, University of Louisville, 1995 to the present, declared that the University of Louisville would strive to become a "nationally pre-eminent metropolitan research university" early in the twenty-first century.

tions, forged an agreement with university, state, and local government officials to manage the U of L hospital and provide health care to indigent patients.[3]

This agreement was signed in June 1994, soon after Swain announced his forthcoming retirement. In January 1995, however, Columbia/HCA suddenly moved its corporate offices from Louisville to Nashville, thereby invalidating its management contract, boiling the blood of local and state officials, and creating another hospital crisis for the university.[4]

Shumaker had little choice but to devote much of his attention during his first months in office to the hospital situation. Spurning Columbia/HCA's bid to continue managing the hospital, in October 1995 the university awarded the contract to University Medical Center, Inc. This action created a new partnership known as UMC, which linked the university with two Louisville non-profit companies, Jewish Hospital HealthCare Services, and Alliant Health System. Under this novel arrangement, which took effect in February 1996, UMC, governed by a twelve-member board containing six appointees named by the U of L board of trustees and three each by the boards of Jewish and Alliant, began operating the hospital, the J. Graham Brown Cancer Center, the Ambulatory Care Building, and related facilities. The fifteen-year contract guaranteed millions in payments to the university for its teaching and research programs, amounts even higher than those provided by Humana, Galen, and Columbia/HCA, and generous subsidies for expansion of the emergency room, improvements at the cancer center, and indigent care. It also reduced competition among area hospitals. Jewish owned twelve hospitals in Kentucky and southern Indiana, including Jewish Hospital in downtown Louisville, while Alliant comprised three Louisville hospitals (Norton Hospital, Kosair Children's Hospital, and Alliant Medical Pavilion) and twenty-three hospitals elsewhere in Kentucky. In 1999 Alliant changed its name to Norton HealthCare.[5]

Matters involving the university's athletic programs also began to demand the new president's attention, just as they had sometimes bedeviled his predecessors. While the university had enjoyed some especially noteworthy accomplishments on the courts

and playing fields during the 1980s and 1990s, by no means was all glorious on the athletic front during that time. In the fall of 1990, for example, the institution suffered from criticism of the academic progress of its athletes, especially basketball and football players. A *Courier-Journal* analysis found U of L's graduation rates trailed those of neighboring University of Kentucky and Indiana University, and of most members of the three schools' respective athletic conferences.[6]

Then in December 1990, *60 Minutes,* the highly rated CBS television weekly news show, portrayed the U of L basketball program as one of those which exploited its athletes without regard for their academic success. *USA Today* noted that fans of opposing schools chanted "Two, four, six, eight, Louisville players don't graduate." Crum countered that many players returned to complete their degrees after the end of the five-year period used to compare schools' rates, while others enjoyed extended professional careers. He and others also noted that U of L's mission encouraged the admission of more "high-risk" students than did many other universities. Some local civil rights leaders and university faculty members, among others, called for the university to make improvements.[7]

Swain had previously announced plans to help athletes return to school after the expiration of their six-year period of scholarship aid. Over Crum's objections, he also had established a new policy requiring team members to have at least a cumulative "C" average in the fall of their junior year and at the beginning of their senior year. Athletes who could not reach this standard would be dismissed from school. The president also committed the institution to the goal of bringing athletic graduation rates up to the national average for NCAA Division I schools within five years. Swain contended that "academic values can prevail over the American sports culture in specific controversies," and, in something of an understatement, called the effort necessary to achieve this objective "a constant battle."[8]

In the midst of these troubling events, U of L accepted a bid to play in football's Fiesta Bowl in Arizona and found itself further embroiled in controversy. That state's voters had just defeated a proposal to create a paid holiday for state workers in honor of Dr. Martin Luther King Jr. In response, the University of Virginia, which had been ranked first in the nation late in the season, had declined Fiesta's bid in favor of a Sugar Bowl invitation. U of L trustee chair Woodford R. Porter Sr., himself an influential African American civic leader, urged acceptance, as did team members, who voted unanimously to go. The university stood to gain as much as $2.5 million, before expenses, for its participation. Furthermore, the game's Phoenix-area sponsors noted that their cities recognized the King holiday and promised an additional $200,000 for minority student scholarships at the schools of the two participants, Louisville and Alabama. One area civil rights leader, however, termed U of L's decision to accept the bid "morally regrettable."[9]

Swain spoke of using a large portion of the bowl revenue to strengthen U of L programs benefitting minority students. He also appointed a committee to advise him on additional ways to spend receipts. Ultimately the athletic association decided to put $200,000 of the anticipated $1.5 million in Fiesta Bowl net revenue into a Martin Luther King Endowment Fund for scholarships for "disadvantaged students of all races," making a total of $400,000 (counting the additional $200,000 from the bowl sponsors); to earmark another $200,000 to help athletes who had used up their eligibility to return to school; and to allocate most of the rest of the money for scholarships for nonrevenue sports and other athletic program projects.[10]

What Swain called a "compromise" was criticized by Porter and some other black leaders and denounced in scathing *Courier-Journal* editorials as not enough money for minority scholarships and too much for other athletic initiatives. In response, Swain promised to find funds to create a campus center dedicated to cultural diversity and to enhance the College of Arts and Sciences' Pan-African studies department. Another trustee argued that when closely examined, nearly $1 million of the bowl proceeds would help minority and disadvantaged students. The Multicultural Center, with offices in the Red Barn and with Linda Wilson as director, opened in the fall of 1991.[11]

Although the specific plans and funding for the Multicultural Center were a direct result of discussions arising out of the Fiesta Bowl controversy, that unit's roots can be traced to the aftermath of an incident of racial prejudice which had occurred a year earlier. In November 1989 a student reported she had been the target of racist notes and a remark to the effect that she did "not belong" in the Panhellenic dormitory. A freshman from Ohio, she was the only African American resident of that building. To show their support for her, more than one hundred students gathered in front of the dormitory. The Black Student Alliance conveyed a list of "demands" to President Swain, among which were calls to eliminate "the segregation of the Panhellenic dorm," to increase the number of African American resident assistants and provide improved training programs for them, institute penalties for racial harassment, remove the Confederate Monument, rename the Confederate Apartments, and create a facility for black students.[12]

Swain responded that he was "deeply distressed that we have apparently had an incident of racial harassment on the Belknap Campus. Such behavior is abhorrent and destructive to the spirit of freedom that must enliven a university. Let there be no mistake about this: *U of L will not tolerate any form of racial harassment!*" The president added, "We must assure that U of L is a welcoming, supportive place for people of all races and ethnic backgrounds." He promised students that the Panhellenic dorm would be fully integrated, that the number of resident assistants who were black would mirror the percentage of black students living in the dorms, that the affected student's dorm fees would be remitted, that a multicultural center would be developed, that the Confederate Apartments (which had never been officially named) would be renamed University Tower Apartments, and that those found guilty of racial harassment would be severely punished. He noted that the university had no authority to move the monument, which had been built on city property long before the university moved to the Belknap Campus site.[13]

About the time of Shumaker's arrival, reports of possible problems in the U of L basketball program began to surface. Following a thorough airing in the press and the university's own investigations, in November 1996 the NCAA placed the program on two years' probation for rule violations centering around a former player's use of two automobiles during the previous year. In the spring of 1997 reports of a subsequent violation emerged, after an assistant basketball coach provided improper benefits to a player's father. During the preceding autumn, Shumaker had said he did not ever want to go through another NCAA investigation. Now he expressed his frustration with the comment, "Compliance with NCAA regulations is not rocket science."[14]

Within two months newspapers were reporting the possibility of serious violations in the U of L women's volleyball program, after the team had completed its best season ever, reaching the regional semifinals in the previous year's NCAA tournament. A few days later Bill Olsen, athletic director since 1980, announced his retirement. Also during this seemingly interminable period of NCAA investigations of U of L athletic programs, an assistant volleyball coach and an assistant basketball coach departed, and another assistant basketball coach was reassigned to noncoaching duties in the athletic department. Ultimately, in September 1998, the NCAA imposed stiff sanctions on the university. Its basketball team was banned from tournament participation following the 1998-1999 season and placed on probation for three additional years. Among other penalties, the number of scholarships available to both the basketball and volleyball teams was also reduced. Shumaker stated that personnel changes had created a long-sought "culture of compliance" in the athletic program.[15]

When Olsen's replacement, Thomas M. Jurich, arrived in October 1997 vowing to rehabilitate what he called U of L's "slightly tainted" athletic image, the football Cardinals were in the midst of their worst season in decades. Upset in its opener against archrival Kentucky, and playing to ever-smaller home crowds, the team went on to post a 1-10 record. Amid some controversy, at season's end Shumaker and Jurich fired head coach Ron Cooper, furnishing him with an extravagant buy-out and quickly replacing him with John L. Smith of Utah State University. Smith's first

team surprised everyone with its 7–4 regular season record. It even played in the postseason Motor City Bowl, where it lost in the school's first bowl game in five years.[16]

LOOKING AHEAD

The election of Paul Patton as governor in the fall of 1995 presented Shumaker with an opportunity to push for an expansion of the university's research and service roles. At his inauguration Patton, who had spoken of being a "higher education governor," pledged to reform Kentucky's higher education system and thus be remembered as the leader who "brought Kentucky out of the backwoods of economic opportunity and made our people prosper in a way that only the dreamers could imagine today."[17]

By then Shumaker, noting that the university had recently been classified a "Research II" (a step up from "Doctoral I") institution by the Carnegie Foundation for the Advancement of Teaching, was speaking openly of the institution's determination to move to the highest level, there joining the University of Kentucky and fewer than ninety other American universities in the "Research I" group. Attainment of Research I status would require university researchers to generate substantially more support from federal funding agencies. The governor, insisting that the universities must play a leading role in the strengthening of the state's economy and pledging to fund their efforts much more generously than did his predecessors, found in Shumaker an enthusiastic ally. In January 1997 Shumaker stated that the University of Louisville would strive to become a "nationally preeminent metropolitan research university" within ten years.[18]

In May 1997 Patton called a special session of the state legislature for the purpose of considering his postsecondary education reform program, which was enacted as House Bill 1. The new law created the Council on Postsecondary Education and made it more powerful than its predecessor, the Council on Higher Education. Echoing Shumaker's words if not his timetable, the law also strengthened U of L's mission, charging the institution to become "a premier,

Paul Patton, elected governor of Kentucky in November 1995, made higher education reform a major objective and found an enthusiastic ally in John Shumaker, who had become president of U of L a few months earlier.

nationally recognized metropolitan research university" by 2020. Furthermore, despite strenuous objections voiced by the University of Kentucky, the statute removed the community college system from UK's control, but envisioned a prestigious advancement for that school by 2020 as well: it was to become "a major comprehensive research institution ranked" in the nation's "top twenty public universities."[19]

The governor's initiative also called for considerably larger legislative appropriations to help the University of Kentucky and the University of Louisville become leading research institutions. Shumaker responded by promoting U of L's ten-year plan, the "Challenge for Excellence," which he had unveiled in January 1997 as a guide for the institution's progress. The plan set lofty goals to be met by 2008. The university would boost its endowment to $500 million; increase the number of its endowed chairs from 25 to 75 and rise to a position of national prominence in selected fields; and double the number of doctoral degrees awarded, to 140 per year.[20]

Shortly after these events, in 1997, United Parcel Service, the area's largest private employer, announced that it faced difficulties in attracting enough part-time workers and spoke about moving opera-

tions elsewhere if it could not find a way to expand its huge Louisville airport hub. During the following winter, Shumaker helped create Metropolitan College, a joint venture with Jefferson Community College and Kentucky Tech, the latter of which was soon renamed Jefferson Technical College. Students enrolled in "UPS U.," as it was inevitable dubbed by local wags, would attend early morning and evening classes tuition-free, sleep during the day in a new U of L dormitory, and ride special buses to their nighttime package-handling jobs at the airport two miles south of the Belknap Campus. UPS responded to this initiative in March 1998 by announcing plans to add six thousand jobs and invest nearly $1 billion to expand its facilities. That fall, eight hundred students enrolled in the program, nearly half of them at U of L.[21]

In the spring of 1998 the state legislature funded the governor's proposal to allocate $110 million for endowed chairs at the state's universities. U of L's share was $33 million. Labeled "bucks for brains" by the press, the program required the universities to match state dollars with private donations and other funds.[22]

Subsequently, in connection with U of L's bicentennial celebration on April 3, 1998, Shumaker announced plans for a $200 million fund-raising campaign. As did the best of his predecessors, the new president wanted the University of Louisville to express the highest values of its community, embody its people's noblest aspirations, and reflect the rich diversity of its population. And as did all of his predecessors, he wanted metropolitan Louisville to consider the university one of its greatest assets and its leaders to labor tirelessly on its behalf.[23]

During the 1998-1999 school year, 68 percent of U of L's 20,857 students were over twenty-one years of age, with an average age of twenty-seven; 92 percent lived off campus; 64 percent were enrolled full-time; 53 percent were female; and 19.6 percent were members of minority groups (10.7 percent African American). The university had 1,203 full-time faculty members, of whom 61 percent were tenured, 90 percent held the doctorate or other terminal degree, 36.4 percent were female, and 17 percent were minority (4.6 percent African American). The average age was forty-eight. In addition, there were 529 part-time faculty members. The staff included 2,614 full-time and 364 part-time employees.[24]

LOOKING BACK

The history of the University of Louisville defies the stereotype of academic tranquility. The institution's earliest predecessor, Jefferson Seminary, was chartered in 1798, but its supporters had to struggle mightily to shape their dreams into a difficult actuality. Fifteen years passed before it opened, and in another sixteen years it was gone. Its successor, the Louisville Collegiate Institute, established in 1837 and soon renamed Louisville College, sputtered along for a few years, but by the mid-1840s it existed in name only. The college was relabeled the "Academic Department" of the University of Louisville in the 1846 statute of incorporation and was given a new building, but it failed to take hold. Six decades passed before the university was able to create a permanent liberal arts college.

The medical school, the university's strongest component and its oldest in continuous operation, grew out of an urban rivalry with Lexington in the early 1830s. By then Louisville had surpassed Lex-ington as the state's largest city and commercial capital, but intellectual primacy still belonged to her inland rival, which could boast Transylvania University and its prestigious medical faculty. With their establishment of the Louisville Medical Institute and the Louisville Collegiate Institute in 1837, the Falls City's leaders believed they could supplant Lexington as "the Athens of the West" as well.

During the medical school's first two decades, however, the university was at the center of a political controversy over public higher education. The incorporation of the University of Louisville proper in 1846 added law and academic departments. The law school survived, but the college, which could not draw from the medical school's coffers, perished. During the remainder of the nineteenth century the university consisted of a medical school and a law school loosely bound together by a common board of trustees. Moreover, although the medical school prospered financially, disharmony within the local medical community afflicted it throughout the nineteenth century.

U of L's development during the nineteenth century mirrors that of medical education in the United States. In that period, medical schools proliferated in response to the nation's geographic and demographic expansion. They competed openly for students and revenue. Eventually, medical leaders recognized the need for consolidation and cooperation to protect their interests, as well as those of their patients.

This new order in medical education followed general trends in higher learning nationwide, as university presidents in Louisville and elsewhere assumed greater authority. Early in the twentieth century, the University of Louisville underwent a rebirth with the revival of the liberal arts college. It also defined the limits of faculty and administrative power, but not without a bloody fight in the late 1920s and sharp skirmishes later in the century. Beginning in the 1920s, African Americans pushed the school toward greater degrees of racial equality. During the 1930s and 1960s general social unrest manifested itself on campus.

Prior to World War II the residents of Louisville may not have been prepared to support a leading university. In 1937 an article in a respected national magazine characterized the city as "an American museum piece," rooted heavily in the past and well satisfied with its social, business, and cultural institutions. According to the author, the town had only enough energy to "lay upon the river bank awaiting the last trump of a Presbyterian God." While the city enjoyed national distinction for the Kentucky Derby and its distilling and tobacco industries, its university was probably no more or less distinguished than many of Louisville's other municipal services and cultural assets.[25]

In any case, the 1930s demonstrated what the university could accomplish under good leadership even with meager resources. Raymond A. Kent, a capable and resilient administrator, brought the university into belated conformity with the progressive era's definition of higher education. The University of Louisville became an institution with the full authority to bestow the professional credentials that established the twentieth-century American middle class.[26]

At this and several other critical junctures in its history, however, the institution failed to solidify its financial base. Jefferson Seminary never prospered and was more often dream than reality. From 1837 until 1860, struggles over money and power afflicted and weakened the university. During the late nineteenth century, rivalries among medical schools prevented the concentration of resources. Early in the twentieth century President A.Y. Ford demonstrated fundraising skills, but the momentum he achieved was lost, as were some outstanding faculty members, under President George Colvin. President Kent probably could have been a more successful development officer under better circumstances.

In the 1950s President Philip G. Davidson saw the university's financial needs and sought municipal and private support to meet them. He turned to state affiliation somewhat reluctantly and, from the vantage point of a later time, perhaps belatedly, and only after having exhausted the other possibilities. Entrance into the state system thrust the University of Louisville headfirst into Kentucky politics. It thus moved U of L's age-old struggle into a new arena, where the institution labored vigorously to maintain

and even enlarge its status and scope as a comprehensive university and to improve its academic quality.

The 1950s and 1960s were wake-up decades for the University of Louisville. At the end of World War II the institution was, at least in some respects, a small, sleepy, somewhat undistinguished university for local white youth who could afford its relatively expensive tuition. The university's few black students attended a division separated from the main campus by color and distance. The ending of the war buoyed the university with an influx of veterans carrying federal dollars for tuition. The closing of the Louisville Municipal College for the first time brought African Americans to its formerly white campuses. Suddenly the university was a truer reflection of Louisville than it had ever been. What was to be its role? Without state affiliation the university's potential for maintaining its appeal to a broader spectrum of its constituency was in doubt. In the 1960s the institution gave up as a quasi-private, quasi-municipal institution. It decided it would become not an urban university—it had always been situated in the city—but would begin a course of action that would lead it in steps toward being a truer, more effective servant—and perhaps leader—of its broader community.

Under the guidance of President Woodrow M. Strickler, the university managed to enter the state system of higher education in 1970 with all its undergraduate, graduate, and professional programs intact. Once achieved, however, this new state status guaranteed little more than a voice in the continuing debate over how to distribute the state's limited higher education budget. It also shook the status quo.

Other members of the system did not necessarily welcome the new arrival. The University of Louisville's chief opponent in the higher education debate was the University of Kentucky. Both schools offered a wide range of graduate and professional programs, and each represented a threat to the other. UK's cautious reaction to this development was quite understandable. Ironically, however, it was the University of Kentucky, not the University of Louisville, that created the more expensive duplicate programs in medicine, dentistry, and law. The situation in the state typified higher education in America, where a variety of public and private entities established colleges and universities. This scattered resources, but also broadened opportunities. The question was how broad the taxpayers of Kentucky could afford to make the opportunities.

In addition to external pressure, state affiliation brought lower tuition and higher enrollment to U of L. Under President James G. Miller, university officials reacted to enrollment growth and a plethora of regulatory demands imposed by Frankfort by assuming the trappings of a large bureaucracy. During the 1970s, after the university left behind a semi-private, semi-municipal tradition to join the state system of higher education, it changed more than it had in any comparable period of its history. Faculty resistance was one symptom of the internal stress that accompanied this rapid change.

Finally, it is worth emphasizing that U of L's fortunes always have been tied to the city of Louisville. The school began as a municipal enterprise, but disappointment with its progress led the city to curtail its appropriations to the university between 1860 and 1910. In 1920 Louisville's black voters defeated a university bond issue, which resulted in the creation of a segregated African American undergraduate division. Following World War II, the movement of taxpaying citizens from the city to the suburbs helped lead to state affiliation. Eventually, municipal funding proved inadequate to the university's mission. Clearly, though, the institution could not have sustained itself as a comprehensive university for long even if it had received stronger support from the county outside the city.

Within the state system, the University of Louisville was assigned a special "urban" mission. For three decades thereafter, chief executives Strickler, Ekstrom, Miller, Swain, and Shumaker worked to maintain and even enlarge U of L's status and scope as a comprehensive university and to improve its academic quality. Strickler provided a link with the past as the school moved into unfamiliar territory. Ekstrom moved in and out of the president's office with apparent effortlessness, as the need arose. Miller had the difficult assignment of presiding during a period of rapid growth and change. Swain was handicapped by waves of budget crises in the 1980s and early 1990s, even as the university's enrollment and endowment continued to increase. Improvement in the state's financial health and the election of an especially supportive governor helped Shumaker position the institution to assume even stronger research and service roles at century's end.

Rightly seeing the University of Louisville as "poor in possessions," Justice Louis D. Brandeis wrote to his nephew Frederick Wehle in Louisville in 1924, "I want the authorities to dream of the University as it should be." He especially wished the school's instructors to be "rich in ideals and eager in the desire to attain them." At those times when the university has allowed itself to envision what it should be, in comparison to what it was, its hopes have virtually always outdistanced the resources necessary to fulfill them. At some points in the past, community leaders and U of L officials foresaw a great university. At other times they seemed satisfied with something far less. It remains to be seen whether or not the university, in what it calls its third century, will achieve the extraordinary distinction it has often boasted, frequently forecast, and occasionally, at least with respect to some of its endeavors, succeeded in reaching.[27]

By the time of U of L's incorporation in 1846, the medical school enjoyed a life of its own in which it had already attained a measure of prominence. Unable to succor its prodigal liberal arts college, however, the university, like an absent parent, exercised scant control over its medical and law schools. For decades these two units, though sisters, scarcely recognized each other as siblings. They lived apart and showed little interest in the well-being of the other. Their eventual welcome of the return of the liberal arts college in 1907 was made more under the duress of accreditation pressures than out of consideration for their university family or the welfare of their community.

By degrees the college made its own way in gown and town, and eventually grew into the institution's largest, though not most influential, unit. Through the years it was joined by schools of dentistry, engineering, music, social work, business, edu-

Long a symbol of the University of Louisville, Auguste Rodin's Thinker, *placed on the steps of the Administration Building and unveiled on March 25, 1949, was a gift of former Louisville Board of Aldermen president Arthur E. Hopkins. This bronze copy, the only one created by the "lost-wax cast" process, may have been the earliest one made, and may have been supervised by Rodin himself.*

cation, justice administration, nursing, allied health, and the graduate school. If not estranged from each other, the university's divisions have often acted as if they were little more than nodding acquaintances. It has been a Balkanization born of habit, practiced by their predecessors, and learned at their own dinner table, not one imposed on them by an outside force.

Unwilling or unable by mid century to forge agreement on common goals and marshal resources to meet them, the University of Louisville in the second half of the twentieth century often tried to be all things to all people, offering the widest range of programs it possibly could. At this it became adept. Stretched thin, its faculty, staff, and administrators alike labored effectively and efficiently. With them, the university fought through obstacles of inadequate funding with the only weapons it had. The commitment and sacrifice of some of its leaders have stood as beacons of encouragement to their colleagues. The university has drawn to it faculty, staff, and administrators who have by dint of extraordinary dedication and hard labor refused to see their work fail. Members of the current generation of U of L employees by and large become firm-jawed and level-eyed when they describe their contributions. Over the last quarter-century, if not longer, they have been overachievers. Most of their programs can correctly claim a measure of success.

Pushing against this tendency, especially during the century's last two decades, has been an opposite notion that the university must channel its never-bountiful resources into those programs most needed to serve its metropolitan area and to reduce or eliminate programs deemed less central to its mission. Presidents Swain and Shumaker exercised power more forcefully and effectively than the institution had been accustomed to experiencing. At the same time they argued that for the university to move to higher levels of academic quality it must foster a greater degree of support from its community.

To his brother Alfred in Louisville in 1925 Brandeis wrote, "To become great, a university must express the people whom it serves, and must express the people and community at their best. The aim must be high and the vision broad; the goal seemingly attainable but beyond immediate reach." To accomplish this level of excellence, the university must reflect the diversity of its community, lead in its appreciation for minorities, and respect and serve the less powerful. It must attract a faculty desirous of performing basic and applied research and eager to teach all ages of students. It must draw students from all sections of the community, teach them well, and work unceasingly to retain them. It must communicate the importance of academic freedom, and allow, even seek out, unpopular opinions. Perhaps if it does these things well, the community it serves will not only want a top-notch research university, but will also help provide the tools the University of Louisville needs to achieve true distinction.[28]

Over the course of a long journey the University of Louisville and its predecessor institutions have fought through what sometimes seemed like insuperable obstacles. The school struggled to maintain financial stability; nursed its fledgling and often neglected liberal arts college to the threshold of maturity; strengthened the role of the president's office; brought a semblance of unity to what was once a collection of more or less independent divisions, called "baronial fiefdoms" by one longtime administrator; improved the quality of its academic programs; and determined to serve thoroughly and well the diverse elements of its community.[29]

On April 3, 1798, a group of Louisville citizens framed a vision of advanced education for their frontier settlement which took root early in the next century. Two hundred years later, as it celebrated its bicentennial, the University of Louisville stood as both beneficiary and caretaker of that vision. Poised at the brink of a new century, it could look back over the course of its long journey and ahead to its promise of even greater achievement.

APPENDIX ONE

DEANS OF THE SCHOOLS AND COLLEGES OF THE UNIVERSITY OF LOUISVILLE

Acting or interim deans are identified (a), unless at some point their status was changed from acting to permanent.

DEANS OF THE COLLEGE OF ARTS AND SCIENCES

John Calvin Willis	1907-1908
John L. Patterson	1908-1922
Warwick M. Anderson	1922-1928
Smiley M. Whinery	1928-1929
Earle B. Fowler (a)	1929-1930
Julius J. Oppenheimer	1930-1957
Guy Stevenson (a)	1957-1959
Richard L. Barber	1959-1972
Martin R. Baron (a)	1972-1973
Thomas H. Crawford (a)	1973-1974
Arthur Joseph Slavin	1974-1977
William G. Bos (a)	1977-1978
Lois S. Cronholm	1978-1985
Joseph Deck (a)	1985-1987
Victor A. Olorunsola	1987-1990
Thomas J. Hynes Jr. (a)	1990-1996
David A. Howarth (a)	1996-1997
Randall Moore	1997-1999
Shirley C. Willihnganz (a)	1999-

DEANS OF THE SCHOOL OF MEDICINE

Lunsford P. Yandell Sr.	1837-1838
Charles Wilkins Short	1838-1841

John Esten Cooke	1841-1842
Jedediah Cobb	1842-1852
Lunsford P. Yandell Sr.	1852-1856
Benjamin Rush Palmer	1856-1857
Lunsford P. Yandell Sr.	1857-1859
Joseph W. Benson	1859-1865
George Wood Bayless	1865-1866
Joseph W. Benson	1866-1867
James Morrison Bodine	1867-1907
Thomas Crain Evans	1907-1911
William Edward Grant	1911-1914
Henry Enos Tuley	1914-1923
Stuart Graves	1923-1928
John Walker Moore	1928-1949
James Murray Kinsman	1949-1963
Donn L. Smith	1963-1969
Douglas Martin Haynes	1969-1973
Arthur Hail Keeney	1973-1980
Donald R. Kmetz	1980-1998
Joel A. Kaplan	1998-

DEANS OF THE SCHOOL OF LAW

Henry Pirtle	1846-1873
William Chenault	1881-1886
Rozel Weissinger	1886-1890
Willis Overton Harris	1890-1911
Charles B. Seymour	1911-1919
Edward W. Hines	1919-1921
Charles B. Seymour	1922-1925
Leon P. Lewis	1925-1930

Neville Miller	1930-1933
Joseph A. McClain Jr.	1934-1936
Jack Neal Lott Jr.	1936-1946
Absalom C. Russell	1946-1957
William B. Peden	1957-1958
Marlin M. Volz	1958-1965
James R. Merritt	1965-1974
Steven R. Smith (a)	1974-1975
James R. Merritt	1975-1976
Harold G. Wren	1976-1980
Norvie L. Lay (a)	1980-1981
Barbara B. Lewis	1981-1990
Donald L. Burnett Jr.	1990-

DEANS OF THE GRADUATE SCHOOL

John L. Patterson	1915-1923
Warwick M. Anderson	1923-1928
John L. Patterson	1928-1935
Guy Stevenson	1935-1961
William J. McGlothlin (a)	1961-1964
John A. Dillon Jr.	1966-1974
Rea T. Alsup (a)	1974-1975
Alan A. Johnson	1975-1976
Richard H. Swigart (a)	1976-1978
X. Joseph Musacchia	1978-1989
Paul D. Jones (a)	1989-1990
Patrick W. Flanagan	1991-1996
Paul D. Jones (a)	1996-1999
Ronald M. Atlas	1999-

DEANS OF THE SCHOOL OF DENTISTRY

James L. Howe	1887-1895
P. R. Taylor	1896-1900
William E. Grant	1900-1918
Henry B. Tileston	1918-1925
John T. O'Rourke	1925-1944
Philip E. Blackerby	1944-1945
Raymond E. Myers	1945-1969
Harold E. Boyer	1969-1972
William J. Meyers (a)	1972-1974
Merwyn A. Landay	1974-1977
Richard L. Miller (a)	1977-1978
Frederick M. Parkins	1979-1984
Edward B. Gernert (a)	1984-1986

Wallace V. Mann, Jr.	1986-1988
Richard L. Miller (a)	1988-1990
Rowland A. Hutchinson	1990-1998
John N. Williams	1999-

DEANS OF THE SPEED SCIENTIFIC SCHOOL

Bennett M. Brigman	1924-1938
Ford L. Wilkinson Jr.	1938-1947
Robert C. Ernst	1947-1969
Harry C. Saxe	1969-1980
Earl R. Gerhard	1980-1990
Thomas R. Hanley	1990-

DEANS OF THE SCHOOL OF MUSIC

Jacques Jolas	1932-1935
Dwight Anderson	1937-1956
Robert Whitney	1956-1971
Jerry Ball	1971-1990
Paul Brink (a)	1990-1992
Herbert L. Koerselman	1992-

DEANS OF THE SCHOOL OF NURSING

Anne D. Taylor	1952-1953
Virginia L. Barker	1979-1980
Regina L. Monnig (a)	1980-1981
Richard H. Swigart (a)	1981-1982
Marion E. McKenna (a)	1982-1984
Justine J. Speer	1984-1994
Paulette Adams (a)	1995-1997
Mary H. Mundt	1997-

DEANS OF THE SCHOOL OF BUSINESS

John R. Craf	1953-1964
Frederick W. Stamm	1964-1968
Carl T. Eakin	1968-1976
William H. Peters	1976-1984
Robert L. Taylor	1984-

DEANS OF UNIVERSITY COLLEGE

William C. Huffman	1957-1973
Roger H. Geeslin (a)	1973-1974
Wendell G. Rayburn	1974-1980
Leicester R. Moise (a)	1980-1982

Deans of the School of Education

F. Randall Powers	1968-1978
Raphael O. Nystrand	1978-1999
Douglas Simpson	1999-

University Librarians

Evelyn Schneider	1919-1965
Wayne Yenawine	1965-1970
Edith Knepper (a)	1970-1971
John Demos	1971-1982
Martha Alexander Bowman	1983-1991
Ralze Dorr (a)	1991-1996
Hannelore Rader	1997-

Deans and Directors of the Kent School of Social Work

Margaret K. Strong	1936-1941
John J. Cronin	1941-1947
Mathilda Mathisen (a)	1947
Howell V. Williams	1947-1955
Mathilda Mathisen (a)	1955
Arleigh L. Lincoln	1956-1962
Kenneth W. Kindelsperger	1962-1971
Howard W. Borsuk (a)	1971
Herbert Bisno	1971-1975
Edward W. Francel (a)	1975-1976
Roger M. Lind	1976-1981
Sam L. Neal (a)	1981-1985
Donald W. Beless	1985-1989
Gerard M. Barber (a)	1989
Thomas R. Lawson (a)	1989-1997
Terry L. Singer	1997-

Deans and Directors of the School of Allied Health Sciences

Richard Swigart (a)	1977-1995
Alfred L. Thompson, Jr. (a)	1995-1998
Roger A. Lanier	1998-

Deans of the School of Justice Administration

David A. McCandless	1969-1971
John C. Klotter	1971-1981
J. Price Foster	1981-1983

Dean of the College of Urban and Public Affairs

J. Price Foster	1984-1991

Deans of the Louisville Municipal College

Rufus E. Clement	1931-1937
David A. Lane	1937-1942
Bertram W. Doyle	1942-1950

Deans of the Jefferson School of Law

Shackelford Miller Sr.	1905-1913
Thomas R. Gordon	1913-1929
Benjamin F. Washer	1929-1950

Deans of Kentucky Southern College

E. Bruce Heilman	1961-1962
John R. Killinger, Jr.	1962-1965
Ray A. Stines (a)	1966-1967
Warren F. Jones	1967-1969

LOUISVILLE MUNICIPAL COLLEGE FACULTY MEMBERS 1931-1951

NAME	HIGHEST DEGREE EARNED	EMPLOYMENT DATES
Howard R. Barksdale	M.A., Fisk University	1943-1951
Antoine Bervin	Licencie en Droit, University of Paris	1947-1948
William M. Bright	Ph.D., University of Illinois	1931-1951
Earl L. Brown	M.A., Boston University	1931-1933
Wilmoth A. Carter	M.A., Atlanta University	1943-1946
Rufus E. Clement	Ph.D., Northwestern University	1931-1937
Floyd W. Crawford	M.A., University of Colorado	1939-1951
John E. Crowe	M.S., Indiana University	1950
Bertram W. Doyle	Ph.D., University of Chicago	1942-1950
Roger Dreyfuss	M.A., Yale University	1947-1951
Rosalind Eagleson	B.A., Fisk University	1945-1946
Donald A. Edwards	M.S. University of Chicago	1936-1944
Augusta M. Emanuel	M.A., Columbia University	1931-1945
William L. Fields	M.A., Indiana University	1943-1950
Susie N. Hagan	M.S., Atlanta University	1948-1950
Henrietta L. Herod	M.A., Radcliffe College	1931-1942
Alphonse Hunnicutt	M.Ed., University of Cincinnati	1948-1951
Thomas D. Jarrett	A.M., Fisk University	1941-1944
James L. Jones	Ph.D., University of Pittsburgh	1934-1935
Juanita E. Lacy	M.A., University of Cincinnati	1949-1951
David A. Lane	M.A., Harvard University	1937-1942
Daniel L. Lawson	M.A., Simmons University	1931-1936
Stanley S. Morris	M.A., Cornell University	1944-1951
Elmer E. O'Banion	M.A., Indiana University	1938-1939
Charles H. Parrish Jr.	Ph.D., University of Chicago	1931-1951
Georgia A. Peters	M.A., Columbia University	1946-1949
James R. Pierce	B.A., University of Toledo	1933-1934
Andrew W. Ramsey	B.A., Butler University	1931-1933

continued

NAME	HIGHEST DEGREE EARNED	EMPLOYMENT DATES
Cassie A. Redden	M.A., University of Illinois	1942-1950
J. Saunders Redding	M.A., Brown University	1934-1937
Dwight T. Reed	B.S., University of Minnesota	1947-1950
George F. Robinson	M.A., Northwestern University	1934-1944
J. W. Sappenfield	Ph.D., Ohio State University	1931-1935
Clark H. Watkins	Ph.D., University of Chicago	1934-1935
Clarence R. White	M.A., Howard University	1940-1942
Forrest O. Wiggins	Ph.D., University of Wisconsin	1945-1947
Hazel B. Williams	M.A., University of Kansas	1932-1944
George D. Wilson	Ph.D., Ohio State University	1935-1951
Henry S. Wilson	Ph.D., Indiana University	1931-1951
Nancy B. Woolridge	Ph.D., University of Chicago	1931-1946

Source: James Blaine Hudson III, "The History of Louisville Municipal College: Events Leading to the Desegregation of the University of Louisville" (Ed.D. diss., University of Kentucky, 1981), 118-119.

NOTES

1. Jefferson Seminary, 1798-1829

1. Jefferson Seminary, Subscription List, April 3, 1798, University Archives and Records Center, University of Louisville (hereinafter cited as U of L Archives); John E. Kleber, ed., *The Kentucky Encyclopedia* (Lexington, 1992), 467-468.

2. Biographical information about the first trustees of Jefferson Seminary can be found in such sources as *Early Kentucky Settlers: The Records of Jefferson County, Kentucky* (Baltimore, 1988), 297, 348, 403, 407, 418, 440; Karen Mauer Green, *The Kentucky Gazette, 1787-1800: Genealogical and Historical Abstracts* (Baltimore, 1983), 7, 23, 132; *Kentucky Encyclopedia*, 21, 139, 242-243; Mary Taylor Brewer, *From Log Cabins to the White House: A History of the Taylor Family*, N.P., N.P., 1985, 319-329; and Samuel W. Thomas, "William Croghan, Sr. (1752-1822): A Pioneer Kentucky Gentleman," *Filson Club History Quarterly* 43 (January 1969), 30-61.

3. Samuel W. Thomas, ed., *Views of Louisville Since 1766* (Louisville, 1971), 22.

4. William H. Littell, ed., *The Statute Law of Kentucky*, 5 viols. (Frankfort, 1809-1819), II, 107-109.

5. R.H. Eckelberry, *The History of the Municipal University in the United States* (Washington, 1932), 23; Alvin Fayette Lewis, *History of Higher Education in Kentucky* (Washington, 1899), 11; *Kentucky Encyclopedia*, 572-573; James C. Klotter, "Two Centuries of the Lottery in Kentucky," *Register of the Kentucky Historical Society* 87 (Autumn 1989), 405-421; Littell, *Statute Law of Kentucky*, II, 378.

6. Littell, *Statute Law of Kentucky*, III, 206-207, 489-490.

7. Butler typically used his middle and last names, omitting his first. Mann Butler, *Valley of the Ohio*, ed. G. Glenn Clift and Hambleton Tapp (Frankfort, 1971), "Preface."

8. Dwayne Cox, "How Old Is the University of Louisville?" *Register of the Kentucky Historical Society* 81 (winter 1983): 59-76; George H. Yater, *Two Hundred Years at the Falls of the Ohio: A History of Louisville and Jefferson County* (2nd ed., Louisville, 1987), 32-37 (this book's 1st ed., published in 1979, was accompanied by endnotes under separate cover, hereinafter referred to as Yater, "Notes" to *Two Hundred Years*); *Kentucky Encyclopedia*, 679-680, 852-853.

9. George A. Hendon, "Notes on the Founding of University of Louisville," December 30, 1947.

10. Lewis Collins, *History of Kentucky*, 2 vols. (Louisville, 1924, originally published 1847), I, 641-642; Jefferson County, Deed Books, July 2, 1813, X, 300-1, Jefferson County Archives; Louisville *Western Courier*, December 20, 1813, April 11, 1814, February 28, 1816; *Louisville Public Advertiser*, August 27, 1814.

11. Henry McMurtrie, *Sketches of Louisville and Its Environs* (Louisville, 1819), 124-125; *Kentucky Acts*, January 3, 1817, 14-15, February 3, 1818, 526, December 21, 1820, 153-154; Jefferson County Court, Minutes, May 15, 1821, X, 19, Jefferson County Archives; *Louisville Commercial*, c. 1885, Richard Ferguson Historical File, Filson Club; *Louisville Public Advertiser*, November 17, 1821, January 14, 1826, September 8, 12, 1827, September 3, 1828.

12. Yater, *Two Hundred Years*, 37-46.

13. Lynn L. Marshall, "The Genesis of Grass-Roots Democracy in Kentucky," *Mid-America* 47 (October 1965): 269-287; *Louisville Public Advertiser*, November 23, 1825, January 14, 21, 1826, February 21, 1829; Louisville, Legislative Records, April 24, 1829, 339-340, Louisville City Archives. Neils Henry Sonne, *Liberal Kentucky, 1780-1828* (New York, 1939), 244 ff., discusses relief party attacks upon Transylvania University in Lexington.

14. David Post, "From the Jefferson Seminary to the Louisville Free School: Change and Continuity in Western

Education, 1813-1840," *Register of the Kentucky Historical Society* 86 (spring 1993): 103-118, describes the rise of public criticism of Kentucky's early "scheme of elite academies."

15. *Kentucky Acts,* January 3, 1830, 262-263; Louisville, Legislative Records, March 6, April 3, and November 27, 1837, 115, 146-148, 370-371, Louisville City Archives; Oliver H. Stratton and John M. Vaughn, eds., *A Collection of the State and Municipal Laws . . . Applicable to the City of Louisville* (Louisville, 1857), 363-367. The other half of the Jefferson Seminary estate went to the county orphan asylum at Middletown.

16. *History of the Ohio Falls Cities and Their Counties,* 2 vols. (Cleveland, 1882), I, 441; J. Stoddard Johnston, ed., *Memorial History of Louisville,* 2 vols. (Chicago, 1896), I, 239; Lewis, *History of Higher Education in Kentucky,* 261-263; Eckelberry, *History of the Municipal University,* 37; William C. Mallalieu, "Origins of the University of Louisville," *Filson Club History Quarterly* 12 (January 1938): 24-41; *Time,* April 5, 1937, 51-52.

17. Dwayne Cox, "How Old Is the University of Louisville?" *Potential,* May 10, 1978; President's Annual Report, 1931-1932, 4, U of L Archives.

18. William C. Mallalieu, Personal Data Sheet, December 10, 1965, Faculty Personnel Records; College of Arts and Sciences, Annual Report, 1935-1936, 32, U of L Archives; *Cardinal,* March 31, 1933.

19. Professor Mallalieu's personal papers in the U of L Archives contain his drafts, which were revised by the Kentucky Writers' Project and published under the title *A Centennial History of the University of Louisville* (Louisville, 1939), hereinafter cited as *Centennial History.* See *Centennial History,* vii, and Mallalieu, Interview, May 27, 1970, U of L Archives.

20. Mallalieu, "Origins of the University of Louisville," 24-41.

21. Monty Noam Penkower, *The Federal Writers' Project: A Study in Government Patronage of the Arts* (Urbana, 1977), 238-248; Urban R. Bell to Henry G. Alsberg, March 1, April 3, 1937, January 26, 1938; Henry G. Alsberg to Urban R. Bell, March 14, 1939; Records of the Federal Writers' Project, National Archives, Washington, D.C.; Mary Burton to Raymond A. Kent, November 19, 1937; Raymond A. Kent to Urban R. Bell, August 8, 1938; Urban R. Bell to Katharine Dryden, August 16, 1938; Records of the Kentucky Writers' Project, University of Kentucky Archives.

22. *New York Times,* February 14, 1937; President's Annual Report, 1936-1937, 5-8, U of L Archives; Flexner, "A Half Century of American Medicine," 29-56, Shafroth, "Modern Standards of Legal Education," 207-240, Bond, "The Black Liberal Arts College as a Societal Force," 309-330, in *A Century of Municipal Higher Education* (Chicago, 1937); Roger M. Williams, *The Bonds: An American Family* (New York, 1971).

23. "Municipal Milestone," *Time,* April 5, 1937, 51-52; *Centennial History,* 13-14, 34-37, 128.

24. Mallalieu, "Origins of the University of Louisville," 24; Eckelberry, *History of the Municipal University,* 9-22; J.H. Easterby, *A History of the College of Charleston* (Charleston, 1935), 94-95.

25. Notice of the *Centennial History,* in *Register of the Kentucky Historical Society* 38 (January 1940): 89-90; *Centennial History,* 11-15.

26. *Courier-Journal,* May 15, 1947.

27. Most notable among the materials Hendon inspected at the University of Chicago was the Durrett Collection, which consisted of manuscript and other records assembled by Louisvillian Reuben T. Durrett. Hendon Personnel Record, Reference Files, U of L Archives; Hendon, Interview, August 13, 1976, U of L Archives; Hendon, "Notes on the Founding of University of Louisville," December 30, 1947, and "Report . . . to President John W. Taylor on Mr. Hendon's Visit to the Harper Library, University of Chicago," May, 1948, Reference Files, U of L Archives.

28. *Courier-Journal,* July 30, 1947, February 9, 1948.

29. *Cardinal,* August 1, 1947, February 14, 1948; *Courier-Journal,* February 10, 1948; "Have Another Party," *Time,* August 11, 1947, 77; Frank L. McVey, *The Gates Open Slowly: A History of Education in Kentucky* (Lexington, 1949), 125-126; Cox, "How Old Is the University of Louisville?" *Register,* 70-71; Cox, "How Old Is the University of Louisville?" *Potential,* May 10, 1978.

30. *Courier-Journal,* February 8, 1948. U of L announcements erroneously described the 1983 graduation ceremony as its "one hundred and eighty-fifth commencement." Such claims, repeated over the years, were based on three assumptions, each incorrect: that the university began offering classes in 1798; held its first commencement in 1799; and has had a commencement every year since then. Morison, "Graduation Ceremonies . . . Number Correct?" *Inside U of L,* June 1983.

31. Creese, "Remembering Mayor Charles P. Farnsley," October 9, 1997, Reference Files, U of L Archives; Yater, *Two Hundred Years,* 217-218; *Kentucky Encyclopedia,* 309.

32. *Louisville* 17 (August 20, 1966), 14-15.

33. J.J. Oppenheimer, Interview, October 24, 1973, U of L Archives. Farnsley received three degrees from the University of Louisville: LL.B. (1930), A.B. (1943), and an honorary doctor of laws (1951).

2. "First Among the Medical Schools of the West"

1. For recent overviews of the history of early Louisville, see Yater, *Two Hundred Years,* 1-60; *Kentucky Encyclopedia,* 574-576; Carl E. Kramer, *Two Centuries of*

Urban Development in Central and South Louisville (Louisville, 1980), 30-64; and Allen J. Share, *Cities in the Commonwealth: Two Centuries of Urban Life in Kentucky* (Lexington, 1982).

2. *Dictionary of American Biography,* ed. Dumas Malone et al. (20 vols., 10 supplements, index; New York: Charles Scribner's Sons, 1928-1996), 8, 60-62 (*Dictionary of American Biography* hereinafter referred to as *DAB*); *Kentucky Encyclopedia,* 396.

3. Mallalieu, "Origins of the University of Louisville," 24-41; Richard H. Wade, *The Urban Frontier: The Rise of the Western Cities, 1780-1830* (Cambridge, 1959), 197-200, 242, 331; Share, *Cities in the Commonwealth,* 26, 28-31, 72; *Centennial History,* 1-16; Sonne, *Liberal Kentucky,* 242-261; John D. Wright, *Transylvania: Tutor to the West* (Lexington, 1975), 99-117; *Kentucky Encyclopedia,* 894-896; Dwayne Cox, "The Louisville Medical Institute: A Case History in American Medical Education," *Filson Club History Quarterly* 62 (April 1988): 197-219.

4. Wright, *Transylvania,* 145-157; WPA Medical Historical Research Project, *Medicine and Its Development in Kentucky* (Louisville, 1940), 90-91; John H. Ellis, *Medicine in Kentucky* (Lexington, 1977), 13-14; Louisville, Legislative Records, October 17, 1836, 23-24, Louisville City Archives; *Louisville Journal,* January 20, 1837.

5. In addition to Caldwell, Cooke, and Yandell, the six original LMI faculty members included Jedediah Cobb of Cincinnati, Henry Miller of Louisville, and Joshua Barker Flint of Boston, Massachusetts. *Kentucky Acts,* February 2, 1833, 300-301; Louisville, Legislative Records, March 6, April 3, 1837, 115, 146-148; *Louisville Public Advertiser,* March 25, 1837, quoted in Yater, *Two Hundred Years,* 51-52; Harriot W. Warner, ed., *Autobiography of Charles Caldwell* (New York, 1968; originally published 1855), 400-401; Emmet F. Horine, "A History of the Louisville Medical Institute and the Establishment of the University of Louisville and Its School of Medicine, 1833-1846," *Filson Club History Quarterly* 7 (July 1933), 133-147.

6. *Kentucky Encyclopedia,* 350, 783; *DAB,* 16, 195-196.

7. Charles Wilkins Short to William Short, November 24, 1844, Short Papers, Filson Club. Statistics compiled from the annual announcements of the Louisville Medical Institute and the Medical Department of the University of Louisville. *Haldeman's Picture of Louisville* (Louisville 1844), 66.

8. Nellie Carstens, "Charles Caldwell, M.D.: A Biographical Sketch" (M.A. thesis, University of Louisville, 1979), 61-89; Emmet F. Horine, *Biographical Sketch and Guide to the Writings of Charles Caldwell, M.D.* (Brooks, Kentucky, 1960), 1-17.

9. Deborah Skaggs, "Charles Wilkins Short: Kentucky Botanist and Physician, 1794-1863" (M.A.

thesis, University of Louisville, 1982), 100-141; Percy Albert Davis, "Charles Wilkins Short, 1794-1863: Kentucky Botanist and Physician," *Filson Club History Quarterly* 19 (July 1945): 131-155, (October 1945): 208-249.

10. Emmet F. Horine, *Daniel Drake, 1785-1852: Pioneer Physician of the Midwest* (Philadelphia, 1961), 324-367; Gerald N. Grob, *Edward Jarvis and the Medical World of Nineteenth-Century America* (Knoxville, 1978), 43-56; James H. Cassedy, *American Medicine and Statistical Thinking, 1800-1860* (Cambridge, 1984), 172-177; Henry D. Shapiro, "Daniel Drake: The Scientist as Citizen," in Henry D. Shapiro and Zane L. Miller, eds., *Physician to the West: Selected Writings of Daniel Drake on Science and Society* (Lexington, 1970), xi-xxii; Joan Titley, "Edward Jarvis, M.D.: A New England Physician's Activities in Louisville, 1837-1842," *Tractions* 3 (1967-1968): 20-23.

11. Samuel D. Gross, *Autobiography,* 2 vols. (Philadelphia, 1887), 1: 96-99; *DAB,* 8, 18-20.

12. Thomas Cary Johnson Jr., *Scientific Interests in the Old South* (New York, 1936), 79, 177-179, 198-199; *DAB,* 17, 163-164.

13. Lunsford P. Yandell to Charles Wilkins Short, June 3, 1838; Charles Wilkins Short to William Short, July 29, 1838; Short Papers, Filson Club; Louisville Medical Institute, *Catalogue* (Louisville, 1838), 6; George M. Bibb, "An Oration Commemorative of Laying the Corner Stone . . ." *Louisville Journal of Medicine and Surgery* 1 (January 1838), insert following p. 250; Haldeman, *Picture of Louisville,* 67; Joan Titley, "The Library of the Louisville Medical Institute, 1837-46," *Bulletin of the Medical Library Association* 52 (April 1964): 353-369; Merija Nonacs, "The Kornhauser Memorial Medical Library: Its History and Development" (M.A. thesis, University of Texas, 1966).

14. Charles Wilkins Short, *Duties of Medical Students During Attendance at Lectures* (Louisville, 1845), 11-23; Daniel Drake, "The Means of Promoting Moral and Intellectual Improvement of Students and Physicians of the Mississippi Valley," in Shapiro and Miller, eds., *Physician to the West,* 295-314.

15. Henry Clay Lewis, "Being Examined for My Degree," in John Q. Anderson, ed., *Louisiana Swamp Doctor: The Life of Henry Clay Lewis* (Baton Rouge, 1962), 165-174; also see Anderson, "Henry Clay Lewis: Louisville Medical Institute Student, 1844-1846," *Filson Club History Quarterly* 32 (January 1959): 30-37.

16. Louisville Medical Institute, *Catalogue* (Louisville, 1837), 3-8; Drake, "Promoting Moral and Intellectual Improvement," 295-314.

17. William G. Rothstein, *American Physicians in the Nineteenth Century: From Sects to Science* (Baltimore, 1972), 88-93; Frederick Eberson, "A Great Purging—Cholera or Calomel?" *Filson Club History Quarterly* 50 (April 1976): 28-35; *DAB,* 4, 384-385; Henry Miller,

"Vulgar Errors in Medicine," *Louisville Journal of Medicine and Surgery* 1 (April 1838): 268-275. Each of the famous "Cooke's Pills" contained two grams of this mercurial compound.

18. Todd L. Savitt, "The Use of Blacks for Medical Experimentation and Demonstration in the Old South," *Journal of Southern History* 48 (August 1982): 331-348; Charles A. Hentz, *Autobiography*, n.d., 64-75, Southern Historical Collection, University of North Carolina, Chapel Hill; Henry Clay Lewis, "Stealing a Baby," in *Louisiana Swamp Doctor*, 151-158; *DAB*, 8, 575-576.

19. Ellis, *Medicine in Kentucky*, 14; WPA, *Medicine and Its Development in Kentucky*, 152-154; "Louisville Marine Hospital," *Western Journal of Medicine and Surgery* 2 (October 1840): 319-320; W.H. Donne, "Wound of the Antrum Highmore," *Western Journal of Medicine and Surgery* 6 (September 1842): 186-189; Eugene H. Conner, "By Many Names: Our City Hospital," *Louisville Medicine* 37 (April 1990), 16-30; Thomas, ed., *Views of Louisville Since 1766*, 47.

20. Charles Wilkins Short to John Cleves Short, February 16, 1848, Symmes, Short, and Harrison Papers, Library of Congress; Drake, "Promoting Moral and Intellectual Improvement," 295-314; Joseph W. Brooks, "On Creosote: A Thesis Submitted to the Managers and Faculty of the Louisville Medical Institute," *Louisville Journal of Medicine and Surgery* 1 (April 1838): 275-294; *DAB*, 3, 216-217.

21. Charles Wilkins Short to William Short, March 2, 1848, Short Papers; Lewis, "Being Examined for My Degree," 164-174; Nancy D. Baird, *David Wendel Yandell: Physician of Old Louisville* (Lexington, 1978), 14-15.

3. From Frontier Academy to City College

1. Charles Caldwell, "A Succinct View of the Influence of Mental Cultivation on the Destinies of Louisville," *Louisville Journal of Medicine and Surgery* 1 (January 1838): 1-34.

2. Louisville, Legislative Records, November 27, 1837, 370-371, Louisville City Archives; Jefferson County, Deed Books, November 21, 1837, LIX, 385-386, Jefferson County Archives.

3. Louisville Collegiate Institute, *Catalogue* (Louisville, 1838), 1ff.; Yater, *Two Hundred Years*, 52.

4. Louisville, Legislative Records, September 22, 1838, 71, Louisville City Archives; Dartmouth College, *Class of Alumni . . . 1813* (Boston, 1854), 34-38; *Louisville Public Advertiser*, September 15, 25, 1838.

5. Thomas D. Clark, *Indiana University: Midwestern Pioneer*, vol. I, *The Early Years* (Bloomington, 1970), 33-45.

6. *Kentucky Acts*, January 17, 1840, 51-52.

7. Skaggs, "Charles Wilkins Short," 108-114.

8. *Louisville Journal*, May 18, 20, 1840; Haldeman, *Picture of Louisville*, 69.

9. William A. McDowell, et al., *At a General Meeting of the Resident Practitioners of Louisville* (Louisville, 1840), 1; Louisville, Legislative Records, August 8, 1842, 218-219, Louisville City Archives; Lunsford P. Yandell, "Dr. McDowell and His Pretensions," *Western Journal of Medicine and Surgery* 7, 2d series (September 1844): 242-247; [William A. McDowell], *Some Account of the Faculty of the Louisville Medical Institute* (Louisville, 1842), 3-5; Louisville Medical Institute, *Some Account of the Origin and Present Condition of the Louisville Medical Institute* (Louisville, 1842), 3ff.

10. Minutes of the Jefferson County Court, Book 18 (June 3, 1844), 681, Jefferson County Archives.

11. Louisville, Legislative Records, December 30, 1845, 82-84, Louisville City Archives.

4. The Emergence of a University

1. Stratton and Vaughn, eds., *A Collection of the State and Municipal Laws . . . Applicable to the City of Louisville*, 363-367.

2. *Biographical Encyclopaedia of Kentucky* (Cincinnati, 1878), 680-682; *Kentucky Encyclopedia*, 681.

3. Louisville, Legislative Records, August 17, 1846, 216; November 23, 1846, 284-285; January 29, 1849, 324; March 28, 1850, 57-58, Louisville City Archives; Board of Trustees, Minutes, August 3, 1846, August 19, 1848, May 13, 1869, U of L Archives; *Public School Laws of Louisville* (Louisville, n.d.), 90-93; Yater, *Two Hundred Years*, 53; Hendon, "Notes on the Founding of University of Louisville," 22-23. The Law Department used the building for a few years, followed by Male High School; see R.C. Riebel, *Louisville Panorama: A Visual History of Louisville* (Louisville, 1954), 48.

4. Stratton and Vaughn, eds., *A Collection of the State and Municipal Laws*, 363-367.

5. James P. Jones, *"Black Jack": John A. Logan and Southern Illinois in the Civil War* (Tallahassee, 1967), 10; Lillian Semple Truman, *The Louisville Law Library* (Louisville, 1912), 14; Law Department, *Catalogue* (Louisville, 1894), 4-6; *Louisville Courier*, August 6, 1946; *Centennial History*, 100.

6. Preston S. Loughborough, *A Digest of the Statute Laws of Kentucky of a Public and Permanent Nature, Passed Since 1834, with References to Judicial Decisions* (Frankfort, 1842); Barbara B. Lewis, Linda S. Ewald, and Donald L. Burnett Jr., "An Aim High and a Vision Broad: A Sesquicentennial History of the University of Louisville School of Law, 1846-1996," in *University of Louisville School of Law Sesquicentennial History & Law Alumni/ae Directory* (Louisville, 1996), xii-xiii.

7. "New Medical School in Louisville" and "A New Medical School," *Western Journal of Medicine and Surgery* 1 (Third series; February 1848) 178-182, 6 (Third Series; July 1850) 89-92; Lunsford P. Yandell to Susan Yandell, May 5, 1850, Yandell Papers, Filson Club; Yandell, *History of the Medical Department of the University of Louisville* (Louisville, 1852), 1-26; Medical Department, *Catalogue* (Louisville, 1872), 17-23; Kentucky School of Medicine, *Catalogue* (Louisville, 1884), 19-27.

8. Yater, *Two Hundred Years,* 61 (this ranking requires viewing New York and Brooklyn as one city); 1851 Kentucky Acts C. 692.

9. *City of Louisville v. President and Trustees of University of Louisville,* 54 KY. 642, 15 B. Mon. 642; *Dartmouth College v. Woodward,* 17 U.S. (4 WHEAT) 518 (1819).

10. *Louisville Democrat,* March 7, 1851; *Kentucky Acts,* March 24, 1851, 231-236, February 28, 1860, 432; *City of Louisville* v. *University of Louisville,* 15 *Monroe* 642 (1855); Hendon, "Notes on the Founding of University of Louisville," 23-29; *Centennial History,* 16-19; Yater, "Notes" to *Two Hundred Years,* 53; Cox, "How Old Is the University of Louisville," *Register,* 60-61.

11. Horine, *Drake,* 360; Horine, *Biographical Sketch and Guide to the Writings of Charles Caldwell, M.D.,* 80-85; Skaggs, "Short," 133-135; Gross, *Autobiography,* I, 103; "Destruction of the University of Louisville," *North American Medico-Chirurgical Review* 1 (March 1857), 306-307; *Louisville Democrat,* June 26, 1857.

12. *DAB,* 8, 60-66; Anna Ruth Spiegel, "The Public Career of James Guthrie" (M.A. thesis, University of Louisville, 1940), 29-89.

13. Randall Capps, *The Rowan Story: From Federal Hill to My Old Kentucky Home* (Bowling Green, Kentucky, 1976), 27-47; Louisville Board of Trade, *A Tribute to William Garvin* (Louisville, 1869), 20-29; "John Hopkins Harney," *Appleton's Cyclopaedia of American Biography,* 6 vols. (New York, 1888-1889), III, 85; Dartmouth College, *Class of Alumni,* 34-38.

14. Medical Department, Faculty Minutes, January 14, 1859, 25-30, Kornhauser Health Sciences Library, University of Louisville (hereinafter cited Kornhauser Library); Burke, *American Collegiate Populations,* 1-9.

5. Civil War Travails

1. Charles Mesmer, "Louisville on the Eve of the Civil War," *Filson Club History Quarterly* 50 (July 1976): 282; *Biographical Encyclopaedia of Kentucky,* 680-682; Nicholas, *Conservative Essays: Legal and Political,* 4 vols. (Philadelphia, 1863-1869), II, 70.

2. Spiegel, "Public Career of James Guthrie," 56-78; Charles J. Bussey, "James Guthrie: Kentucky Politician and Entrepreneur," in James C. Klotter and Peter J. Sehlinger (eds.), *Kentucky Profiles: Biographical Essays in Honor of Holman Hamilton* (Frankfort, 1982), 57-71; Robert S. Cotterill, "James Guthrie—Kentuckian, 1792-1869," *Register of the Kentucky Historical Society* 20 (September 1922): 293-296; Cotterill, "The Louisville and Nashville Railroad, 1861-1865," *American Historical Review* 29 (July 1924): 700-707.

3. Baird, *David Wendel Yandell,* 34-58; *DAB* 17, 440-441.

4. Medical Department, *Catalogue* (Louisville, 1863), 3; Hambleton Tapp and James C. Klotter (eds.), *The Union, the Civil War, and John W. Tuttle: A Kentucky Captain's Account* (Frankfort, 1980), 151; William Quentin Maxwell, *Lincoln's Fifth Wheel: The Political History of the United States Sanitary Commission* (New York, 1956), 9, 189, 318-319; Yater, *Two Hundred Years,* 85.

5. Benson Court Martial, January 7, 1865, Records of the Judge Advocate General, National Archives; Medical Department, Faculty Minutes, September 6, 1864, 76-77, Kornhauser Library.

6. B.R.S. Boemond, Testimony, July 29, 1867, Freedman's Bureau Records, National Archives; *Louisville Commercial,* January 16, 1868. George W. Bayless, who had served as dean pro-tem following Benson's arrest, was elected dean in February 1865. Back in harness briefly during 1866-1867 session, Benson was succeeded as dean by James Morrison Bodine in February 1867.

7. Lewis, Ewald, and Burnett, "An Aim High and a Vision Broad," xi, and *Centennial History,* 96.

8. *Louisville Journal,* May 17, June 22, 1866; Medical Department, Faculty Minutes, April 12, 1865, 80-81, Kornhauser Library.

9. Micah Saufley to Sallie Rowan, October 6, 1865, January 17, 1866, Saufley Papers, Southern Historical Collection, University of North Carolina, Chapel Hill; Baird, *David Wendel Yandell,* 58-64; Medical Department, Faculty Minutes, August 15, 1865, 85, Kornhauser Library.

6. Competition, Consolidation, and Reform

1. William G. Rothstein, *American Physicians in the Nineteenth Century: From Sects to Science* (Baltimore, 1972), 85-100, 287-297; Martin Kaufman, *American Medical Education: The Formative Years, 1765-1910* (Westport, 1976), 109-126.

2. Ellis, *Medicine in Kentucky,* 17-22; Baird, *David Wendel Yandell,* 93-94; *DAB,* 7, 90; Dwayne Cox, "From Competition to Consolidation: Medical Education in Louisville, 1850-1910," *Filson Club History Quarterly* 66 (October 1992): 562-577; Horine, "A Forgotten Medical Editor: Edwin Samuel Gaillard (1827-1885)," *Annals of Medical History,* 3rd series, 2 (September 1940), 375-382.

3. *Kentucky Encyclopedia,* 150; *Biographical Encyclopaedia of Kentucky,* 13-14.

4. Medical Department, Faculty Minutes, June 2, 1873, 263, Kornhauser Library.

5. Ellis, *Medicine in Kentucky,* 18-20; *Louisville Medical News,* January 1, February 19, 1876.

6. Statistics compiled from the annual announcements of the Medical Department of the University of Louisville.

7. Abraham Flexner, *Report on Medical Education in the United States and Canada* (New York, 1910), 230; Simon Flexner, "A Half Century of American Medicine," 33-34; John Allan Wyeth, *With Sabre and Scalpel: The Autobiography of a Soldier and Surgeon* (New York, 1914), 327-329; *Cumberland County News,* October 28, 1976.

8. *Cardinal,* April 16, 23, 1936; *Salt Lake City Desert News,* August 12, 1891, Genealogical File, Kornhauser Library.

9. *Cardinal,* April 16, 23, 1936; Simon Flexner, "A Half Century of American Medicine," 29-56.

10. Medical Department, Faculty Minutes, May 16, 1868, 175, Kornhauser Library.

11. *Cardinal,* April 16, 23, 1936; *Kentucky Statutes* (1894), Chapter 36, Section 13335, 532; *Centennial History,* 66-69; Arch E. Cole, "Historical Sketches of Departments in the Medical School," *Kentucky Medical Journal* 35 (March 1937), 124, 127-128; *Journal of the American Medical Association* 45 (August 9, 1905), 444. Disinterment as a method of procuring cadavers for use in medical education, though illegal, was practiced widely in Europe and the United States during the nineteenth century. See Suzanne M. Shultz, *Body Snatching: The Robbing of Graves for the Education of Physicians in Early Nineteenth Century America* (Jefferson, NC), 1992.

12. Medical Faculty, Minutes, March 29, 1866, 93; February 20, 1867, 135-6; May 15, 1869, 209-10; May 14, 1874, 280; June 9, 1877, 305-6; June 27, 1879, 327; May 8, 1884, 359, Kornhauser Library; Kaufman, *American Medical Education,* 133-140; University of Louisville, *Annual Announcement* (Louisville, 1878), 5, 12-13.

13. Baird, *David Wendel Yandell,* 59-84. Yandell was president of the AMA in 1872. Other U of L medical school graduates and faculty who have served as AMA president include Paul F. Eve (1857), Henry Miller (1859), Samuel David Gross (1868), Tobias G. Richardson (1878), Theophilus Parvin (1879), Austin Flint (1884), Joseph McDowell Mathews (1899), John A. Wyeth (1902), Lewis S. McMurtry (1905), Irvin Abell, Sr. (1938), Elmer Lee Henderson (1950), and Hoyt D. Gardner (1979). Of these, only Wyeth and Mathews did not serve on the U of L faculty. Morris Fishbein, *A History of the American Medical Association, 1847 to 1947* (Philadelphia, 1947).

14. Johnston, *Memorial History of Louisville,* II, 456-459; Medical Department, *A Testimonial to James Morrison Bodine* (Louisville, 1910), 7; Medical Department, Faculty Minutes, March 3, 1881, 337, Kornhauser Library.

15. Joseph N. McCormack, ed., *Some of the Medical Pioneers of Kentucky* (Bowling Green, Kentucky, 1917), 100-102; "Theodore S. Bell," *Louisville Past and Present* (Louisville, 1875), 305-318; Ford and Ford, *History of the Falls Cities and their Counties,* I, 444-445.

16. David W. Yandell, "A Discourse on the Life and Character of Dr. Richard Oswald Cowling," *American Practitioner* 25 (March 1882): 129-148.

17. *Biographical Encyclopaedia of Kentucky,* 114, 400-401; H.A. Cottell, "The Life and Character of Professor Edward Rush Palmer," *American Practitioner and News* 21 (April 4, 1896): 241-253; *Courier-Journal,* March 13, 1884; Maxwell, *Lincoln's Fifth Wheel,* 70-75.

18. *Biographical Cyclopedia of the Commonwealth of Kentucky* (Chicago, 1896), 450-452, 511-513; "Joseph M. Mathews," Records of the Kentucky Writers' Project, University of Kentucky Archives; Sherrill Redmon, "Professor's Sex Ed Courses Delighted Medical Students," *Inside U of L,* May 2, 1988.

19. Kramer, *Two Centuries of Urban Development,* 65-81; Yater, *Two Hundred Years,* 71-76, 101-104, 118-121.

20. Medical Department, *Catalogue* (Louisville, 1868), 7; *Louisville Medical News,* January 8, 1876; Medical Department, Faculty Minutes, February 26, 1876, 291; February 14, 1877, 301-302, Kornhauser Library; Louisville Medical College, *Catalogue* (Louisville, 1884), 15.

21. Medical Department, *Catalogue* (Louisville, 1880), 2, 4, 7.

22. "University of Louisville Medical Department," *American Practitioner and News* 3 (March 5, 1887): 155-157; Medical Department, *Catalogue* (Louisville, 1884), 9.

23. Kaufman, *American Medical Education,* 133-140; Dean F. Smiley, *History of the Association of American Medical Colleges, 1876-1956* (n.p., 1957), 1-24; Medical Department, *Catalogue* (Louisville, 1877), 4, (1880), 4; Judith Walzer Leavitt, "'Science' Enters the Birthing Room: Obstetrics in America Since the Eighteenth Century," *Journal of American History* 70 (September 1983): 281-304.

24. C.K. Caron (comp.), *Caron's Louisville Directory* (Louisville, 1887), 32-34; "Medical Schools in the United States," *Journal of the American Medical Association* 45 (August 9, 1905): 444; *Centennial History,* 69.

25. Annual catalogues of the Medical Department of the University of Louisville, the Kentucky School of Medicine, the Louisville Medical College, and the Hospital College of Medicine all contain numerous examples of the schools' promotional literature on the city, as well as exaggerated descriptions of their own physical plants and other benefits.

26. Kaufman, *Medical Education,* 154-159; Ellis, *Medicine in Kentucky,* 20-21; *Centennial History,* 79-80;

University of Louisville, *Annual Announcement* (Louisville, 1891, 1893, 1896, and 1898), 5-6, 9-10, 11-12, and 12-14. Statistics compiled from the annual announcements of the Medical Department of the University of Louisville. For a dramatic example of the U of L medical school's role in popularizing the new germ theory of disease, see Sherrill Redmon, "U of L Doctor Solved Mystery of the 1891 Poison Wedding," *Inside U of L,* September 19, 1988.

27. *Centennial History,* 81-86; Arthur Dean Bevan, "Cooperation in Medical Education and Medical Service," *Journal of the American Medical Association* 90 (April 1928), 1173-1181; Ellis, *Medicine in Kentucky,* 56-57.

28. *Courier-Journal,* June 20, 1907, June 10, July 19, 29, 1908; *Louisville Herald,* June 20, 1908; Board of Trustees, Minutes, March 26, 1909; James F. Hopkins, *The University of Kentucky: Origins and Early Years* (Lexington, 1951), 258-259; *Centennial History,* 81.

7. The Late Nineteenth-Century Law School

1. Medical Department, *Catalogue* (Louisville, 1872), 29.

2. Robert Stevens, *Law School: Legal Education in America from the 1850s to the 1980s* (Chapel Hill, 1983), 20-91; Board of Trustees, Minutes, March 22, 1881, U of L Archives; *Centennial History,* 107-108.

3. Law Department, *Catalogue* (Louisville, 1896), 7-9; H. Levin, ed., *The Lawyers and Lawmakers of Kentucky* (Chicago, 1897), 767; *Louisville Law Examiner,* February 10, 1976.

4. *DAB* 17, 440-441, *Kentucky Encyclopedia,* 840-841.

5. Law Department, *Catalogue* (Louisville, 1896), 7-9; Board of Trustees, Minutes, March 22, 1881, U of L Archives; Levin, *Lawyers and Lawmakers,* 767; *DAB,* 9, 440-441; *Centennial History,* 103-104.

6. For biographical information on the law faculty see Levin, *Lawyers and Lawmakers,* 83-84, 145, 158-159, 184, 191-193, 293-294, 481; Johnston, *Memorial History of Louisville,* I, 355-356, 388-390; *Biographical Encyclopaedia of Kentucky,* 533; "Peter B. Muir," *Biographical Cyclopedia of the Commonwealth of Kentucky,* 10-11; Jonathan Truman Dorris, "William Chenault, 1835-1901: One of the Founders of the Filson Club," *Filson Club History Quarterly* 19 (April 1945): 67-85; *Kentucky Encyclopedia,* 112-113, 840-841.

7. Levin, *Lawyers and Lawmakers,* 299-302; *DAB,* 4, 314, 20, 304-305; James P. Jones, *"Black Jack,"* 10; Thomas D. Clark, "Reuben T. Durrett and His Kentuckiana Interest and Collection," 353-378, Edward M. Walters, "Reuben T. Durrett, the Durrett Collection, and the University of Chicago," 379-394, *Filson Club History Quarterly* 56 (October 1982).

8. *Centennial History,* 111.

9. *Centennial History,* 109-112; *Colonel* (1909), 134-135; Board of Trustees, Minutes, April 26, 1894, U of L Archives.

10. *Centennial History,* 110; Dwayne Cox, "You've Come a Long Way, Betty Coed," *Louisville* 29 (February 1978): 19-20.

11. William R. Johnson, *Schooled Lawyers: A Study in the Clash of Professional Cultures* (New York, 1978), xi-xvii.

12. Rothstein, *American Physicians in the Nineteenth Century,* 85-100, 282-297; Kaufman, *American Medical Education,* 36-77, 109-163.

13. Laurence R. Veysey, *The Emergence of the American University* (Chicago, 1965), 302-317; Paul M. Gaston, *The New South Creed: A Study in Southern Mythmaking* (New York, 1971), 189-214; *Kentucky Encyclopedia,* 936-937.

14. *Kentucky Encyclopedia,* 724-725.

15. John A. Garraty, *The New Commonwealth, 1877-1890* (New York, 1968), 1-32; C. Vann Woodward, *Origins of the New South, 1877-1913* (Baton Rouge, 1951), 436-448.

8. The Rebirth of the Liberal Arts College

1. *Centennial History,* 140-141; *Louisville Times,* October 31, 1917.

2. Robert Worth Bingham to Charles F. Granger, November 30, 1904, Mayor's Office Records, Filson Club; Yater, *Two Hundred Years,* 145-164; *Kentucky Encyclopedia,* 80.

3. Board of Trustees, Minutes, February 23, April 30, 1906, March 12, April 26, June 5, 1907, U of L Archives; *Courier-Journal,* April 26, 1907; *Centennial History,* 118-119.

4. College of Liberal Arts, Courses and Rules (Louisville, 1907), 5-31; *Centennial History,* 120, 126.

5. Board of Trustees, Minutes, March 27, 1907; *Centennial History,* 120-121.

6. The first graduates included twelve who earned bachelor's degrees (five male and seven female) and six master's (three male and three female); 1908-1909 Catalog (Louisville, 1908), 12, 28; 1909-1910 Catalog (Louisville, 1909), 34; *Centennial History,* 122.

7. Board of Trustees, Minutes, June 2, 1937, U of L Archives.

8. Ruth Wilson Cogshall, Interview, February 24, 1977, U of L Archives.

9. *Centennial History,* 133-134; Evelyn J. Schneider, "The Library," *Alumni Bulletin* 2 (February 1928), 9; Schneider, "The University Library," *Alumni Magazine* 1 (December 1938), 4-5; Joyce E. Bruner, "The History of the University of Louisville Libraries" (M.S. thesis, University of North Carolina, 1953), 58-63.

10. Evelyn Schneider, Interview, February 24, 1977, U of L Archives.

11. Duke University, *Alumni Register,* October, 1952, 205, 223; *Cincinnati Inquirer,* July 29, 1962, Reference Files, U of L Archives; *Centennial History,* 129-130.

12. Austin R. Middleton to A.Y. Ford, September 24, 1925; Middleton to John L. Patterson, September 18, 1928, Faculty Personnel Records; Ruth Wilson Cogshall, Interview, May 28, 1976; William Furnish, Interview, December 7, 1976, U of L Archives; Middleton, *The University of the Americas* (Louisville, 1938), 1-4.

13. Cotterill, "Southern Railroads and Western Trade, 1840-1850," *Mississippi Valley Historical Review* 3 (March 1917): 427-441; Cotterill, "The Telegraph in the South, 1845-1850," *South Atlantic Quarterly* 16 (April 1917): 149-154; Cotterill, "Early Agitation for a Pacific Railroad," *Mississippi Valley Historical Review* 5 (March 1919): 369-414; Cotterill, "The Louisville and Nashville Railroad, 1861-1865," *American Historical Review* 29 (July 1924): 700-715; Cotterill, *A History of Pioneer Kentucky* (Cincinnati, 1917); Gottschalk, *Jean Paul Marat: A Study in Radicalism* (New York, 1927); Gottschalk, *The Era of the French Revolution, 1715-1815* (New York, 1929); Ware, *The Industrial Worker, 1840-1860* (Boston, 1924); Ware, *The Labor Movement in the United States, 1860-1895: A Study in Democracy* (New York, 1929); Marguerite Lorenz, "Kentucky as a Confederate State" (M.A. thesis, University of Louisville, 1925); Jennie Angell Mengel, "The Neutrality of Kentucky in 1861" (M.A. thesis, University of Louisville, 1925); Jessie Munday, "The Railroads of Kentucky, 1861-1865" (M.A. thesis, University of Louisville, 1925).

14. *Colonel* (Louisville, 1909), 141, 152, 154, 156, 162, 178, (1910), 184; *Centennial History,* 135-136; Deborah Skaggs, "U of L Women Courted Basketball in 1908," *Potential,* February 9, 1980; Salem Ford Papers, U of L Archives.

15. *Colonel* (1909), 155, 159, (1911), 81; David Wallechinsky, *The Complete Book of the Olympics* (New York, 1984), 65.

16. *Colonel* (1909) 152, (1910), 105-114; Janet Hodgson, "Early Team Found Success on Baseball Diamond," *Inside U of L,* April 17, 1989.

17. *University of Louisville 1997-98 Basketball Information Guide* (Louisville, 1997), 118; *Centennial History,* 135; *Colonel* (1909), 156.

18. James S. Junot, "Who Was Louisville's First Head Football Coach," *Scorecard,* August 1988; *Centennial History,* 135-136.

19. *Centennial History,* 136; *Colonel* (1909), 162; Cox, "You've Come a Long Way, Betty Coed," 19-20; Florence Daisy McCallum Papers, U of L Archives.

20. *Colonel* (Louisville, 1909), 130-131, 178, (1911), 169, 172-173.

21. *Centennial History,* 138, 184; Reference Files, U of L Archives.

22. College of Arts and Sciences, Faculty Minutes, December 16, 1915, 10; April 29, 1916, 20-21, U of L Archives; *Centennial History,* 185.

23. Flexner, *Report on Medical Education in the United States and Canada,* 229-231; also see Flexner, *Abraham Flexner: An Autobiography* (New York, 1960), 73-88.

24. Board of Trustees, Minutes, August 29, 1910, and College of Arts and Sciences, Annual Report, 1913-1914, 7-12, U of L Archives; College of Arts and Sciences, *Catalogue* (Louisville, 1913), 3-4, and *Catalogue* (Louisville, 1915-1916), 20; *Centennial History,* 131.

25. *Centennial History,* 138-139.

26. James H. Cassedy, *Medicine and American Growth, 1800-1860* (Madison, 1986), 67-72; James G. Burrow, *Organized Medicine in the Progressive Era: The Move Toward Monopoly* (Baltimore, 1977), 14-28; Dwayne Cox, "Medical Education in the South: The Case of Louisville, 1837-1910," in John David Smith and Thomas H. Appleton Jr., eds., *A Mythic Land Apart: Reassessing Southerners and Their History* (Westport, 1997), 43-56.

27. Burton J. Bledstein, *The Culture of Professionalism: The Middle Class and the Development of Higher Education in America* (New York, 1976), 287ff.

28. *Centennial History,* 128; *Louisville Times,* June 7, 1910; Louisville Board of Trade, Resolution, February 23, 1910, Legislative Records of the City of Louisville, Supplementary Series.

29. Robert H. Wiebe, *The Search for Order, 1877-1920* (New York, 1967), 133-163.

9. Campus and Academic Expansion

1. *Kentucky Encyclopedia,* 341; Ford Hall, Dedication Program, December 3, 1982, U of L Archives.

2. Law Department, *Catalogue* (Louisville, 1909), 5-6; *Centennial History,* 146-148; *Colonel* (1911), 42.

3. A.Y. Ford to Leon P. Lewis, November 15, 1923, President's Office Records, U of L Archives; Neville Miller, "Justice Brandeis and the University of Louisville School of Law," *Filson Club History Quarterly* 34 (April 1960): 156-159; Lewis, Ewald, and Burnett, "An Aim High and a Vision Broad," xiv-xvi.

4. Laurence Lee Howe, Interview, April 1, 1977, A.Y. Ford to Alfred Z. Reed, March 24, 1923, President's Office Records, U of L Archives; *U of L Alumni Magazine* (September 1939), 8; Stevens, *Law School,* 92ff.

5. Skaggs, "Jefferson School of Law," *Inside U of L,* April 8, 1985; Lewis, Ewald, and Burnett, "An Aim High and a Vision Broad," xxii-xxv; and Vince Staten, *Law at the Falls: A History of the Louisville Legal Profession* (Dallas,

1997), 49-53; Jefferson School of Law Records, U of L Archives.

6. Robert N. Miller to Louis D. Brandeis, June 29, 1925, Leon P. Lewis to Robert N. Miller, February 21, 1925, Brandeis Papers, U of L Law Library; Bernard Flexner, *Mr. Justice Brandeis and the University of Louisville* (Louisville, 1938), 57-84; Alpheus T. Mason, *Brandeis: A Free Man's Life* (New York, 1956), 587-593.

7. Janet Hodgson, "Louis Dembitz Brandeis," *U of L Magazine* 6 (summer 1987), 16-17; Lewis, Ewald, and Burnett, "An Aim High and a Vision Broad," xvii-xxi.

8. *Courier-Journal,* November 3, 4, 7, 1914; A.Y. Ford to Stuart Graves, November 18, 1922, President's Office Records; President's Annual Report, 1922-23, 12-13, 21, U of L Archives; *Centennial History,* 166-168; *Inside U of L,* March 1983; Yater, *Two Hundred Years,* 157.

9. Dental Department, *Catalogue* (Louisville, 1918), 8; Ellis, *Medicine in Kentucky,* 74; Margaret Merrick, "School of Public Health Had U of L Ties," *Inside U of L,* April 16, 1990; University of Louisville, *Catalogue* (Louisville, 1919), 124.

10. The commonwealth's first dental school may have been the Transylvania College of Dental Surgery (not affiliated with Transylvania University in Lexington), which existed for three months in 1850-1851. *Kentucky Encyclopedia,* 177, 262-263; Fred A. Engle Jr., "Central University of Richmond, Kentucky," *Register* 66 (July 1968), 291-292; Robert L. Sprau, "History of the University of Louisville School of Dentistry," *Journal of the Kentucky State Dental Association* 8 (January 1956): 15; Sprau and Edward B. Gernert, *History of Kentucky Dentistry, 1636-1910* (Louisville, 1960), 97-134; *Centennial History,* 149-153. According to one source, the U of L School of Dentistry is the tenth oldest of the nation's fifty-four dental schools and the fifth oldest west of the Alleghenies. American Association of Dental Schools, *Admission Requirements of U.S. and Canadian Dental Schools: 1998-99* (35th ed., Washington, DC, 1997).

11. *Centennial History,* 153-156. Dental college dean William Edward Grant (1872-1936), who received his D.D.S. and M.D. degrees from the Hospital College of Medicine in 1894 and 1897, respectively, is not to be confused with U of L Medical Department dean William Edward Grant (1845-1920), who received his M.D. from the Kentucky School of Medicine in 1887.

12. *Centennial History,* 168-172.

13. *Colonel* (Louisville), 75, 83, 117, (1910), 68, (1912), 82; E.E. Butler, Post Mortem Report on Cocaine Annie, January 3, 1916; Isabel Blacklock Limpp to Douglas M. Haynes, December 17, 1971; Roscoe H. Beeson to Stuart Graves, August 26, 1926, Medical School Student Records, U of L Archives; *Courier-Journal,* August 5, 1976.

14. "Woman and Her Physician," *American Practitioner* 3 (January 1871), 13; "Should Women Practice Medicine?" *American Practitioner and News* 11 (June 20, 1891), 414-415; Cox, "You've Come a Long Way, Betty Coed," 19-20.

15. Reference Files, U of L Archives.

16. College of Arts and Sciences, Faculty Minutes, February 10, October 4, 1917; Board of Trustees, Minutes, April 19, 1917, May 10, September 5, 1918; Ruth Wilson Cogshall, Interview, May 28, 1976, U of L Archives; "College War Service," and John L. Patterson, "A Plan for Government Service," *The Nation* 106 (May 4, 1918): 524-525, 527-528; *Centennial History,* 123-124, 132-133; Carol S. Gruber, *Mars and Minerva: World War I and the Uses of Higher Education in America* (Baton Rouge, 1975), 213-252.

17. *Courier-Journal,* May 26, October 8, 1918; College of Arts and Sciences, *Catalogue* (Louisville, 1919), 67; Board of Trustees, Minutes, October 8, 1918, U of L Archives.

18. Board of Trustees, Minutes, April 19, May 24, October 8, 26, 1917; March 21, 22, July 1, 1918; March 26, 27, 1921; Law School Matriculation Book, 1911-1930, U of L Archives.

19. Fred C. Koster, Interview, November 22, 1978, U of L Archives; *Thoroughbred* (Louisville, 1926), 204, (1929), 137; *Inside U of L,* November 17, 1986.

20. *Kentucky Acts,* March 23, 1916, 510-511; *Centennial History,* 145-146.

21. Board of Trustees, Minutes, May 24, 1917, March 21, 1923; *Centennial History,* 146, 174, 185-186; Walter L. Creese, *Report on Belknap Campus with Facts, Pictures, History, Observations and Comments, for Ready Reference* (Louisville, 1954), 5-6.

22. George C. Wright, "Blacks in Louisville, Kentucky, 1890-1930" (Ph.D. diss., Duke University, 1977), 156-157; Wright, *Life Behind a Veil: Blacks in Louisville, Kentucky, 1865-1930* (Baton Rouge, 1985), 208-209; Wright, "William Henry Steward: Moderate Approach to Black Leadership," in Leon Litwack and August Meier, eds., *Black Leaders of the Nineteenth Century* (Urbana, 1988), 287-288; Raymond Wolters, *The New Negro on Campus: Black College Rebellions of the 1920's* (Princeton, 1975), 3-28, 340-350.

23. James Blaine Hudson III, "The History of Louisville Municipal College: Events Leading to the Desegregation of the University of Louisville" (Ed.D. diss., University of Kentucky, 1981), 24-36; Lawrence H. Williams, *Black Higher Education in Kentucky, 1879-1930: The History of Simmons University* (Lewiston, New York, 1987), 94, 149.

24. Board of Trustees, Minutes, March 3, 1916, March 21, April 3, 1923; Juliet R. Belknap to A.Y. Ford, April 23, 1923; A.Y. Ford to Juliet R. Belknap, April 24, 1923, President's Office Records, U of L Archives; *Courier-Journal,* March 4, 1923; *Centennial History,* 185-186; Douglass L. Stern, "A History of the Site of Belknap

Campus from 1850 to 1923" (History 235, University of Louisville, 1974); Creese, *Report on Belknap Campus,* 6, 14, 41, and *passim;* Shively, *Belknap Campus—Its History* (Louisville, 1959); Carl E. Kramer et al., *Louisville Survey East* (Louisville Historic Landmarks and Preservation Districts Commission, 1980), 100, 209.

25. *Inside U of L,* April 1982.

26. Yater, *Two Hundred Years,* 79-80, 113, 134, n. 1; Johnston, *Memorial History of Louisville,* II, 339; Mary R. Block, "Child-Saving Laws of Louisville and Jefferson County, 1854-1894: A Socio-Legal History," *Filson Club History Quarterly* 66 (April 1992), 232-251.

27. Louisville Common Council, Minutes, February 13, 1862, and Louisville Board of Aldermen, Minutes, February 13, 1862, Microfilm Edition; "First Annual Report of the . . . Louisville House of Refuge . . . for the Year Ending December 31, 1866," Louisville Municipal Reports, Microfilm Edition; "University of Louisville Belknap Campus Historic District," National Register of Historic Places Inventory Nomination Form, 1976, Reference Files; Stern, "A History of the Site of Belknap Campus from 1850 to 1923," 8; U of L Archives. Also see Creese, *Report on Belknap Campus,* 12; "Louisville and Its Defenses," *Courier-Journal,* September 30, 1956; Robert E. McDowell, *City of Conflict: Louisville in the Civil War, 1861-1865* (Louisville, 1962), 61, 174-175, 206-208; Thomas, *Views of Louisville Since 1766,* 128; and Yater, *Two Hundred Years,* 87, 113, n. 1.

28. Morison, "What Is the Oldest Building on the Belknap Campus?" *Inside U of L,* January 1982.

29. Stern, "University of Louisville and Belknap Campus from 1900-1939: Its Historical Significance" (Fine Arts 593, University of Louisville, 1974); Shively, *Belknap Campus—Its History,* 6.

30. *Thoroughbred* (Louisville, 1925), 66, (1926), 188; *Centennial History,* 134-135, 178-179; Associated Press, Feature Service, June 21, 1928; *Holland's Magazine of the South,* September, 1928; Boyd Martin Scrapbooks, U of L Archives; Glenn Taylor, "The Architectural History of the Belknap Playhouse: A Credit to C.J. Clarke," *Filson Club History Quarterly* 72 (July 1998), 260-287. Hollywood stars Ned Beatty and Warren Oates both acted in productions in the Playhouse during their U of L student days.

31. *Alumni Monthly,* March, 1927, 6-7, 9, December, 1927.

32. B.M. Brigman to A.Y. Ford, July 11, 1923, Speed Fund; Declaration of Trust, February 15, 1924, Ruth L. Koch Papers, U of L Archives; Tom Owen, "Speed School," *Inside U of L,* September 24, 1984.

33. Raymond Schnur, Interview, December 14, 1978; Edwin Franz, Interview, November 16, 1978, U of L Archives; Robert C. Ernst, "Reflections on Engineering," Speech to the Louisville Conversation Club, March 2, 1987, Reference Files, U of L Archives.

34. Dwayne Cox, "The Cardinal: A Record of Student Life," *U of L Magazine* (spring 1985), 18-19.

35. In 1966 the *Cardinal* became the *Louisville Cardinal.*

36. *Centennial History,* 185.

37. *Thoroughbred* (1925), 77; Fred C. Koster, Interview, November 22, 1978. Yearbooks tell the story of Greek activities at U of L: homecoming events, parties, service to the community, fraternity and sorority houses, and the annual Fryberger Sing. For a list, with founding dates, see Jack Anson and Robert Marchesani Jr., *Baird's Manual of American College Fraternities* (20th ed., Indianapolis, 1991), II-100, and "Bicentennial Views," *U of L Magazine* 16 (fall 1997), x.

38. *U of L News,* April 13, May 25, October 12, December 7, 1928, April 4, 1929; Laurence Lee Howe, Interview, April 1, 1977, U of L Archives; Dwayne Cox, "Howe and 'Leopard Sweat,'" *Inside U of L,* October 7, 1985; William E. Leuchtenburg, *The Perils of Prosperity, 1914-1932* (Chicago, 1958), 140-177.

39. *U of L News,* November 2, 1928.

40. At the very end of his administration Ford and the trustees amended the university's charter to make it explicit that the authority for budgetary allocations lay in the central administration, not in the individual units, as had been the case; *Centennial History,* 192.

10. President vs. Faculty

1. Dwayne Cox, "The Gottschalk-Colvin Case: A Study in Academic Purpose and Command," *Register of the Kentucky Historical Society* 85 (winter 1987): 46-68; Kitty Conroy, "George Colvin: Kentucky Statesman and Educator," *Bulletin of the Bureau of School Service . . . University of Kentucky* 16 (March 1944): 5ff.; *Kentucky Encyclopedia,* 217; Frank L. McVey to George Colvin, July 15, 1926, George Colvin to Frank L. McVey, July 24, 1926, President's Office Records, University of Kentucky Archives.

2. Veysey, *Emergence of the American University,* 263-341.

3. George Colvin to Board of Trustees, January 25, 1927, President's Office Records, U of L Archives.

4. "Report on the University of Louisville," *Bulletin of the American Association of University Professors* 13 (October 1927), 429-469; George Colvin to Hill Shine, October 6, 1926; Hill Shine to George Colvin, October 6, 1926, Shine Personnel Record, U of L Archives; *Centennial History,* 124-125; *Courier-Journal,* December 26, 1926.

5. George Colvin to Yancy Altsheler, February 29, 1928, Altsheler Personnel Record; George Colvin to Alfred Selligman, March 23, 1927, George Colvin to Helm Bruce, April 16, 1927, George Colvin to Ernest S. Clarke,

December 7, 1927, Warwick M. Anderson to George Colvin, April 2, 1928, President's Office Records; U of L Archives.

6. "Report on the University of Louisville," 432; Louis R. Gottschalk to H.W. Tyler, March 31, 1927, American Association of University Professors Records, AAUP Headquarters, Washington, D.C.

7. "Report on the University of Louisville," 429; Louis R. Gottschalk to Board of Trustees, April 5, 1927, President's Office Records; Board of Trustees, Minutes, April 7, 1927; U of L Archives. *Courier-Journal,* March 17, May 7, 1927; George Colvin to Louis R. Gottschalk, February 16, 1927; Louis R. Gottschalk to H.W. Tyler, March 16, 31, 1927; Rolf Johannesen to H.W. Tyler, March 31, 1927, AAUP Records.

8. "Report on the University of Louisville," 429; Louis R. Gottschalk to Board of Trustees, April 5, 1927, President's Office Records; Board of Trustees, Minutes, April 7, 1927; U of L Archives. Louis R. Gottschalk to H.W. Tyler, March 16, 31, 1927, Rolf Johannesen to H.W. Tyler, March 31, 1927, AAUP Records.

9. *Courier-Journal,* April 1, 1927; *Louisville Times,* April 13, 1927; *Centennial History,* 192, 197, 210; William Belknap to William Heyburn, April 4, 1927, Presidents Office Records, U of L Archives; Leo J. Raub to H.W. Tyler, May 9, 1928, AAUP Records.

10. Simeon E. Leland to W.T. Semple, May 12, 1927, AAUP Records.

11. "Report on the University of Louisville," 429ff.

12. A.O. Lovejoy, "Memorandum of the Louisville Report," September 26, 1927, AAUP Records; *DAB,* Supplement 8, 480-483; Daniel J. Wilson, *Arthur O. Lovejoy and the Quest for Intelligibility* (Chapel Hill, NC, 1980), 118-121.

13. Frederick J. Kelly, *Report of a Study of the Curriculum of the College of Liberal Arts of the University of Louisville* (Louisville, 1927), 3ff., and Frank L. McVey, *Report on the Organization of the University of Louisville* (Louisville, 1927), 4ff., U of L Archives; *Centennial History,* 196-201, 209, 216. McVey's report was adopted with a few changes by the trustees on April 2, 1928.

14. George Colvin to Frank L. McVey, January 7, 1928, President's Office Records, University of Kentucky Archives; *U of L News,* July 31, 1928; Robert N. Miller to Louis D. Brandeis, January 3, 1928; "Reprint of Published Statements of Certain Trustees of the University of Louisville Concerning Conditions in that Institution," May, 1928; U of L Archives.

15. Perhaps in an attempt to right a wrong, the university invited Gottschalk to participate as a guest of honor in the celebration of U of L's sesquicentennial in 1948. Twenty years later Gottschalk served as Bingham Professor of Humanities. In 1970, he was awarded an honorary doctorate by the university, and in 1975 the old Social Sciences Building, one of the oldest on Belknap

Campus and home of the history department, was named for Gottschalk.

16. Louis D. Brandeis to Robert N. Miller, July 31, 1928, Brandeis Papers.

11. Academic Respectability

1. J.J. Oppenheimer, "Raymond Asa Kent, 1883-1943," *Educational Record* 24 (April 1943): 148-56.

2. *National Cyclopaedia of American Biography,* 62 vols., supplements, indices (New York, 1893-1984), XXXII, 436; *Courier-Journal,* April 11, 1937, July 2, 1939; Raymond A. Kent to John W. Barr Jr., January 13, 1940, Faculty Personnel Records, U of L Archives; Bledstein, *Culture of Professionalism,* 129-158.

3. *Courier-Journal,* July 2, 1939; Sinclair Daniel to John L. Patterson, May 29, 1929, H.W. Arant to Raymond A. Kent, February 28, 1936, Raymond A. Kent to A.B. Chandler, November 19, 1936, President's Office Records, U of L Archives; Deborah Skaggs, "The University of Louisville School of Law, 1925-1939: The Struggle for National Accreditation" (History 605, University of Louisville, 1976); *Inside U of L,* February 1983; Lewis, Ewald, and Burnett, "An Aim High and a Vision Broad," xxvi-xxvi; *Centennial History,* 240-246.

4. School of Law, Annual Report, 1931-1932, 2-3, 1938-1939, 12, U of L Archives; Stevens, *Law School,* 155ff.

5. School of Medicine, *Catalogue* (Louisville, 1939), 16-40; Sidney Isaac Kornhauser, "Facilities for the Study of Anatomy," *Kentucky Medical Journal* 12 (March 1937): 17-19. In 1959 the medical library, now called the Kornhauser Health Sciences Library, was named in his honor.

6. Arthur H. Keeney, Interview, March 14, 1980, William Keller, Interview, October 12, 14, 1978, U of L Archives.

7. S. Spafford Ackerly, Interview, December 7, 1977, U of L Archives; *Centennial History,* 168.

8. School of Dentistry, Annual Report, 1929-1930, 15-18; 1930-1931, 11-12; 1938-1939, 12-19, U of L Archives; Sprau, "History of the University of Louisville School of Dentistry," 15-18.

9. "To University of Louisville Chemical Engineering Students," c. 1940, Ford L. Wilkinson to Raymond A. Kent, October 31, 1938, April 13, 1940, Ford L. Wilkinson to A.W. Lissauer, February 17, 1939, President's Office Records, U of L Archives; Howard E. Bumstead, "The Utilization of Grapefruit Waste" (M.C.E. thesis, University of Louisville, 1940), 23-26.

10. Dale Patterson, "Eastern Parkway Relocation Altered U of L's Master Plan," *Inside U of L* (November 5, 1989), 6; Samuel W. Thomas, Louisville Since the Twenties (Louisville, 1978), 74, 240; Ruth L. Koch and W. Roscoe

McIntosh, *History of Progress in Engineering Education: Speed Scientific School, 1925-1969* (Louisville 1969), 4-6, 14, 18-20; Yater, *Two Hundred Years,* 206; Margaret Merrick, "Speed Library Once Served as Home of Industrial Research," *Inside U of L,* November 29, 1987. The Institute of Industrial Research, successor to the Division of Industrial Research, closed in 1974. After renovation, its building housed the Laura Kersey Library of Engineering, Physical Sciences, and Technology, named for the longtime head of the Speed library.

11. J.J. Oppenheimer, "Curriculum Reconstruction in the College of Liberal Arts," in B. Lamar Johnson, ed., *What About Survey Courses* (New York, 1937), 130-50; College of Arts and Sciences, *Catalogue* (Louisville, 1934), 32-37; *Centennial History,* 217-218.

12. William F. Ekstrom, "In Honor of Ernest C. Hassold," April 14, 1977, Reference Files, U of L Archives. For a favorable assessment of Hassold and other members of the Arts and Sciences faculty by a student of the late 1930s and early 1940s, see Benjamin L. Reid, *First Acts: A Memoir* (Athens, GA, 1988), 138-147. Reid was awarded the Pulitzer Prize for biography in 1969 for *The Man From New York: John Quinn and His Friends,* a subject which had drawn his interest while he was a U of L undergraduate.

13. This building later became known as the Art Studio. It was razed in 1979 to make way for the Ekstrom Library. *Potential* 3 (February 23, 1977), 6; *Centennial History,* 223-224, 227.

14. Raymond A. Kent to John Erskine, January 3, November 19, 1931; John Erskine to Raymond A. Kent, January 16, 1933; Fanny Brandeis to Raymond A. Kent, March 21, 1935; Raymond A. Kent to Jacques Jolas, March 23, 1934; Raymond A. Kent to Fanny Brandeis, February 23, 1935, President's Office Records, U of L Archives.

15. Irv Frank, "History of the School of Music," School of Music Programmatic Planning Review, 1980, 11, Reference Files, U of L Archives; Oscar Bryant, "Solid Gold: Music Turns 50," *U of L Magazine* 1 (winter 1983): 10, 12; *New York Times,* June 18, 1998.

16. Graduate Division of Social Administration, Annual Report, 1937-1938, 1-4; 1938-1939, 1-4; 1940-1941, 1-3, U of L Archives; Howard E. Hollenbeck, "A Housing Project in Louisville—Its Social Interpretation: A Study of College Court" (M.S.S.W., University of Louisville, 1940), 99-108.

17. Norman J. Ware to Warwick Anderson, January 23, 1928, Personnel Records, U of L Archives.

18. Deborah Skaggs, "Kent School's Centennial Year," *Inside U of L,* January 27, 1986.

19. Fernandus Payne to Raymond A. Kent, November 5, 1934; Raymond A. Kent to A.W. Homberger, November 18, 1938, President's Office Records; University Librarian, Annual Report, 1930-1931, 6; 1932-1933, 9, U of L Archives; Morison, "How Many

Buildings Have Housed the U of L Library," *Inside U of L,* November 1982. Some of the history masters theses of the period include Carl Richmond Fields, "The Know-Nothing Party in Louisville" (1936), Flora Heitz, "A Comprehensive Survey of Cultural Movements in Louisville during the Nineteenth Century" (1937), Edward J. Johnson Jr., "A Social and Economic History of Louisville, 1860-1865" (1938), Patrick Sarsfield Kirwan, "Henry Watterson and World War Propaganda" (1939), Anna Ruth Spiegel, "The Public Career of James Guthrie" (1940), Lolla Wurtele, "The Origins of the Louisville and Nashville Railroad" (1939), and Attia Martha Bowmer, "The History of the Government of the City of Louisville" (1948).

20. President's Annual Report, 1935-1936, U of L Archives; *Cardinal,* October 14, 1932.

12. A Dream Deferred

1. For coverage of this trend in Louisville, see Wright, *Life Behind a Veil.*

2. For a comprehensive treatment of LMC, including events leading to its establishment, see two studies by J. Blaine Hudson: "The Establishment of Louisville Municipal College: A Case Study in Racial Conflict and Compromise," *Journal of Negro History* 64 (spring 1995), 111-123, and "History of Louisville Municipal College," the latter first cited in chapter nine. Also see George D. Wilson, *A Century of Negro Education in Louisville, Kentucky* (rev. ed.; Louisville, 1986), 111-122, and *Centennial History,* 212-215. On the bond issues and their aftermath, see Wright, "Blacks in Louisville," 368-378; Wright, *Life Behind a Veil,* 208-209, 271-272; and John A. Hardin, *Fifty Years of Segregation: Black Higher Education in Kentucky, 1904-1954* (Lexington, 1997), 39-41. Also see Lowell H. Harrison and James C. Klotter, *A New History of Kentucky* (Lexington, 1997), 389. The phrase "a dream deferred" was used by the African American writer Langston Hughes; see Arnold Rampersad, ed., *The Collected Poems of Langston Hughes* (New York, 1994), 387, 388, 426.

3. *Kentucky Encyclopedia,* 258-259; Hudson, "History of Louisville Municipal College," 20; Richard Allen Heckman and Betty Jean Hall, "Berea College and the Day Law," *Register* 66 (January 1968), 35-52; James C. Klotter, *Kentucky: Portrait in Paradox, 1900-1950* (Frankfort, 1996), 152-153; and George C. Wright, *In Pursuit of Equality, 1890-1980,* vol. 2 of *A History of Blacks in Kentucky* (Frankfort, 1992), 144-148.

4. The State Normal School for Colored Persons was chartered in 1886 and went through several name changes: in 1902 it became the Kentucky Normal and Industrial Institute for Colored Persons; in 1926 Kentucky State Industrial College for Colored Persons; in 1938 Kentucky

State College for Negroes; in 1952 Kentucky State College; and in 1972 Kentucky State University. See John Hardin, *Onward and Upward: A Centennial History of Kentucky State University, 1886-1986* (Frankfort, 1987); Klotter, *Kentucky: Portrait in Paradox*, 156-157; and *Kentucky Encyclopedia*, 285-287, 514-515.

5. For a full treatment of Simmons University, see a work first cited in chapter nine, Lawrence H. Williams, *Black Higher Education in Kentucky, 1879-1930: The History of Simmons University*, 79-80, 99-126, *passim*. Also see Wright, *In Pursuit of Equality*, 132; Hudson, "History of Louisville Municipal College," 19, 23; and *Kentucky Encyclopedia*, 609, 821-822.

6. Hudson, "History of Louisville Municipal College," 23, 33-35; Wright, *Life Behind a Veil*, 272; Hardin, *Fifty Years of Segregation*, 48-49; Harrison and Klotter, *A New History of Kentucky*, 395-396.

7. Williams, *Black Higher Education in Kentucky*, 58; *Centennial History*, 212, 214-215; *Kentucky Encyclopedia*, 855.

8. *Courier-Journal*, November 4, 1930; Hudson, "History of Louisville Municipal College," 14, 35-36.

9. Simmons University Records and LMC Scrapbook, Louisville Municipal College Records, U of L Archives; Board of Trustees, Minutes, May 15, 1935; *Kentucky Encyclopedia*, 583-584, 822; Hudson,"History of Louisville Municipal College," 35, 43; Williams, *Black Higher Education in Kentucky*, 53; *Centennial History*, 214-215.

10. *Courier-Journal*, November 11, 1952, November 8, 1967, March 28, 1977, August 13, 1983. Rufus E. Clement was a son of George Clement, a Louisville black leader and a bishop in the AME Zion Church; Stone to Linda Wilson, August 18, 1993, LMC Collection, Multicultural Center, University of Louisville. For a list of LMC faculty members and their years of service, see Appendix Two.

11. "Louisville Municipal College for Negroes: Preliminary Announcement of Opening," September 1, 1930, LMC Collection, Multicultural Center, University of Louisville; Hudson, "History of Louisville Municipal College," 48, 54, 61; and Louisville Municipal College, *Catalogue* (Louisville, 1931), 7-9. The U of L Archives has preserved administrative files, faculty papers, photographs, and other LMC records; the Oral History Center contains interviews with LMC students, faculty, and administrators; and the Multicultural Center has collected additional LMC materials, such as photographs, memorabilia, and student reminiscences.

12. Hudson, "History of Louisville Municipal College," 1, 36-64; George D. Wilson, "Footprints in the Sand—Kentucky Sand," 1982, 74-240, Wilson Papers, U of L Archives. LMC faculty were not considered part of the University Senate, nor did that body exercise any authority over the college.

13. David A. Lane, Interview, June 10, 1976, U of L Archives; Hudson, "History of Louisville Municipal College," 47-53.

14. President's Annual Report (1936), 24; LMC Scrapbook, Louisville Municipal College Records, U of L Archives; Shively, Interview, December 18, 1978, U of L Archives; Wright, *Life Behind a Veil*, 139.

15. Sue C. Greathouse, "Student Life at Louisville Municipal College, 1931-1951," Social Science 542, University of Louisville, 1985, U of L Archives.

16. Hudson, "History of Louisville Municipal College," 45; Greathouse, "Student Life at Louisville Municipal College"; Carridder M. Jones, "Bantam Bonds: Louisville Municipal College," *U of L Magazine* (winter 1997), 14-15.

17. The LMC student newspaper went by several names through the years, e.g. the *Blah, Bantam Bugler, Bantam Call, Bantam Herald*, and *Bantam*.

18. Hudson, "History of Louisville Municipal College," 46.

19. *Louisville Defender*, October 19, 1946; *Courier-Journal*, October 20, 1946; LMC Scrapbook, Louisville Municipal College Records, U of L Archives.

20. *Louisville Defender*, January 17, 1948; LMC Scrapbook, Louisville Municipal College Records, U of L Archives. Dwight Reed left LMC after the 1948-1949 basketball season for a head coaching position at Lincoln University. John Crowe, his successor, coached the 1949 football team and the 1949-1950 basketball squad. Willie Lewis served as the LMC's head coach during its final year, guiding the 1950 football and 1950-1951 basketball squads.

21. Greathouse, "Student Life at Louisville Municipal College," 6.

22. *Courier-Journal*, April 28, 1946.

23. L. Dale Patterson, "Municipal College Met Needs of Blacks before Integration," *Inside U of L*, February 20, 1989.

24. Hudson, "History of Louisville Municipal College," 68-75; Hardin, *Fifty Years of Segregation*, 89-96.

25. Hudson, "History of Louisville Municipal College," 76-79; Wright, *In Pursuit of Equality*, 185.

26. *Cardinal*, March 25, 1949.

27. *Courier-Journal*, March 30, 1949.

28. *Cardinal*, April 8, 1949; *Courier-Journal*, April 9, 1949.

29. *Cardinal*, January 21, February 18, 1949.

30. James A. Crumlin to Board of Trustees, September 30, 1949, U of L Archives; *Courier-Journal*, October 1, 1949; Hudson, "History of Louisville Municipal College," 76-82; *Kentucky Encyclopedia*, 258.

31. Hudson, "History of Louisville Municipal College, 82-84; Raymond E. Meyers to John W. Taylor, April 17, 1950, U of L Archives.

32. *Cardinal*, April 28, 1950; Hudson, "History of Louisville Municipal College," 76-116; Hardin, *Fifty Years*

of Segregation, 98-99, 102; *Kentucky Encyclopedia,* 583, 634; "Report of the President, 1947-1951," 20, U of L Archives. In February 1951 the U of L Board of Trustees decided to admit black students who wished to attend the 1951 summer session rather than have them wait until the fall 1951 semester. The University of Kentucky admitted blacks to its undergraduate programs in 1954 after the U.S. Supreme Court's decision in *Brown v. Board of Education.* That ruling struck down the court's 1896 "separate but equal" ruling in *Plessy v. Ferguson* and invalidated the Day Law. Davidson's "first in the South" boast referred to universities. In Kentucky, four colleges preceded U of L in desegregation: Berea, Bellarmine, Nazareth, and Ursuline, the latter three all Catholic colleges in Louisville.

33. Hudson, "History of Louisville Municipal College," 92-93.

34. Board of Trustees, Minutes, November 6, 1950; Hudson, "History of Louisville Municipal College," 97-98.

35. Hudson, "History of Louisville Municipal College," 102.

36. Hudson, "History of Louisville Municipal College," 102-106; *Kentucky Encyclopedia,* 287.

37. Hudson, "History of Louisville Municipal College," 93-107.

38. C.H. Parrish Jr., Interview, November 20, 1981; G.D. Wilson, "Footprints in the Sand," 240; Hudson, "History of Louisville Municipal College," 106; Ekstrom, *Recollection of the University of Louisville* (Louisville, 1996), 9.

39. Hudson, "History of Louisville Municipal College," 115; Sue C. Greathouse, "Student Life at Louisville Municipal College."

40. Morison, "Why, What and Where Is Parrish Court," *Inside U of L,* July 1982.

13. Famine, Flood, and War

1. *Centennial History,* 248; William Manchester, "Louisville Cashes in on Culture," *Harper's Magazine* 211 (August 1955), 78-79; Yater, *Two Hundred Years,* 201, 213.

2. *Cardinal,* October 21, November 4, 1932, April 18, September 19, 1935; *The "L" Book* (Louisville 1933), 24.

3. Speed Scientific School, Annual Report, 1931-1932, 2; 1933-1934, 3, B.M. Brigman to George F. Zook, August 3, 1933; Ford Wilkinson to Raymond A. Kent, February 27, 1940, President's Office Records, U of L Archives.

4. Raymond A. Kent, *An Open Season for Youth* (Louisville, 1935), 1-18; President's Annual Report, 1934-1935, 15-17; Raymond A. Kent to James M. Yard, June 18, 1934, Yard Personnel Record; Raymond A. Kent to

Herbert Agar, July 20, 1938; Raymond A. Kent to Andrew Broaddus, February 26, 1939, President's Office Records, U of L Archives.

5. Report of Operative Number Four, November 18, 1930; Report of Operative Number Nine, November 19, 1930, President's Office Records, U of L Archives; Margaret Merrick, "Campus Eats," *U of L Magazine* 14 (summer 1996), 22-23.

6. Cox, "The Cardinal," 18-19.

7. Student Health, Annual Report, 1930-31, 2, U of L Archives; *Cardinal,* January 6, 1933; *Courier-Journal,* December 1, 1934. The university's student health service was begun in 1930; Morison, "How Long Have We Had a Student Health Service," *Inside U of L,* May 1984.

8. *Cardinal,* December 2, 1938; George C. Lighton to Ernest Hassold, November 16, 1937; George C. Lighton to Rhodes Jackson, November 18, 1937, Hassold Papers, U of L Archives.

9. Harvey C. Webster, "Communist Party Activity," c. 1953, Webster Papers, U of L Archives.

10. Ray H. Bixler, "The Psychology Department at the University of Louisville, 1907-1953," *Filson Club History Quarterly* 57 (July 1983), 257-263; Morison, "How Long Has U of L Had a Department of Psychology?" *Inside U of L,* October 1983; William B. Pirtle to Edward S. Jouett, January 17, 1935; Joseph Lazarus, affiant, April 25, 1935, President's Office Records, U of L Archives.

11. *Ellis Freeman* versus *James T. Merriwether,* Jefferson Circuit Court, 244182 (1935-1937), Jefferson County Archives; Clifford Wright, affiant, April 15, 1935; Grant Hicks, affiant, May 4, 1935, President's Office Records; Anne H. Bowers, "The Ellis Freeman Case" (History 528, University of Louisville, 1981), 1ff., U of L Archives; Cathy Sutton, "They Did It in the 30's, Too," *Thoroughbred* (Louisville, 1970); Clyde Crews, *Spirited City: Essays in Louisville History* (Louisville, 1995), 60.

12. *Alumni Magazine* 3 (September 1940), 3; 6 (January 1945), 3-4; Neville Miller to Raymond A. Kent, October 24, 1940; Raymond A. Kent to Barnard Flexner, November 17, 1938; Leon J. Solomon to John Walker Moore, October 15, 1947, President's Office Records, U of L Archives; Gerhard Herz, "Personal Recollections," in E.R. Hagemann (ed.), *Albert Schweitzer* (Louisville, 1965), 24-30; Inge Witt, "Justus Bier: Man of Vision," *North Carolina Museum of Art Bulletin* 12 (1974): 9-26.

13. John H. Gruber, "Remarks of Dr. Henry G. Hodges at the Playhouse," September 30, 1934; Morris D. Waldman to Charles W. Morris, October 23, 1934, Jewish Community Federation Records, U of L Archives; *Kentucky Encyclopedia,* 756; Janet Hodgson, "Rauch Planetarium Honors a Rabbi's Life of Dedication," *Inside U of L* (February 6, 1989), 6.

14. B.M. Brigman to Raymond A. Kent, May 20, 1930, B.M. Brigman, "Report on the Activities of the

Department of Buildings and Grounds," January 1, 1931, Koch Papers; Buildings and Grounds, Annual Report, 1931-1932, 8.

15. R.B. Stewart to Einar W. Jacobsen, March 29, 1946, President's Office Records, U of L Archives; *Centennial History*, 246-247.

16. *Kerr v. City of Louisville*, 111 *Southwestern Reporter* 2nd ser., 1046 (1937); Ellis, *Medicine in Kentucky*, 77; R.B. Stewart to Einar W. Jacobsen, March 29, 1946, Raymond A. Kent to Frank L. McVey, July 21, 1934, W.S. Learned to J.J. Oppenheimer, May 19, 1933, President's Office Records, U of L Archives.

17. President's Annual Report, 1930-1931, 23-29, 1932-1933, 16-17, 1936-1937, 20; J. Garland Sherrill to Board of Trustees, April 13, 1934; R.B. Stewart to Einar W. Jacobsen, March 29, 1946, President's Office Records, U of L Archives.

18. Board of Trustees, Minutes, May 1, 1940; *U of L Alumni Magazine* (November 1941): 7.

19. Flexner, *Mr. Justice Brandeis and the University of Louisville*, 7-56; Anna Blanche McGill, comp., *The Libraries of the University of Louisville* (Louisville, 1934); *Guide to the Papers of Louis Dembitz Brandeis at the University of Louisville, Microfilm Edition* (Louisville, 1980), 10-11; Janet Hodgson, "Brandeis Was a Lifelong Supporter of the University," *Inside U of L* (November 19, 1984), 4; Hodgson, "Louis Dembitz Brandeis," 16-17.

20. Morison, "High Water Mark at U of L," *U of L Magazine* 5 (winter 1987), 19; Leland R. Johnson, *The Falls City Engineers: A History of the Louisville District, Corps of Engineers, United States Army* (Louisville, 1974), 203-204.

21. Crews, *Spirited City*, 37; Yater, *Two Hundred Years*, 200; Kramer, *Two Centuries of Urban Development*, 148-151.

22. President's Annual Report, 1936-1937, 5-8, U of L Archives.

23. Tom Owen, "University Campuses Suffer Minor Damage," *Cardinal*, January 12, 1987.

24. *Centennial History*, 250-251.

25. *Cardinal*, February 11, 1937.

26. Also see Board of Trustees, Minutes, April 19, 1937.

27. College of Arts and Science, Annual Report, 1939-1940, 1-2; 1940-1941, 4, U of L Archives; *Cardinal*, November 24, 1939, November 29, 1940; Read, *Atrocity Propaganda, 1914-1919* (New Haven, 1941), 285-286.

28. President's Annual Report, 1940-1941, 9-20; College of Arts and Sciences, Annual Report, 1940-1941, 2; Speed Scientific School, Annual Report, 1940-1941, 2; School of Law, Annual Report, 1940-1941, 8-10; School of Medicine, Annual Report, 1940-1941, 10; Dean of Women, Annual Report, 1941-1942, 7-8, U of L Archives; *Cardinal*, September 19, 1941.

29. *Cardinal*, December 12, 1941, January 9, 1942;

Ford L. Wilkinson to Raymond A. Kent, October 6, 1942, President's Office Records; World War II Alumni/faculty Files, 1941-1945; E.R. Hagemann, Interview, March 4, 18, 1977, U of L Archives; Morison, "How Many U of L Students Lost Their Lives in World War II?" *Inside U of L*, November 1983.

30. Sprau, "History of the University of Louisville School of Dentistry," 17-18; *Courier-Journal*, April 21, 1943; George Yater, "When the Navy Invaded U of L," *U of L Alumni Magazine* (fall 1990), 22-23.

31. L. Dale Patterson, "Sailors, Barracks Gave U of L Naval Flavor," *Inside U of L*, October 31, 1988. Originally occupying the area where Schneider Hall was later built, the four barracks were moved a short distance to the southeast. Referred to as temporary, they served the needs of a cramped campus for thirty-six years before they were torn down in 1979 to make way for the Chemistry Building.

32. Yater, "When the Navy Invaded U of L," 23; Mike Smith, *Top of the Cards: A Look Back at 10 University of Louisville Basketball Teams* (Louisville, 1995), 23.

33. Ford L. Wilkinson to S.E. McKerley, June 13, 1944, President's Office Records, U of L Archives; *Courier-Journal*, August 29, 1943.

34. Deborah Skaggs, "WW II Changed the World . . . and U of L," *U of L Magazine* (summer 1985), 20-21; James G. Schneider, *The Navy V-12 Program: Leadership for a Lifetime* (Boston, 1987), 76-78, 257, 305, 328, 482; "ROTC Cards," *U of L Magazine* 13 (summer 1995), 5; *Louisville Times*, April 6, 1976; Reference Files, U of L Archives.

35. *Courier-Journal*, February 27, 1943; Schneider, *Navy V-12 Program*, 233.

36. "Kent School of Social Work," *Alumni Magazine* 7 (October 1944), 6, 11; Mary Ann Millet, letter to author, August 28, 1997. Annie Ainslie Halleck was the widow of Reuben Post Halleck, longtime principal of Male High School; see Patricia K. Bowling, "Reuben Post Halleck: A Biography" (M.A. thesis, University of Louisville, 1968), 33-36.

37. Ernest C. Hassold, "Comment on Jacobsen," April 25, 1977, Hassold Papers, U of L Archives.

14. The "Golden Age"?

1. John M. Houchens to Einar W. Jacobsen, April 12, 1946, News Release, June 12, 1948, President's Office Records, U of L Archives; Rollin E. Godfrey, "A Study of the Academic Success of Veteran Former Probation Students in the College of Arts and Sciences" (M.A., University of Louisville, 1947), 76; *Courier-Journal*, August 4, 1948; *Cardinal*, May 16, December 19, 1947; *New York Times*, August 10, 1947, July 11, 1948.

2. President's Annual Report, 1950-1951, U of L Archives; *Cardinal*, September 26, 1947.

3. News Release, June 12, 1948, President's Office Records, U of L Archives; *Courier-Journal,* August 4, 1948; *Cardinal,* May 16, December 19, 1947; *New York Times,* August 10, 1947, July 11, 1948; Yater, *Two Hundred Years,* 217-220; President's Annual Report, 1947-1948, 7-8; President's Annual Report, 1948-1949, 7; President's Report, 1947-1951, 17-19, U of L Archives; *Alumni Bulletin* 1 (April 1948), 1; Board of Trustees, Minutes, March 24, 1948; Merrick, "U of L Students Combine Jobs, Family Life, and College Through the Years," *U of L Magazine* 11 (fall 1992/winter 1993), 14-16.

4. *Louisville Times,* October 9, 1972; Reference Files, U of L Archives.

5. For four years beginning in 1946 Van Duyn and her husband Jarvis A. Thurston taught in the English department; while in Louisville they started the literary magazine *Perspective: A Quarterly of Literature,* which they edited until 1967. Michael Burns, ed., *Discovery and Reminiscence: Essays on the Poetry of Mona Van Duyn* (Fayetteville, 1998), 151-155; *Courier-Journal* December 20, 1987; Steve Brockwell, "A Way with Words," *U of L Magazine* 5 (winter 1987), 5-7; *Directory of American Scholars* 2(6th ed., New York, 1974), 672.

6. *Courier-Journal,* July 30, 1948; Bulletin of the Neighborhood Colleges (Louisville 1948), 9, U of L Archives. In April 1948, U of L students had the opportunity to write, produce and announce their own once-a-week radio program on WGRB. Called "Cardinal-of-the-Air," the program was affiliated with the school's student newspaper. It offered news, features, and interviews, all pertaining to U of L. For information about this activity and others involving U of L radio broadcasts, see *U of L Alumni Bulletin,* February 1928; *U of L Alumni Magazine,* March 1940; and *Cardinal,* April 16, 1948.

7. Ekstrom, *Recollection,* 4; Yater, *Two Hundred Years,* 218-219.

8. Ekstrom, *Recollection,* 8; Leslie Shively, conversation with author, October 2, 1997.

9. Board of Trustees, Minutes, April 11, 1951, and Ekstrom, *Recollection,* 8-9.

10. Philip G. Davidson, Interview, February 14, March 1, April 5, 1976, U of L Archives; Edwin Mims, *History of Vanderbilt University* (Nashville, 1946), 456-457; Paul K. Conkin, *Gone with the Ivy: A Biography of Vanderbilt University* (Knoxville, 1985), 421, 440-443, 455, 479. Longtime President's Assistant Turner began her career as a part-time employee in the registrar's office two years after enrolling as a student in 1928 and retired five presidents later, in 1972.

11. J.J. Oppenheimer to Philip G. Davidson, December 2, 1948, Davidson Papers; Davidson, Interview, March 1, 1976; Davidson, "What Sort of University Do We Want," November, 1951, President's Office Records, U of L Archives.

12. Maurer later won an out-of-court settlement for Hollywood's unsolicited use of his work, *The Big Con* (New York, 1940).

13. Harvey C. Webster, *On a Darkling Plain: The Art and Thought of Thomas Hardy* (Chicago, 1947), Richard M. Kain, *Dublin in the Age of William Butler Yeats and James Joyce* (Norman, 1962), and Mary E. Burton, ed., *The Letters of Mary Wordsworth, 1800-1855* (Oxford, 1958); President's Annual Report, 1965-1966, 4. Margaret Strong (sociology) and Hilda Threlkeld (education) became full professors in 1930 and 1934, respectively. For a first-person account of the establishment of the Ph.D. program in English, see Ekstrom, *Recollection,* 17-19.

14. Gerhard Herz, "Toward a New Image of Bach, Parts I and II," *Quarterly Journal of the Riemenschneider Bach Institute* 1 and 2 (October 1970 and January 1971): 9-27 and 7-28; "Bach's Religion," *Journal of Renaissance and Baroque Music* 1 (June 1946): 124-138; "The Performance History of Bach's *B Minor Mass,*" *American Choral Review* 15 (July 1973): 5-21.

15. Manchester, "Louisville Cashes in on Culture," 81-82; Share, *Cities in the Commonwealth,* 110-119; Jeanne Belfy (ed.), *The Louisville Orchestra New Music Project: Selected Letters* (Louisville, 1983), 9-13.

16. Justus Bier, *Tilman Riemenschneider: His Life and Work* (Lexington, 1982), was a condensed version of the original four-volume biography published in German between 1925 and 1978. Also see Bier, "Carl C. Brenner: A German-American Landscapist," *The American-German Review* 17 (April 1951), 20-25, and Witt, "Justus Bier," 5-21.

17. Laurence Lee Howe, *The Pretorian Prefect from Commodus to Diocletian, A.D. 180-305* (Chicago, 1942), 63-64; "Historical Method and Legal Education," *Bulletin of the American Association of University Professors* 36 (summer 1950), 346-356. Samuel Eliot Morison praised Howe's views on historical writing in his presidential address to the American Historical Association: "Faith of a Historian," *American Historical Review* 56 (January 1951): 263.

18. *New York Times,* May 31, 1970; Ray L. Birdwhistell, *Introduction to Kinesics* (Louisville, 1952); *Courier-Journal,* May 19, 1970.

19. Speed Scientific School, Freshman Handbook, 1950-1951, 2, 23, 26; 1959-1960, 2, U of L Archives.

20. University of Louisville, Freshman Handbook, August 1949, 33, 36, U of L Archives. U of L biologist William Furnish, whose boyhood home adjoined the campus, witnessed albino squirrels there in the 1930s. Thane Robinson, another U of L biology professor, believed there were enough albinism genes among the U of L squirrel population to form two white ones each generation. Morison, "How Long Have White Squirrels Inhabited the Belknap Campus?" *Inside U of L,* July 1983.

21. Morison, "What Is the Origin of the University's Flag?" *Inside U of L,* September 1982; Janet Hodgson, "The Great Flag Debate," *U of L Magazine* 12 (winter 1994), 11; *Courier-Journal,* September 27, 1959; Creese, "What Are We Celebrating Today," *Egghead* 1 (spring 1959), 35-38; and Reference Files, U of L Archives. For additional information on Creese, see Tom Owen, "Creese Left an Enduring Mark on U of L Architecture," *Inside U of L,* January 26, 1985.

22. *Thoroughbred* (1939), 158, (1950), 84-85; Morison, "When Did the U of L Band Begin to Play at the Kentucky Derby," *Inside U of L,* June 1, 1984; Tom Owen, "U of L's Marching Band has an Erratic History," *U of L Magazine* 3 (fall 1984), 22-23; Reference Files, U of L Archives.

23. University of Louisville, Handbook of Student Activities, c. 1950, 2, Dean of Men, Annual Report, 1956-1957, 1; Dean of Women, Annual Report, 1954-1955, 2, U of L Archives; *Cardinal,* March 6, 1952, March 10, 1967. Following Hilda Threlkeld, Doris Stokes began her service as dean of women in the mid-1950s; David Lawrence, who served as dean of men in the 1950s, became dean of students in 1963. Both Stokes and Lawrence retired in 1978.

24. Merrick, "Campus Eats," 22-23.

25. Dale Patterson, "Dorms Essential—Even at Commuter Schools," *Inside U of L* (February 5, 1990), 6.

26. Patterson, "Dorms Essential," 6. The university finally created a full-fledged housing office, headed by Harold Adams, in 1971. Known for his understanding ear for students' concerns, Adams was memorialized by the naming of the main walkway leading to the Student Activities Center.

27. Ekstrom, *Recollection,* 9.

28. *Cardinal,* October 23, 1958.

29. *Cardinal,* March 11, October 4, 11, 25, November 1, 8, 1963, March 10, 1964.

30. *Courier-Journal,* January 27, 1986.

31. Davidson, Interview, February 15, March 1, 1976, U of L Archives; *Louisville Times,* September 7, 1978; *Courier-Journal,* September 22, 1982; *Potential,* July 2, 1975; University of Louisville, *Cardinal Football* (Louisville, 1982), 50-51, 53, 63.

32. *Kentucky Encyclopedia,* 58.

33. Western Kentucky University was close behind— African Americans Clem Haskins, the future WKU All-American who was also recruited by U of L, and Dwight Smith joined the Hilltoppers' freshman squad the following year, 1963. Sam Smith was a leading scorer in his first varsity year, was declared academically ineligible, and eventually transferred to Kentucky Wesleyan College, where he achieved stardom. Whitehead sat out for the second half of his sophomore year because of academic problems, but returned as a valuable member of the 1964-1965 and 1965-1966 teams. Houston earned letters for all three years; he also served as assistant basketball coach at U of L, 1976-1989, and as head coach at the University of Tennessee, 1989-1992. For an account of the perspectives of Houston, Hickman, and Dromo on the integration of U of L basketball, see Smith, *Top of the Cards,* 82-84.

34. Mike Smith, "Someone Special," *U of L Magazine* 14 (spring 1996), 15-17; *Kentucky Encyclopedia,* 58-61, 914; Dave Kindred, *Basketball: The Dream Game in Kentucky* (Louisville, 1975), 131-140; John Dromo, Interview, December 19, 1981, U of L Archives. Forced by a heart attack to retire as head basketball coach after the ninth game of the 1970-1971 season, Dromo was succeeded for the remainder of that year by Howard Stacey.

35. The basketball team has also played in the Missouri Valley (1964-1975) and Metro (1975-1995) conferences. In 1995 U of L helped form Conference USA (C-USA). News Release, September 22, 1949, President's Office Records, and Board of Trustees, Minutes, December 9, 1949, U of L Archives; *Courier-Journal,* October 11, December 20, 1949; *Kentucky Encyclopedia,* 504-505.

36. *University of Louisville 1997-98 Basketball Information Guide* (Louisville 1997), 115.

37. *ESPN College Basketball Magazine* (1995-1996), quoted in *University of Louisville 1996-97 Basketball Information Guide* (Louisville 1996), 93.

38. Reference Files, U of L Archives; *University of Louisville 1996 Baseball Media Guide* (Louisville 1996), 36, 40-42.

39. Morison, "Did U of L Really Win the Old GE College Bowl," *U of L Magazine* (spring 1983), 24-25.

40. Ekstrom, *Recollection,* 19.

41. *Inside U of L,* June 1982; Otis A. Singletary (ed.), *American Universities and Colleges,* 10th ed. (Washington, 1968), 568-572; Carl Abner, et al., to Philip G. Davidson, April 16, 1962, President's Office Records, U of L Archives. U of L doctoral programs added during this period included chemistry (1951), chemical engineering (1955), anatomy, biochemistry, microbiology, pharmacology, physiology, and biophysics (1956), biology (1958), psychology (1963), English (1965), interdisciplinary studies (1967), and physics (1970). U of L's "Study of Higher Education, Phase I, Submitted to the Council on Public Higher Education," 1970, 4-7, President's Office Records, U of L Archives, discusses the development of these programs.

42. *Courier-Journal,* November 6, 1952; Walter Creese, "Recommendations from 'Final Report on Belknap Campus,'" November, 16, 1953, President's Office Records; Laurence Lee Howe to Frank Howe, June 11, November 16, 1967, Howe Papers, U of L Archives; Shively, *Belknap Campus—Its History,* 13-22. For an account of the development of urban renewal in Old Louisville and its effect on the university, see Kramer, *Two Centuries of Urban Development,* 227-229.

43. Carl E. Kramer, *Old Louisville: A Changing View*

(Louisville, 1982), provides a detailed discussion of Old Louisville's rise, decline, and revival. Theodore Brown and Margaret Bridwell, *Old Louisville* (Louisville, 1961), remains a useful reference tool on the subject. Also see Yater, *Two Hundred Years,* 238-239, and Samuel W. Thomas and William Morgan, *Old Louisville: The Victorian Era* (Louisville, 1975).

44. Funded by the Kentucky Women's Confederate Monument Association, the Confederate Monument was completed in 1897, years before the university occupied the Belknap Campus. See Morison, "The Confederate Monument: A Landmark that Almost Wasn't," *Inside U of L* (December 3, 1984), 4, and "U of L Alumnus Solves the Monument Mystery," *Inside U of L* (January 14, 1985), 4.

45. Morison, "How Did U of L Acquire Robbins Hall?" *Inside U of L,* January 1984.

46. *Inside U of L,* April 1982.

47. Morison, "What Was Shipp Street, and Whatever Happened to It?" *Inside U of L,* April 1982.

48. Morison, "Has Parkway Field Always Been Part of U of L?" *Inside U of L,* June 1982.

49. *The American Eagle,* February, 1953, Reference Files, U of L Archives; *The American Mercury,* May, 1953, 111-114; Laurence Lee Howe to Bud and Dorothy Haley, June 16, 1953, Howe Papers; Harvey C. Webster to John Ryan, c. 1953, Webster Papers, President's Annual Report, 1952-1953, 9-10; U of L Archives; *Alumni News,* January, 1954. For a first-person account of the role of the U of L chapter of the American Association of University Professors in opposing the requirement of a faculty loyalty oath in the spring of 1950, see Ekstrom, *Recollection,* 6-8; for another faculty member's comments on the university's posture during this period, see Walter L. Creese, "A Short Report on the University of Louisville," August, 1959, Reference Files, U of L Archives.

50. International Center, Annual Report, 1953-1954, 10-11, U of L Archives; *Cardinal,* April 26, 1951; *Courier-Journal,* December 12, 1961, February 3, 1963; Tom Owen, "Belknap Coffee Tree Marks Early Hope for United Nations," *Inside U of L,* October 3, 1988; Janet Hodgson, "Louisville's Center for International Affairs," *Inside U of L,* February 19, 1990.

51. Board of Trustees, Minutes, April 19, 1950; Myrdal, "Social Trends in America and Strategic Approaches to the Negro Problem," *Phylon: The Atlanta University Review of Race and Culture* 9 (1948), 209; B. Edward Campbell, "Brief History of the Southern Police Institute and School of Police Administration," in Joseph Rosenfeld (ed.), *University of Louisville School of Police Administration, Southern Police Institute: Yesterday, Today, Tomorrow* (Louisville, 1976), 5-6; and Oscar Bryant, "Policing Pioneers," *U of L Magazine* 12 (summer 1994), 15-17. Gunnar Myrdal received an honorary degree when he spoke at President Woodrow Strickler's inauguration in 1968; *Cardinal,* November 22, 1968.

52. Raymond A. Dahl, "The Southern Police Institute's Seminar Programs," in Rosenfeld (ed.), *University of Louisville School of Police Administration,* 8; Dahl, "David A. McCandless, 1905-1971," in Rosenfeld, 16.

53. Omer Carmichael and Weldon Jones, *The Louisville Story* (New York, 1957), 18-35.

54. Board of Overseers, Minutes, May 31, 1950, 1-2; Board of Trustees, Minutes, April 19, 1961; *Cardinal,* March 3, 10, May 3, 17, 1961; April 17, May 1, 1964; April 21, May 5, September 23, 1967; *Louisville Times,* March 10, 1960; C.H. Parrish to Whitney Young Sr., March 25, 1962, Parrish Papers, U of L Archives; Merrick, "Campus Eats," 22-23.

55. Charles G. Talbert, *The University of Kentucky: The Maturing Years* (Lexington, 1965), 190-193.

56. *Courier-Journal,* July 22-24, 28-30, 1948; *Alumni Bulletin* 2 (September 1948), 1.

57. Philip G. Davidson to Lyman Dawson, February 3, 1961, President's Office Records, U of L Archives; Yater, *Two Hundred Years,* 223, 229-230; *Courier-Journal,* August 26, 1956, July 30, 1961; *Louisville Times,* May 14, 1970; Dwayne Cox, "The University and the Hospital: A Historic Relationship," January, 1981, University Archives Information Requests, U of L Archives. For a description of the planning, design, and construction of the U of L Health Sciences Center and other nearby medical facilities in the context of urban renewal, see Kramer, *Two Centuries of Urban Development,* 223-225. This effort was aided by the approval of a $5 million city bond issue in November 1957; Yater, *Two Hundred Years,* 223.

58. Ellis, *Medicine in Kentucky,* 77-78; Davidson, Interview, February 14, 1976; *Alumni News,* February 14, 1956; Board of Trustees, Minutes, August 3, 1956; Board of Overseers, Minutes, January 31, 1956, U of L Archives; Raymond E. Myers, "Why Two Dental Schools in Kentucky," *Journal of the Kentucky State Dental Association* 8 (January 1956), 9-14.

59. Davidson, Interview, February 14, 1976; Randall Green to Lee P. Miller, January 14, 1960, President's Office Records; Board of Trustees, Minutes, January 20, November 5, 1960, U of L Archives; *Louisville Times,* November 4-5, 1960; Morison, "Churchill Downs . . . to U of L," *Inside U of L,* April 1984.

60. Louis F. Muller, conversation with author, September 8, 1998.

61. *Courier-Journal,* February 11, 1965.

62. Board of Trustees, Minutes, June 2, 21, 1955, January 20, 1965; Morison, "Money for Athletics Is a Question That's Been Raised Before," *Inside U of L,* August 27, 1984.

63. *Courier-Journal,* February 11, 12, 1965.

64. *Courier-Journal,* February 12, 1965.

65. Board of Trustees, Minutes, February 11, 1965; *Courier-Journal,* February 12, 1965.

66. *Courier-Journal,* February 12, 1965; Ekstrom, *Reflections,* 45-46.

67. Laurence Lee Howe, "Campus Recollections, 1925-1976," c. March, 1977, 5-6, Oral History Files, U of L Archives. William F. Ekstrom, who came to U of L in 1947 and headed the English department through much of the Davidson era, echoed Howe: "Faculty-Administration relations had never been better." Ekstrom, *Recollection,* 45.

15. Statehood

1. Yater, *Two Hundred Years,* 145, 229, 241.

2. Kris W. Kindelsperger, "A Study of Factors Leading to the Entrance of the University of Louisville into the State System of Higher Education in Kentucky" (M.A., University of Louisville, 1976), 9-20.

3. Kindelsperger, "Entrance . . . into the State System," 23-28.

4. Ibid., 28-33.

5. Kindelsperger, "Entrance . . . into the State System," 33-34; Heald, Hobsen and Associates, "Report to the Joint Committee Regarding the University of Louisville and the State System of Higher Education: Alternatives and Consultants' Recommendations" (March 1967); and Lisle Baker to John Oswald and Philip G. Davidson, November 24, 1967, President's Office Records, U of L Archives.

6. *Courier-Journal,* June 11, 1967; John W. Oswald, Interview, August 10-12, 1987, University of Kentucky Archives.

7. Philip G. Davidson, Interview, February 14, March 1, 1976; William J. McGlothlin, Diary, August 7-8, 1967, McGlothlin Papers, U of L Archives.

8. "There was no doubt that we had waited too long, but how we would have fared is another matter." Ekstrom, *Recollection,* 48.

9. Ekstrom, *Recollection,* 43-44, 47-48; *Courier-Journal,* March 30, 1968.

10. Dee Akers, Interview, February 1, 1976; William J. McGlothlin, "Summary of Events," September 18, 1967, McGlothlin Papers, U of L Archives.

11. Executive Committee, University of Kentucky Board of Trustees, Minutes, March 6, 1968, President's Office Records, University of Kentucky Archives; Akers, Interview, February 1, 1976, U of L Archives; Kindlesperger, "Entrance . . . into the State System," 44-46; Ekstrom, *Recollection,* 48-49; Susan Converse, "U of L: In the Beginning," *University of Louisville Bicentennial Commemorative Program* (Louisville, 1998).

12. William McGlothlin to Philip G. Davidson, March 14, 1968, Davidson Papers; *Courier-Journal,* March 10, 13, 1968.

13. Kindelsperger, "Entrance . . . into the State System," 49; Oswald, Interview, University of Kentucky Archives; Harrison and Klotter, *A New History of Kentucky,* 396-397; Joint Committee on the Affiliation of the University of Kentucky and the University of Louisville, Report, June, 1969, l, President's Office Records; Council on Public Higher Education, Legislative Implications Related to the Six Alternatives as Recommended by Heald, Hobsen and Associates, August 29, 1969, 2, President's Office Records; Otis A. Singletary, Interview, June 8, 1976; Akers, Interview, April 1, 1976; U of L Archives.

14. Otis A. Singletary to Woodrow M. Strickler, October 23, 1969, President's Office Records, U of L Archives.

15. Woodrow M. Strickler to Otis A. Singletary, October 30, 1969, President's Office Records, U of L Archives; *Courier-Journal,* October 12, November 8, 1969.

16. Eleanor Turner to Philip G. Davidson, November 23, 1969, Davidson Papers; Akers, Interview, February 1, 1976, U of L Archives.

17. Harrison and Klotter, *A New History of Kentucky,* 396-397; Lowell H. Harrison, *Kentucky's Governors, 1792-1985* (Lexington, 1985), 175-178; *Kentucky Encyclopedia,* 538, 684-686.

18. Interview with Louie B. Nunn, June 18, 1998, U of L Archives; *Courier-Journal,* January 8, 9, 22, March 21, 1970; *Louisville Times,* January 1, 1972.

19. Board of Trustees, Minutes, January 7, 21, 28, February 6, March 18, April 15, May 20, June 17, June 29, 1970, U of L Archives.

20. President's Annual Report, 1971, 1; Interview with Louie B. Nunn, June 18, 1998, U of L Archives.

16. Student Unrest

1. Mary S. Donovan and D. Patricia Wagner, *Kentucky's Black Heritage* (Frankfort, 1971), 139-140; *Cardinal,* April 12, 19, 1968.

2. *Courier-Journal* May 1, 2, 1969.

3. *Cardinal,* May 9, 1969; Woodrow M. Strickler, Interview, March 20, 1974; James Blaine Hudson III, Interview, August 11, 18, 1980; Eleanor Turner to Philip Davidson, May 18, 1969, Davidson Papers, U of L Archives; Ekstrom, *Recollection,* 62-64. Hudson and five others were tried, convicted, and dismissed from the university. They appealed and in 1970 were acquitted. Four were readmitted in the fall of 1969; Hudson and the remaining student, Robert L. Martin Sr., were readmitted in the spring of 1970. The Office of Black Affairs became the Office of Minority Affairs in 1976.

4. Board of Trustees, Minutes, November 17, 1965; Student Petitions in Student Government Association Records; Dean of Students, Annual Report, 1969-1970, l; U of L Archives. *Cardinal,* January 6, 1967, December 12, 1968.

5. *The Harpoon*, February, 1968; *The Bloomin' Newman*, November 10, 1969; *The Other Side*, March 6, 1969.

6. *The Thinker*, November 19, December 10, 1968, February 11, 1970; Laurence Lee Howe to Frank Howe, December 10, 1967, Howe Papers, U of L Archives.

7. *Cardinal*, December 6, 1968, October 3, 1969; *Thoroughbred Magazine* 1 (Louisville, 1970), 2-7, 42-43; Laurence Lee Howe to Frank Howe, December 24, 1967, Howe Papers, U of L Archives; Merrick, "Campus Eats," 23.

8. Woodrow M. Strickler, Statement on American Foreign Policy in Cambodia, May 6, 1970; Evelyn Blanford and Tom Owen to Woodrow M. Strickler, April 7, 1969; William J. Boughey to Woodrow M. Strickler, April 7, 1969, President's Office Records, U of L Archives; *Cardinal*, March 28, 1969; *Louisville Times*, April 1, 12, 1969; *Courier-Journal*, April 1, 2, 9, 1969; Cox, "The Cardinal," 19.

9. *Courier-Journal*, May 16, 1972; *U of L Magazine* (summer 1995), 5; *Cardinal*, October 8, 1994, February 23, 1995. The Life Sciences Buiding was dedicated in 1970. The Humanities Building was finished in 1974; in 1979 it was named for Barry Bingham Sr., publisher of the *Louisville Courier-Journal*, and his wife, Mary.

10. Kindelsperger, "Entrance . . . into the State System," 52; Shirley Harmon and Norman C. Lewis, "They Whom a Dream Hath Possessed: A History of Kentucky Southern College, 1962-1969," (Louisville, 1999); Kentucky Southern College Records, U of L Archives; Steven T. Hurtt, "The Closing of a College: An Analysis" (Ed.D. dissertation, Indiana University, 1977); Lowell H. Harrison, *Western Kentucky University* (Lexington, 1987), 180-181.

11. Kindelsperger, "Entrance . . . into the State System," 53, 81; Ekstrom, *Recollection*, 44-45.

12. *Courier-Journal*, May 17, 1968.

13. Eleanor Turner to Philip G. Davidson, March 12, 1970, March 26, 1971, Davidson Papers, U of L Archives; Ekstrom, *Recollection*.

14. Ekstrom, *Recollection*, 70.

15. *Courier-Journal*, February 2, 1976; Eleanor Turner to Philip G. Davidson, January 23, 1972, Davidson Papers; E.R. Hagemann to Harvey C. Webster, May 18, 1970, Webster Papers, U of L Archives.

17. Growing Pains

1. Board of Trustees, Minutes, February 19, 1973; *Louisville Times*, February 20, 1973.

2. Davidson to Family, October 8, 1973, Davidson Papers, U of L Archives.

3. President's Annual Report, 1979, 31; Middleton to David Grissom, April 9, 1980, President's Office

Records; Ekstrom, Interview, July 13, 1982, U of L Archives; Ekstrom, *Recollection*, 85; *Courier-Journal*, April 29, 1977; *Kentucky Encyclopedia*, 165.

4. *Louisville Times*, March 31, April 21, 22, September 16, 1977.

5. President's Annual Report, 1977, 3-6, U of L Archives. Also see Cathy Lynn Cole, "A Historical Perspective of the Kentucky Council on Higher Education" (Ph.D. dissertation, Southern Illinois University, 1983), 337-355. In 1977 the Council on Public Higher Education became the Council on Higher Education.

6. President's Annual Report, 1965-1966, 4; "Urban Studies Center," (Louisville 1969), 5; "The Urban Studies Center: Past, Present and Future" (Louisville 1980), 3; Reference Files, U of L Archives.

7. "Urban Studies Center" (Louisville 1969), 4; *Courier-Journal*, December 15, 1971.

8. *Inside U of L*, September 8, 1995; "The Urban Research Institute: Responding to Society's Needs for Twenty-Five Years" (Louisville 1991), 2-10.

9. Ekstrom, *Recollection*, 85. Funding for the pendulum was provided by the U of L Foundation and retired biology professor Louis Krumholz; Roger E. Mills, "A Report on the Foucault Pendulum at the University of Louisville," March 15, 1990, Reference Files, U of L Archives; *Louisville Times*, March 23, 1978; *Cardinal*, January 25, 1990.

10. *Louisville Times*, October 7, 1976; *Courier-Journal*, April 14, July 21, 1976, April 13, 1980. The Belknap Campus became a preservation district on the National Register of Historic Places in 1976; Taylor, "Architectural History of the Belknap Playhouse," 283-287.

11. Elbert, Interview, June 13, 27, 1983, U of L Archives.

12. *Courier-Journal*, September 6, 1974; *Cardinal*, September 13, October 18, 1974; *Alumni Newspaper*, Autumn 1974, 4.

13. Morison, "Bald Cyprus Tree Destroyed by Lightning—Was It the Oldest?" *Inside U of L*, July 1984; Anna Kearney, "Library's Development Built Around Tree," *Inside U of L*, May 4, 1987. Muller worked in Buildings and Grounds, which had long been referred to as "B & G," from 1956 until 1984. It was renamed Physical Plant about the time the Ekstrom Library opened.

14. Wynn Egginton and Wayne Childers, "Twenty Years: Tracing Threads of Change and Continuity," *Cardinal Principles* 3 (summer 1988), 2-7. On the history of the Louisville Normal School and the Louisville Colored Normal School, which also closed in 1935, see "Twenty-Fourth Report of the Board of Education of Louisville, Ky.," and "Louisville Colored Normal School Record Book," Jefferson County Public Schools Archives.

15. Frank, "History of the School of Music," 26; *Courier-Journal*, April 13, 1947; Yater, *Two Hundred Years*, 156-157, 180. In February 1969 the body of a

female music student was found behind the Reynolds Building. This tragedy hastened the music school's abandonment of the building and was a factor in the subsequent enlargement of the U of L police force. The murder went unsolved for three years. *Courier-Journal,* February 5, 6, 1969, November 4, 17, 1972; *Louisville Times,* June 29, 1973; *Cardinal,* February 7, 1969; Ekstrom, *Recollection,* 65.

16. Frank, "History of the School of Music."

17. Bryant, "Solid Gold," 11-15. In 1999 the concert hall was named for music school benefactor Margaret Comstock.

18. Francis M. Nash, *Towers over Kentucky: A History of Radio and TV in the Bluegrass State* (Lexington, 1995), 124; *Courier-Journal,* December 4, 1975, June 10, 1976, March 28, 1993; Reference Files, U of L Archives.

19. *Courier-Journal,* August 3, 1994.

20. *Inside U of L,* March 1984.

21. Morison, "School of Nursing . . . Years Ago," *Inside U of L,* March 1, 1984.

22. *Courier-Journal,* April 16, 1974; *Louisville Times,* April 22, 1975; Board of Trustees, Minutes, March 26, 1979.

23. President's Annual Report, 1979, 31, U of L Archives; John A. Dillon, Interview, May 16, 1978; A.J. Slavin, Interview, May 31, June 6, 28, 1983, U of L Archives; Ekstrom, *Recollection,* 79.

24. Alan A. Johnson, Interview, July 21, September 29, 1978, U of L Archives; Johnson to the Graduate Faculty, c. November 15, 1976, September 5, 1980, Reference Files, U of L Archives.

25. *Louisville Times,* October 31, 1977, August 8, 1978; *Courier-Journal,* October 27, 1977, January 5, 1979; Faculty Senate, Minutes, September 7, 1977, 7, September 10, 1980, 4, U of L Archives.

26. *Louisville Times,* October 9, 1974, December 5, 1978; Administrative Memorandum 74-22-1, Administrative Handbook, U of L Archives; *Potential,* December 21, 1977; *Louisville Defender,* April 7, 1977.

27. *Louisville Times,* June 6, November 28, 1981; *Courier-Journal,* May 26, 1979, July 18, 1980; Arthur H. Keeney, Interview, September 28, 1981, U of L Archives; Jack Gourman, *The Gourman Report: A Rating of Graduate and Professional Programs in American and International Education* (Los Angeles, 1980), 54-57.

28. Gourman, *The Gourman Report,* 54-57; *Courier-Journal,* October 11, 1974, November 18, 1977; *Louisville Times,* October 25, November 21, 1978, May 26, 1979; "Questioning the Bar Exams," *Time,* February 25, 1980, 44.

29. *School of Law Catalogue, 1996-1998* (Louisville 1996), inside front cover; Board of Trustees, Minutes, April 19, 1950.

30. Skaggs, "Jefferson School of Law," *Inside U of L,* April 8, 1985; Oscar Bryant, "Carl Perkins: Rustic

Representative," *U of L Magazine* 2 (summer 1983): 2-4; President's Annual Report, 1965-1966, 4; *Kentucky Encyclopedia,* 716-717, 970.

31. This reorganization, which resulted in a consolidated system known as the University Libraries, was initiated by President Miller in 1980 and completed under President Swain in 1982. The law school's library remained a part of that school and was not made a component of the new system. Faculty Senate, Minutes, May 5, 1971, 2-4; James Grier Miller to Steven Smith, September 30, 1980, Dean's Office Records, University Libraries, U of L Archives; Board of Trustees, Minutes, September 27, 1982; *Louisville Times,* January 10, 1980. Also see Dee Garrison, *Apostles of Culture: The Public Librarian and American Society, 1876-1920* (New York, 1979), and Orvin Lee Shiflett, *Origins of American Academic Librarianship* (Norwood, New Jersey, 1981). For an overview of the U of L libraries written by a longtime library administrator, see Ralze Dorr, "A Brief History of the University of Louisville Libraries, 1837-1996," *Owl* 13 (May, June 1998), 1-3, 1-3.

32. Demos, Interview, June 2, 1982, U of L Archives.

33. Graduate School, *Catalogue* (Louisville, 1980), 27-30; Louis D. Brandeis to Frederick Wehle, October 28, 1924, President's Office Records, U of L Archives; Brandeis to Alfred Brandeis, February 18, 1925, Melvin I. Urofsky and David W. Levy (eds.), *Letters of Louis D. Brandeis* (5 vols.; Albany, NY, 1971-1978) V, 163-164. The Oral History Center was started in the Department of History by Charles R. Berry. Under Carl G. Ryant, his successor, it moved to the University Archives in 1978.

34. President's Annual Report, 1978, 9-15, 1979, 17-23; A.J. Slavin, Interview, May 31, June 6, 28, 1983, U of L Archives; Dana Fischetti, "Mirroring Human Behavior," *Et Ultra* (summer/fall 1998), 6-9.

35. *Cardinal,* March 31, 1978; Wini Breines, *Community and Organization in the New Left, 1962-1968: The Great Refusal* (New York, 1982), 150; *Courier-Journal,* March 9, 1974, March 24, 1977; *Louisville Times,* January 25, 1979.

36. *Cardinal,* April 8, 1977, April 13, 1979; Cox, "The Cardinal," p. 19; Larry Hovekamp, "The Cardinal War for Independence," *U of L Magazine* 7 (spring 1989), 18-19.

37. *Louisville Times,* December 11, 1982; *Courier-Journal,* November 6, 1982; *Louisville Scholar,* February 11, March 10, May 6, 1983.

38. University of Louisville, *Fact Book: Fall 1979* (Louisville, 1980), 23; Yale Daily News, *The Insider's Guide to the Colleges* (New York, 1978), 210-212; *Potential,* July 14, 1976; *Louisville Times,* May 31, 1977, February 14, 1979; *Courier-Journal,* February 2, 1976, February 27, 1977.

39. *Louisville Times,* March 26, 1976; Morison, "How Long Has the *Minerva,* U of L's Student Yearbook, Been Published?" *Inside U of L,* October 1982; Margaret

Merrick, "Yearbooks Display Student Lifestyles through the Years," *Inside U of L*, October 19, 1987; *Centennial History*, 182-183. The yearbook version of the *Kentucky Cardinal* appeared in 1922 and 1923 as the final spring issue of the *Kentucky Cardinal* magazine, a literary monthly published from December 1921 through April 1925.

40. The dental school claims U of L's first yearbook, though it appeared before that unit became part of the university. While still attached to Central University, the Louisville College of Dentistry's students were included in Central's *Cream and Crimson* as early as 1895.

41. Merrick, "Campus Eats," 23.

42. Louisville Times, December 11, 1975; Michael Daniel, "Old Red," *Thinker* (March 1979), 33-34; Sheila Joyce, "Barn Raising: The Comeback of U of L's Red Barn," *Louisville Today* 3 (January 1979), 59-60; John Chamberlain, "Barn to Be Wild," *U of L Magazine* 2 (winter 1984), 22-24; Shane Armstrong and Bill Noltemeyer, "Howe We Care," *U of L Magazine* 13 (summer 1995), 6-7; *Cardinal*, October 8, 1994. Other students credited with the initial capturing of the Red Barn were Michael E. Geralds, Lance O. Mabry, Robert B. McGeachin, and R. Danny Miller. During his three terms as head of the Union for Student Activities (1972-1975), Robert E. Merrick's work in scheduling events demonstrated that the Red Barn fulfilled student needs unmet elsewhere in the university. M. Thomas Boykin, Kenneth J. Minogue, and others helped start the Red Barn Alumni Association in 1985. That group singled out Woodrow M. Strickler, William R. Davidson, Harry M. Sparks, and David H. Lee among U of L administrators instrumental in saving the building. George J. Howe, conversation with author, September 24, 1998. Student involvement in Red Barn programming was commended in George D. Kuh, et al., *Involving Colleges: Successful Approaches to Fostering Student Learning and Development Outside the Classroom* (San Francisco, 1991), 92.

43. Daniel, "Old Red," 33; Joyce, "Barn Raising," 59-60; Chamberlain, "Barn to Be Wild," 23-24.

44. "The Red Barn Report," Reference File, U of L Archives. Jaklin Klugman finished third in the 1980 Kentucky Derby.

45. University College, *Catalogue* (Louisville, 1972), 418-420.

46. President's Annual Report, 1956-1957, 17-18; Board of Trustees, Minutes, July 17, 1957.

47. Merrick, "U of L Students Combine Jobs, Family Life, and College Through the Years," 15-16.

48. Reference File, U of L Archives.

49. University of Louisville, *Cardinal Football* (Louisville, 1997), 151; *Courier-Journal*, December 13, 1970, January 4, 1973, December 1, 15, 1974; *Louisville Times*, October 30, 1981.

50. University of Louisville, *Cardinal Basketball* (Louisville, 1982), 9; "Cardinal Phobia," *Sports Illustrated*,

March 22, 1982, 11; *Courier-Journal*, June 29, 1983; *Inside U of L*, January 1983; *Kentucky Encyclopedia*, 244. U of L basketball's string of forty-six consecutive winning seasons began in 1944 and ended in 1990; University of Louisville, *Cardinal Basketball* (Louisville, 1997), 134.

51. *Louisville Defender*, May 19, 1977; *Louisville Times*, August 28, 1974, November 11, 1980; *Courier-Journal*, November 12, 1980, April 22, October 2, 1981; *Cardinal*, September 25, 1981.

52. *Lady Cardinal Basketball 1997-98 Media Guide* (Louisville 1997), 56.

53. *Women's Center News* 6 (fall 1998), 2; *Courier-Journal*, April 25, 1998; Christopher Lasch, *The Culture of Narcissism: American Life in an Age of Diminishing Expectations* (New York, 1979), 181-219.

54. Board of Trustees, Minutes, May 6, 1936, January 18, 1956, March 20, 1963, June 17, 1970, July 19, 1976, October 17, 1977. The board of trustees adopted the "Organization of the University of Louisville Together with Laws Creating and Affecting Same" on May 6, 1936; for this and other governance documents, see Reference Files, U of L Archives.

55. Administrative Memoranda 79-9, 76-13, 76-20, Administrative Handbook; A.J. Slavin to Vice Presidents and Deans, March 7, 1977, Reference Files, U of L Archives; Ekstrom, *Recollection*, 60, 93-95.

56. William Furnish, Interview, April 4, 1977, U of L Archives.

57. William F. Ekstrom, "Reflections on the University of Louisville Experience," May 8, 1982, Reference Files, U of L Archives; Ekstrom's commencement address of May 9, 1982, was published in condensed form as "See Life Steadily and See It Whole," *U of L Magazine*, 1 (fall 1982), 16-17.

58. *Alumni News*, September 29, 1978; Board of Trustees, Minutes, June 25, 1979; Ekstrom, *Recollection*, 99.

59. Ekstrom, *Recollection*, 88.

18. An Agent for Change

1. *Cardinal*, January 11, 1980; *Louisville Times*, September 18, November 25, 1980.

2. Ekstrom, *Recollection*, 100-101.

3. Ekstrom, *Recollection*, 101-102; *Courier-Journal*, February 14, 1981. The food processing plants south of Eastern Parkway were also responsible for the distinctive soybean or peanut oil aromas that visited the Belknap Campus from time to time.

4. *Courier-Journal*, December 2, 1980.

5. Donald C. Swain, letter to author, April 4, 1998.

6. *Courier-Journal*, January 27, April 11, September 18, December 27, 1981; *Louisville Times*, September 18, 1981.

7. *Courier-Journal,* April 30, May 5, 1981; Swain to author, April 4, 1998.

8. Conner, "By Many Names," 29; *Courier-Journal,* July 31, 1981, January 5, 1982.

9. *Kentucky Encyclopedia,* 624; Katherine Vansant, "U of L Enters a New Kind of Public-Private Partnership," *U of L Magazine* (spring 1983): 3-5.

10. William F. Ekstrom, Interview, July 13, 1982; Norbert F. Elbert, Interview, June 13, 1983, U of L Archives; Vansant, "U of L Enters a New Kind of Public-Private Partnership," 3-5; Conner, "By Many Names," 29-30; *Courier-Journal,* November 6, 1982, March 2, April 30, 1983, April 2, 1986.

11. *Courier-Journal,* November 25, 1980, July 24, 1981; *Cardinal,* August, 1981.

12. *Louisville Times,* March 12, 1982; *Courier-Journal* March 13, 1982; Katherine Vansant, "An Urban University Forms an Urban College," *U of L Magazine* 2 (summer 1983), 5.

13. The Continuing Studies Division was formed to coordinate offerings in this area. *Louisville Times,* March 29, April 24, 1982; *Courier-Journal,* March 6, 1983; *Undergraduate Catalog 1994-1996* (Louisville 1994); *Inside U of L,* September 10, 1993; Swain to author, April 4, 1998.

14. *Courier-Journal,* February 8, March 6, 1983. For information about U of L's fund-raising campaigns in the twentieth century, see Morison, "Current Endowment Campaign . . . and Past Fund Drives," *Inside U of L,* April 1983.

15. *Kentucky Encyclopedia,* 665; Grawemeyer Award Records, U of L Archives. Psychology, the fifth award, was slated to be given first in 2000. For more information, see Allen E. Dittmer, Paul J. Weber, and Gene March, *The Power of Ideas: The University of Louisville Grawemeyer Awards,* forthcoming.

16. Allen R. Hite, a U of L law school graduate, had served as a trustee; Marcia S. Hite, a painter, had attended the Art Center school. *Courier-Journal* May 20, 1947; Dario A. Covi, "An Account of the Interpretation and Implementation of the Hite Bequest and a Statement of Goals and Recommendations," November 1, 1962, Reference Files, U of L Archives; Janet Hodgson, "A Historical Look at the Louisville School of Art," *U of L Magazine* (fall 1989), 14-15; Jennifer Recktenwald, "Independent Expression: The Allen R. Hite Institute at 50," *U of L Magazine* 15 (fall 1996), 22-24.

17. *Alumni Magazine* (January 1945), 3-4.

18. The old Art Center facility became U of L's Honors Building, located between Stevenson Hall and the Interfaith Center. The Ph.D. in art history was the College of Arts and Sciences' second Ph.D. program in the humanities area awarded by the University of Louisville; the School of Music's music history department developed a joint Ph.D. program in musicology with the University of Kentucky, but that degree was awarded by UK. The terms fine arts department and Hite Institute were often used interchangeably.

19. University of Louisville, *Inauguration of President Donald C. Swain* (Louisville, 1981), 1; *Courier-Journal,* October 5, 1981, July 14, 1983; *Louisville Times,* December 2, 1980; Donald C. Swain to University Faculty and Staff, April 29, 1982; University of Louisville, *The Quest for Excellence* (Louisville, 1981), 10-17, Reference Files, U of L Archives.

20. *Courier-Journal,* November 26, December 14, 1990, February 26, April 16, May 21, October 29, 1991, January 17, April 23, 28, 1992; President's Annual Report, 1965-1966, 4. For an account of how another state university dealt with, and was affected by, Kentucky's higher education budget cuts of the 1980s, see Harrison, *Western Kentucky University,* 264-276.

21. *Courier-Journal,* October 29, 1991, January 17, April 23, 28, 1992.

22. *Courier-Journal,* October 22, November 10, December 16, 1992, June 15, 1993; Swain to author, April 4, 1998.

23. *Courier-Journal,* October 24, 1989; University of Louisville, *Fact Book: 1990-1991* (Louisville 1991), 21; Harrison and Klotter, *A New History of Kentucky,* 397.

24. *Courier-Journal* January 16, 22, April 9, 10, 1992.

25. *Courier-Journal,* February 4, 5, 19, April 1, 15, May 13, September 2, 1993; Board of Trustees, Minutes, September 26, 1994.

26. "Enrollment Management: A New Competitive Market—Part 1 of 2," *The Faculty Connection,* Spring 1997; *Kentucky Encyclopedia,* 295; University of Louisville, *Fact Book: 1994-1995* (Louisville, 1995), 22; Swain to author, April 4, 1998. Ph.D. programs begun under Swain included industrial engineering, computer science and engineering, art history, urban affairs, visual sciences, and civil engineering, the latter in cooperation with the University of Kentucky. The Speed School's first Ph.D. program, in chemical engineering, had been established in 1955.

27. *Cardinal,* March 29, 1968.

28. *Courier-Journal,* February 28, 1989.

29. *Courier-Journal,* October 3, 8, 15, November 7, 8, 9, 1991; University Librarian's Office Records, U of L Archives.

30. Computer Board Records, 1966-1971; "A Recommended Six-Year Plan for Computing Activities and Facilities at the University of Louisville, 1974-1980" (Louisville, 1973), President's Office Records, U of L Archives.

31. *Courier-Journal,* December 4, 1985, February 3, 1990; *Inside U of L,* June 24, 1994. In 1997 the Louisville Area Chamber of Commerce and the Greater Louisville Economic Development Partnership merged to form Greater Louisville, Inc., The Metro Chamber of Commerce.

32. *Courier-Journal,* November 17, 19, 22, 29, December 6, 1988, February 8, March 1, April 18, May 1, 1989.

33. Morison, "How Many Times Have the Teams Met," *Inside U of L,* May 1983.

34. *Courier-Journal,* July 2, 5-6, 14, 1977, January 1, 1978, March 14, 1984.

35. *Sports Illustrated,* March 22, 1982, 11; *Courier-Journal,* June 29, 1983; University of Louisville, *Cardinal Basketball* (Louisville, 1997), 118-119.

36. *Courier-Journal,* July 26, 1981, February 28, 1984, April 2, 1991.

37. *Kentucky Encyclopedia,* 799.

38. *1990 U of L Football Media Guide* (Louisville, 1990), Reference File, U of L Archives; *USA Today,* October 31, 1990.

39. The record attendance for a football game at Cardinal Stadium was set on September 5, 1991, when 40,457 fans saw Louisville lose to Tennessee; it was also the first U of L home game televised by ESPN. *Courier-Journal,* January 29, 1993; *1995 Louisville Football Media Guide* (Louisville, 1995), 18, 74-75.

40. *Courier-Journal,* May 17, 1996; Oscar Bryant, "75 Years and Building," *U of L Alumni Magazine* (winter 1994), 17-18; "On Campus," *U of L Alumni Magazine* 15 (fall 1996), 4.

41. *Courier-Journal,* July 12, 1990, November 6, 1991, April 3, August 20, 1992, January 29, October 2, December 22, 23, 1993, December 21, 1994, September 6, 1998.

42. Reference Files, U of L Archives.

43. *Courier-Journal,* April 13, 1996, April 4, 1998, April 6, 1999; Reference Files, U of L Archives.

44. Reference Files, U of L Archives.

45. Reference Files, U of L Archives.

46. Hardin, *Fifty Years of Segregation,* 116-117; William A. Kaplin and Barbara A. Lee, *The Law of Higher Education* (3rd ed.; San Francisco, 1995), 801-804; John B. Williams III, ed., *Desegregating America's Colleges and Universities: Title VI Regulation of Higher Education* (New York, 1988), 3-53, 77-81; *Chronicle of Higher Education,* January 26, 1981, February 17, 1988, July 19, 1989. Robert A. Dentler, D. Catherine Baltzell, and Daniel J. Sullivan, *University on Trial: The Case of the University of North Carolina* (Cambridge, MA, 1983), 1-15, places the Adams case in historical context.

47. University of Louisville, *Fact Book: Fall 1982* (Louisville, 1983), 33; *Fact Book: 1995-1996* (Louisville, 1997), 28-29, 42-43. For a critical overview of the Reagan administration's responses to calls for desegregation in U.S. higher education, see Gary Orfield, *Inequality Accepted and Approved: The Abandonment of Civil Rights Enforcement in Higher Education* (Chicago 1989).

48. Sydney Schultze, "Enriching the Curriculum: Formation of the Women's Studies Program," in Mary E. Hawkesworth, ed., *Feminist Intervention: Equality Work in a Gendered Institution,* forthcoming; Fonda R. Bock, "Resounding Voices," *U of L Alumni Magazine,* Fall 1996, 20-21; *Louisville Times,* February 18, 1975.

49. *Louisville Times,* March 3, 1975; Schultze, "Enriching the Curriculum."

50. *Courier-Journal,* January 17, 1991; Lucy M. Freibert, "Teacher as Catalyst: Updating the University Infrastructure," in Hawkesworth, *Feminist Intervention;* and "University of Louisville Women's Center: Beginnings, 1991-1996" (Louisville 1997).

51. Freibert, letter to author, April 21, 1998; Freibert, "Teacher as Catalyst," 18; Reference Files, U of L Archives. For information on U of L school songs, see Tom Owen, "U of L 'Alma Mater' Has Noted Past," *U of L Magazine* (summer 1984), 28. Collette M. Murray served as vice president for development and alumni, 1985-1988.

52. "Meeting the 21st Century: Access, Opportunity and Achievement: Report of the Task Force on the Status of Women" (Louisville 1994), 3, 25-29, passim; *Courier-Journal* July 21, 1994, November 16, 1996, July 12, 1997.

53. *Chronicle of Higher Education,* August 29, 1997, August 28, 1998; *Courier-Journal,* October 13, 1997, March 21, August 27, 1999.

54. President's Annual Report, 1951-1952.

55. Michael A. Lindenberger, "Great Greek Years," *U of L Magazine* 17 (winter 1998), 23-24. For a professor's memories of serving as faculty advisor to one U of L fraternity for fifteen years, see Ekstrom, *Recollection,* 12-14.

56. Board of Trustees, Minutes, June 18, 1952.

57. School of Business *Bulletin* (Louisville 1953), 11; John R. Craf and William H. Peters, "The School of Business: 1953 to 1978 and Beyond" (Louisville 1978); *Courier-Journal,* April 16, 1987.

58. *Inside U of L,* September 8, 1995.

59. *U of L Undergraduate Catalog, 1998-2000* (Louisville 1998), 88; *U of L Graduate Catalog, 1997-1999* (Louisville, 1997), 48-52, 118, 133-134.

60. *Courier-Journal,* December 1, 1990; *School of Law Catalogue, 1996-1998,* 11.

61. Two U of L dental school graduates have served as president of the American Dental Association: Carl A. Laughlin (1932) and James H. Gaines Jr. (1961). Another, James Edwards (1955), was governor of South Carolina and secretary of energy under President Ronald Reagan.

62. Oscar Bryant, "Going Strong at 100," *U of L Magazine* 5 (summer 1986), 12-14, and Calvin Miller, "Word of Mouth," *U of L Magazine* 11 (spring 1993), 8-11.

63. Koch and McIntosh, *History of Progress in Engineering Education,* 8-10.

64. *Courier-Journal,* October 27, 1940; *Time,*

November 11, 1940, 54; "Trauma Surgery at the University of Louisville," *Suture-Line,* October 31, 1986, 1-3.

65. *Courier-Journal* October 30, 1994, July 13, 1997; *Business First,* December 2, 1996; *Kentucky Encyclopedia,* 624; Kevin Rayburn, "Healing Hands," *U of L Magazine* 13 (summer 1995), 12-15; *Time* (August 3, 1998), 65.

66. Robert Hadley, "McConnell Center Attracts Future Leaders," *U of L Alumni Magazine* 12 (spring 1994), 12-14; "McConnell Center Report," November 1, 1997, Reference Files, U of L Archives.

67. Bryant, "Solid Gold," 11-15; U of L School of Music 1983-1985 *Bulletin* (Louisville, 1983), 9.

68. Board of Trustees, Minutes, January 27, 1997; *U of L Graduate Catalog, 1997-1999,* 121-122; Ekstrom, *Recollection,* 98.

69. Kevin Rayburn, "Fresh Approaches: Revamping Teacher Education at U of L," *U of L Alumni Magazine,* Summer 1994; "NCATE Board of Examiners Report: Continuing Accreditation Visit to University of Louisville," October 1996, 16-17; Harrison and Klotter, *A New History of Kentucky,* 391-393; Swain to author, April 4, 1998.

70. Rosenfeld (ed.), *University of Louisville School of Police Administration,* 8-9. The SPI Building, erected in 1956 to house the Kentucky Education Association, was named McCandless Hall in 1985.

71. Campbell, "Brief History," 5-6.

72. Rosenfeld (ed.), *University of Louisville School of Police Administration,* 9, 18-21.

73. Lynnell Major, "Healing Arts," *U of L Magazine* 7 (summer 1988), 2-4; *U of L Graduate Catalog, 1997-1999,* 76.

74. Health Sciences Center Executive Council, Minutes, February 22, 1978, U of L Archives; *Inside U of L,* October 4, 1996; *U of L Undergraduate Catalog, 1998-2000,* 42.

75. Ekstrom, *Recollection,* 91-92; *Inside U of L,* May 7, 1999.

76. *Courier-Journal,* June 16, 1994.

77. Carl Brown, "Presidential Legacy," *U of L Magazine* 13 (summer 1995): 10.

19. Looking Ahead, Looking Back

1. *Inside U of L,* June 24, 1994.

2. *Courier-Journal,* April 16, 1995.

3. *Courier-Journal,* November 12, 1992; June 11, October 3, 1993; March 4, 1994.

4. *Courier-Journal,* July 1, 1994, January 11, 1995.

5. *Courier-Journal,* October 17, 1995, February 8, 1997, December 18, 1998; Kevin Rayburn, "21st Century Partners," *U of L Magazine* (spring 1996): 12-14; Barbara

Zingman and Betty Lou Amster, *A Legendary Vision: The History of Jewish Hospital* (Louisville, 1997), 149-152.

6. *Courier-Journal,* September 2, 3, 1990.

7. *Courier-Journal,* December 24, 25, 1990; *USA Today,* June 18, 1991.

8. Swain, "College Presidents Must Clean Up Mess in Athletic Programs," *USA Today,* April 1, 1991. U of L's 1996 graduation rate for athletes was 63 percent; the NCAA Division I average that year was 59 percent; Marty Benson, ed., *The 1996 NCAA Division I Graduation-Rate Report* (Overland Park, KA, 1996), 268, 624.

9. The bowl's announcement of money for minority scholarships touched off another controversy when an official of the civil rights division of the U.S. Department of Education contacted the Fiesta Bowl, asserting that race-based scholarships were illegal. Later, after his department threatened to halt federal aid to institutions of higher education offering scholarships based on race, the U.S. secretary of education resigned under pressure from the Bush administration, which then announced that Alabama and Louisville could accept the bowl's offer of minority scholarship funds. *Courier-Journal,* November 13, 18, December 5, 7, 13, 19, 1990. Also see Paul J. Weber, "Healthy Turmoil at U of L," *Courier-Journal,* December 16, 1990.

10. Swain, "Why Louisville Accepted the Fiesta Bowl Bid," *New York Times,* November 18, 1990; Board of Trustees, Minutes, November 26, 1990; *Courier-Journal,* February 20, 1991.

11. *Courier-Journal,* February 22, 24, March 11, 14, 1991; *Cardinal,* October 24, 1991; *Inside U of L,* November 18, 1991; Reference File, U of L Archives.

12. *Cardinal,* November 9, 30, 1989, October 21, 1991.

13. Swain to Members of the University of Louisville Community, November 14, 1989; Swain to Members of the Black Student Alliance, November 17, 1989; President's Records, U of L Archives.

14. *Courier-Journal,* June 29, July 1, September 22, 1995, May 3, 1997.

15. After U of L appealed the ban on postseason play, the NCAA conceded making errors in its own procedures and allowed the basketball team to compete in tournaments at the end of the 1998-1999 season. *Courier-Journal,* June 28, July 4, 24, September 24, 1997, April 16, 18, September 23, 1998, February 6, 1999.

16. *Courier-Journal,* October 22, November 20, 25, December 18, 1997. Cooper received about $1.8 million, an amount judged sufficient to produce $1 million after taxes. In 1993 Louisville had beaten Michigan State University in the Liberty Bowl.

17. *Courier-Journal,* December 13, 14, 1995, May 31, 1997.

18. Minutes, Board of Trustees, January 27, 1997; *Inside U of L,* January 31, 1997; *Courier-Journal,* August 11, 1995, January 29, 1997.

19. KRS 164 Sec. 2(2)(b) and (c), and Sec. 65(1); *Courier-Journal,* May 31, 1997.

20. "Challenge for Excellence: U of L's Vision for the Next Decade" (Louisville, 1998), 8-13. By early 1999 the number of endowed chairs had risen to fifty-one. *Courier-Journal,* January 30, July 12, 1997, March 21, 1999.

21. Dana Fischetti, "World Class Hub," *U of L Magazine* (winter 1999): 10-13; *Courier-Journal,* April 15, 1999.

22. *Courier-Journal,* April 2, June 23, 1998, February 16, 1999.

23. *Inside U of L,* April 10, 1998.

24. University of Louisville, *Fact Book: 1998-1999,* passim.

25. George R. Leighton, "Louisville, Kentucky: An American Museum Piece," *Harper's Magazine,* September 1937, 400-421.

26. See Bledstein, *Culture of Professionalism,* 287ff.

27. Flexner, *Mr. Justice Brandeis and the University of Louisville,* 5.

28. Ibid., 1.

29. Ekstrom, *Recollection,* 40.

INDEX